# Reforming
# Sex

# Reforming Sex

The German Movement for Birth Control
and Abortion Reform, 1920–1950

ATINA GROSSMANN

OXFORD UNIVERSITY PRESS

*New York    Oxford*

Oxford University Press

Oxford   New York
Athens   Auckland   Bangkok   Boston   Bombay   Buenos Aires
Calcutta   Cape Town   Dar es Salaam   Delhi   Florence   Hong Kong
Istanbul   Karachi   Kuala Lumpur   Madras   Madrid   Melbourne
Mexico City   Nairobi   Paris   Singapore   Taipei   Tokoyo   Toronto   Warsaw

and associated companies in
Berlin   Ibadan

First published in 1995 by Oxford University Press, Inc.
198 Madison Avenue, New York, New York 10016

First issued as an Oxford University Press paperback, 1997

Oxford is a registered trademark of Oxford University Press

Library of Congress Cataloging-in-Publication Data
Grossmann, Atina.
Reforming sex : the German movement for birth control
and abortion reform, 1920–1950 / Atina Grossmann.
p.  cm.   Includes bibliographical references and index.
ISBN 0-19-505672-8; 0-19-512124-4 (pbk.)
1. Birth control—Germany—History—20th century.
2. Contraception—Germany—History—20th century.
3. Abortion—Germany—History—20th century.
4. Eugenics—Germany—History—20th Century.   I. Title.
HQ744.5.G4G76   1995
363.9'0943—dc20   94-13050

1 3 5 7 9 8 6 4 2

Printed in the United States of America
on acid-free paper

# — preface —

This book describes a mass social movement for accessible birth control and legal abortion that included several hundred-thousand working-class members of grassroots sex reform leagues, physicians who staffed birth control clinics and lectured on sexual hygiene, and political activists and health officials who campaigned for abortion law reform. The movement transgressed conventional political and professional divisions and encompassed Social Democrats, Communists, independent feminists, intellectuals and professionals, even contraceptive manufacturers and "quack" abortionists, as well as thousands of people seeking safe, inexpensive, and available birth control and sex advice.

*Reforming Sex* focuses first on the organization and politics of the movement for sex reform during the tense, chaotic, and immensely innovative years of the late Weimar Republic. It goes on to discuss the fate of German sex reform (and sex reformers) both within and outside Germany from 1933 until the end of the immediate postwar period around 1950. The book crosses conventional chronological and geographic boundaries. It spans the political divides of 1933 and 1945 and insists that the movement extended well beyond Germany's borders. I believe that this focus can shed a new and different light on the persistent controversies over continuity and break in modern German history, the singularity and comparability of National Socialism, and especially the degree to which the Third Reich can or should be integrated into a long-term development of modernity and a technologized society. To put it another way, I hope that by expanding the view beyond Germany and interrupting—although certainly not ignoring—the usual focus in studies of social

medicine, eugenics, or feminism on the bitter end of Nazism and the Holocaust, I can join this seemingly endless argument in a different and useful way.[1]
The history of German sex reform is international and cannot be told only
within the confines of an internal German narrative defined by the descent
into National Socialism.

The shift is important because increasingly historians, especially of science, social welfare, and medicine, have fixed on "biomedical" politics and
a particularly "modern" scientific and technocratic arrogance as explanatory models for the triumphant and relatively straightforward progress of
National Socialism from "Weimar to Auschwitz."[2] When I first began re-
searching this topic many years ago, I was amazed to discover that, as I wrote
at the conclusion of my dissertation, sex reformers often spoke a language of
social health and eugenic hygiene, of "fit and unfit" that "often sounds bizarre
and even frightening to post-1945 and post-Auschwitz ears."[3] By now it has
become something of a cliché to note what I worked so hard to understand
then: that the National Socialists expropriated eugenic health notions associated with sex reform and social medicine, as well as the "progressive" dream
of an efficient centralized state health system, in the service of an ultimately
genocidal racial hygiene program.

The recent emphasis on "The Genesis of the 'Final Solution' from the Spirit
of Science," as Detlev Peukert has provocatively put it, now poses new and
particular problems for an analysis of Weimar campaigns for sex reform and
social health.[4] Certainly, both the lay activists and medical professionals, many
of them members of the Communist or Social Democratic parties, who
labored to legalize abortion and institutionalize birth control and sex counseling within the national health system, were committed to the propagation
of a healthy and fit *Volk* as well as to what they understood as the rationalization of sexuality, a term first introduced in 1912 by the German demographer
Julius Wolf to characterize modern sexual and procreative behavior, especially
changes in women's social role and the birth rate decline.[5]

It is undeniable that heavily researched and compellingly argued recent studies have powerfully remapped the grid in which we attempt to understand the
social and political history of modern Germany and "The Genesis of the 'Final
Solution.'"[6] Fifteen or twenty years after the (re)discovery of the Weimar sex
reform movement,[7] we now must incorporate into our analysis not only the
postmodern assault on feminist and Marxist as well as liberal notions of progress
and progressive but also the total collapse of the Soviet social and political experiment that inspired so many sex reformers to envision a new human "race"
of sexually and socially healthy women and men.[8]

But the focus on continuities in "biopower" and biomedical thinking (itself revisionist and to which my earlier work contributed) also presents us
with conceptual and political problems of historical interpretations that
strongly privilege continuity over change. It lends itself to an accusatory history of Weimar that detects the long arm of social control everywhere, ex-

tending its almost unbroken reach from the beginning of Enlightenment faith in universalist reason and intensifying it with the consolidation of the scientific professions and the welfare state by the turn of the century. Recent histories of German medicine and eugenics admit to one degree or another the need to differentiate among various groups of eugenicists or racial hygienists and present at times some rather hagiographic nostalgia about the loss of reform-minded Jewish doctors and social workers.

Finally, however, they all seem to impute to social welfare in general, from the imperial era on, a kind of slippery slope trajectory of inexorability that led in a perhaps bumpy but nevertheless logical line to forced sterilization, euthanasia, and then genocide. Even those studies that scrupulously describe the diverse politics of eugenicists and point out the highly contested nature of German population policy from 1870 to 1945, such as conflicts during Weimar between national and local authorities, and differences in the Third Reich between populist ideologues and elitist technocrats, seem to conclude that Weimar reform initiatives were "precursors" of Nazi policies.[9]

The apparently necessary conclusion of this new history has been that no matter what its humane and socialist intentions, the aggressive interventionist social medicine of the 1920s social reformers, with its eugenic language and faith in state intervention, paved the way for and softened up both the general population and medical and social welfare professionals for support of Nazi population policy—another utopia expropriated and gone wrong.

I want to argue something different: that despite all amply proven continuities in medicine, population policy, racial hygiene, and eugenics, and especially among geneticists and racial hygienicists in universities and research institutes, the Nazi seizure of power in 1933 represented a radical break for those who advocated reform of paragraph 218 of the penal code which criminalized abortion and the establishment of birth control and sex counseling clinics. I want to insist that for sex reform and social medicine there was no seamless path, not even a slippery slope, but rather a convoluted and highly contested route.

In order for the ideological and discursive continuities in hygiene, eugenics, and technocratic medical authoritarianism to work and be enforced, and in order for the National Socialists to appropriate the language both of maternalism and scientific eugenics and make it useful for their own coercive, hierarchical, and terroristic aims—as they certainly did—there first had to be a dramatic break. The institutions in which those discourses had operated and the people who developed and applied them in clinical practice had to be eliminated. And when those discourses were reoperationalized and the institutions were reopened by the Nazis, for example, as hereditary and racial welfare clinics, they may have sounded and looked similar, containing some of the same ideology, but they employed for the most part different people with a different understanding of social health. In a radically changed political context, the elements of a consensus about motherhood, eugenics, and rationalized sexuality fit together very differently.

We need of course to develop a nuanced and complex analysis of modern German history that balances the various elements of continuity and discontinuity, peculiarity and comparability. Clearly, this is not an either/or story. Historians of science, medicine, and social welfare have now demonstrated in great, sometimes chilling, detail the remarkable durability over time and regime of an underlying consensus about the paramount importance of motherhood and eugenics for a healthy family and state.[10] But this book is meant to show that the emphasis on long-term continuities in eugenic worldview about hierarchies of fitness and reliance on state and expert control, and the exposure of truly breathtaking continuities in personnel if not in explicit ideology after 1933 and 1945, can be as blinding as it has been eye-opening.

We often tend to conflate the positions, both institutional and political, of sex reformers who worked in municipal and health insurance clinics with those of social welfare bureaucrats in state agencies and researchers in universities and institutes. We sidestep or overinterpret the significance of gender and status differences among reformers and "helping professionals." In some analyses, necessary critiques of professional control tend toward a demonization of all physicians, and modernity is seen as an assault by the medical profession on some putative "natural" realm of female power.[11] Stressing, however rightfully, the continuous hegemony of a consensus on the importance of eugenic health and responsible motherhood from at least the end of the nineteenth century through the post–World War II period tends to obscure how variously those goals were defined and imposed by different authorities at different times under different regimes.

These exposés of continuity—until recently heftily resisted by many mainstream German historians and professionals—have now done their work so successfully that a new level of revision and nuance becomes necessary: in relation to sex reform and social hygiene, it must be said that there was also— if certainly not only—a profound and irrevocable break in 1933 that could not and would not be reversed after 1945 and that left its marks on the postwar development of population and family policy in both German states. Finally, for all of their virtues in undermining the *Betriebsunfall* (industrial accident) or demonic ("mad scientist") versions of National Socialism, as well as the benign narrative of the modernizing welfare state, continuity arguments threaten to efface what *also* needs more careful attention: the dramatic degree of discontinuity after 1933, as well as the continuities after 1945, some of which reached back to Weimar and attempted to repress the intervening twelve years.

Chapter 1 provides a brief historical introduction, alerting readers to highlights of social developments that have been extensively discussed elsewhere. Chapter 2 discusses the development of sex reform organizations in the 1920s, emphasizing the important role of physicians and the international, especially the American, birth control movement as well as the Bolshevik model publicized by the German Communist party. Chapter 3 discusses the institutionalization of sex reform in municipal and health insurance prenatal and birth control clinics, especially in Berlin. I stress the contradictory ways in which the movement aimed both to empower and regulate women and the working class. Sex reform physicians accepted the pervasive social health and eugenics discourse that valorized healthy motherhood and divided society into hierarchies based on notions of the "fit and unfit, valuable and asocial,"[12] as well as on gender. Yet they also provided spaces where women could exercise the right to control their fertility and sexuality. I pay particular attention to the ways in which gender differences structured and disrupted these discourses, and to the relationship in the clinics between rhetoric and practice.

Chapter 4 details the forceful mobilization, spearheaded by the Communist party in 1931, for the legalization of abortion and also discusses how and why abortion became such a potent political and social issue during the depression. Chapter 5 documents the ultimate failure of the abortion reform campaign and related efforts to establish a unified sex reform organization as the Weimar welfare state collapsed. It also sketches the radical visions of a new sexuality and comradeship between women and men that leftist sex reformers developed in the latter years of the republic. Chapter 6 on continuity and discontinuity describes the simultaneous destruction of the movement and the institutionalization of a comprehensive National Socialist population and racial hygiene policy.

Chapter 7 follows Weimar sex reformers into exile, notably to the countries that had exercised such a powerful influence on them during the Weimar years: the United States and the Soviet Union. It describes how, in the United States (and also England, Scandinavia, Palestine, and Australia), exiled German sex reformers were deradicalized, incorporated into, and helped to shape international Planned Parenthood. It also discusses the divided fate of those who went into Soviet exile. It is important to complete their biographies—so drastically interrupted with the collapse of the Weimar Republic—not only because they are inherently interesting, often adventurous, and still relevant for all those who are concerned about the politics of reproduction and the body, but because they underline once again how much this is a story that cannot be closed in 1933.

Chapter 8 describes the reemergence in altered form of the debate about abortion and paragraph 218, and of family planning initiatives, as American and Soviet models again influenced population policy in the postwar Germanies. Chapters 7 and 8 together thus provide a new historical, comparative perspective on some of the guiding people and ideas of post-1945 family planning and population control programs. I am pursuing these questions in a new research project on the politics of rape, abortion, and family planning in the post–World War II period.

Having outlined what this book is about and what its intentions are, I need to say something about what it is not about. I am very much aware that for a study of *reforming sex*, I have remarkably little to say about *sex* or *sexuality*.

Weimar sex reform focused on improving certain procreative and heterosexual practices. An open and unsentimental approach to sexual activity and
discourse was a crucial marker of modern identity in Weimar, but how that
related to pleasure and desire (or for that matter consumption), and the multiple understandings of gendered and sexed bodies that historians—influenced
by feminist, "queer," and postmodern theory—have come to ponder in recent years, remains for me very much open to question. I hope to address
some of these issues in future work.

I should also address another obvious absence in this study. Weimar Germany developed a lively and richly complicated homosexual rights movement
and gay subculture. Again, although I note clear overlaps, this book traces a
movement primarily concerned with stabilizing and rationalizing heterosexuality and procreation. Numerous scholars are currently working on gay and
lesbian history in Germany; some attention is just beginning to be paid to problems of consumer culture. I look forward to increasing crossing of interests
and fields on a wide range of topics in social, medical, and cultural studies.[13]

Finally, I should add that the far-reaching nature of German sex reform is
reflected in the breadth and eclectic nature of my research. I consulted archives
and conducted interviews in the United States, Great Britain, Sweden, Israel,
the Federal Republic of Germany, and the German Democratic Republic. I
was fortunate to be able to still take advantage of the wealth of information
becoming available in the various collections of the former GDR. Like so many
students of German history and politics, I found that my work was both en-
riched and delayed by the fall of the Berlin Wall and the new research possibilities—oral, visual, and written—it opened up. I have no doubt that there is
considerably more material on German sexual and population politics to be
found, especially in the archives of the former GDR and Soviet Union.

*New York*                                                          A.G.
*March 1994*

# — acknowledgments —

This book has been a long time in the making and has accompanied me through multiple personal and professional changes. Both I and the political and intellectual milieu I inhabit were quite different when I first became intrigued with the German sex reform movement, and I have incurred innumerable debts in the process of trying to figure out how to tell a story in the 1990s that I began to think about in the 1970s. Luckily, I was not alone in this venture, and I am happy to acknowledge—inevitably inadequately—the support that kept me going.

To start with the crucial institutional level, I am grateful for research and travel funding and leave time—never enough it seems, but indispensable— to the American Council of Learned Societies, the National Endowment for the Humanities summer fellowship program, the German-American Academic Exchange Service, and Columbia University's Councils for Research in the Humanities and Social Sciences and Junior Faculty Development Leave. A large crew of archivists, librarians, colleagues, and interview partners facilitated my access to source materials, some of them—like the Weimar sex magazines that Gudrun Schwarz and I excavated from the basement of the West Berlin *Staatsbibliothek* in the late 1970s—buried and forgotten since 1933. I am particularly grateful to Dr. Jürgen Wetzel of the *Landesarchiv* Berlin, Ilona Kalb of the Humboldt University archive, Esther Katz of the Margaret Sanger Papers Project, Sabine Schleiermacher of Hanover University, and the by now world famous Herr Lange, formerly of the Institute for the History of Marxism Leninism in East Berlin and now a part of the *Bundesarchiv*. Veterans of the sex reform movement and their children and grandchildren gave generously of their time and knowledge, often proud to tell their stories, sometimes (especially at the earlier stages) amazed that anyone was still interested.

Like many of my good friends, I have been extraordinarily fortunate in participating on both sides of the Atlantic in a longstanding and ongoing network of personal and scholarly exchange in German and feminist history. In New York, the German Women's History Study Group has nurtured and critiqued this book, prodded and comforted me, as it has many others. Molly Nolan and Marion Kaplan have been especially steadfast in their clever mixing of stern pushing and unconditional support; I relish our collective work and look forward to more. In Berlin, Carola Sachse, Elisabeth Meyer-Renschhausen, Gabriele Czarnowski, and Dagmar Reese (and Tilla Siegel when she's in town) never fail to stimulate, provoke, and feed me; we are still in the midst of a collaboration begun in Annemarie Tröger's oral history seminar at the Free University in the late 1970s. At Columbia, my colleagues Martha Howell, Betsy Blackmar, Deborah Levenson, and most recently Victoria de Grazia have brightened Fayerweather Hall and taught me a great deal about what it means to be a teacher/scholar/activist. And in cyberspace, Geoff Eley and Bob Moeller, masters of the encouraging and perceptive e-mail message, have sustained me through many a long night at the computer. I didn't manage to follow all of their suggestions and insights, but I've stored them on the hard disk and will return to them as I continue my work.

The list of those to whom I owe thanks is very long. Nancy Lane, my editor at Oxford, has been patient and supportive for longer than she should have needed to be. Amy Hackett's keen editorial eye and organizational sense gave me perspective at crucial moments. Let me mention also other colleagues and friends who helped me keep body and soul together: Dolores Augustine, Bonnie Anderson, Renate Bridenthal, Jane Caplan, Deborah Hertz, Claudia Koonz, Jan Lambertz, and Nancy Reagin from the German Women's History Study Group; and Ann Alter, David Bernstein, Miriam Frank, Eike Geisel, Amos Grunebaum, Miriam Hansen, Pamela Hort, Mechthild Küpper, Peter, Barbara and Ghilia Lipman-Wulf, Michael Muskal, Susan Ochshorn, Andy Rabinbach, Mindy Roseman, Debby Rosenberg, Tom Sedlock, Ruth Sedlock, and Sally Stein.

PS 75 Manhattan, Purple Circle Day Care Center, Erika Busse Grossmann, and Marie Keyes Jackson (a miraculously stable and understanding presence) taught, cared for, and helped raise my children (and thereby me). All of us engaged in the work/family/community juggling act know how incalculable my debt to them is. Max and Nelly Mecklenburg have lived with this project more than they wanted to; their tempting offers of distraction and alternative ways to spend one's weekends convinced me that it was time to stop. The same is surely true of Frank Mecklenburg; computer wizard and *Lebenskünstler*, he was always there and I thank him.

Finally, this book owes much to the memory of my two "fathers": my actual father Hans Sigismund Grossmann and my *Doktorvater* Harold L. Poor. Both told great Weimar stories, loved to live, died too soon, and would have been glad to know this done.

# — contents —

# — abbreviations —

| | |
|---|---|
| AfG | Arbeiter Vereine für Geburtenregelung (Workers Associations for Birth Control) |
| AfVG | Arbeitsgemeinschaft für Volksgesundung (Working Group for the Restoration of the Health of the *Volk*) |
| AIZ | *Arbeiter Illustrierte Zeitung* (Workers Illustrated Newspaper) |
| AMSO | Arbeitsgemeinschaft Marxistischer Sozialarbeiter (Working Group of Marxist Social Workers) |
| ARSO | Arbeitsgemeinschaft sozialpolitischer Organisationen (Working Group of Social Political Organizations) |
| ARWO | Arbeiterwohlfahrt (Workers Welfare) |
| BArch(K) | Bundesarchiv Koblenz |
| BArch(P) | Bundesarchiv Potsdam (former Zentrales Staatsarchiv DDR) |
| BArch(Sapmo) | Stiftung Archiv der Parteien und Massenorganisationen der DDR im Bundesarchiv (formerly Institut für Geschichte der Arbeiterbewegung, Institut für Marxismus-Lenismus, Zentrales Parteiarchiv der SED) |
| BDÄ | Bund deutscher Ärztinnen (League of German Women Doctors) |
| BDF | Bund deutscher Frauenvereine (Federation of German Women's Associations) |

BDM        Bund deutscher Mädel (League of German Girls)

BfM        Bund für Mutterschutz und Sexualreform (League for the
           Protection of Motherhood and Sex Reform)

BKR        Bund der Kinderreichen (Federation of Large Families)

DFDA       Demokratischer Frauenbund Deutschlands Archive
           (Democratic Women's League of Germany)

EpS        Einheitskomitee (or Verband) für proletarische
           Sexual Reform (Unity Committee—or league—for
           Proletarian Sex Reform)

FWA        Friedrich Wolf Archiv. Akademie der Künste (former GDR)

GESEX      Gesellschaft für Sexual Reform (Society for Sexual Reform)

GStA       Geheimes Staatsarchiv Preussischer Kulturbesitz, Dahlem

HARA       Max Hodann Papers, Arbetarrörelsens Arkiv, Stockholm

IAH        Internationale Arbeiter Hilfe (International Workers Aid)

IPPFA      International Planned Parenthood Federation Archives,
           David Owen Centre for Population Studies, University of
           Wales, Cardiff

KJVD       Kommunistischer Jugend Verband Deutschlands
           (Communist Youth)

KPD        Kommunistische Partei Deutschlands (German Communist
           Party)

LAB        Landesarchiv Berlin

*Liga*     Liga für Mutterschutz und soziale Familienhygiene (League
           for Protection of Mothers and Social Family Hygiene)

MASCH      Marxistische Arbeiter Schulung (Marxist Evening School)

MSPS       Margaret Sanger Papers, Smith College

*NG*       *Neue Generation* (BfM)

NSDAP      National Socialist German Workers Party (National
           Socialist Party)

*PS*       *Proletarische Sozialpolitik* (ARSO)

RAfBF      Reichsausschuss für Bevölkerungsfragen (Committee for
           Population Questions)

RAHV       Reichsausschuss für hygienische Volksbelehrung (Committee
           for Hygienic Education of the *Volk*)

RF         Rockefeller Foundation Center Archives, Pocantico Hills

RFB        Roter Frontkämpfer Bund (Red Front-Fighters League)

RFMB       Roter Frauen und Mädchen Bund (Red Girls and Women's
           League)

| | |
|---|---|
| RGA | Reichsgesundheitsamt (Department of Health) |
| RGO | Revolutionäre Gewerkschaftsopposition (Revolutionary Trade Union Opposition) |
| RH | Rote Hilfe (Red Aid) |
| RMI | Reichsministerium des Innern (Ministry of the Interior) |
| RV | Reichsverband für Geburtenregelung und Sexualhygiene (National League for Birth Control and Sexual Hygiene) |
| *SA* | *Sozialistischer Arzt* (Socialist Physician) |
| SAD | Staatsarchiv Dresden |
| Sanger LC | Margaret Sanger Papers, Library of Congress |
| SBZ | Sowjetische Besatzungszone (Soviet occupation zone) |
| SED | Sozialistische Einheitspartei Deutschlands (Socialist Unity Party) |
| *SH* | *Sexual-Hygiene* (RV) |
| SMA | Sowjetische Militäradministration (Soviet Military Administration) |
| SPD | Sozialdemokratische Partei Deutschlands (Social Democratic Party of Germany) |
| VKB | Verband der Krankenkassen Berlins (Berlin Health Insurance League) |
| VSA | Verein Sozialistischer Ärzte (Association of Socialist Physicians) |
| WLSR | World League for Sex Reform |

# Reforming
# Sex

# one

# Introduction
## New Women and Families
## in the New Germany

Rejection of childbirth has virtually become a public movement.[1]

The transformed woman wants more than to be a mother, she also wants to be a woman. Women are fleeing Nora's doll house not just in isolated cases but in battalions (*Heerenstärke*).[2]

### New Women and New Families

Conducted just at the midpoint of the Weimar Republic's brief turbulent existence, the 1925 German census served to confirm the widespread contemporary perception of a nation in the grip of rapid demographic and social transformation. Most dramatically, the "new" women of the "new" German Republic were, it seemed, becoming less motherly, both quantitatively and qualitatively. Average family size had dropped to one child per family.[3] Depending on one's point of view, the modern nuclear family had arrived or women were on a birth strike. Of the total population of 62,410,619, 96 percent lived in families,[4] but the families they lived in were significantly different—particularly for the urban working class—than those of the pre–World War I era. The traditional large proletarian families of the *Kaiserreich,* symbolized by Heinrich Zille's and Käthe Kollwitz's renderings of hordes of children tugging at the skirts of pregnant mothers, while still a staple of both right- and left-wing political propaganda, were becoming a remnant of a prewar past. They were nostalgically mourned by some and discarded as patently dysfunctional—indeed "asocial"—in the modern world by others. In any case, while still visible, they were becoming a minority.

The birth rate in Germany had been steadily declining since the late nineteenth century,[5] but the trend toward smaller families did not appear as a mass working-class phenomenon until after the First World War.[6] According to the census, the average working-class household now consisted of 3.9 persons.[7]

War and defeat exacerbated longstanding anxieties about depopulation as well as eugenic quality, and aroused increased medical and governmental concern about the survival of the *Volk* and the labor and military capabilities of the coming generations.[8] For the first time in German history, the alarmed population expert Hans Harmsen announced in 1931, "The urban proletariat has relinquished its function as the strata of population increase."[9]

Demographers focused their attention on so-called net reproduction rates that measured "replacement levels," and Germany, it was generally acknowledged, had the lowest postwar net reproduction rate of any country in Europe except Austria.[10] By 1933, the national birth rate, which had reached 25.9 per 1000 population in 1920 in the immediate aftermath of the war, dropped to 14.7, the lowest in Europe.[11] Overall, the national fertility rate was one-half of what it had been at the turn of the century.

Metropolitan Berlin, with its invigorating "air, its vitality, and tempo,"[12]— "babylonian, profound, chaotic, powerful"—as enchanted urban chroniclers described their city,[13] was also "sterile Berlin" with the lowest birth rate of any city in Europe.[14] In the years 1871 to 1880, the German capital had boasted a birth rate of 43.1 per 1,000 population; by 1923, the figures had drastically dropped to around 9.9.[15] Moreover, this decrease was primarily caused by a decline in marital fertility. Working-class women were joining the wives of white-collar employees, civil servants, and professionals in consciously limiting the size of their families. In 1933, just over 35 percent of all the married couples in Berlin were childless, twice the national average.[16] In September 1928, at the height of postwar and postinflation prosperity and before the depression even began, the Prussian minister for social welfare issued a special memorandum on the birth rate decline that determined:

> There is no doubt that the limitation of births is willful. Intercourse is rationalized, at least by the greater part of the population. People simply do not want more than one or two children.[17]

At best the "two-child system" was establishing itself, still below the three child "replacement level" decreed necessary by demographers. And Berlin, it seemed, was well on its way "from the one-child to the no-child system."[18]

Such statistics prompted a massive debate among politicians, population policy experts, physicians, sociologists, and social policy planners about the meaning of these changing fertility patterns. Raging across the political spectrum, the discussion produced apocalyptic visions of the collapse of German *Kultur* and the danger of innundation by Slavic hordes from the East and other foreigners rushing in to fill the vacuum[19]—fears surely aggravated by the revolutionary upheavals in Russia—as well as earnest attempts to talk about a necessary "rationalization" of the population increase.[20] Behind all the discussions there lurked questions about the role of the "new woman": Was the modern woman too selfish, too physically degenerated by the luxuries of civilization, or too exhausted from the rigors of wage labor to reproduce? Had she gone, as Ernst Kahn suggested in a famous book published in 1930, on a birth strike?[21]

Modernity, it seemed to many observers, had come to the new republican Germany with a vengeance. Rapid rationalization of production and the work process, financed in part by extensive American investment, including the introduction of scientific management and assembly lines, and new standards of speed, efficiency, and productivity, was accompanied by—and dependent on—a much remarked-upon rationalization and scientifization of everyday life. Dr. Otto Neustätter's Health Calendar for June 1926 noted:

> No period in history makes such demands on people as ours. Telegraph, telephone, radio, railroads, automobile, airplanes, media, work pressures, hectic pace of life—industrialization, mechanization, Americanization of our whole modern lifestyle force people into an unprecedented tempo of life.[22]

Key to mastering these challenges—indeed central to the social project and "modern" identity of the Weimar Republic—were attempts to reconcile motherhood with paid work, and to produce "new women" and new families capable of efficiently and lovingly managing housework, sexuality, maternity, and wage earning. Women seemed to be both on the cutting edge of modernity and a bastion of stability in a rapidly changing world. They were located in such traditional sectors as agriculture and the home and in the most advanced sectors of assembly-line production and the "new" white-collar occupations.

In an encounter of public and domestic spheres that had been greatly intensified by the expansion of state intervention in World War I and affirmed by the social welfare promises of the Weimar Constitution, women also were increasingly visible, as clients and caregivers, in public health and social service agencies.[23] As workers, wives, and mothers, they were both at home in, and burdened by, a fast-paced modern age which repositioned public and private space, restructured male and female roles, and undermined "organic" values. Women appeared, therefore, in many conflicting and overlapping guises as modernity's agents, victims, and mediators. Indeed, they personified emblematically and in their social roles the "crisis of modernity" that shook Germany after the First World War.[24]

As the twin pressures of nerve-wracking new work processes and the traditional wage differential between male and female workers were added to the burden of endless unpaid labor at home, women emerged as quintessential rationalized workers: they earned little and were very productive. Most German women, in fact, still worked at tasks defined as traditional, either as unpaid workers within the family and household or within family enterprises. And, despite the widespread concern about young unskilled female workers replacing experienced, skilled male workers, women only rarely displaced men. In fact, far from precipitating a female invasion of male labor preserves, rationalization tightened, indeed, institutionalized, the modern sexual division of labor.[25] Yet, rationalized work and family patterns affected even those women who did not directly work in the new sectors of the economy. While not significantly increasing the proportion of women in the labor force, rationalization reorganized it in such a way that women stood at the forefront: in assembly-line factories; in mechanized offices with typewriters, filing cabinets, and switchboards; behind the sales counters of chain stores; and in the expanded social service bureaucracies of a welfare state.

Persistent government, scientific, and media declarations of "crisis" stemmed in part from the conflation of two phenomena which appeared to magnify each other: the declining birth rate and the so-called "crisis" in marriage. Women were getting married in record numbers, but nevertheless it seemed as though there were neither enough men nor babies to go around. The "surplus women problem," attributed to the decimation of war, was a staple of social commentary. Between 1.7 and 1.8 million German men had been slaughtered in the war, approximately 15 percent of all men between the ages of 20 and 40—an ominous figure for women of marriageable and childbearing age.[26] The 1925 census counted 30,196,823 males and 32,213,796 females, still leaving a "surplus" of over two million women.[27]

Widespread assumptions about masses of sadly single women may have been partly wishful thinking: it was after all a matter of interpretation whether a woman was "surplus" by force of demographic circumstance or "single" by choice. A small but visible minority of women, often intellectuals and professionals, but also committed members of the working-class movement, consciously chose not to marry and to live in unlicensed "marriage-like" relationships with life companions (*Lebensgefährten*).[28] Urban white-collar workers were also mostly single, largely by virtue of their youth. Yet their (still) unmarried status caused anxiety; social observers feared that the "working girl," having tasted the pleasures of urban mass culture, would resist settling into a life of maternity and housework.[29]

In fact, the percentage of women getting married had been steadily rising, just as clearly as the birth rate had been steadily declining.[30] But the new married woman, in contrast to a putative "old" one, did not necessarily give up paid employment, immediately embark on motherhood, or seek to create a large family. The "crisis" was constructed not only by the high visibility of single women but also by a larger number of marriages producing fewer children.

Images of decay and degeneration attended fears about a "*Volk* without youth," which could not reproduce itself. In 1910, one-third of the population had been under 15; by 1925, only one-quarter.[31] The approximately two million war-related casualties on both battlefront and homefront, followed by the devastating flu epidemic of 1918–1919, magnified the perception of an overaged population. Experts warned that postwar Germany was not only sterile but geriatric; even toy manufacturers complained of a slump.[32] At the same time, however, the coming of age of the turn of the century "baby-boom" generation produced an impression of hectic overcrowding and an exacerbation of gender and generational tensions.[33]

Furthermore, the general shift toward smaller working-class families and the decline in the traditional "birth rate differential" between bourgeoisie and proletariat meant that those proletarian families that did remain large were generally not the healthy "child-rich" families celebrated by church and nationalist groups.[34] New divisions emerged within the working class between the respectable and hardworking, deemed intelligent and disciplined enough to adapt to the new conditions of married women's labor, urban housing shortage, inflation, and unemployment by restricting family size, and an "underclass" commonly called "degenerate" and "asocial" well before the Nazi takeover.

Ironically, the expansion of health facilities and insurance coverage, especially for women and children, with its corollary improved monitoring of health conditions, fanned fears about population quantity and quality. Doctors in urban insurance and welfare practices confirmed what health insurance statistics reported: a rise in nervous disorders and suicide, especially for women of childbearing age; women workers called in sick less often but for longer periods and more serious ailments than their male colleagues.[35] In general, the nature of disability had changed. If improved hygiene and medications had reduced the number of infectious diseases, "modern" ailments such as cancer, cardiovascular diseases, emotional stress and suicide, and hazards from chemical and electrical products were increasing. The assembly-line tempo in both factory and office was placing nervous disorders at the top of the list of occupational diseases, especially among women.[36] Economic rationalization led, on the one hand, to a purging of "unproductive" elements from the work force, creating a new category of the "asocial," dependent on public assistance and subject to public supervision; on the other hand, it increased pressures on those remaining in the work force.

The acute housing shortage of the postwar years also exacerbated social tensions. According to the 1925 census, 117,430 Berliners were homeless and another 47,000 were living in basically uninhabitable temporary shelters such as attics and cellars.[37] Despite the efforts of Social Democratic municipal administrations and trade unions to finance innovative housing projects during the relatively stable mid-1920s, not enough was built and what was built was often too expensive for working-class occupants. Only 13.8 percent of the housing available in the Reich on January 1, 1930, had been built after the war.[38] Many new projects became architectural showplaces for an elite while the majority of the working-class population made do in extremely overcrowded prewar dwellings.[39]

Despite the promise of the Weimar Constitution to give housing priority to large families, and the pervasiveness of pronatalist rhetoric among all

political groups, new housing generally provided no more space than did the
much maligned dark and dank prewar back courtyard (*Hinterhof*) apartments.
The modern architecture of the 1920s, streamlined and determinedly func-
tional, was clearly designed for a smaller family; the new domestic culture
mandated sparse and efficient homes. The working-class and popular press,
stores, and exhibitions campaigned against ornament and *kitsch*, and the
wasted space in an underutilized parlor (*gutes Zimmer*).[40]

## The New Germany and the Welfare State

The grand and contradictory visions of an interventionist welfare state that
aimed simultaneously to protect, regulate, and emancipate Germans in a new
republic were inscribed within the Weimar Constitution. Article 109 guaranteed basically equal rights and responsibilities for male and female citizens
while Article 119 promised social protection for the family, especially large
families. Marriage was affirmed as the foundation of family life at the same
time that the rights of illegitimate children were protected. The sanctity of
the family was asserted but the state undertook final responsibility for rear-
ing children. Other sections boldly posited the right of all Germans, especially
the "child-rich," to decent housing, as well as the right to work and right to
compensation if no appropriate gainful employment could be found. Committed to the preservation of health and working ability as well as the encouragement of childbearing, the constitution promised adequate social insurance
for all citizens, and especially for mothers.[41]

At the same time, official national policy aimed to replace the catastrophic
manpower losses of the war and raise the dwindling birth rate. Alongside the
generous pro-natalist incentives promised by the constitution, the penal code,
adopted in 1871, and the civil code, essentially unchanged since 1900, deployed
punitive measures to protect the family and stimulate population growth.
Paragraph 218, even as amended in 1926, prohibited any abortions that were
not strictly medically indicated. Paragraph 184.3 outlawed the advertising,
display, and publicizing of contraceptives as objects intended for "indecent"
use, although selling or manufacturing contraceptives was not forbidden.
While steadily on the rise, divorce remained difficult and expensive. The link-
age of high fertility with national health and stability, rooted in nostalgic
memories of a prewar Germany that no longer existed, was so deeply ingrained that government officials never relinquished the hope of raising the
birth rate despite overwhelming evidence of a demographic shift that resisted
all efforts at correction.

The rapid and ambiguous development of Weimar social, health, and
population policy has been carefully described by historians—and indeed was
extensively documented at the time—so it will be only briefly rehearsed here
as a background for the following chapters. During the period of relative stabilization from 1924 to 1928, a swift spread of public health services, pregnancy,

maternal- and infant-care clinics, school health facilities, venereal disease treatment programs, and marriage counseling centers promoted increasing health consciousness, at least among the urban population. Germans in the 1920s were, it seemed, preoccupied as never before with health, nutrition, vitamins, exercise, gymnastics, and the healing properties of nature and body culture.

State and legislative efforts on a national, provincial, and local level both hampered and spurred the work of sex reformers, as a series of legal and legislative reforms streamlined government control of work and family life and ushered in what Paul Weindling has called—not entirely without irony—"a golden age of health education and propaganda."[42] For the Weimar welfare state, despite its broad promises and even conspicuous successes in some large cities, remained in many ways "a ramshackle edifice that had insecure financial foundations and great gaps in its cover."[43] Still buffeted by war, inflation, and an insecure international position, the various levels of government—in cooperation with business and advertisers—tried to implement social and population policy on a wide array of fronts: counseling centers, health programs, exhibitions, special events, committees, conferences and seminars, and innumerable publications and reports.

Publicity campaigns such as "National Baby Week" and large health and hygiene shows were designed to improve Germany's diplomatic and commercial status, promote advertising and consumption of German products, and encourage adherence to rational, cost-efficient health guidelines. In October 1926, for example, the Reich Ministry of the Interior and Department of Health subsidized the city of Berlin for hosting the first International Congress for Sex Research, not because of any great sympathy for the topic, but out of eagerness to attract distinguished foreign guests to a Germany that still felt itself an international pariah.[44] In Düsseldorf, a city anxious to promote its wares and its recovery from the ignominy of French occupation, national and local government and private industry together sponsored a massive 400,000-square-meter exhibition dedicated to "health, social welfare, and fitness (GESOLEI)."[45] Educational films and booths allowed manufacturers to advertise and display new consumer goods in an atmosphere that suggested the compatibility of profits and patriotism. Given the lackadaisical level of mass consumption in Weimar Germany, however, such exhibits were as much about showcasing German know-how and efficiency as they were about urging purchase of products. In Dresden in the same year, an elaborate Hygiene Museum was opened that also celebrated German "order, cleanliness and comfort."[46]

This push to improve health and raise eugenic awareness during the stabilization era dovetailed with a series of remarkable initiatives by which national and provincial authorities, through legislation and decree, claimed increased authority over Germans' health and well-being. On February 19, 1926, the Prussian Ministry for Social Welfare, an island of Catholic Center party control in an SPD state, issued a decree calling for the establishment of official medically directed marriage counseling centers to advise prospective mates and parents about their eugenic fitness for marriage and procreation. Social welfare officials conceptualized the centers as a direct alternative to the birth control services already being offered by nonstate organizations and clinics. Their goal was to encourage "responsible" marriages likely to produce "healthy and high-quality offspring" and conversely to prevent the procreation of the "unfit"; not by encouraging contraception, but rather by preventing socially and eugenically undesirable sexual relations and marriages. Prussia thereby served notice that despite municipal and local support for birth control services, state policy disavowed any attempt to artificially limit population growth.[47] As if to buttress the point, a long awaited but extremely limited national abortion law reform was finally pushed through the Reichstag in May 1926. While punishments were minimized, the principle was maintained that abortions were illegal, other than those strictly necessary to preserve life and health of the mother.

The first Prussian counseling center, directed by the eugenicist physician F. K. Scheumann, opened in eastern Berlin's working-class Prenzlauer Berg district on June 1, 1926. By the end of the year, 77 counseling centers had been set up in Prussia, and 52 more were in the planning stage, many of them in smaller towns and rural areas. Nationwide, 111 official counseling centers existed in 1926; by 1933 there would be about 200. But the Department of Health conceded that apart from the relatively well-frequented Prenzlauer Berg clinic, the centers were barely utilized.[48] Citizens were more interested in safe inexpensive contraceptives and general sex advice than in premarital health certificates or testing their physical fitness for marriage and procreation. Furthermore, most clients were already engaged in "biological marriage" and could not be dissuaded from an existing sexual relationship, however dysgenic. Ambitious plans to set up accurate eugenic files also foundered on the obvious unreliability of information presented by the clients.[49] Despite the notable lack of public enthusiasm, and the admitted impossibility of making scientifically valid judgments about fitness for procreation, government health officials refused to relinquish the idea, hoping that improved publicity would increase interest.

The Prussian decree, intended to counter unauthorized birth control services, actually only confirmed the absurdity of expecting a population to gear its sexual activities according to (dubious) eugenic guidelines. Indeed, it drew attention to and benefitted the independent facilities that did try to meet the demand for birth control and sex advice. In 1927, the Ministry of Labor and Social Welfare in Saxony issued its own call for the establishment of official marriage counseling centers as part of its social welfare agenda. Expressing a somewhat different intent from that of the Prussian decree, and in a step toward state support, the Saxon guidelines recommended sex and birth control counseling in the hope of combating infant mortality, illegitimacy, and illegal abortions, while also lauding the possibility of applying eugenic data gathered in the centers to the identification and treatment of criminals.[50]

Despite the strict emphasis on moral probity and reproductive fitness, the public and the media perceived the establishment of such state-sponsored centers as a sign of sexually more open times. As we shall see in the following chapters, their very existence (especially if like the Berlin site, they did make referrals for birth control in cases of supposedly compelling medical or eugenic need) subverted their own intentions and sanctioned ongoing public discussion about "the crisis of marriage," and the need for birth control and sex education.[51] On the Prenzlauer-Berg center's first anniversary, the *Berliner Tageblatt* gleefully reported the case of a middle-aged woman with an overeager husband who wondered whether it was safe to add a little bromide to his tea.[52]

Passage of several other ambitious regulatory and protective reforms also marked parliamentary and political life in the mid-1920s. Reponding in part to longstanding demands of the bourgeois women's movement, as well as to medical and eugenic concerns, the Reichstag on February 18, 1927, passed the Law for the Prevention of Venereal Disease, which provided that medical authorities assume what had previously been police functions in the treatment and prevention of sexually transmitted diseases. The law broke a long tradition of freedom of choice in health care (*Kurierfreiheit*); since 1869 trade regulations had allowed homeopathy and other popular health movements to flourish. By making it a felony for anyone without a medical license to examine or treat reproductive organs, it signaled an attack, not only on the lay midwives, homeopaths, and folk healers who traditionally had a role in gynecological and obstetrical care, but also on the proliferating lay self-help leagues.[53] Passed over KPD and some SPD objections, the new law offered the government a potentially potent weapon for its harassment of the sex reform movement.[54] This resulted, however, not in the demise of the leagues but in an intensification of their efforts to ally with sympathetic physicians to provide clients with medically sound contraceptives and advice.

Like most Weimar population policy, the venereal disease regulations were ambiguous in that they actually facilitated some access to birth control by permitting advertisements for condoms as a means of preventing infections. In Berlin, to the consternation of many conservative and clerical groups worried about the decline in public morality, local authorities assured that condoms were easily available from vending machines at hairdressers, restaurants, cafes, and bars, and from toilet attendants.[55] At the same time that Social Democratic and Communist officials were pressing for the distribution of birth control information in marriage and sex counseling centers, conservative and clerical groups were mounting counteroffensives as evidenced by the passage in 1926 of a rather ineffectual law against "Filth and Trash" (*Schund und Schmutz*).[56]

In another major assertion of welfare state initiative, a Law for the Protection of Mothers, promulgated on July 16, 1927, expanded the provision of prenatal and maternity benefits. The law offered insured women workers a maternity allowance of three-quarters of their wage for four weeks prior to and six weeks after delivery, with protection from dismissal during that time, making Germany, at least on paper, a world leader in the provision of maternity benefits.[57] In this case, however, general pro-natalist principles did not override the traditional welfare state strategy of insuring citizens as workers. In practice many German women were not eligible or simply could not afford to take advantage of the provisions, preferring to continue working as long as possible in order to supplement their wages with their maternity allowance.[58] At the same time that maternity and delivery coverage was improved, regulations governing birth and delivery, particularly licensing and training procedures for midwives, were tightened.

The republic's clear commitment to an expanded state role in social welfare and public health, the ongoing barrage of demographic and social data, and the insistent and pervasive sense that both the war and the rationalization of the economy had fundamentally altered everyday life and especially family life, set the stage and provided the framework for the movement described in this book. Weimar's "crisis of modernity" moved reformers to emphasize the rationalization of sex and reproduction as integral to the organization of a modern progressive republic. Antonio Gramsci, in his famous essay on "Americanism and Fordism," put this conviction in extreme form, referring to sexuality:

> The exaltation of passion cannot be reconciled with the timed movements of productive motions connected with the most perfect automatism. . . . The truth is that the new type of man demanded by the rationalization of production and work cannot be developed until the sexual instinct has been suitably regulated and until it too has been rationalised.[59]

If the new economy and new social institutions required a new type of man, they also and most especially required a new type of woman and family. As the woman's fashion magazine *Die Neue Linie* (*The New Line*) declared in 1930: "Housewife, mother and working woman. The synthesis of these three lifestyles is the problem of the age."[60] Indeed, women's newly visible presence in public spaces—at the workplace, in politics, or in social welfare institutions—even as they continued to be responsible for home, health, and procreation, seemed only commensurate with a generalized scientifization and bureaucratization that the industrial psychologist Fritz Giese termed the "neutralization of modern life through technology."[61]

Weimar sex reformers aspired to confront this neutralization with a reformed gendering and sexualization—especially refeminization of women—through a "rebirth of the body." The development of, and support for, working-class and female sexual and procreative behavior adequate to a technologized world were crucial factors in this process. While often deeply divided on other political issues, sex reformers shared in and helped to formulate a consensus around the necessity of rationalization and human economy in both production and reproduction.

Throughout the twenties and early thirties, sex reformers gained influence in local governments dominated by Communist and Social Democratic officials and played an important role in municipal health departments and health insurance systems. All of their innovations, in public health and social medicine, in maternal and infant care, in birth control and sex counseling, were, as we shall see, placed under severe strain by the economic and political crisis in late Weimar Germany. But both the initiatives of the stabilization years and the attacks on them during the depression provided for an unlikely coalition of doctors and grassroots activists to build a social movement that could both medicalize and politicize the urgent popular demand for birth control and information on sexuality.

# two

# "Prevent: Don't Abort"

## The Medicalization and
## Politicization of Sexuality

**Birth Control, The Challenge of the Times.**

Workers! . . . Girls! . . . Women! . . . let yourself be counseled and
avoid abortions that can destroy your bodies. . . . Proletarians! The
more you love your children, the more you should think about their
welfare and your responsibility! Come to us! We can help you prevent
unhappiness!

RV leaflet, ca. 1930[1]

Prevention of pregnancy belongs in the hands of the doctor.[2]

In 1932, the Berlin gynecologist Hans Lehfeldt published an article in which he
documented the remarkable growth of what he termed "a people's movement"
(*Volksbewegung*) for birth control and sex education during the twelve years of
the Weimar Republic. The appearance of such an essentially favorable report
written by a physician in a journal edited by the eugenicist and social hygienist
Hans Harmsen was a sign of how broad and diverse this social movement for
the reform of sexual and procreative regulations and practices had become.[3]
Lay leagues claimed over 150,000 members—including sympathetic physicians—and their influence stretched well beyond those who formally joined.
Their journals, meetings, and makeshift counseling centers were highly visible
throughout much of Germany, and birth control and sex education services
were available in numerous municipal and health insurance clinics.[4]

An eclectic coalition of political actors constituted this sex reform movement (*Sexualreformbewegung*). Some came from commercial leagues selling
birth control products; others were members of the Communist and Social
Democratic parties or smaller working-class political groups. They were
joined by representatives of the medical profession, state agencies, and
the international birth control movement, embodied by the globe-trotting
American birth controller Margaret Sanger. All were united by the convic-

tion that sexuality was better regulated than repressed, and that it was more sensible to manage and steer the birth rate decline than to mourn it. They adhered to a motherhood-eugenics consensus which assumed that motherhood was a natural and desirable instinct in all women, only needing to be properly encouraged, released, and regulated, and which understood the bearing of healthy offspring as a crucial social task. In the search for effective birth control and sexual advice, they both clashed and cooperated in campaigns to limit births and promote sexual hygiene.

Sex reformers undertook the practical work of establishing birth control and sex advice counseling centers that took as their motto, "better to prevent than to abort." They also organized mass and parliamentary campaigns for the reform or abolition of paragraph 218 and the legalization of abortion. Across a wide political spectrum, they shared a vision of a "healthy" modern society in which access to legal abortion, contraception, eugenic sex education, and general social welfare would assure a new "rational" social order that was both stable and humane and that would promote both collective welfare and individual happiness.

The Weimar movement began with the collapse of the Wilhelmine regime at the end of World War I and the chaos of defeat and revolution. A perceived rise in venereal disease, and dissolute mores (*Verwilderung der Sitten*), as well as the spread of a relentlessly publicized "abortion scourge," provoked grave anxiety about social health and the future of the family, but also publicized and gave impetus to sex reform initiatives. The early Weimar press was filled with reports on meetings to oppose the repressive sex codes, especially paragraph 218, as well as advertisements touting all manner of "rubberwares" and remedies for "women's troubles." A typical ad for a vaginal syringe helpfully announced that, "it is forbidden to insert this during pregnancy since same will then be terminated."[5] The huge German pharmaceutical industry produced something like 80–90 million condoms annually—24 million just from the Fromms Act Company—and about 150 other birth control products. With profit margins estimated at 800–1,300 percent, manufacturers were happy to fill the demand of a thriving self-help market in birth control.[6] The Ministry of Interior and the newly established national Department of Health (*Reichsgesundheitsamt*, RGA) worried helplessly about a rising rate of illegal abortions, apparently facilitated by the many suspicious syringes and douches flooding the market. Brazen salespeople often hawked their wares right at the factory gates, selling and lecturing to women workers on their lunch hour.[7]

At the same time, the advent of the new republic, and reports of the revolutionary family and sexual codes being legislated in the young Soviet Union, also raised hopes that a "new morality" of responsible birth control and companionate sexual relations could be reflected and institutionalized in a reformed legal code. In the immediate postwar years, particularly during the brief hiatus between the abolition of imperial censorship and the institution of new restrictions by the Weimar authorities in 1922, topics that had previously remained "hidden away in . . . professional journals—or else become the domain of pornography" entered mass popular culture and became an integral part of public discourse.[8] The first films attacking restrictions on abortion and homosexuality were produced as part of a wave of so-called "enlightenment films." In the newly constituted Reichstag, proceedings began to reform the sections of the imperial penal code regulating sexual behavior.

Sexual science enjoyed a new vogue and legitimacy as defeated Germany maintained its position as the international leader in the field. In 1919, Prussia's new Social Democratic state government offered homosexual rights campaigner Magnus Hirschfeld—whose Scientific-Humanitarian Committee had been battling since 1897 for reform of paragraph 175, which outlawed sodomy and other sex crime laws—a mansion in Berlin's fashionable Tiergarten district to house his library of over 20,000 volumes and 30,000 photographs. He immediately set up the Institute for Sexual Science and inaugurated a pioneer sex counseling clinic.[9] Weekly public question-and-answer sessions in the institute's Ernst Haeckel Hall fielded queries such as, "What is the best way to have sex without making a baby?" "What is the most absolutely reliable contraceptive?" or "How long do condoms last?" and became popular evening outings for Berliners.[10]

The counseling strategies pioneered by Hirschfeld and his colleague Max Hodann set the style for later municipal and health insurance clinics as well as for private birth control and sex counseling clinics. A controversial and eccentric figure, long known as a homosexual and champion of congenital and "third sex" theories of homosexuality, Hirschfeld combined a deep faith in scientific and technological "treatment" and "correction" with a commitment to direct social action, which led him into alliance with lay leagues and the Communist party (KPD). Hirschfeld treated the panoply of sexual problems from unwanted pregnancy to heterosexual dysfunction, and from venereal diseases to the most bizarre "perversions," with a pragmatic approach that insisted on asking not, "who is at fault," but "what is at fault."[11]

In 1921, Hirschfeld's institute hosted a preliminary meeting of the World League for Sex Reform (WLSR), which would become a gathering place for sex reformers from Russia, Japan, Europe, and the United States between 1928 and 1933.[12] Enjoying increased freedom of expression and political support, German sex reformers hoped to continue the tradition begun in 1911, when the first international conference for birth control was convened in Dresden. Led by independent feminist Helene Stöcker, the League for the Protection of Motherhood and Sex Reform (*Bund für Mutterschutz und Sexualreform*, BfM)—founded in 1905—continued its fight for a "new ethic" of women's right to sexuality and unwed motherhood, and maintained its preeminent position of intellectual (and moral) leadership within the sex reform movement.[13]

A unique organization, with a relatively small membership of about 2,000, in which notions of "free love" and pacifism mingled with support for the

Soviet Union, contact with the Communist party, and an affinity to the "home-less" intellectuals of the Weimar left, the BfM—together with the Institute for Sexual Science—was a major innovator in providing sex counseling services for youth and unmarried women.[14] The middle-class Federation of German Women's Associations (*Bund deutscher Frauenvereine*, BDF), however, which had split in 1908 when a majority of members voted against the abolition of paragraph 218, persisted in its avoidance of controversial positions on sexuality or birth control in the Weimar period.[15] The Society for Sexual Reform (*Gesellschaft für Sexual Reform*, GESEX), established in 1913 under the leadership of Dr. Felix Theilhaber, continued to rally left-wing intellectuals against paragraphs 175 and 218 of the penal code. The Association of Socialist Physicians (*Verein Sozialistischer Ärzte*, VSA), also first founded in 1913, functioned as an important forum for Social Democratic and like-minded—in the Weimar Republic, many of them were Communists—doctors who took as their motto Rudolf Virchow's famous dictum that physicians were "the natural advocates of the poor."[16]

After the war, GESEX and the VSA were key to the emerging alliance between radical professionals and lay leagues, which would be central to Weimar sex reform. Increasingly, a new emphasis on service and political activism shifted attention away from taxonomies of the "esoteric" and "deviant" such as masturbation, homosexuality, and the "plagues" of prostitution and venereal disease, toward the stabilization and encouragement of "normal" family and heterosexual relations.

In a lively marriage of commerce and politics, the first postwar birth control leagues such as the Federation of the Active (*Bund der Tätigen*), founded in 1922 in Bavaria, Saxony, and Silesia, were essentially clever business schemes by birth control manufacturers and distributors. Called "lay leagues" to distinguish them from existing sex reform organizations composed of intellectuals, sexologists, and physicians, they were initially local commercial organizations that catered to a German proletariat that was now actively participating in the birth rate decline that had characterized the bourgeoisie since the end of the nineteenth century. Popular associations advocating natural healing and "lifestyle reform" (*Lebensreform*), such as nudism or vegetarianism, provided cadres and political orientation.

Largely independent of the intellectual prewar sex reform tradition but influenced by press, legal, and parliamentary discussions about reforming the sex code, lay groups recruited working-class members who had little access to sympathetic physicians and were reluctant to pay high pharmacy or mail-order prices for contraceptives. Their propaganda was informed by a vaguely anticapitalist and neo-Malthusian rhetoric, which appealed to class resentment with the subversive premise that the working class, too, had the right to sexual pleasure without suffering the consequences of unwanted pregnancy.[17] Drawing on socialist and anarchist traditions, as well as from the health, sports, and youth movements of the Wilhelmine era, the lay leagues became an integral

part of working-class culture and of the broad new consumer culture developing in Germany after the First World War.[18]

To compensate for their relatively low prices, the leagues offered business-
men a large concentrated market, with accessible membership lists and advertising space in journals and newsletters. Moreover, they provided relative
immunity from paragraph 184.3, which restricted dissemination of birth control information, since publicity within an organization was not deemed public
advertising. Manufacturers competed for product endorsements from lay
league functionaries and traveling salespeople, and later from doctors who
recommended birth control methods in clinics or lectures. Some entre-
preneurs, like the pharmacist and abortionist Paul Heiser, formed "Workers
Associations for Birth Control" just to sell their own special contraceptive con-
coctions. Even the venerable Magnus Hirschfeld seems to have been bribed
(albeit not very lucratively) into unscrupulous promotion of certain brands.[19]

By 1924, as postwar unrest and inflation eased, and the economy briefly
and precariously stabilized, exclusively commercial ventures began to lose
power and influence, and the first independent lay birth control organizations
appeared. Relying on traditions of self-help and folk medicine, lay reformers
were nonetheless increasingly insistent that the working class also had a right
to the benefits of scientific progress. Anarchosyndicalists and socialists of
various stripes, along with lay healers and homeopaths, established "Associations for Sexual Hygiene and Life-Style Reform." Two groups based in
Saxony formed official sex reform organizations that had their own nationally distributed journals and a combined membership of 13,000. Other groups
continued to split, splinter, reform, and splinter again.[20]

By the mid-1920s, sex reform activists were explicitly demanding medical
supervision of birth control services and state regulation of contraceptive
production. Although some continued to accept funds or free samples from
manufacturers, leagues generally purchased and resold at cost affordable and
accessible birth control products such as spermicidal suppositories. These
commercial items were supposed to replace traditional methods of coitus
interruptus or douching immediately after intercourse, which were thought
to hinder sexual gratification, and, because of their high failure rate, contrib-
ute to the abortion "scourge." Lectures and question-and-answer sessions con-
veyed the insights of "enlightened, nonjudgmental" medicine and psychoanalysis to a wide audience. But, while health professionals generally saw in
the expansionist welfare state an opportunity to increase their influence and
prestige, they often anxiously opposed these attempts to appropriate and
popularize their knowledge and techniques.

Countless name changes and legalistic tricks reflected sex reformers' eagerness to escape the lingering stigma of profiteering, and the police harassment
to which they were subjected on the grounds of violating paragraphs 218
and 184.3 and various antiquackery and antiobscenity regulations. Reformers
aimed to demonstrate their scientific legitimacy to a medical profession that

accused them of health-endangering quackery as well as unethical politicization of purely medical issues. At the same time, they sought to prove their
socialist credentials to working-class parties critical of a single-minded focus
on family limitation derisively termed Malthusian and individualistic. Thus,
lay activists sought professional aid and credibility even as they criticized the
moralistic and class bias of most medical professionals; they generated self-
help groups to meet their immediate needs, while demanding support and
legitimacy from political parties, the state, and the medical profession.

By the crucial transition year 1928, just before the economic crisis hit with
full force, the lay leagues had joined government agencies and the medical
profession in preaching the dangers of quack abortions and overpriced patent
medicines. Increasingly, self-help was defended not as a matter of principle
but as an unfortunate necessity blamed on the lack of social responsibility
demonstrated by the vast majority of German physicians. Lay sex reformers
resented their lack of access to the latest developments in contraceptive and
sexological research, which were reported on at birth control and medical
congresses. Slowly and halfheartedly, they abandoned their mistrust of science and academic medicine, and actively enlisted the support of the small
but committed minority of physicians sympathetic to campaigns for birth control and sex counseling—partly out of political principle, and partly in the hope
of gaining influence over a growing grassroots movement that required medical control.

The incipient cooperation between left-wing physicians and the lay leagues
drew on a pool of a couple thousand mostly Socialist and Communist doctors. Centered in Berlin, they were organized in the Association of Socialist
Physicians (VSA), as well as in the League of German Women Doctors (BDÄ)
that had been formed in 1924 and counted about 900 members nationally by
1933. With a membership that was half Social Democratic, 20 percent Communist, and 30 percent unaffiliated, and a subscriber list of 2,000 for its journal *Der Sozialistische Arzt* (*The Socialist Physician, SA*), the VSA offered members a unique opportunity to meet and debate such issues as "Birth Control
and Socialism"—the theme of the 1928 national convention.[21] Remarkably,
professional solidarity and a common interest in the promotion of social
hygiene and preventive medicine overcame some of the otherwise bitter
political differences between Communists and Social Democrats; it also
helped compensate for the isolation progressive doctors faced in the profession as a whole.[22] Many of the most outspoken women physicians in the Berlin
BDÄ local were also VSA members.

Increasingly, urban doctors with large insurance and welfare practices
believed that rational medical practice necessarily involved building a reformed society that prevented poverty and disease and thereby promoted
good health. Birth control, after all, was already widely practiced among the
population, largely without benefit of medical advice; when contraception
failed, women resorted to illegal abortions. The only way to combat the "abor-

tion scourge" was to legalize and then regulate the provision of abortion and contraception. In an expanding welfare state committed to heightening health consciousness, combating the economic misery of the proletariat, and stabilizing family life in all classes, birth control, and—for that matter—control of broad postwar changes in sexual values and activity, required medical expertise and intervention. As we shall see, VSA and BDÄ members were the stalwarts staffing the municipal medical outposts in large cities as well as a central force in Weimar campaigns for sex reform. Sex reform doctors thus served to legitimize and supervise lay sex reform while at the same time incensing conservative colleagues who did not want their profession sullied by involvement with the "gutter politics" of birth control and abortion.

### Medicalization of the Lay Movement: The RV

The first major lay sex reform organization with substantial support from doctors, the National League for Birth Control and Sexual Hygiene (*Reichsverband für Geburtenregelung und Sexualhygiene*, RV) was founded in the summer of 1928.[23] It resulted from a merger of several lay organizations that wanted to liberate themselves from ties to birth control manufacturers and cooperate with doctors and sexologists in GESEX. Each group maintained considerable local autonomy, but combined they created an instant national membership of 12,000, subscribing to a single journal *Sexual-Hygiene* (*SH*). They also formed a loose association with the 19,000 subscribers to the *Weckruf* (*Reveille*), published by the People's Federation for the Protection of Mothers in Silesia.

The RV remained committed to its lay roots, insisting that physicians should serve members on a volunteer basis and not take over and determine policy. To prove the point, the RV appointed an exclusively lay leadership. A former carpenter from Nuremberg, Franz Gampe, was named business manager; Wilhelm Schöffer, who became editor of *SH*, was a former lay GESEX activist.[24] In large part because of its GESEX and VSA links, the RV successfully recruited physicians to write for its journals, lecture to members, and work in counseling centers examining women and fitting contraceptive devices. The passage of the 1927 Venereal Disease Law, which criminalized any nonmedical treatment of genital disorders, had made this cooperation with physicians not only a matter of conviction but also of legal necessity.

The RV was committed to the working-class movement but carefully avoided party affiliation, fearing both takeover by Communists and the fierce splits between Communists and Social Democrats that afflicted many avowedly socialist organizations. Many of its members probably voted Social Democratic, but were impressed by the reports from the Soviet Union of improved maternal and child health care, legalization of birth control and abortion, reform of marriage and divorce laws, and the decriminalization of consensual sexual acts. Referring proudly to the revolution in family and sexual codes ordered by the Bolsheviks, the KPD had, since its inception in 1919, treated access to legal abortion and birth control as serious political issues. In party propaganda, paragraph 218 served as a prime example of class injustice and bourgeois hypocrisy: sanitoria doors stood open to women who could pay for a therapeutic abortion justified as "medically necessary" while working-class women were condemned to quacks and hazardous, potentially deadly, "self-help."

But for both Social Democrats and Communists, birth control presented something of an ideological conundrum. Prewar mainstream Social Democracy had rejected neo-Malthusianism as individualist self-help, preferring to rely, as Clara Zetkin and Rosa Luxemburg insisted, on power in numbers. Dissidents, such as the physician Julius Moses (and the revisionist Eduard Bernstein), had in 1913 unsuccessfully called for a working-class birth strike to deny the ruling class "cannon fodder" and a "reserve army of labor."[25] Moses now served as a population policy spokesman for the SPD in the Weimar Reichstag; unlike the KPD, which consistently called for decriminalization, his party remained divided on how best to reform paragraph 218. The RV, with its mixed Communist, socialist, and independent membership, strenuously insisted that capitalist political and economic policies, not babies, caused social misery, but also recognized the social necessity of birth control and abortion reform. Occasional slippage into neo-Malthusian rhetoric and, by the end of 1928, cooperation with that most devout single-issue birth controller, Margaret Sanger, notwithstanding, the RV advocated birth control not as a check on overpopulation or a panacea for the world's social ills but as a survival tactic for the hard-pressed working class:

> Even if the birth control movement cannot be the ideal solution for the liberation of humankind, under the currently prevailing economic system, it is the only thing that can save the family from hunger and misery.[26]

Socialists, RV supporters insisted, were obliged to consider the situation of individual families (not individual women), whose limited resources had to be effectively allocated through a rational program of "human economy" (*Menschenökonomie*). It did, indeed, matter whether a weekly income of 50 RM had to feed a family of two, four, or ten.[27] The RV's programmatic demands reflected this short-term focus. They included abolition of paragraphs 218 and 184.3 and the legalization of medical abortions, availability of birth control on prescription through the health insurance system or through communal welfare for the uninsured, public support for indigent pregnant women, and three months of pre- and postdelivery financial support for mothers. Defined as part of a future socialist revolution, these goals were also demands on the existing capitalist state, designed to test its limits and presumed to find it wanting. But the RV also had high expectations of what a state could do for sexual health, demanding a "perfectly functioning state-run sexual welfare system" that would guarantee safety, reliability, and affordability.[28] In the interim, accurate information on reliable contraceptives would protect working-class families from overpriced quacks.[29]

The RV (and other lay leagues) promoted family limitation primarily as economic self-defense, and not to enhance sexual pleasure. It privileged regulation and discipline as working-class virtues directed against the chaos and disorder of capitalism. Just as trade unions and party organizations imposed a hopefully internalized political and work discipline on working-class families, so the sex reform leagues facilitated the internalization of a sexual self-discipline that the proletariat was so often accused of not having. The sex-reformed working class would not provide the ruling class with cannon fodder or a reserve army of labor; neither would it fulfill its reputation of being licentious and "asocial."

Sex reform did intend to increase the pleasure quotient in proletarian daily existence, but in a responsible, rationalized fashion that would contain potentially dangerous erotic impulses, break the mold of the "large, degenerate, asocial" family, and spread the bourgeois privilege of small, healthy, and well-cared-for families. As the RV's Dr. Lehfeldt argued in a popular "marriage" advice booklet, "In erotic matters it would even be unscrupulous not to use reason . . . and [like animals] copulate without considering the consequences."[30] Proper use of birth control, however, could heighten sexual satisfaction and thereby stabilize marriages and in turn the entire nation. In that sense, the willingess to use birth control became for progressives almost as much a test of character and morality as the rejection of birth control was for certain religious and conservative groups.

This vision of social respectability and domestic happiness was tightly linked to the eugenic notions that coexisted with the language of class consciousness. Rehearsing the oft-quoted Nietzschean proverb, "Don't just reproduce, but also upgrade,"[31] the RV posed birth control as genetically responsible as well as politically correct, and projected a eugenic utopia of "consciously conceived free-spirited quality people."[32] As one birth control clinic physician typically formulated it: Sex reform was understood as a form of "applied eugenics . . . a science concerned with sexual relationships which should be individually satisfying and best suited to produce children healthy in body and mind" as well as "human beings of greater humanity and individuality."[33] For many league members, birth control clearly meant more than mere economic survival; it promised healthier families, stronger marriages, and more time and money for activism in the class struggle.

Nevertheless, the insistent framing of sex reform as a primarily economic issue may help to explain male dominance of the lay leagues, and why skilled but unemployed male workers were so prominent in their leadership. These were, after all, groups devoted to distributing contraceptive devices intended for women and providing education in sexual techniques that would make their partners more satisfying lovers. As the ostensible family breadwinners, however, men were urgently interested in family limitation. Moreover, birth control and sex advice could help husbands by stabilizing and harmonizing marital relations within the working-class family.

The lay leagues' relationship with the women they aimed to serve and educate was much more problematic. Male sex reform activists, like trade union, SPD, and KPD organizers, regularly expressed frustration at their failure to mobilize women. RV leader Gampe complained that, "All the legal paragraphs cannot cause as much trouble for our work as the shame and modesty among the women and girls of broad sections of the working people."[34] Women were continually berated for passivity, even as some leagues urged them to run for office and even to elect special women's representatives.[35] At the same time,—and in stark contrast to the medical and Communist sex reform movement where women, especially doctors, were prominently involved—membership in the working-class lay leagues was implicitly male, as reflected in such typical *SH* announcements as: "Attendance of all members with wives is mandatory," or: "Members come one and all. All of you bring your wives."[36]

When Dr. Hans Lehfeldt published his comprehensive survey of lay sex reform in 1932, he estimated a total membership of 113,000 but hastened to add that, "The actual number is considerably higher . . . most importantly because . . . the wives of the members who are often especially active in the movement have been overlooked."[37] RV branches willing to organize activities specifically for women found that they were much more successful in attracting them. Some groups reluctantly realized that separate evenings helped women "loosen their tongues" and talk frankly about their bodies and sexual needs.[38] In Hamburg two male physicians successfully attracted participants for a series of women-only courses where they used a "phantom model" to teach about the female body and various forms of birth control.[39]

If women were blamed for "false modesty" and inhibitions against discussing sex, the membership as a whole was criticized for its apolitical consumerism. Lay leagues pleaded with their members to participate actively in the movement and "not merely profit from it."[40] Clearly, lay sex reform's major appeal was the services—information and products—it provided, and not the opportunity for political organization. The lay movement was perhaps not quite the "ersatz religion" some Communist sex reformers bemoaned,[41] but it did go well beyond supplying contraception information and remedies. It also provided advice on general health issues such as the advisability of surgery, natural healing, sports, gymnastics, nutrition, and body care, as well as potential connections to sympathetic and inexpensive, or even free, doctors. Some, especially Communist, physicians were well known for their willingness to perform illegal abortions safely and for a reasonable (or no) fee. Finally, the lay leagues played an important role in popularizing the notion that sexual repression was unhealthy, that better sex had the potential of creating better human beings, better families, and better children, and that when it came to achieving better sex, it was best to ask your doctor for advice.

However, for people outside large cities like Berlin, Hamburg, and Frankfurt, where birth control could be obtained from supportive physicians and some municipal and health insurance clinics, the "your-doctor-knows-best" policy was difficult to enforce. Few physicians were willing to donate their time to suspect organizations with meager budgets. Despite the venereal disease law, nonlicensed folk healers and homeopaths continued to provide many medical services in lay leagues' counseling centers. By 1933, the RV had over 200 affiliated locals with some kind of counseling service, but only three—in Berlin, Hamburg, and Nuremberg—had real medical support.[42] Even the very active Hamburg RV only provided contraceptive distribution without benefit of medical examination every Tuesday and Friday between 7 P.M. and 9 P.M.

Doctors explained the proper use of birth control in large lectures with blackboards, slides, and exhibitions of devices. Women in the audience were given the address of a contraceptive distribution center and a referral to Dr. Rudolf Elkan, an agreeable local general practitioner. While such large meetings reached many more people at one time than would have been feasible in a doctor's office, they also compensated for a medical profession that remained, in Dr. Elkan's words, mostly "opposed and apathetic."[43] Like other leagues with even less support from physicians, the RV set up mobile ("flying") counseling centers (*fliegende Beratungsstellen*) where a single doctor, accompanied by a traveling league functionary, made regular visits to outlying nonurban areas, such as in Saxony and Thuringia, bringing contraceptive samples and slide shows to those with the least access to medical birth control services.

The RV grew rapidly, becoming the most influential, if not the largest, mass sex reform league. It was unique in its political but nonpartisan stance, independence from commercial ties, broad membership, and attention to both lay and medical constituencies. Between 1928 and 1930, it expanded from 136 to 192 locals, providing 15,526 subscribers to *Sexual-Hygiene* (*SH*).[44] Within two years the Hamburg branch organized 1,500 members who met every fourth Tuesday of the month for lectures on such themes as "Introduction to Population Politics; Anatomy and Physiology of the Sex Organs; Theory and Techniques of Contraception; Surgical and Infectious Women's Diseases; Race Theory, Eugenics, and Sterilization; and, The Extermination of Unfit Life." Knowledge of the latest eugenics and race hygiene theories was considered just as necessary as information on birth control techniques or prenatal development of fetal life as presented in Dr. Wilhelm Liepmann's popular filmstrip, *Fetal Life*.[45] In reference to the use of the phrase "extermination of unfit life" (literally, "life unworthy of life"), *SH* pointedly noted that it was admittedly a bit "harsh," and should not imply any inferiority on the part of cripples;

nevertheless it was appropriate because when it came to the regulation of procreation, collective welfare and fitness for reproduction should be the primary concern.[46]

The RV/GESEX Counseling Center was established in 1930 in a proletarian district in central Berlin. Run on a volunteer basis by two doctors, Hans Lehfeldt and Franz Hirsch, the storefront center was financed by contributions from trade unions, leftist Social Democrats, and anarchist groups. Doctors fitted and distributed samples of diaphragms and cervical caps donated by manufacturers. Such clinics served as convenient laboratories for testing birth control products and technology, and some of the first experiments with the original IUD (Gräfenberg ring) were carried on in the RV clinic. While trying hard to remain within legal bounds, doctors stretched the letter of the law to provide women with certificates attesting to the medical necessity of abortions. In accordance with what were perceived as socialist principles, both married and unmarried women were treated, and Drs. Hodann, Lehfeldt or Hirsch conducted regular question-and-answer evenings.[47]

Clients were offered Dr. Lehfeldt's pamphlet, *Das Ehe-Buch* (*The Book of Marriage: A Guide for Men and Women*), which promised to fight the "abortion epidemic" through "timely prevention of pregnancy." Lehfeldt gave simple explanations of the female reproductive system and accurate information on the female fertility cycle (something not to be taken for granted in birth control literature). He acknowledged that abstinence was the only surefire birth control method but suggested that anyone who thought that was a viable alternative could close the book right away! Like virtually all sex reformers, Lehfeldt discouraged coitus interruptus—the only universally available and free method—as both unreliable and sexually frustrating, and recommended that women rely on a mechanical/chemical combination of diaphragm and spermicide. Along with the obligatory exhortation that, "Prevention of pregnancy belongs in the hands of the doctor,"[48] and the defensive rhetoric about combating the need for abortions, the brochure offered for a minimal fee solid sympathetic contraceptive information to anyone who read it.[49]

The RV's journal, *Sexual-Hygiene* (*SH*), was another important source of advice, a self-proclaimed weapon in the campaign against "sexual illiteracy."[50] Attractively printed on glossy paper and nationally distributed, it had by 1932 an official circulation of 21,000, which did not represent all its readers since only one copy was sent to a household and many were handed out for free.[51] *SH* carried simply written educational articles that avoided some of the more melodramatic features of other lay journals. In 1929, for example, issues introduced Freud's ideas of psychoanalysis, explained mechanical and chemical birth control methods, publicized the campaign to abolish paragraph 218, and warned women that since male sperm was crucial to female health and vitality, coitus interruptus was also an undesirable contraceptive method for them (lest they become "dried out").[52] In keeping with alarmist social hygiene tenets about the dangers of national degeneration, *SH* also carried eugenic

horror stories of children conceived in drunken lust who grew up doomed
to disease or criminality. More positively, *SH* exhorted:

> Our time needs women who know their bodies, who are familiar with the laws
> of enlightened eroticism—and who in harmony with the ancient ideals of the
> beauty of body and soul will give life to healthy children.[53]

## Lifestyle Reform: Body, Machine, and Commerce

The RV, like all of sex reform, and much of the socialist and youth movements, drew heavily from an older tradition of lifestyle reform (*Lebensreform*)
that espoused a panoply of causes ranging from holistic medicine to nudism,
antivivisection, antiimmunization, vegetarianism, health foods, consumer
food cooperatives, suburban garden towns, artisanal craftsmanship, and various semireligious trends such as parapsychology, theosophy, Rudolf Steiner's
anthroposophy, and graphology as well as "modern" goals of improved housing and sanitation. *Lebensreform* also often propagated a diffuse antimodernism,
overlapping with *völkisch* sentiments, which saw industrialization and urban-
ization as corrupting evils. Despite its close cooperation with many left-wing
Jewish doctors, the RV was not immune to the "proletarian anti-Semitism"
that inflected parts of the working-class movement. An *SH* editorial in 1930
responded to complaints about anti-Jewish personal advertisements by re-
minding its readers: "The proletarian Jew is our comrade. We must combat
the Jewish bourgeoisie with its capitalism and nationalism just as much as
National Socialism."[54]

Still, unlike many *Lebensreform* advocates, and in contrast to *völkisch* population experts, sex reformers refused to accept a necessary contradiction between
technology and nature. Indeed a machine's potential for flawless technical
precision made it a model for the possible perfection of the human body—
which could become just as sleek, reliable, and efficient as a machine. Scathing
in their critique of capitalist inhumanity, sex reformers devoutly believed in
the perfectability of the human race. Thus they urged careful cultivation of
the body, working to coax it into greater feats at work, on the sports field, or
in bed.

The lay leagues' mid-1920s conversion to the value of medical expertise
stood in uneasy relationship to the traditional distrust of "regular" allopathic
medicine in *Lebensreform* and people's health movements. The communist sex
reform physician and playwright Friedrich Wolf, for example, championed
"diet, movement, air and water, fresh fruit, whole wheat bread, vegetables,
butter, milk" as "the best doctors in the world."[55] Like the proper use of birth
control and sexual hygiene, such a regimen represented proletarian self-help,
offering freedom from the dubious ministrations of the reactionary medical
profession and building up strength for struggle. Natural healing therefore
was propagated not only as something that could be purchased as a patent

medicine but as the cornerstone of a people's health (*Volksgesundheit*) movement. The working class, youth, and trade union movements translated the "lifestyle reform" (*Lebensreform*) stress on nature and "light, air, sun" into collective activities such as hiking, swimming, and rowing, which would promote comradely contact between the sexes, political discussion, and sex education, as well as healthful escape into the outdoors from the confines of urban labor.

Doctors committed to preventive medicine insisted that good health could best be achieved not by human or animal experimentation, immunization, or the profession's "injection mania" but by proper hygiene, fitness, nutrition, and decent living conditions.[56] They suggested a diet without meat, low in salt and spices, and rich in whole wheat bread, steamed vegetables, spinach juice, muesli, soft cheese, yogurt, celery, red beets, and chamomile and lavender tea.[57] Common prescriptions for physical fitness included breathing techniques, and mud baths, massage, and morning exercise to stimulate skin and metabolism. Recommended sports included skiing, skating, water sports, and hiking. Clothes were to be loose and comfortable.

Intent on counterbalancing the perceived physical and psychic deficits of urban life, sex reformers touted the weekend as a time for cultivating body fitness rather than drinking, carousing, or competitive sports. Mass entertainments like cinema, soccer, boxing, and other spectator sports were viewed with great suspicion. Leisure and relaxation were not to be left to chance, any more than were sex and health; they too needed to be organized, rationalized, set up in the most time-efficient manner for maximum benefit. Some of the admonitions for abstinence from alcohol and cigarettes, clean, well-ventilated separate bedrooms for parents and children, and "a pleasant bathroom for every home" must have seemed quite exotic to a working-class audience.[58] Dr. Wolf reassured his readers that he had lived "as a vegetarian for more than twenty years and is still not debilitated or dim-witted."[59] Women were of course responsible for enforcing unfamiliar regimes of household and sexual hygiene, as well as budgeting for, buying, and preparing in an appetizing manner foods, such as carrots, cabbage, tomatoes, and sauerkraut, which contained the proper balance of vitamins and minerals, while resisting expensive stimulants like coffee and tea.

Sex reform periodicals and films glorified, indeed fetishized, the ancient Greek ideal of the harmony of body and soul and the pure beauty of the naked body in motion.[60] Well-scrubbed physical attractiveness was linked to eugenic health; ugliness to ill health and degeneration. Sexologists tinkering with hormone therapies experimented with "fountain of youth" cures. The emphasis on healthy motherhood and its new connection to fulfilled female sexuality presupposed a new fascination with the female body as an object of active strength and beauty rather than simply as a static object of ornament. Gymnastic systems especially designed for women, modern dance, and light athletics gained popularity; in general, the stress on sports and outdoor activities served to display especially the female body in novel and unexpected ways. Journals were filled with semipornographic photographs of well-toned unclothed bodies, which were of course always defended as depictions of wholesome nudity.[61] The "Body School (*Körperschule*) Adolf Koch" in Berlin, for example, proudly reported that in the six years of its coeducational existence, not a single case of venereal disease had occurred among its 78 percent unmarried membership—a clear sign of the moral and hygienic superiority of its sensible and "natural" approach to sexuality.[62]

Dr. Max Hodann's advice column in *SH* served as an extension of the counseling center or the doctor's consulting room. It reflected sex reformers' scientifically objective and determinedly matter-of-fact approach, and outlined a body regimen clearly meant to be both disciplinary and emancipatory. Hodann, who was widely known and beloved as the author of sex education booklets for children and youth, defined sexuality as the most natural thing in the world, which would flourish in an atmosphere of openness and good common sense.[63] To the question, "Is daily intercourse advisable?" the good doctor replied, "If it feels good, why not."[64] To the concerned husband who wrote, "My wife can only come when she's on top. What can I do about this?" Hodann sensibly riposted, "If one position is more satisfying than another, there's absolutely no reason not to enjoy it."[65] He reassured readers that masturbation was harmless—in moderation—and admonished them not to marry anyone with whom they had never had sexual relations.[66]

Under the rubric "Dr. Hodann answers," he gave advice on birth control methods, treatment for vaginal discharge, tight vaginas, and menstrual cramps, and how to avoid exhaustion after intercourse and premature ejaculation.[67] Eclectic in his scientific allegiances, Hodann recommended hormone treatment for vaginal dryness, but suggested Freudian psychoanalysis for a more intractable case of "frigidity."[68] In this manner, Hodann specifically intended to translate into accessible didactic language not only Freudian theories on sexuality but also the flowery but highly precise prescriptions for mutual sexual fulfillment contained in Th. Van de Velde's sex manual *Ideal Marriage,* which had first appeared—to great press attention (and satire)—in German translation in 1928.[69] *Sexual-Hygiene* therefore provided valuable sexual and medical advice to working-class readers, especially those in small towns and rural areas who otherwise relied on quacks and traveling salespeople. It also offered clients access to mail-order contraceptives or the opportunity to obtain them in closed meetings without the embarrassment and additional expense of purchasing them at the local pharmacy.

*Sexual-Hygiene* was not the only sex reform forum in Weimar Germany or the only one to call upon the expertise of Max Hodann and other "sex doctors" like Hirschfeld, Elkan, or Lehfeldt. The journal *Ideal Lebensbund (Ideal Life Union),* for example, contained a mixture of mildly titillating nude photographs, lightly erotic fiction, and a good deal of birth control information. By 1928, it had changed its name several times, from *Kultur-Ehe* to *Ideal-Ehe* to *Ideal-Lebensbund*, presumably both to evade legal prosecution on obscenity charges and to find a title that suggested companionship rather than legal marriage. Max Hodann chose its pages to announce that, "It is certain that monogamy is a catastrophe. The new path is still not clearly defined."[70] Over the course of a year, it covered a wide variety of topics: the hereditary nature of criminal characteristics; "misunderstood" (i.e., frigid) wives; hypnosis, sadism, and masochism (in a special issue on the "erotic"); advice on how to find a marriageable man; diet; and tips on "scientific" matchmaking by handwriting analysis.[71]

Wherever the ubiquitous Hodann published, he always used his dual authority as physician and working-class activist to plead for tolerance and run interference for "people in trouble."[72] In another typical column, he counseled parents not to punish a daughter whose love letters they had found, and instead to give the young couple time to get to know each other sexually before being forced into marriage:

> The pressures of everyday life, the disruptive power of habit can only be overcome through experience, erotic experience, and where would young people get this? They are fed sex propaganda, they are being titillated by shrill advertising of revues and by erotic, lewd publications, but nowhere are they given an inkling of how serious a matter eroticism is.[73]

In their column "Out of Sexual Misery," Magnus Hirschfeld and Maria Krische, the editors of the journal *Aufklärung*, (*Enlightenment*) offered similarly direct advice, defending single women's right to sexual activity and motherhood, and brusquely informing a jealous husband that his wife's lesbian affair was none of his business so long as she also served him well sexually: "There is no property right to the body of another. Or do you see your wife as your slave?"[74] In other lay journals, readers could study Van de Velde's graphs charting the path to mutual orgasm, and instructions for how to use a diaphragm diagrammed by Hirschfeld himself.[75]

*Sexualnot* (*Sexual Misery*), published by a small lay group, in 1928 promised guidance on "How to Keep the Family Small, Hygiene, Eugenics, and the Culture of Marriage and Sex Life."[76] Subscribers were offered graphic descriptions of the sexual misery of the proletariat and exhorted to class solidarity against a barbarous—indeed cannibalistic (*menschenfressender*)—capitalist and patriarchal state (*Vaterstaat*). In a pro-birth strike argument much more explicit (and florid) than Social Democrats or Communists would have been willing to make, women were presented both as victims forced to produce cannon and factory fodder—"bled to death" along with male workers and soldiers—and as potential heroines who would resist "stock-mongers out for booty" by refusing to "surrender their bodies to the demands for more children." Eugenic and maternalist discourse was fused with the language of class conflict, capitalism indicted as unhealthy and dysgenic, and a romantic, almost mystical, focus on nature intertwined with a worship of scientific progress. In a future, more just and humane postrevolutionary world, women's resistance to childbearing would wither away. They would "voluntarily . . . make available their bodies in the interest of society, thereby ascending of their own free will to their position as both the bearers and the servants of human society," thus fulfilling their natural role as "biological capital."[77]

In the meantime, however, sex reform journals presented seemingly endless horror stories—guaranteed to evoke outrage over an unjust law—about desperate victimized women unable to feed their families or obtain a safe abortion, who committed suicide or infanticide, or died from botched illegal abortions. In Essen in 1928, for example, a worker in a local factory gave birth at work, took the baby home in a briefcase, and tried to burn it; the woman was arrested and committed suicide in her cell. In Berlin in 1929, a 15-year-old girl was found dying in the street, the victim of a quack abortion. In Metzingen in December 1928, a 29-year-old woman died of poisoning after attempting a self-induced abortion.[78]

Left-wing "sex doctors" like Max Hodann, Hans Lehfeldt, Rudolf Elkan, Hertha Riese, and Wilhelm Reich, and their lay allies painted a dismal picture of proletarian sexual misery (*Sexualnot*), defined by inadequate medical care, sex education, privacy, sanitary facilities, and leisure time, and compounded by women's double burden of housework and wage labor. In this melodramatic script, deliberately counterposed to the lighthearted fare offered by most mass circulation periodicals, couples were forced to make love half-clothed and in constant fear of being disturbed, sometimes in parks and alleyways. Forced to share rooms and sometimes beds with relatives and boarders, children were exposed to quick and brutal sex. Prostitutes anxious to complete their transactions trained men to eschew foreplay and promoted premature ejaculation, which led to "frigidity" in women and sexual discord in marriage. In the face of such living conditions, the supposedly "natural" working class was portrayed as more deprived sexually than a bourgeoisie with access to sex information, medical contraception, and safe if not entirely legal abortions.[79]

One revealing short story in *Sexualnot* depicted a marriage on the rocks because Herr Kocha, the unemployed husband, refuses to do any housework to relieve his still employed wife. The resentful wife, with two children and seven abortions behind her at age 27, fears further pregnancies and additional work. She withdraws sexually from her husband, but is reluctant to leave him "because he was ready subtly to adjust to her physical idiosyncrasies and thus knew how to lead her to sexual fulfillment. She had learned from her girlfriends that this was something few men did . . . , in spite of all the bickering, she was really quite fond of him."

Frau Kocha's reluctant rebuffs push the decent but amorous Fritz into the arms of other women, thus raising the specter of venereal disease and divorce. Obviously, the "partial solution, birth control," could serve here: it could not provide a job for Fritz, nor would it resolve the housework conflict, but it would facilitate a happy sexual relationship between man and wife, which would presumably lighten all other burdens. At a critical point in the story, a traveling sex reformer materializes as *deus ex machina*. Despite the inevitable advances from Frau Kocha, who is presumably thrilled to find a male knowledgeable in contraception, he refuses to be led seriously astray, explaining to his client that she is suffering from a social problem that can be solved not through infidelity but rather by joining his lay league and purchasing his products. Finally, Fritz returns home penitent, and the relationship begins anew with plenty of reliable birth control provided by the wandering sex reform activist.[80]

Considering the nature of some of the advice offered in *Sexualnot*, such as the "fact" that coitus interruptus caused insanity, and that a woman's "safe" period begins right before the middle of the menstrual cycle, one wonders how long their conjugal bliss lasted. Nevertheless, even the more disreputable journals and leagues served to spread information about birth control, as well as about new styles of heterosexual companionship and erotic technique; league activities such as hikes and dances also offered opportunities for making contacts and forming relationships. And even ostensibly disrespectable journals like *Ideal Lebensbund*, which were frequently confiscated as obscene, counted physicians like Hirschfeld and Hodann as their authors. Curiously, in an era when political groups were at great pains to distinguish themselves from one another, sex reform was consistently marked by the blurring of lines and the transgression of conventional left/right political categories. In everyday practice, the themes of commerce, hygiene, pornography, marriage reform, and sexual pleasure were constantly intermeshed.

## The Liga: Lay Leagues as Mass Organizations

Although lay and medical sex reform groups moved closer to one another in the later 1920s, strong separatist currents remained. In response to the continuing opposition of the medical establishment, the lay League for Protection of Mothers and Social Family Hygiene (*Liga für Mutterschutz und soziale Familienhygiene*, referred to here as *Liga*) was established in 1929 as a direct competitor to the socialist and medically oriented RV. An outgrowth of a smaller group established by a birth control manufacturer in 1925, the *Liga* quickly became the largest lay group in Germany.[81] The *Liga* and its journal *Liebe und Leben* (*Love and Life*) captured the attention of right-wing pro-natalist groups, government experts, and police in a way that the SPD-leaning RV had not. The *Liga*'s twisted history and the presence of former Communists and others with a criminal record of sex code violations in its leadership made it more susceptible to surveillance, even though the *Liga* itself was determinedly apolitical and resented the KPD members who threatened to infiltrate its ranks.[82]

The *Liga* was probably more typical of lay sex reform leagues than the relatively well-organized and respectable RV. It was strongest in very poor industrialized regions like Mansfeld in Thuringia, but also in Catholic areas such as Bavaria, Württemberg, and Rhineland-Westphalia. The semiofficial Federation of Large Families (*Bund der Kinderreichen*, BKR) reported to the Department of Health (RGA) that more than 60 of its own members had been drawn to a *Liga* meeting in the Ruhr, all wanting information on "how to avoid having more children." The "captivating" female lecturer "spoke as if possessed by the devil" and convinced "hundreds . . . to join the organization just to acquire the contraceptive offered." Especially "working-class women [had] hung on every word of the lecture as if hypnotized." The memo concluded accusingly, "What will we come to if these products are distributed in such a mass way?"[83]

Such rapid-fire appeal fanned the flames of "birth strike" paranoia among government officials and nationalist population experts. Much to the frustration of the police and the ministries of Interior and Health, birth control leagues could not be prosecuted under paragraph 184.3, prohibiting the public advertising of contraceptives, since products were offered only to members, however brief or opportunistic the membership. Police and government agencies were very limited in their ability to repress the proliferation of unregulated "groups which hide behind many different names," and "are highly skilled in getting around legal regulations."[84]

A 1930 court case in Bochum, in the heavily industrialized and Catholic Ruhr region, offers an unusual insight into the labyrinthine and ambivalent workings of a lay sex reform league caught among commercial considerations, its need to supply political education and contraceptive services to members, and the pressures imposed by state legal authorities. The trial illustrated how porous were the lines between public service, business, and politics.

One male and two female members of an organization functioning under the name "League for Sexual Hygiene and the Protection of Mothers," as well as other similar-sounding titles presumably designed to complicate police surveillance, were charged with violating paragraph 184.3. The league claimed a commitment to combating abortion, venereal disease, and hereditary disorders through the dissemination of birth control. Anyone over 18 was eligible to join by paying dues ranging from 20 to 40 Pfennig, and a joint membership for married couples was available. The organization was contractually obligated to distribute exclusively tubes of spermicidal paste with the peculiar name "Three Monks Antispermin," formerly marketed as "Satisfaction is domestic happiness." The league bought the tubes at the wholesale price of 1.25 RM, resold them for 1.50 RM to organization middlemen, who in turn sold to members for 2RM, which was still one-half of the drugstore price. Offering active members an opportunity to earn a commission, this system was undoubtedly an attraction for working-class or unemployed men.

The defendant Mr. F was accused, together with his wife and another woman, of holding a series of birth control meetings throughout the Bochum region for which he received travel expenses plus an honorarium of 3 RM to 5 RM for each lecture. Unemployed local citizens publicized league events with leaflets promising "Good News" and free Three Monks samples. At meetings, the mechanics of birth control were explained and demonstrated with the aid of a slide show, and the audience of about 80 to 100 people was informed that the "riches of children" should be reserved for the ruling class. One slide demonstrated the insertion of the spermicide into the vagina and in another a pregnant woman was shown on her knees (begging for an abortion?) before a nurse who dangled a tube in her hand, with the caption: "And why don't you use Three Monks?" Mr. F remembered to add that Three Monks offered excellent protection against venereal disease.

The defendants admitted the accuracy of the facts but insisted that the prohibition on "public advertising" did not apply because the audience had joined a private society by signing their names and paying dues. They also tried to turn the 1927 venereal disease law to their advantage, since it sanctioned publicity for products intended to prevent VD, a loophole commonly used by birth control advocates. The court dispensed with this argument on the ground that disease prevention was clearly not the primary purpose of Three Monks; moreover, the meeting had been publicly advertised and guests were allowed to withdraw from their "membership" immediately following the lecture. Three Monks was "useful for indecent purposes" because it could be obtained by unmarried as well as married people. The court concluded that the league had been established "at the instigation" of a birth control manufacturing firm "in order to create a better market" for its products.

Mr. F was found guilty of violating paragraph 184.3 and the two female codefendants were convicted of aiding and abetting with malice aforethought. Irrelevant to the legal judgment but presumably of great interest to Three Monks' consumers was an expert witness's certification that the products were safe and effective contraceptives.[85] For the audience at sex reform league meetings, business arrangements between "reformers" and contraceptive manufacturers were of less concern than the relatively easy and nonembarrassing access to reasonably reliable, reduced-rate birth control products and information.

The confused legal and political conditions with which both law enforcement authorities and sex reform leagues had to contend were illustrated by a diametrically opposed court judgment handed down that same year in Saxony. There, the district court in Chemnitz ruled that local birth control advertising did not violate paragraph 184.3 because contraceptive devices were widely used by respectable people and not for indecent purposes. Moreover, the court explicitly noted that this paragraph from the 1871 penal code did not do justice to such realities of "modern times" as companionate marriage and the Weimar Constitution's equal recognition of illegitimate children. Since birth control did not offend a mature adult's sense of decency, it should not be considered obscene. The RGA carefully recorded this decision, as it had the Bochum case, and consoled itself that the Saxon ruling had only local significance.[86] In fact, the Chemnitz decision reflected the widespread accept-ability and practice of birth control among all segments of the population.

Despite police harassment, the *Liga* continued to grow and gradually also gained sympathy from parts of the medical profession. Its first national con-ference in October 1929 in Berlin attracted representatives from the Berlin Health Insurance League (*Verband der Krankenkassen Berlins*, VKB), the *Bund für Mutterschutz* (BfM), the GESEX, and the RV. The presence of Drs. Hodann, Hirschfeld, and Hertha Riese of the Frankfurt BfM showed the many over-lapping affiliations within sex reform and the increasing degree to which even purely "lay" leagues now sought medical support.[87]

Until 1931, the *Liga*'s Berlin office had referred members to the RV / GESEX center in central Berlin and to two clinics run by Max Hodann; in 1931 it set up its own clinic directed by Dr. Ludwig Levy-Lenz, held in ill repute by some RV colleagues as an abortionist.[88] The author of a textbook on abortion tech-niques, Levy-Lenz carefully distanced himself from "exploitative quacks" and claimed to provide both contraceptive and fertility advice only after a com-prehensive medical exam.[89]

As with much sex reform prescription, Levy-Lenz's advice was highly clini-cal but at times unconventional. Attempts to induce pregnancy included experiments with artificial insemination, hormone treatment, surgery, and finally, the suggestion to try another partner! Other curatives for marital boredom—obviously a problem from which he himself suffered since he rather frequently switched wives—included well-calibrated doses of pornog-raphy, and failing that, separate bedrooms. In the view of many Weimar sex therapists, nothing so quickly cooled sexual ardor as encountering a sleepy, disheveled partner "when many a husband is apt to serve rather as a hot water bottle than as a lover."[90] In line with Van de Velde's cures for frigidity, Levy-Lenz recommended diligent male application of tongue and finger in pursuit of the vaunted simultaneous orgasm during intercourse—an event carefully pinpointed on the inevitable graphs in sex manuals and journals that purported to plot scientifically women's fundamentally different—slower and more dif-fuse—patterns of arousal and satisfaction.[91]

Max Hodann also popularized Van de Velde's streamlined lovemaking discipline with its step-by-step instructions for orgasm in his own publications, while cynically referring to him as "the most famous of these salvage experts" for bourgeois marriage.[92] In tracts intended for a working-class readership, Max Hodann bluntly declared that, "There is no such thing as a frigid woman, only incompetent men" and added in his kindly but authoritarian manner that, "The sexual personality of a woman unfolds only under the hands of a man.[93] The eroticization of marriage and the rationalization of sexuality through matter-of-fact education about birth control and sexual technique was in-tended to heighten heterosexual satisfaction, lessen female resistance, guard against the "plagues" of venereal disease, prostitution, incest, and abortion, and thereby encourage the production of happy, healthy children conceived in passionate but rationally considered intercourse. In an effort to match the rationalization of industry with a rationalization of the body, clinics and sex manuals attempted to institutionalize certain standards of eugenically sound and socially responsible sexual behavior.

The goal was to produce a better product, be it a healthy child or a mutual orgasm: under the right (usually future) circumstances, preferably both. Moreover, as doctors in counseling centers repeatedly pointed out, frigidity was a threat to fertility as well as to satisfactory heterosexuality. Sex reformers devoutly believed that better sex would make for happier marriages and more and healthier children. One physician proudly reported his solution in a case involving six years of infertility: the husband was ordered to wear a thick condom in which a hole had been carefully made with a needle. The reduced stimulation prolonged intercourse, the wife was able to have an orgasm for the first time, and within six months she was pregnant![94] A Lamarckian belief in the power of the environment to affect hereditary characteristics meant that many doctors believed that the quality of the intercourse during which a baby was conceived influenced the quality of the product. Orgasm was stylized into a eugenic measure as well as a family-stabilizing event; pleasure was instrumentalized for the motherhood-eugenics consensus. With such concerns in mind, Levy-Lenz, along with other sex doctors, was willing not only medically to puncture a hymen to alleviate the "trauma of the first night" but to reconstruct it, if that seemed indicated, in the interests of "eroticizing" marriage.[95]

## Politicization: The Communist Party and Sex Reform

By the late 1920s, both physicians and the Communist party, observing the success of the lay leagues with envious and somewhat bewildered attention, became more interested in harnessing the energy and momentum of groups that were—in a repeatedly used phrase—springing up everywhere like mushrooms. Thus, almost from the outset, the sex reform movement was shaped by two apparently opposed forces: medicalization and mass politicization. The KPD was poised in 1928 for new initiatives that could distinguish it from the reformist SPD and broaden its appeal among progressive professionals and intellectuals otherwise skeptical of rigid party dogma. The KPD had raised the abolition of paragraph 218 as a major demand since its founding in 1919, and from the early 1920s on, the KPD was also arguing that contraception, not abortion, must be the solution to the problem of family limitation.

The Women's Commission in party headquarters formulated what would be the standard KPD position throughout the Weimar period: "a society not able to provide women with the material means for motherhood," also had "no right to demand that women take on the cares and burdens derived from motherhood."[96] Sexual politics provided a way for the KPD, always in thrall to Comintern directives from Moscow, both to develop a popular mass line (especially in its mass social welfare organizations) and to propagandize the virtues of a Soviet Union which had been the first country in the world to legalize abortion and formulate a comprehensive program for "the protection of mother and child."[97]

In 1928, the KPD actively joined the ranks of the sex reform movement with the formation of the Working Group of Social Political Organizations (*Arbeitsgemeinschaft sozialpolitischer Organisationen*, ARSO). The brainchild of the KPD's mass-organizing genius Willi Münzenberg, this subgroup of the International Workers Aid was to become the primary KPD representative in social welfare and abortion reform campaigns.[98] Left-wing sex reform organizations such as ARSO made demands for expanded state support the center of their platforms, even as they railed against the politics of the existing national government. Composed primarily of professionals and intellectuals and led by two KPD Reichstag deputies, Martha Arendsee and Siegfried Rädel, ARSO, like the sex reform movement in general, aimed to promote the spirit of self-help, assist members in fully exploiting the existing welfare system, and make further demands on the state. During the crisis years after 1928, ARSO's bitter critique of the "reactionary and bourgeois" Social Democratic social welfare system would be forced to shift—at least partially—to demands against its dismantling.

ARSO served as an umbrella organization integrating the work of numerous KPD interest groups responsible for various supposedly marginal constituencies—from youth and prisoners to war invalids, intellectuals, and women.[99] To help members negotiate the complex web of the existing social service bureaucracy and set up alternative services, ARSO could draw on a sophisticated cadre of Communist and fellow-traveling health and social welfare professionals strategically located in municipal posts, such as the Berlin health commissioners Max Hodann (Reinickendorf), Richard Schmincke (Neukölln), and Ernst Joel (Kreuzberg). Indeed, the first major ARSO conference in July 1928, attended by 700 people, was held in the building housing the Prussian Landtag.[100]

Promulgated in 1929, ARSO's sex-political platform was very similar to the RV's, displaying the desire for increased medical supervision and faith in the benefits of state control and regulation of birth control common to all sex reform groups. Specifically, it demanded abolition of all penalties for abortions performed by doctors, preferably in a hospital, within the first three months; state and health insurance funding of medically prescribed abortions and contraceptives; sex counseling centers supported by health insurance and municipal authorities; training for physicians in the techniques of contraception and safe abortion; and state control and manufacture of contraceptives. Although ARSO—like the RV—did not fail to note "that birth control forms only a part of the demands for a proletarian health program," its demands remained within the framework of Weimar social policy; contraception and abortion services were to be integrated into the already existing comprehensive national health insurance system.[101]

During the 1927 Reichstag debates on the Law to Combat Venereal Disease, KPD delegates had argued that limiting the right to treat sexual organs to licensed medical doctors would limit the proletariat's possibilities for self-help and only extend state police powers into workers' personal lives.[102] But by 1929, ARSO members also saw state control over birth control production and marketing as a reasonable extension of the government's responsibility to protect its citizens against harmful or fraudulently marketed products. Even as ARSO was attacking the state and the medical profession, and the Interior and Health ministries and the police were surveilling its activities as thoroughly as they did any potentially subversive Communist group (or alleged KPD front), ARSO sought to have doctors and government do their job better.

All sex reform politics reflected these continuing tensions between two internally contradictory sets of demands: attacks on the state, yet calls for it to heighten intervention in the daily life of the proletariat; criticism of the medical profession for neglecting social issues, while calling for medicalization of the birth control and abortion reform movement. The Communist physician Martha Ruben-Wolf defensively (and typically) insisted that birth control could only be a partial solution: there had to be a political—not just medical-technical—response to "misery, rationalization, pension-squeezing, cutbacks in social welfare, lowering of wages" because "Pills won't help there!"[103] But the entire thrust of the ARSO, and indeed RV, political program suggested that pills, that is, medical intervention, would help—and not just any pills but pills produced and regulated by state agencies. Whether those state agencies were to be the currently existing ones or those established by some future revolutionary regime was never entirely clear.

### Internationalism, Bolshevism, and the Americanization of Sex Reform

So far, this story of the rapid development of a mass sex reform movement in Weimar Germany has been told as an internal German narrative, with an occasional nod in an eastward direction toward Bolshevik experiments in the Soviet Union. But German sex reform worked very much in an international context. It was profoundly influenced both by the Soviet model propagandized by the KPD and its affiliated groups, and by the American birth control movement, personified particularly by Margaret Sanger and her European representative Agnes Smedley.

From 1920 to the Nazi takeover in 1933, Germany remained a center of sexological research and sex reform innovations, and German sex reformers were an influential presence at numerous international birth control and sex reform congresses. On July 1, 1928, sex reformers gathered in Copenhagen for the first meeting of the World League for Sex Reform (WLSR) since Hirschfeld's attempts to revive the prewar movement at the Berlin conference in 1921.[104] Under the leadership of Magnus Hirschfeld, Danish physician Hans Leunbach, and the British birth controller Norman Haire, and with the honorary participation of sexologists August Forel and Havelock Ellis, the WLSR encompassed a motley crew of sex reformers from around the world, including radicals like Wilhelm Reich and Alexandra Kollontai, nonsocialist Anglo-American birth controllers, and even representatives from Japan and India. Committed to the motto *Per Scientam ad Justitiam*, carved into the ornate doors of Hirschfeld's Berlin institute, the WLSR argued that a program respecting science and nature would inevitably lead to justice, tolerance, and a better and more humane society, in which love and healthy sexuality would thrive. Sexual repression was irrational; reform was rational:

> Our World League wants to supplant the sexual order, which it views as sexual disorder, with new sexual ethics, based on a scientific understanding of human nature and adapted to present-day conditions.[105]

The WLSR's 10-point manifesto subscribed to the general consensus about the paramount importance of healthy motherhood and eugenic hygiene while incorporating goals of the various pre- and postwar sex reform initiatives, from birth control and women's rights to tolerance of sexual "deviants." The WLSR was, however, more concerned with homosexual rights and "abnormal" sexuality than was the lay movement with its emphasis on family and birth control; moreover, its program did not explicitly mention abortion. In another concession to international cooperation, it was also silent on socialism, although clearly influenced by the Soviet model of revolutionizing human relations through a state program of maternal and child health care, legalization of birth control and abortion, reform of marriage and divorce laws, and the general decriminalization of consensual adult sexual acts.

The platform proposed (1) a medical model of sexual deviance in exchange for civil rights and toleration; (2) sexual equality and birth control justified in terms of responsible and rationalized childbearing; (3) political and economic equality of the sexes; (4) sexual equality for women; (5) freedom of marriage and divorce from state control; (6) birth control to encourage responsible childbearing, not sexual license; (7) consideration of eugenic factors in childbearing; (8) protection of unwed mothers and illegitimate children; (9) prevention of prostitution and venereal disease; and (10) medicalization and psychiatrization of sexual disorders since they were not crimes, sins, or vices, but "more or less" pathological symptoms whose expression in acts between consenting adults should be tolerated and not legally proscribed.[106]

WLSR members shared a breathtakingly innocent faith in "progress" and the ability of science and technology to regulate and solve human problems.

Believing medicalization and psychiatrization to be more enlightened and humane than criminalization, they valorized physicians as more objective and therefore trustworthy and sympathetic than church or state. A further congress in London in 1929, organized by Norman Haire, reinforced the organization's medical focus.[107]

Among noted sex reformers, only Margaret Sanger, fearing that the WLSR's association with homosexuality, abortion, and Communism would undermine her determined single-issue focus on contraception, resisted all attempts to get her to participate. Her absence from the WLSR, however, in no way foreclosed her involvement in the international birth control movement. The latter encompassed not only WLSR members but eugenicists and birth controllers who rejected the sex reform label and were defining positions that would come to be identified after the Second World War with Planned Parenthood.

The extraordinary correspondence between the American radical Agnes Smedley, then living in Berlin, and Margaret Sanger reveals how much the German sex reform movement and especially the development of Berlin's pioneering network of birth control and sex counseling clinics relied on American moral and financial support.[108] Ironically, at the same time that Sanger was smuggling German-made diaphragms and contraceptive creams, via Canada, into the United States—where they were still illegal—she also became a missionary of medical birth control to the homeland of sexual science and the inventors of the diaphragm. The frequent charge by the German clerical and nationalist right wing that the sexual emancipation of women and the rationalization of birth control and sexuality were driven by alien Bolshevik and American influences was not without basis.

The extensive lay movement and the deep involvement of working-class political movements in sex reform, as well as the broad (both legal and illegal) market in contraceptives and abortifacients, were peculiarly German. But American money and the insistent pressure by Sanger and Smedley for the establishment of birth control clinics on the model of Sanger's New York clinic were the crucial factors in the remarkable melding of women doctors, Communist municipal officials, sex reformers, and Social Democratic health insurance officials into an alliance able to initiate a comprehensive program of clinic-based birth control and sex advice programs in Berlin. In this sense, as we shall see in the next chapter, the translation of German sex reform principles into the practice of birth control clinics run by physicians has to be judged as part of the Americanization process that was so important to the rationalization of everyday life in Weimar Germany.[109]

In the fall of 1927, 200 delegates from approximately 30 nations had gathered on Sanger's initiative for a world population congress in Geneva. Primarily concerned with the danger of overpopulation, especially in the non-Western world, participants affirmed that population studies should be carried on in a strictly "scientific, nonpolitical" manner. German representatives included the racial hygiene experts Erwin Baur and Eugen Fischer, who would move on to successful careers in the Third Reich, as well as the conservative Social Democratic social hygienist Alfred Grotjahn, whose seminars at the University of Berlin trained a whole generation of German sex reformers of various political persuasions.[110]

Also present was the young Dr. Hans Harmsen, a Grotjahn protégé who, armed with funding from the Rockefeller Foundation, was just beginning to make his mark as a demographic researcher and population policy expert for the Inner Mission, the Protestant Church's social welfare organization.[111] Fifty years later, he still remembered the excitement of that first post–World War I international population conference and his infatuation with the captivating American woman who had apparently made it all possible. He coyly remembered his encounter with Sanger: "I was a young man, and I danced with her the whole night . . . and right then and there the real importance of that question of birth control began to dawn upon me."[112]

Always willing to cross political lines in her determined quest to gain acceptance for birth control, Sanger moved on from Switzerland to Berlin at Smedley's urging. There, her meetings with women doctors, her sanctioning of Smedley's close cooperation with Communist physicians, and most importantly, her financial subsidies, made possible the formation of a German Committee for Birth Control, whose members—drawn from the RV/GESEX, KPD, SPD, and VSA—would organize and staff a network of birth control and sex counseling centers run by health insurance and municipal authorities in Berlin.

Smedley's difficult personal life and passionate commitment to international revolution never interfered with her devoted friendship with the (no longer socialist) Sanger. Sanger was unfailingly loyal to her politically radical and emotionally labile friend, providing her with money to pay her doctors and her analyst. From 1926 until the end of 1928, when Smedley left Berlin for new adventures in China, Sanger regularly sent funds and supportive letters that showed her bemused rather than worried by Smedley's dealing with radicals and Communists.[113] Politically conservative birth control advocates such as the admiring Harmsen, however, were clearly discomfited by those associations, as well as by Sanger's unapologetic defense of women's sexual freedom. They feared that the American "apostle of birth control" did not fully grasp the degree to which "the problem of birth control is in this country immediately and to a large degree connected with agitational-political demands."[114]

Sanger had indeed originally hoped to convene a large public birth control conference in Berlin. But firm opposition from potential allies among German feminists, gynecologists, and social hygienists, such as Harmsen and Dr. Anne-Marie Durand-Wever of the BDÄ, persuaded her that it would be more prudent to gather on neutral ground in Switzerland those "individuals (no matter what their political or religious affiliation) who are working directly in clinics where information on contraception is given."[115] Even as secret meetings were held in Grotjahn's office to block Sanger's plans for a mass event in their city, no one among the politically diverse set of Berlin physicians interested in social hygiene and birth control seriously (or openly) wanted to alienate their radical medical colleagues "who really had something to say about the field" or American financial support and contacts.[116] Finally, therefore, it was only Sanger's uniquely broad range of contacts and her pledge to assure "the freest discussion from a strictly technical point of view"[117] that would allow her to invite a very broad spectrum of German sex reformers, many of whom had never even met, to the landmark 1930 Zurich conference on birth control.

## The Zurich Conference

The international Conference for Birth Control held in Zurich from September 1 to 5, 1930, marked a major turning point for German sex reform and its relationship to the international movement. Along with the far more radical WLSR Congress held in Vienna only a few days later, it highlighted and sharpened controversies about medicalization and politicization, demarcating once again the differences between the American and German models of birth control work. Over 100 selected delegates from all corners of the globe attended what had become an "experts only" conference. They were enjoined to avoid all issues of "politics, religion, and morality" and to discuss contraception, abortion, sterilization, and further research areas in a strictly medical manner.

The astonishingly broad group of delegates ranged from staunch Communists like Martha Ruben-Wolf, who represented both the Committee for Birth Control and Soviet physicians, to Hans Harmsen, who rejected abortion but supported contraception and sterilization. The list of German delegates read like a virtual "Who's Who" of sex reformers, also including Drs. Anne-Marie Durand-Wever from the Berlin BDÄ; Ernst Gräfenberg, developer of the IUD; Georg Manes and Rudolf Elkan from the Hamburg BfM and RV; Hans Lehfeldt and Felix Theilhaber from the Berlin RV/GESEX; Lotte Fink and Hertha Riese from the Frankfurt BfM; Reni Begun from the Berlin VSA and BDÄ; Ludwig Levy-Lenz from the *Liga*; Charlotte Wolff from the Berlin health insurance league; Max Hodann from the municipal Berlin centers; F. K. Scheumann from the state-sponsored counseling center in Berlin-Prenzlauer Berg; and one of the few nonphysicians, Auguste Kirchhoff, from the Bremen BfM.

Already at the 1929 WLSR Congress in London, Dora Russell had noted the "remarkable . . . number of courageous and intelligent professional women from Germany."[118] A lay journal reported that in Zurich, too, women "were the driving force."[119] Unlike working-class women in the lay leagues, women doctors, psychologists, and social workers were able to claim a particular credibility in the medical sex reform movement on the basis of their extensive experience as women treating women and children in insurance and welfare clinics. However, they were notably more silent when it came to the scientific research papers on hormonal secretions or sterilization methods that often preoccupied male colleagues at such conferences.

Despite all admonitions to avoid ideological conflicts, the Zurich conference was characterized by carefully controlled tensions between men and women, and between single-issue birth controllers and those committed to a broader program of social and sexual reform. Controversy arose over abortion and whether it should even be considered as a birth control method.[120] Most German delegates, both men and women, socialists and nonsocialists, were distrustful of the single-issue focus on contraception urged by Sanger and her Anglo-American cohorts. For her part, Sanger complained that the Germans "seemed to be so full of theories and opinions . . . that their practical knowledge seems to have been sacrificed."[121] She insisted, in a phrase that rings more disturbing in retrospect than it would have then, on the "cool, scientific conviction that today contraception as an instrument in racial progress is on the way to be reliable and efficient and may in the very near future be perfected."[122]

Despite their own serious internal divisions, exacerbated by the tense campaign for the September 1930 Reichstag elections, the German delegates all shared the experience of living in a nation in the grip of massive unemployment and social instability. Influenced by the lay and working-class movement, German sex reformers located birth control as one issue among many of sex hygiene, social welfare, and overall social change. Relatively secure about the basic legality of contraception, they worried, like their Soviet and Scandinavian comrades, about price, easy accessibility, and uncooperative and hostile medical associations. Still seeking to legitimize birth control, their American colleagues were more likely to promote professionalization and a single-issue focus on birth control. Hodann and Riese both pointedly noted that only pressure from the lay leagues had led physicians to consider seriously the question of contraception and its inclusion in medical practice and training. Birth control was not only a matter of expert research and methods but also of access; rather than attacking the lay organizations, doctors should cooperate with them.

The carefully crafted compromise resolutions called for the abolition of all laws restricting birth control information, the inclusion of birth control in medical school curricula, standardized terminology in research reports (for example, was a pessary a diaphragm, a cervical cap, or a suppository?), and the exact listing of the contents of all products in order to undercut commercial exploitation. By a hotly contested vote of 22 to 19, the conference also urged that sterilizations be performed (if necessary without cost) on people who were not able to use birth control properly. Abortion, the focus of so much German sex reform effort, was not mentioned.

The connections forged among birth control advocates in Zurich were last-ing. A few years later, when numerous delegates were forced to emigrate from Nazi Germany, they proved, as we shall see in Chapter 7 on sex reform in exile, to be lifesaving. A model successful professional conference that offered not only stimulating scientific papers but also dinners and dances on the *Kurhaus* terrace, a twilight boat trip on the lake, and an excursion into the Alps, the 1930 gathering in many ways led directly to the formation of Inter-national Planned Parenthood after the war. Certainly the "general harmony and mutual respect" finally achieved facilitated cooperation for the remain-ing years of the republic among the combative group of German sex reform physicians who had attended.[123]

Indeed, Kate Stützin, the underemployed and endlessly energetic wife of a Berlin urology professor and sexologist, was inspired to offer herself as a unifying figure and to organize an umbrella group, the Center for Birth Con-trol (*Arbeitszentrale für Geburtenregelung*), for all doctors involved in birth con-trol. Stützin quickly moved into the vacuum left by Smedley's departure for China, replacing Ruben-Wolf as Sanger's most regular German correspon-dent. Subtly but definitively, she shifted Sanger's focus from the close ties with the KPD, which had been mediated by Smedley, to those with more conser-vative birth controllers, like Harmsen, who were suspicious of legalized abor-tion and the lay movement.

The 1930 WLSR Congress in Vienna met right on the heels of the Zurich conference. Several delegates traveled from one to the other on a journey to a rather different political universe. The Vienna event was enthusiastically supported by the socialist city government; the local press paid the delegates admiring attention, and the mayor hosted a wonderful banquet. A crowd-pleasing adjoining exhibit showcased every variety of birth control devices. One participant recalled the conference as "a real Viennese sensation."[124] In contrast to the scientific tone in Zurich, speaker after speaker detailed the "sexual misery" of those groups denied fulfillment by social forces: Wilhelm Reich discussed the proletariat in general, while others dealt with prisoners, mental patients, and single women. The insistence on understanding and treating sexual problems in social context culminated in one speaker's an-nouncement that, "The ultimate therapy for frigidity and homosexuality is socialism."[125]

Whatever the differences among lay and medical, socialist, Communist, and unaffiliated reformers, it was clear by the end of 1928, and certainly by 1930, that supportive physicians would be welcomed in the lay movement. The generally increasing involvement by doctors produced a mixture of skep-ticism and hope in the lay movement, which had after all based its early exist-ence on the unwillingness of doctors to cooperate. As discussed earlier, al-though lay organizations were committed to introducing medicalized birth control and rationalized sexual techniques to the working class, they were wary of encouraging total dependency on a medical profession that was gen-

erally disinclined to meet its needs. Thus, they were all the more dependent
on those relatively few physicians who were able to balance their commitment to medical expertise with a dedication to social justice. Ironically, the
very resistance of most German physicians to birth control helped to open
working-class lay sex reform to medicalization. The insistence on proletarians' right to protection from quacks and hazardous abortions through effective medical birth control was cast as a class-conscious position: class justice
required the working class to have access to the same benefits that the bourgeoisie was able to buy. Thus, those doctors willing to cooperate with the
lay working-class movement acquired a great deal of legitimacy and influence
within it.

The Weimar sex reform movement was, as we have seen, continuously
in contact and in dialogue with the American birth control movement; at several points, as the next chapter will detail, American money and influence
were decisive. Yet, the story of German sex reform diverges in crucial ways
from the trajectory described in Linda Gordon's pathbreaking study of the
U.S. birth control movement, in which professionals took over a cause that
radicals and socialists had deserted.[126] In Germany, by contrast, an active
grassroots working-class movement forced professionals, in a sense, into the
birth control struggle. Lay sex reform actively solicited medical cooperation
as necessary to its struggle for legitimacy and freedom from commercial domination, and to provide truly useful services to its constituencies. Yet, in Germany, medicalization was not entirely synonymous with professionalization,
insofar as most of the professionals involved were radicals on the margins of
their own medical establishment and understood themselves to be working
in the service of the working-class movement.

Radical professionals were in many ways the critical group in the German
sex reform movement; far from pressing depoliticization, they saw politicization as going hand in hand with medicalization. While still connected to their
bourgeois (often Jewish) background, training, and professional identity, they
were nonetheless committed in one form or another to the working-class
struggle. They pressured their own profession from within, in medical journals and at medical conferences; however, as "politicals" they were often
discredited within its higher echelons, underlining once again the importance
of differentiating within a given occupation when discussing the process of
professionalization. Still, as the cooperation within the VSA, BDÄ, or RV demonstrated, remarkably durable professional networks helped medical sex reformers bridge some of the political polarizations that marked Weimar politics in ways closed to lay activists. In fact, the German case is instructive
precisely because it illustrates the fallacies of setting up rigid categories of
"popular" and "professional."

Medical sex reformers occupied a peculiar position straddling popular
movement and professional concern. Their campaign for birth control, therefore, always encompassed dual tasks: the need to educate the masses, but also

the need to educate colleagues and pressure the profession to be more responsive to the masses. Continually invoking the dangerously high illegal abortion rate, they warned that the lay movement would revert to commercial domination and reliance on lay healers if rebuffed by physicians.

The movement remained marked by the tension between the idioms of science and politics—both claiming objective truth. If these German doctors were sometimes frustrated by insufficent and irregular use of counseling centers, they were often amazed and touched by the response to their advice manuals and lectures. Sex reform physicians—a significant number of them women—therefore fulfilled a dual project of empowerment and control: they broke through the wall of ignorance about reproductive and sexual matters, enabling working-class women to take more control over their fertility, but also reinforced the image of the physician as a kindly but powerful authority. The commitment to self-help in the form of working-class leagues and a language of class struggle did not preclude a belief in the promise of state and medical control and technological efficiency to guarantee social stability and human happiness. Sex reform embraced and furthered medicalization even as it attacked the medical profession. Thus, progressive professionals mediated among the lay movement, medical and women's organizations, the state, and political parties.

After 1928, increasing numbers of doctors worked in RV, *Liga*, Bund für Mutterschutz, and—as we shall see in the next chapter—municipal and health insurance counseling centers. For the first time, they faced the challenges of distributing contraceptive devices and information on a large scale in a clinic environment, rather than in their private practices. As reliable birth control became both more available and more widely publicized, counseling centers in large cities and especially in Berlin became a central site for Weimar innovations in sexual politics and population policy.

## — three —

# Birth Control, Marriage, and Sex Counseling Clinics
## The Administration of Sex Reform

Fortunately, "puritanical" America has sent us not only the dancing girl, but it has sent us also the woman, Mrs. Margaret Sanger.[1]

Don't enter marriage blindly.
Go for counseling.
There can be no happy marriage without physical and mental health.
Marriage may not last without conscious planning.
Children cannot thrive without healthy genes.[2]

The marriage, sex, and birth control clinics established by municipal and health insurance officials in German cities during the Weimar Republic constituted a remarkable experiment in the publicly funded "management of sexuality" and procreation.[3] Physicians and social workers used them as laboratories in which to implement and contest the politics of medical sex reform. They tried—with varying degrees of success—to translate into clinical practice their ambition to produce, via satisfying heterosexuality, healthy offspring at well-timed intervals. At the same time, the centers' reports on the emotional, sexual, and material impoverishment of working-class life became raw data for constructing a new highly ideologized vision of sexuality that called for combating both frigidity and dysgenic births. Doctors' experiences in clinics both radicalized their commitment to reform of the laws restricting abortion and contraception, and increased their attraction to eugenic sterilization.

The establishment of a network of birth control and sex counseling centers depended on two conditions unique to Germany. First, the existing national public health and social insurance system was formally committed to the provision of preventive and social health services. Second, Germany had a mass working-class movement, with a militant Communist party pressuring a reluctant SPD, and a mass lay movement of birth control advocates pressuring the KPD, the SPD, and the medical profession. The key players, as the previous chapter concludes, were left-wing professionals: simultaneously members of working-class parties and state employees, they worked in local government and Social Democratic–dominated health insurance funds. With access to and legitimacy in multiple social universes, doctors and social workers served as crucial links among political movements, professionalized social welfare systems, and the everyday life of the proletariat.

Germany's state welfare system offered a language of cost effectiveness, eugenics, and maternalism in which to couch demands for birth control and sex education services. The existing health insurance and social welfare network was certainly not universal; in many respects it was "mean, penny-pinching, and inadequate."[4] Yet, as inscribed in the Weimar Constitution and local ordinances, the state acknowledged responsibility for and interest in social health, the welfare of family and children, and the reproduction of the labor force, thereby claiming the right to intervene in "private" matters. Birth control, abortion, or sterilization were not, however, among the many services, from prenatal care to massages, that were offically provided and funded. Although, by 1931, over 200 state centers in Prussia, established according to the 1926 Ministry of Social Welfare decree, counseled on fitness for marriage and procreation, they were not supposed to discuss birth control.[5]

These contradictions opened a political and rhetorical space in which sex reformers could demand contraception and even abortion as part of a national preventive health program. Most reformers did not move beyond the prevailing consensus on the importance of healthy motherhood and eugenic fitness and employed the idiom of social health, medicalization, cost effectiveness, and national welfare. Yet, as this chapter details, defensive rhetoric notwithstanding, every aspect of these so-called marriage and sex counseling centers (*Ehe-und Sexualberatungsstellen*) or clinics was disputed at great length, in the popular and working-class press and in professional medical publications of all political casts. The history of these institutions and the sometimes arcane controversies that accompanied their development reveals a great deal about Weimar politics of sexuality and reproduction.

## The Development of Health Insurance Clinics in Berlin

By the mid-1920s, the clinics (*Ambulatorien*) of the Berlin Health Insurance League (*Verband der Krankenkassen Berlins* [VKB]) became a primary site of innovation and contention about the mass provision of birth control and sex counseling. They were themselves the result of an ongoing bitter dispute about money and professional prerogatives between private physicians organized in the powerful Hartmann Bund and the giant, mostly Social Democratic, German health insurance funds that burgeoned during Weimar.

In 1923, at the height of the inflation, Berlin private doctors admitted to insurance practice (*Kassenärzte*) went on strike against the VKB's management. Tired of collecting insurance reimbursements rendered worthless by inflation, and generally incensed at the bureaucratic and fiscal power the health insurance fund exercised over their professional lives, the doctors vowed to accept only cash payments rather than insurance vouchers (*Krankenscheine*). When this action left most of its patients without medical care, the VKB established walk-in clinics to provide emergency medical care for its insurees. Some Social Democratic and Communist physicians employed by the VKB found themselves in the unusual position of strikebreakers against their own guild.[6]

In April 1924, as the economy stabilized, a state arbitration court decision legitimized the new clinics but also allowed patients to resume use of their insurance vouchers with approved private physicians. The VKB guaranteed the survival of the clinics by extending services to family members of the insured. Between 1924 and 1928, the health insurance system expanded to cover almost 22 million people out of a population of 66 million; the number of insured women rose especially fast.[7] By 1927, the Berlin insurance league had a budget of almost 5 million RM and an annual patient load of 3,100,604. Every day, more than 700 employees in 40 clinics treated over 10,000 people for conditions ranging from tuberculosis and influenza to cancer, puerperal fever, and "neurosis."[8] Jubilant VKB officials were convinced that they were engaged in a major innovation in urban social and preventive medicine that could serve as a model for mass health care in the modern age.

In the vision of the mostly socialist and Communist (many of them women) doctors staffing the clinics, community-based health care would replace such custodial institutions as hospitals and asylums, thereby meeting the increasingly complex health needs of a basically healthy—but ever more emotionally and physically stressed—population. VKB officials insisted that only community-based clinics dedicated to social hygiene, as much as to individual cures, could provide poor and working-class populations with the high-quality medical care that they required. Presenting a clear alternative to the private medicine practiced in Germany, even by those physicians connected to the health insurance system, the clinics provided a range of innovative medical services aimed more at preventive than acute care, such as orthopedic gymnastics, sports medicine, speech therapy, and mental health services.[9]

Central to this holistic vision of social medicine and absolutely crucial to the development of birth control, marriage, and sex counseling services were the VKB's prenatal- and infant-care clinics (*Schwangerenfürsorge*). They were set up after the strike in 1924 at the same time as the League for the Protection of Mothers (*Bund für Mutterschutz*, BfM) opened its first birth control and sex counseling centers in Hamburg, Frankfurt, Mannheim, and Breslau. In 1926 the VKB also took over the women's hospital (*Cecilienhaus*) directed by the noted gynecologist Wilhelm Liepmann. By late 1927, at the apex of the stabilization period, four women physicians and several female social workers were handling almost 16,000 consultations annually at 18 maternal and infant-care clinics.[10]

Women doctors, who were a minority within the exclusive ranks of private physicians with health insurance eligibility but were prominent among the ranks of public health physicians, became the dominant force in the prenatal clinics. They worked in welfare offices, schools, and the marriage and sex counseling centers run by local Berlin districts, and by Helene Stöcker's BfM. Female physicians were particularly visible in Berlin, where in 1932, 722 of the city's 6,785 doctors were women.[11] Many of them (at least 270) were also Jewish, although for most of the leftist public health doctors, that identity did not take on special meaning until 1933, when their "non-Aryan" status forced them from their posts.[12] Women directed 5 of the 16 municipal marriage counseling centers, and all 5 of the physicians staffing the VKB prenatal and birth control clinics were women.[13]

Dr. Alice (Goldmann-) Vollnhals, a graduate of Dr. Alfred Grotjahn's seminar in social hygiene at the University of Berlin, and her all-women team of doctors and social workers used the new prenatal clinics to pioneer a comprehensive health service for women that included advice on childrearing and contraception as well as on healthy pregnancy, childbirth, and breastfeeding. Explicitly conceived as centers for the protection of women (*Frauenschutz*), the clinics also provided aid in cases of wife battering, child abuse, drug addiction, alcoholism, incest, rape, suicide, disturbed children, infertility, overcrowded housing, evictions, and unemployment; in addition they made referrals for therapeutic abortions and sterilizations. Services included home visits and family counseling, childbirth and infant-care classes, complete medical exams, laboratory tests, dental care, education in hygiene, nutrition, and physical fitness (fruit, vegetables, and vitamins, swimming, sunning, gymnastics, and the "now-so-modern weekend"), even advice on comfortable clothing and home furnishings—in short, everything to decrease infant mortality, illegitimacy, and illegal abortion and to ensure healthy offspring in a healthy family.[14]

In the wake of their dramatic expansion, the battle over the clinics intensified, and in 1928 state arbitration was once again required. Whereas the 1924 ruling had guaranteed the existence of the clinics, the 1928 decision made major concessions to the threatened private doctors. New clinic positions now had to be filled by insurance-approved doctors (*Kassenärzte*) who would be allowed to work part-time while maintaining their private practices, a policy that betrayed the VKB's commitment to employing full-time physicians. Current medical staff, however, was forbidden to engage in private practice. Furthermore, clinic treatment would only be provided for family dependents, while the insured themselves had to take their vouchers to private doctors.

In a curious demonstration of the Weimar state's shifting and ambivalent attitude toward working mothers, insured women wage earners could still use clinic advice services but were to be sent back to private doctors for treatment or medication. There they might well receive decent obstetrical care, but no access to the coveted contraceptives or an all-women team of doctors and social workers prepared to provide sex and family counseling. Over one-third of all clinic patients were insured members who had voluntarily chosen the supportive atmosphere of the clinics rather than the hurried services of busy private health insurance physicians. Women knew that clinic doctors regularly distributed contraceptives, while health insurance regulations did not permit reimbursement for birth control prescribed by private doctors.

The VKB reluctantly agreed to the government's restrictive regulations despite "lively protest" from members and working-class organizations. Vollnhals and her colleagues in the prenatal clinics insisted that clinic care was not a second-class substitute for those without their own doctors but a superior, more modern, rational, and humane alternative. Asserting that counseling and medical services, and maternity care and birth control, should always be linked, Vollnhals refused to separate dependent and wage-earning women, and continued to treat all women who came to her clinics. Her abrupt retirement in 1930, and her replacement as director by a male physician, was probably linked to this conflict.[15]

Infuriated by the government ruling and the resulting decline in eligible patients, Dr. Kurt Bendix, director of the VKB's clinic network, decided on a bold counterattack. He moved to further extend health insurance services to insured workers and their families in the form of marriage and sex counseling clinics. A radical socialist, Bendix was profoundly convinced that only medically reliable birth control, prescribed by doctors sensitive to a woman's social as well as medical situation, could halt the "national scourge" of abortion and thereby meet the mandate of Section 363 of the National Insurance Code to provide preventive and not only curative care. But his decision to establish freestanding clinics specifically dedicated to birth control and sex counseling was also driven by the relentless efforts of Margaret Sanger's Berlin representative Agnes Smedley, the KPD's Dr. Martha Ruben-Wolf, and the Committee for Birth Control they had formed after Sanger's visit in December 1927.

Bendix's audacious action created a dilemma for Social Democratic social welfare officials. Bendix was not only defending his health insurance model against conservative anti–Social Democratic private physicians but was also confronting his own party comrades in Prussia's state government. They had handed over the Ministry of Social Welfare to Catholic Center party officials, who in 1926 instituted marriage counseling that explicitly rejected birth control, thereby disavowing the services provided by the traditionally Social Democratic health insurance fund. The SPD's familiar role as an advocate of working-class and trade union interests, increasingly understood as including a commitment to birth control and abortion reform, clashed with the

SPD's government coalitions with the Catholic Center, as well as with its own sexually conservative familialist social politics.[16]

## Berlin Health Insurance, the Committee for Birth Control, and Sanger's American Model

At this point, Bendix's dilemma fortuitously intersected with the interests of American birth controller Margaret Sanger and her friend Agnes Smedley.[17] On December 6, 1927, on her way home from the Population Congress in Geneva, Sanger created a stir when, at the invitation of the Berlin League of German Women Doctors (BDÄ), she lectured on birth control to a large and contentious crowd at the Charlottenburg Town Hall. Rather unwittingly, she touched off a bitter debate between Dr. Martha Ruben-Wolf, the militant Communist abortion rights advocate, and Alfred Grotjahn, a right-wing Social Democrat who opposed all but the most restricted access to abortion.[18] Smedley used her friendship with BDÄ leader Dr. Hermine Heusler-Edenhuizen to set up a follow-up meeting with about 20 women doctors in Sanger's hotel room. The American visitor offered the group a monthly stipend of $50 for three years in order to set up and maintain birth control advice bureaus.

Like many of her colleagues, Dr. Heusler-Edenhuizen—whom Smedley described as "an aristocrat, a nationalist in her politics, . . . But on women she is as straight as ever woman can be"[19]—routinely signed petitions for reform of paragraph 218 and was apparently quite prepared to perform discreet abortions in her private women's clinic. But like Anne-Marie Durand-Wever, who joined the effort to prevent Sanger from holding her large birth control congress in Berlin, she was nervous about the drama surrounding Sanger's visit. Despite the financial temptation, she was not willing to commit her organization to a controversial public campaign to establish birth control clinics on the American model.[20] Annoyed at the BDÄ's caution on birth control services despite its outspoken stance for abortion law reform, Smedley quickly discerned that when it came to birth control her staunchest and most reliable comrades were to be found among the Communist party physicians. She thus formed a close personal and political alliance with the general practitioner Martha Ruben-Wolf.

Smedley and Sanger's vision of a birth control clinic was quite different from the various kinds of counseling services already available in Germany; it offered neither the tolerant sex counseling provided by Magnus Hirschfeld's Institute for Sexual Science, nor the comprehensive family services to which the women doctors in the prenatal clinics were committed, nor the eugenic premarital counseling that the Prussian state vainly tried to impose on its citizenry. Smedley proudly reported to Sanger that their planned clinic would be "the first one to run on straight B.C. [birth control] lines."[21] It would operate under strict medical supervision, "pure and simple, with no homosexual-

ity or venereal diseases or tubercular appendages," and not "mixed up with
motherhood, sickness. . . . etc." Admitting that she was "perhaps conservative" on this issue, she professed herself "willing to fight on B.C. but not on
homosexuality."[22]

By April 1928, the Committee for Birth Control, inspired by Sanger, organized by Smedley, and clearly separate from the BDÄ, was well on its way. It
initially included the Communist city councilman and health commisssioner
from the Neukölln district, Dr. Richard Schmincke; Dr. Max Hodann, sex
reform gadfly and municipal physician in Berlin Reinickendorf; Mathilde
Winternitz, a young Communist gynecologist who worked in the Charité
university hospital; Alfred Dührssen, a noted gynecologist and pioneer in tubal
ligation sterilization techniques; and Ruben-Wolf; as well as the only two
nonphysicians, Helene Stöcker and Smedley. Despite her fears about competition for the BfM, the iconoclastic Stöcker was persuaded to become a loyal
member. Like Hodann and Ruben-Wolf, Stöcker looked to the Soviet Union
as a model of enlightened sexual and population policy and was therefore
unafraid to enter into coalitions with KPD members. Smedley reported with
pride that her "peach of a committee," of whom "3 are Communists, 3 are
non-Communists and I'm the rest!," was a model of nonpartisan cooperation,
sweetened by the regular arrival of Sanger's American dollars. Smedley confessed that she preferred the Communists because, unlike her friends within
the BDÄ whose "lady-like lack of interest in the Clinic idea repelled me," they
"are willing to fight."[23]

Sanger herself was "astonished that in the very country where we were
purchasing our contraceptives" activist women doctors were skeptical about
her single-minded approach to establishing birth control clinics.[24] BDÄ physicians' resistance to the Sanger model may well have had less to do with an
unwillingess to fight—they were, after all, quite vocal on abortion—than with
a reluctance to give up the maternalist vision of centers for "protection of
women" that animated their work in the prenatal clinics. Smedley, for her
part, was absolutely determined to maintain her distance from the kinkier
sides of German sex reform:

> B.C. methods are normal, healthy things used by normal persons, and I am
> uncompromisingly [sic] to have B.C. mixed up in any particular with any form
> of perversion. Why I wouldn't even want it mixed up with religion or Catholi-
> cism or other forms of perversion![25]

In public she also was careful to downplay Sanger's role, wanting both to
protect her friend from open alliance with Communists and the birth control movement from nationalist charges of foreign conspiracy to reduce the
German birth rate. As Smedley wrote to Sanger, only partly tongue-in-cheek,
"And I want the Clinic to open and be run without the firing of one gun."[26]

Sanger provided the Committee for Birth Control with $500 to launch the first clinic, scheduled to open on May 1, 1928, in Neukölln. However, the local KPD councilman Dr. Schmincke was stymied by bureaucratic and political problems, and his irritated party comrade Ruben-Wolf determined that the committee needed further reinforcements, even from the usually suspect SPD.[27] In a remarkable coup, Ruben-Wolf persuaded (or bullied) Dr. Bendix to join. Catching him just at the moment when he was seeking revenge for the 1928 ruling restricting VKB services, she cleverly played on Social Democratic fears of KPD competition in municipal elections, and on more general concern over women voters, if the SPD yielded the sex reform field to its Communist rivals.

As Smedley wrote triumphantly to Sanger, the "ruthless . . . Frau Dr. Wolf has manipulatated Dr. Bendix. . . . He works so hard for fear the Communists will do more than he."[28] In this case, the bitter competition between Communists and Social Democrats on all governmental levels, and particularly the substantial KPD presence in Berlin's politics and administration, served as a spur to innovative action. Certainly, Communist, Social Democratic, and "bourgeois" city officials and physicians shared anxieties about the proliferation of lay, commercially oriented, "wild" birth control centers lacking full medical supervision.

Bendix was to prove an indispensable ally. With his institutional support and Sanger's financial aid, it quickly became possible to set up five (eventually seven) marriage and birth control counseling centers under the auspices of the Health Insurance League's (VKB) clinic network. Even the best-organized lay and private centers offered only intermittent medical supervision. They generally advised and referred but did not directly examine women or do fittings for diaphragms or cervical caps. The VKB clinics, however, could provide modern medical equipment and facilities, and the regular services of trained and committed physicians. Only the Czech-born Dr. Winternitz had to be sacrificed because "the *Ambulatorium* objected to any but a German physician being put in."[29] Thus, the institutionalization of birth control services in Berlin was achieved by the link between the Committee for Birth Control, primarily organized by the American radical Smedley and the Communist Ruben-Wolf, and the Social Democrat Bendix's Health Insurance League.

The first clinic where "Birth control is very specifically the central point of our activity" opened July 1, 1928, on the premises of the health insurance offices in Neukölln.[30] On opening day, 15 women turned up, over half of them, as Smedley reported, pregnant and "desperately asking for abortions . . . [whom] we simply have to turn . . . away."[31] The center was initially open (much to Sanger's annoyance) only four hours a week, in the evening and on Thursday afternoon, in order to provide convenient hours for both housewives and working people. Two doctors, one male and one female, and a social worker instructed women in the use of a Ramses diaphragm with

Sanger's special recipe for lactic acid spermicide. The popular creams Patentex and Antibion were also tested for their effectiveness, and in a typical example of contraceptive overkill, doctors additionally urged patients to douche after each sexual encounter. After a free medical exam and fitting, a contraceptive device was sold to patients at cost and on the spot. As clinic doctors noted, referring to private centers like those of the BfM, which only provided advice and referrals, "If we were to limit ourselves to advice and not also provide the means . . . all our efforts would be utopian."[32]

Sanger's money was crucial to the pioneer operation; in its first year the Committee for Birth Control received a total of $1,200 (5,025 RM), much of it used to sponsor the Neukölln clinic. On October 1, 1928, the VKB inaugurated four more facilities. Having succeeded in officially introducing birth control services into the health insurance network at five locations (in addition to the services already provided by the prenatal clinics), the committee was assured by Sanger of a monthly $100 stipend for two more years. In a bid to regain the independence that had been exchanged for the mass outreach and powerful resources of Bendix's organization, the Committee then moved to open its own autonomous clinic. Max Hodann offered to serve as medical director of a smaller alternative center in Berlin-Reinickendorf where he served as municipal physician. Now closely associated with the RV as well as the Committee for Birth Control, he was eager to leave his position at the Institute for Sexual Science, held in ill repute by many of his comrades both because of Hirschfeld's activities in the homosexual rights movement and his alleged bribe taking from contraceptive manufacturers.[33]

Fortified by Sanger's money and the VKB's commitment to running birth control clinics, the Committee hoped that a center completely freed from government control or funding could avoid the arguments and misgivings about the restrictions of paragraph 184.3 and the limits on insurance prescription of contraceptives, which bedeviled the VKB's activities. While serving a more limited number of clients, an independent clinic would better focus on contraceptive research and experimentation, physician training, and political propaganda. Sanger's dollars provided contraceptives, supplies, and salaries for two doctors in Reinickendorf, as well as additional funding for two BfM clinics in Berlin and one directed by Dr. Hertha Riese in Frankfurt.[34] The committee invested in a typewriter, and mail asking for advice poured into Hodann's makeshift office. Plans were made for a doctors' seminar on birth control. Mass sex education meetings attracted 1,500 to 2,000 people, where Martha Ruben-Wolf, "a woman with children of her own, dignified and white-haired," held her working-class audience spellbound.[35]

Just before she departed for China at the end of 1928, Smedley tried to explain her Berlin experience to Sanger:

It is different than your Committee in America. The driving force from the beginning has been Communist, although we have tried to give it a general

representative character. . . . Here in Germany we do not need respectable
women to give B.C. a respectable name. It is already respectable, and only the
working class is denied the methods.

And lest Sanger still was not convinced, Smedley added a postscript designed
to prepare her correspondent for her successor as primary German contact,
the dedicated and energetic Ruben-Wolf. In Berlin she noted, Communists
were "perfectly respectable and one is to be found in almost every intellectual family. . . . They are not to be scoffed at. Here you can be a Communist
and be welcome in every gathering of intelligent people."[36]

The committee's cooperation with the VKB produced a successful network
of birth control services in Berlin. In 1928, their first year, five VKB centers
logged 2,705 first visits, the vast majority requests for birth control from married or "affianced" working-class women.[37] Additionally, the prenatal-care services that continued to provide birth control handled 16,929 cases.[38] A year
later, the number of clients had increased by several thousand, and the VKB
opened two more sex counseling centers. Seven clinics now supplied a range
of contraceptives, including diaphragms, IUDs, and suppositories.[39] Furthermore, doctors in the VKB's 18 prenatal clinics also referred women for clearly
medically indicated abortions and sterilizations, although this was of course
not advertised.[40]

In December 1928, the Committee for Birth Control responded to this new
situation of widely available public birth control services by organizing the
first doctors' course on birth control ever conducted in Germany. Held at
Langenbeck-Virchow Hospital in Berlin, the seminar marked the first time
that a large group of physicians had so openly moved to confront the growing competition from lay leagues. Especially doctors who worked in urban
clinics realized that combating the much bemoaned "plague" of illegal abortions required physicians trained in the use of, and willing to prescribe, contraceptives.

Approximately 200 doctors, most of them members of the VSA and/or
BDÄ, came together to discuss experiences and methods. They met in a highly
charged partisan atmosphere; mainstream medical journals had refused to
place announcements for such a dubious gathering, Virchow hospital administrators were harassed, and conservative birth controllers such as Hans
Harmsen refused to participate. Nevertheless the conference drew a crowd
of very respectable obstetricians and gynecologists. Professor Walter Stoeckel,
chief of women's services at the prestigious Charité and by no stretch of the
imagination a sex radical, lectured on birth control. Ernst Gräfenberg touted
the "elegance" of his controversial new IUD, much to the horror of colleagues
who warned about its dangers; others discussed x-ray and surgical sterilizations or artificial insemination. The program exhibited much the same
balance between political and scientific topics characteristic of WLSR congresses.[41]

The 1928 three-day seminar was such a success that five all-day sessions
were held later that winter. Lilly Ehrenfried, a young hospital resident, was
so inspired by her participation in the 1929 course that she immediately set
up sex counseling hours at the welfare office in working-class Prenzlauer Berg
in eastern Berlin. Impressed that the "evil Communists" were the only ones
willing directly to address the topic of birth control, she also joined a study
tour to the Soviet Union, explaining that:

> A doctor must, after all, be able to give some kind of answer to the wives of
> the unemployed when they ask about how to limit their families. How else are
> we supposed to gain their trust? Not through hypocrisy in this crucial ques-
> tion![42]

The central question facing physicians was however never adequately resolved: Should the decision to use contraception—and, by implication, to have
an abortion—be made by the woman alone, with the physician essentially
her agent helping carry out her choice, or should control finally rest with the
doctor? The resolutions passed by the assembled physicians avoided the issue,
by demanding simply that health insurance should fund birth control along
with other preventive measures.[43] Tensions between lay and medical reformers, of course, remained a staple of sex reform politics. The newly formed
RV, which had its own aspirations to medical respectability, complained that
it had not been taken seriously enough at the medical seminar in December.[44]
Yet, remarkably, the Committee for Birth Control had succeeded in getting
a diverse group of physicians, including some with "professor" titles, to discuss birth control, despite opposition from their own professional organizations.

These widely publicized medical birth control initiatives promoted further
growth of a wide variety of marriage counseling services. Given the ambigu-
ity of the term *Eheberatung*, the distinct emphases in different centers on sex,
contraceptive, or eugenic counseling, and the very limited number of hours
some centers were open, the actual number of facilities can only be estimated.
But, by the end of the Weimar Republic, there were at least 40 installations
in Berlin, ranging from the original clinic at the Institute for Sexual Science,
to private doctors' offices and health insurance and state clinics, that offered
some form of marriage, birth control, and sex counseling.[45] Most municipal
health offices in Berlin's districts included birth control advice with their
eugenic and psychological marriage counseling, as did two centers run by the
BfM in Kreuzberg and Friedrichshain. Additionally, the KPD International
Workers Aid (IAH), the RV-GESEX, the *Liga*, and the Committee for Birth
Control all ran their own centers.

The Health Insurance League prenatal clinics also dispensed birth control
services to pregnant and postpartum women. Women doctors in the BDÄ
who had kept their distance from Sanger and Smedley's initial efforts to open

independent clinics were especially involved in the BfM, municipal, and VKB centers. Furthermore, in the fall of 1928, the bourgeois Municipal League of Berlin Women's Associations (*Stadtverband Berliner Frauenvereine*) had established a "Confidential Counseling Center (*Vertrauenstelle*) for Married and Engaged Couples" in Charlottenburg. Run by BDÄ members Anne-Marie Durand-Wever and Annie Friedländer, it provided guidance on sex, marriage, and divorce (and a mail depot for "women in trouble") but referred the middle-class clientele to private physicians for birth control.[46]

Durand-Wever, herself an activist for abortion reform, noted that her center tried to avoid, "all matters of a controversial nature" because "it does not want to antagonize large groups of women who have widely divergent views on such subjects."[47] Still, notwithstanding the differences in the scope and breadth of services provided and in an indication of how widespread the trend had become all over Germany during the second half of the Weimar Republic, 43 cities from Altona to Witten (and not including Berlin) reported in a 1931 national survey that they maintained some kind of marriage counseling program.[48]

## Debates About Birth Control Clinics: Rationalized Medical Care and the Welfare State

The rapid expansion of counseling centers that openly dispensed birth control provoked fierce debate, chiefly among doctors of varying political persuasions. Embedded in medical controversies over funding, staffing, contraceptive methods, and the ethics of providing birth control in public clinics were intensely political questions. At professional meetings and in the pages of medical and public health journals, as well as in the daily press, doctors argued about the limits of social insurance coverage for a modern welfare state, the proper venues for providing mass health care, and their professional identity in an age of spiraling technology and shrinking resources—disputes that also interrogated the nature of gender and sexual relations in a modern rationalized society. These battles over money, turf, and jurisidiction became increasingly bitter as the general trend toward rationalization—centralization, specialization, and cost cutting—in medical care was intensified by economic crisis at the end of the 1920s.

Some questioned the legitimacy of providing medical services of any kind in a public clinic setting. Status-conscious health insurance physicians (*Kassenärzte*), most of them male, who were reimbursed for seeing patients in private consultation, observed the growing popularity of birth control and family-care clinics with trepidation and resentment. They contended that clinics restricted free choice of doctors by patients, and of medication and therapies by physicians; promoted impersonal, overspecialized, and bureaucratized "Americanization" and "desouling" of medicine; and thereby disrupted the sacrosanct relationship between healer and patient, which was, after all, especially important when dealing with such delicate matters as sex and procreation.

This was a curiously disingenuous position for doctors so often accused of completely avoiding these "delicate" issues. More likely, their antagonism was driven by fears of losing clientele and fees. The strict regulations and long waiting lists for health insurance eligibility, and the oversupply of physicians, especially in large cities, had led to intense competition for the guaranteed patient pool and steady income of an insurance practice (*Kassenpraxis*).[49] Doctors were all too aware that many working-class women only sought a physician's services if they were pregnant or had other gynecological problems. They worried about degradation by association with the "gutter politics" of birth control, and by extension, abortion. But they were also alarmed that so many women defected to lay midwives or quacks, or increasingly to the mail-order and storefront services of lay leagues, because doctors could not legally provide abortions or insurance-subsidized contraceptives and often knew precious little about such matters.

Clinic supporters retorted that changes in the nature of disease and disability, caused by the rationalization of the German economy, required a shift in focus from acute care and compensation to illness and accident prevention, both at home and in the workplace. In a modern welfare state, health education, rehabilitation, and physical fitness were more cost effective than intervention after damage had been done. As scientific employees and public servants, doctors were bound to use the most modern technology and medical expertise to provide services to as many people as possible, including the apparently healthy. Clinics were generally located in district "houses of health," proud modern edifices, some newly built in 1928 or 1929. In the famous *Gesundheitshaus am Urban* in Kreuzberg, for example, school health services, a general polyclinic, sports medicine, marriage and sex counseling, tuberculosis, venereal disease, mental health, and substance abuse treatment were all provided, along with a lecture hall for an audience of 500, a library with health education books and magazines, and an exhibition room.[50]

The availability of consulting specialists and expensive sophisticated diagnostic equipment in a central location assured better and more cost-effective care, avoiding false diagnoses or duplication of services. Medical knowledge, clinic advocates declared, had advanced far beyond the comfortable diagnostic intuition of the friendly family doctor (*Hausarzt*). Simply prescribing a pill for a headache was no longer medically or fiscally responsible; proper treatment required that its cause first be established by laboratory tests. The VKB aggressively attempted to restructure medical care in Berlin by establishing its own facilities for x-rays or medicinal baths and by limiting the numbers and types of drugs that were eligible for reimbursement. Private doctors, pharmaceutical companies, and pharmacists of course resented the competition from this new "big business," while clinic doctors pointedly noted that the real assembly-line medical care was provided by private *Kassenärzte* who processed large numbers of patients daily in order to maximize their income.[51] Insurance and public health officials thus positioned themselves as the guarantors of rational economical medical care.

For a profession that never seemed to feel secure about its social and scientific status, this emphasis on inexpensive primary and preventive care was highly problematic. The use of tools such as orthopedic gymnastics, health education, or "healing warming" radiation therapy did not always conform to the narrow rules of academic medicine, nor did it satisfy many doctors' desire for complex surgical and drug intervention. Many doubted the wisdom of doctors trained to repair acute disorders engaging in large-scale hygienic projects such as campaigns against alcoholism, venereal disease, drug addiction, illegal abortion, and general sexual misery (*Sexualnot*). Clinic and public health doctors, however, most of them general practitioners rather than highly trained specialists, believed that health insurance should extend medical control to groups not previously considered needy, such as those requiring birth control, speech therapy, or child guidance. They favored continuing surveillance not only of one diseased individual at certain discrete times but of the entire body politic in a process akin to that later described by Jacques Donzelot as the "hygienization" of the "whole social enclosure."[52]

Municipal and health insurance clinics were therefore deeply implicated in the general Weimar discussion—which escalated with the economic crisis beginning in 1929—about the breadth and costs of public and semipublic welfare institutions. Critics from the nationalist right, in particular, suggested that the continued expansion of health insurance coverage and an ever-widening definition of problems requiring therapeutic intervention (for example, sexuality) led to a corrupt, profligate welfare state bureaucracy that in turn created a nation of weaklings (*Verweichlichung*). Coddled by an overly generous health-care system that rewarded malingering by paid sick leave, conservatives argued, Germans were lapsing into a veritable addiction to health care and doctors' visits. Thus the clinics became highly visible contested ground in the larger debate over the "crisis of confidence" in medicine and the proper limits of social insurance coverage and funding.[53]

### Debates on Public Management of Birth Control and Sexuality

It should be clear by now that agitation against the clinics by physicians was generally not directed against birth control per se but represented a defense of private medical practice and opposition to making birth control a public and thereby "degraded" political issue. Even the firmest opponents were not necessarily against the discreet medical prescription of contraception—or indeed abortion—in the seclusion of the consultation room. On another level, however, the debate over dispensing birth control in clinics was directly inflected by the matrix of anxieties and hopes stirred by the "new woman" and by changes in the family and labor market. Conservatives such as the Catho-

lic gynecologist August Mayer anguished that birth control clinics were "part
of a process towards dissolution of the family, the state, and I believe it is no
exaggeration if we say, this is the beginning of the decline of the West."[54] Still
others worried that counseling might heighten already strained tensions between the sexes and within families by offering a space to vent hostilities and
collect incriminating information. (For example, some citizens reportedly
tried to use the state marriage centers as detective bureaus to gather data on
prospective mates.)

Disputes over the existence of clinics could not be separated from conflicts
about the propriety of public (hence state) support for birth control and sex
education. The majority of doctors, whatever their individual policies in
regard to contraception (and, as we shall see in the next chapter, abortion),
were unalterably opposed to the "socialized" clinic model. Opposing them
was the committed minority of politically active doctors, most of them members of the SPD or KPD, many of them women and Jews, gathered in the
VSA and the BDÄ, who firmly believed that public bureaucracies could and
should provide the broadest possible medically supervised distribution of birth
control as part of their general investment in social medicine. Between them
were a growing number of elite physicians, such as the gynecologist Ludwig
Fränkel, who pleaded for insurance reimbursement of birth control precisely
in order to avoid ceding the field to quacks, salespeople, or clinics.[55]

Although the use or prescription of birth control was not illegal in Germany, paragraph 184.3 of the penal code prohibited the advertising, publicizing, or display of contraceptive devices as "objects intended for indecent use";
furthermore, health insurance did not reimburse for contraceptive services
by private doctors. Remaining within this framework but reversing the conclusion, clinic officials countered that birth control was moral or ethical
(*sittlich*) precisely because it encouraged health, personal discipline, and social
responsibility. Doctors committed to sex reform insisted that the availability
of birth control in public clinics and through the national insurance system
would neither promote licentiousness nor subvert a national population policy
still officially committed to raising the birth rate. Rather it would simply
rationally manage and supervise the ongoing, unregulated, and unobservable
use of quack remedies, coitus interruptus, illegal abortions, and products sold
by lay leagues. Birth control methods prescribed by professionals would encourage habits of regularity and discipline and protect women's capacity for
future pregnancies, perhaps even assuring that *more* healthy children would
be born and raised.

As Dr. Hertha Riese caustically pointed out at a national congress of gynecologists, doctors could influence only "the methods used in regulating population numbers, i.e., whether it is done through contraception, child murder,
abortion, through illness, death or suicide."[56] Clinics did not steal patients
from private doctors; indeed, as one professor of gynecology remarked, offering "advice on sexual matters . . . one of the most intimate topics there is,

offers the best opportunity to gain the public's trust."[57] Once examined, registered, and helped by the clinic system, female and working-class patients, "who might never have thought of going to a doctor," would then "find their way from the counseling centers to the physician's consulting room."[58]

VKB doctors deployed a commonplace rhetoric of fiscal responsibility, social rationalization, and eugenic health (as well as nationalism) to defend the doubtful legality of distributing contraceptives in their clinics. They invoked paragraph 363 of the national insurance code's injunction to provide preventive as well as curative care, contending that birth control preserved the health of the *Volk*, while medical neglect would only increase the "ballast" of the unfit. At the same elite gynecology conference, RV Drs. Lehfeldt and Hirsch asked their colleagues why the national health system should pay to battle epidemics, but not the national epidemic of illegal abortions?[59] In a rationalized cost-conscious insurance system, funding of sterilization, contraception, and abortion was surely preferable to the expense of caring for the disabled and unwanted.

Physicians increasingly understood that cynically telling a woman to avoid pregnancy without carefully prescribing an appropriate "means of protection" would only further reduce the profession's already precarious credibility and drive women to quacks.[60] Women, after all, continued to be most vulnerable to illness and death during the childbearing years from 30 to 40, a statistic that was explained by high incidences of suicide, childbirth complications, and of course illegal abortions.[61] With a touch of irony, VKB clinic chief Dr. Bendix claimed that while birth control counseling could hardly further reduce the low birth rate among the working class, it would certainly reduce abortion, as well as infant and child mortality.[62] He also sharply criticized the hypocrisy of colleagues who denounced clinic-based gynecological services as degrading, pointing out that:

> In their private practice they meet only women of the upper classes, and the women they see in their clinics are removed from their own milieu, they lie in airy rooms, in clean beds, are bathed, and their relations with the professor are limited to examination and treatment.[63]

Medical sex reformers never fully agreed on whether birth control was good per se or a necessary evil. Painstakingly balancing advantages and drawbacks, some welcomed family limitation as rational quality control, while others couched their support in terms of stimulating childbearing by reducing maternal and infant mortality.[64] Sex reform doctors shared many of their conservative colleagues' fears about sexual license and dysgenic breeding. They too fretted that better educated and more responsible couples, both working and middle class, would limit births, while the "asocials" would reproduce, or that counseling about possible genetic disabilities and birth control options might further weaken Germans' already fragile desire for children.

But, finally, sex reformers were convinced that there was no sense in lamenting a mythical past of large happy families. They knew that, "Whoever has a chance to take a really good look at life as we do . . . knows that love can neither be forbidden nor prevented"; realistically their alternatives were to "either be stuck with the ghastly effect of abortion or else bring order and method to the question of contraception."[65] Thus they anxiously searched for birth control methods and means of distribution and education that would best preserve medical privileges while providing maximum access. Communist and socialist physicians, in particular, struggled to reconcile their competing agendas of medicalization and self-help. They sought to assure that birth control provision and counseling became a respectable medicalized domain, but also wanted to avoid overdependence on a generally resistant medical profession.

Constantly confronted with these bitter debates, clinic staffs were defensive about the legality and ethics of their work. Wrapping themselves in the consensus language of motherhood, eugenics, and cost effectiveness, they stressed that they were not condoning immorality or promiscuity; on the contrary, they were saving marriages and producing healthy children at minimal cost. The latter argument became ever more urgent with the onset of the depression when insurance funds were under enormous pressure to cut expenses, just when the number of insured working patients was declining and the welfare caseload was swelling. Counseling center reports were filled with case histories of the most "degenerate," the most "asocial," the most handicapped, who had been mercifully prevented from procreating. If only one unfit birth were avoided, one center director noted, the state would immediately save 92,000 RM.[66]

Poignant case histories were publicized as much for their propaganda as for their scientific value. Doctors reported on the 39-year-old wife of a porter who claimed to have had 20 pregnancies, 18 of which she had aborted; the 37-year-old wife of a stoker who had two living children and five abortions including several with fever; the 34-year-old wife of an unemployed mechanic, with two children, five abortions, and one premature birth. Patients were invariably described as being in extremely poor health and as having unsuccessfully attempted to use various kinds of birth control methods. In an interesting twist, however, while propaganda for birth control and legalized abortion usually invoked the trope of overburdened mothers with hordes of children tugging at their frayed skirts, and most clinic clients reported numerous pregnancies, very few clients actually had more than two children.[67] Counseling centers were not so much creating as confirming and abetting the existence of the smaller proletarian family and women's determination to limit births.

## Debate Over Staffing, Methods, and Scope of Service

Even for supporters, medical responsibility for birth control raised complex questions of control and autonomy. Doctors quarreled over whether effective birth control required regular medical supervision; whether it should be available to the unmarried as well as the married, those with many children and those who wanted no children at all, those in dire economic straits and those desiring birth control for other "personal" reasons; and finally, they disagreed over whether birth control was the responsibility of the man, the woman, or the couple. Was it a right available to all or a privilege to be granted to the medically or socially needy and deserving? Municipal and health insurance clinics generally drew their guidelines deliberately broadly to cover women "who had no male breadwinner to support them," who had given birth within the past two years, and most inclusively, those for whom, "another child would jeopardize the economic survival of the family."[68] In practice, most clinics conveniently redefined "marriage counseling" to denote "biological marriage"; hence they served any sexually active woman.[69]

Closely connected to doctors' arguments about choice of methods and products were debates over staffing, particularly about appropriate medical personnel. Psychiatrists and venereologists both claimed special expertise while gynecologists insisted they were the only ones sufficiently informed about the indications and contraindications for each contraceptive method. Others, more skeptical about gynecologists' grasp of birth control and suspicious of their propensity to use the clinics for experimentation with new methods, felt that compassion and "healthy common sense" were most likely to be found among the less elite ranks of general practitioners. Some male doctors suggested that only men were equipped to deal with the sexual problems of both men and women.[70] In general, however, women doctors were acknowledged as necessary to the clinics' success, if only because their special gifts of "sympathy, insight, and tact" encouraged women to confide their intimate needs.[71]

The nature and scope of the services provided was also at issue. Should they be limited, as Smedley and Sanger pleaded, to birth control; or should clinics offer more comprehensive advice and treatment for sexual and marital problems, infertility, and fitness for marriage and procreation? Differences about the importance of access versus the need for medical regulation also affected debate on proper contraceptive methods. Physicians tended to recommend the proper medically certified mechanical/chemical combination, while lay activists and some of their medical allies often preferred simple spermicidal suppository creams because "really cheap simple methods which are nevertheless effective" were more likely to be used.[72]

Medicalized sex reform presented women with a complicated double message: first, take control of your own bodies, learn about and use birth control, but in the final analysis, enter into an alliance with your doctor, because only your doctor knows for sure. Birth control should be easy enough for women to utilize, but not easy enough to eliminate the need for medical supervision. This message was reinforced by harrowing warnings about the dangers of illegal abortions and quack remedies, or even the wrong choice of contraceptive. In an attempt to buttress their professional standing, and faced with formidable competition from laypeople, doctors sought to establish birth control as a complicated medical specialty that had no simple solutions. In this scenario, the variety of methods available and the need to tailor the method to the individual woman meant that the proper choice required careful examination by an expert physician. In other words, if doctors were to be forced to involve themselves in so mundane and indelicate a matter as birth control, then it should at least be packaged as something requiring sophisticated medical skills. Thus, at the same time that sex reform was demanding inexpensive, safe, accessible, and easy-to-use birth control, it was mystifying the entire process by turning it into a medical event. Stringent medical supervision (preferably under state control) was presented as the only alternative to exploitation by quacks.

Physicians' at times almost hysterical stress on the complexities and potential hazards of various contraceptives was not without irony in view of the abysmal level of ignorance within most of the medical profession on all questions relating to contraception. Although doctors did learn how to perform surgical abortion procedures (dilation and curettage), it took the pharmacist and quack abortionist Paul Heiser to develop the suction method, and most doctors had never even seen a diaphragm. Dr. Hertha Nathorff, who daily provided women with contraceptives at her Charlottenburg clinic, recalled learning nothing about birth control as a young resident in obstetrics and gynecology at major university clinics:

> Really . . . I was at the Women's Clinic in Heidelberg, I was at the Women's Clinic in Freiburg, I had *never*[very loud] heard the word birth control [*Geburten-regelung*]. I knew nothing about a so-called diaphragm, but one day I took over for a colleague and in came a woman with a diaphragm and said I should put it in place for her. I stared at the thing, "I'm so sorry, but you have to wait until the doctor comes back herself." And when my colleague came back, I told her about it: "What could that have been?" She answered: "And this one calls herself a doctor?"[73]

Her colleague Dr. Reni Begun complained in the VSA journal that birth control research was not "even remotely on a par with . . . the rest of medical progress" where "otherwise every mini-problem" was subjected to "hair-splitting investigations."[74] Undaunted, doctors mobilized an arsenal of ideological if not very scientific weaponry about the enigmatic nature of female biology and the skill required to manage it, in order to convince women of physicians' superior knowledge.

Prescriptions for contraceptive use were sometimes so convoluted and unappetizing that it hardly seems surprising that many women were reluctant to use them or used them improperly, and that—much to the frustration of their providers—couples often trusted to luck and illegal abortion. Consumers were urged to purchase not only a diaphragm or pessary but also one of myriad contraceptive creams on the German market—for example, Contrapan, Speton, Semori, Patentex, or Antibion—as well as an applicator for proper insertion and an irrigator for douching.[75] The suggestion to douche after intercourse, even if a reliable contraceptive had already been used, exemplified the kind of recommendation that might well have struck women as unpleasant, uncomfortable, and for the many without running water, quite impossible. The glorification of mutual sexual satisfaction also rang ironic in view of the complicated instructions for proper birth control practice. Perhaps the equally detailed prescriptions for sexual technique were necessary to help overcome the obstacle course of proper contraceptive routine!

Indeed, use of contraception required instilling in most, especially working-class, women, a fundamentally new and narrower understanding of birth control. Since many working-class women did not define themselves as "pregnant" until after "quickening," a properly developed birth control consciousness necessitated first of all a novel and sharper distinction between abortion and contraception. This in turn dictated shifting the domain of fertility control from women's networks to doctors and clinics. In the process, the rhetoric of "expertise" tended to escalate and continually clashed with the competing priorities of easy availability and use. Ironically, in the course of fighting for the right to "private choice" in reproduction, sex reformers first had to construct abortion and contraception as distinct and public issues.

Sex reform's constant reminders that there was no magical formula for trouble-free birth control were also intended to counter fraudulent and exaggerated claims by manufacturers, such as the Antibion spermicide advertisements (alluding to Van de Velde's widely read sex manual) promising that, "The prerequisites for an ideal marriage are thus now available in the form of this blessed medical invention."[76] Sex reformers desperately wanted to install doctors, rather than salespeople, as the purveyors of "scientific," not quack or commercial, products. Yet doctors were also not above touting their favorite creams as not only fully effective against pregnancy and venereal disease but also as vaginal lubricants to assure sexual pleasure.

Clinic records served the political agenda of proving that birth control could be safe, effective, and efficiently distributed on a mass scale, but they also served research and commercial purposes. They were cited in advertisements as well as medical journals, and a doctor's recommendation of one particular brand in scientific forums, working-class newspapers, or in the counseling centers could have an important impact on contraceptive sales, a fact not unnoticed by manufacturers, who often supplied clinics with free samples.[77]

Judgments about methods also implied judgments about how much women or the lower classes (or both) could be trusted, and how much they were capable of learning and understanding. Doctors overwhelmingly preferred the so-called Anglo-American diaphragm and spermicide (mechanical and chemical) combination pushed by Sanger, but only for women "intelligent" enough to use it properly. If correctly used, a 3-RM diaphragm was reliable and harmless, and could last several years; compared to suppositories or condoms, which had to be constantly repurchased, it was also quite economical. Cervical caps and IUDs, which required more medical intervention, were recommended "for women of low intelligence," and of course sterilization remained as a last resort when women consistently failed as contraceptors.

The new silkworm-ring IUD, promoted by Berlin gynecologist Ernst Gräfenberg as the solution for women unwilling or unable to use a diaphragm, provoked the fiercest disputes. He extolled it as an "elegant" method that obviated the need for messy paraphernalia and forethought. But many doctors were convinced that the "magic ring," which used silk strands to block sperm that got past the cervical stem, worked by creating potentially dangerous infections or irritations.[78]

Remarkably absent from most of the debate was any serious suspicion that gender conflict and power differentials between men and women might continue to complicate birth control even if all technical problems were to be solved. Ultimately, of course, the dramatically high number of criminal abortions offered the most persuasive argument for expanding birth control access and counseling. Even those who vigorously supported the decriminalization of abortion did not question that it was "better to prevent than to abort." Most so-called counseling centers run by lay leagues still operated with little medical help, but the rapid development in Berlin of a birth control clinic network under municipal and health insurance auspices affirmed the existence of a general consensus on the desirability, if not the specific character, of medical control of birth control and sex counseling.

## Women Doctors: A Different View

Women doctors, on the front lines as clinic staff, walked a fine line in these political and medical debates about the role of doctors and the proper parameters of social insurance coverage in the German republic. As self-defined advocates for women, they claimed a special legitimacy in the new and hotly contested area of marriage, sex, and birth control counseling. They understood female resistance to cold and unsympathetic doctors and insisted that their dual experience as physicians and as women lent them privileged insight into women's intimate lives. They prided themselves on treating sexual and marital complaints within the total context of a woman's life (*Lebenstotalität*) rather than as problems to be simply fixed by medical intervention.

Women distinguished themselves from even their progressive male colleagues by insisting on their specific responsibility to other women, and on the ethical as well as political and technical aspects of marriage, sex, and birth control counseling. They frequently criticized doctors whose research interests led them to "completely forget about the patient from whom these bacilli had just come."[79] This holistic "woman-oriented" approach to medicine as more social than scientific was even inscribed in the gendered terminology of medical hierarchy. Women defined themselves as clinicians (*Ärztinnen*) rather than scientists (*Medizinerinnen*) and used a language suffused with maternalist and essentialist rhetoric.[80] Highly visible in urban clinics, women physicians were perceived—in somewhat distorted and overstated fashion—as the vanguard of sex reform. As one anxious observer noted:

> It is no accident that the directors and organizers of the new sexual counseling centers are often women doctors. Filled with a feeling of humanity, with sympathy for their sisters and the sanctity of their mission, hypnotized by the successes of the Anglo-American women pioneers, these leading women present themselves as the apostles of a new era and are convinced that they will have the last laugh over a backward patriarchal morality.[81]

Yet, female physicians were also in the vanguard of the campaign to medicalize family life and women's bodies. Indeed, in many ways, their alternative definition of medicine as a humane social undertaking facilitated the process of medicalization by embracing interventionist medicine as progressive, modern, and caring. Critical of sterile academic medicine (*Schulmedizin*), they nevertheless wanted to lure women away from "backward quackery" into the bureaucratic public health system. In the name of protecting and serving women, clinic physicians were committed to the most rationalized and potentially impersonal form of medical organization. Centralized clinics, they argued, enabled early detection and treatment through the use of laboratory tests, complete physicals, and systematic record-keeping; they also encouraged cooperation with social workers and social service agencies.

In fact, women physicians were actively competing with midwives and lay "wise women" for the loyalty and trust of female patients. Many of the "back-street" abortionists they so maligned were midwives whose livelihoods were increasingly threatened by tighter licensing procedures, the general decline in births, and the takeover by physicians of much of the limited obstetrics work still available. In rather sharp contrast to the single-issue birth control focus championed by Smedley and Sanger, German women doctors envisioned birth control services connected to both prenatal services and a comprehensive family medicine program. By defining public health clinics as communities of women, they sought to reconcile efficient modernity and the rationalization of reproduction with warm maternalism.

Female clinic doctors thus defended women's right to birth control but also worried that therapies focused exclusively on contraception and sex education would pressure young women into unwanted sex, as well as obscure more fundamental problems of inequality and family burdens. They wanted to protect their patients from premature and unwanted sexual activity and childbearing, but also—and not without trepidation—sought to give them the means to control their own bodies. Based on daily clinical evidence, women doctors were suspicious about the hazards of sexual freedom that birth control might facilitate, but were also impassioned about the dangers of limiting access to contraception and abortion. They were angered by the willful ignorance about birth control of their male medical school professors and hospital chiefs. Lilly Ehrenfried remembered that as a resident she was told, "Doctors do not concern themselves with such matters." When she then "naively" asked, " 'But how do you do it with your wife?' he gave me an angry look and walked out of the room."[82]

The rhetorical stress on women's sexual fulfillment and the new partnership and comradeliness in relations between the sexes had not altered the assumption that disciplined contraceptive use—even during the pleasures of "sex-reformed" intercourse—remained primarily women's responsibility. Constantly negotiating paradoxes, women doctors recognized women's need for independence from men's (unreliable) willingess to practice coitus interruptus or use condoms, but also suggested that birth control should be a shared duty, since a man should not be relieved of birth control responsibility "on the basis of his carelessness."[83]

Female physicians, however, were also remarkably prescient about the dangers of medicalized birth control, sounding a rare note of warning about the threat posed by progressive physicians' zeal for experimenting with new contraceptive techniques such as the IUD. Alice Goldmann-Vollnhals, the staunch birth control advocate, lamented:

> As if it were simply a matter of course, birth control is primarily practiced with methods to be used on the woman. One wants to "protect the poor woman from the fact of unwanted pregnancy." But on the other hand, we claim to want to fight malignant tumors, to reduce female diseases. We don't bother to think about whether it should be a matter of course that women carry within themselves foreign objects which we know can lead to unpleasant irritations, even though we also continue to believe that irritations can cause cancer. The woman carries the burden of reproduction. She has the pain of childbirth, the dangers of the childbed and the effort of nursing. Now the woman is also supposed to undertake the elimination of the consequences of sexual relations.[84]

Some lay female activists were even more pointed; referring to the Zurich birth control conference, Auguste Kirchhoff of the Bremen BfM complained that, "Precisely as a woman, one repeatedly got the uneasy feeling that, to put it crassly, one was not yet out of the guinea pig stage."[85]

Women doctors preferred the diaphragm as a harmless method that required minimal medical supervision and encouraged individual responsibility. It forced women to touch their genitals and thereby overcome the "false modesty" that hindered gynecological care and birth control counseling, as well as sexual satisfaction. Clinic physicians railed against the "backwardness" and passivity of poor women who came in pregnant time after time, unable to use birth control properly or articulate their sexual problems. But, at the same time, they were distressed by the sexual shamelessness of the young single women who came to them demanding birth control. For these matter-of-fact doctors, many of whom themselves led unconventional private lives, one of the most shocking effects of urban modernity was young women's readiness not only to separate sex from procreation but also to divorce sex from love. The tenuous and constantly shifting line between sexual emancipation and whoring was never clearly defined, especially for those who considered themselves most avant-garde. Dr. Hertha Nathorff recalled an encounter with one tough young clinic patient:

> Once I began to preach a moral lesson because she didn't know if this one or that one was the father. "This is outrageous, at your age I was still going to school, I didn't even know about such things." Then she said, "Well, I certainly wouldn't want to be as stupid as Frau Doktor." So I said, "You're right, I would have been happier if you had been a little stupider."[86]

But women clinic doctors were also determinedly unsentimental and realistic. Treating pregnant women and prescribing birth control, they were privy, as other physicians were not, to confessions of sexual anxiety and dissatisfaction. Both married and unmarried women were sexually active and needed to be safeguarded from abortions. Both women and men needed information to combat the newly identified "epidemic" of female "frigidity," which was preoccupying sex reformers, psychologists, and all those seeking to repair postwar strains between the sexes and awaken women's "will to a child." They were all too familiar with what Agnes Smedley had described, with her customary frankness, in a letter to Sanger from Berlin as that "most awful nervous tension" that caused her and many other women "to lie awake in bitterness all night long, while a man slumbers peacefully."[87]

Women physicians aimed to meet this need for sex advice, while protecting women with careful treatment and counseling. Along with providing birth control, they promoted a particular vision of responsible companionate heterosexuality. Nathorff was proud of her personal touch; a woman who complained about her husband's insensitivity was brusquely advised to preserve her marriage but was also given some tips on cunnilingus: "Everything very simple, very honest, very matter-of-fact. But still esthetic."[88] Dr. Käthe Becher of the Spandau clinic agonized over the "indifference, . . . passivity and indolence" caused by exhaustion, hopelessness, and poverty. Yet she also championed sex advice and fittings for diaphragms that could be immediately taken home as empowering antidotes for patients too poor to buy them and too ignorant to avoid falling prey to quack products.[89]

For women clinic doctors, trying simultaneously to help, supervise, and discipline, eugenic hygiene and social order were key to women's management of the double burden. But in their view, this goal also required women's right to control their fertility. They saw no contradiction in combining lessons in social respectability and eugenic hygiene with a fierce devotion to improving social conditions and meeting the particular needs of their diverse patient pool of single working girls, working-class housewives, and working mothers. Claiming, if not fully controlling their clinics as women's spaces, they loved their work and were proud of the specifically female approach to clinic medicine in which "the medical side was only half the job."[90]

Women doctors, tied to their professional identity and social welfare employment, did of course aim to exert social control over other women. But it is crucial to stress that clinic doctors were also responding to genuine demand from women desperate for birth control and sex information. In a complex negotiation similar to the one Linda Gordon describes in her nuanced analysis of American social workers and their clients, neither woman professional nor woman client got exactly what she wanted, but both got something and the service provided was changed in the process.[91]

## Doctors, Clinics, and Sterilization

It was no accident that women and socialist physicians arguing for legal abortion and distribution of contraceptives were also among the most avid proponents of eugenic sterilization and were likely to use a terminology that divided women into the responsible worthy and the "asocial." As the foot soldiers of medical sex reform and social medicine toiling in the trenches of the counseling centers and insurance practices, they knew how hopeless it might be to get an alcoholic husband to hear a "no" or to tolerate contraceptive use. Women professionals' daily experience in working-class neighborhoods provided continuing evidence of the apparent validity of many eugenic and social health arguments. Overcrowded urban housing did produce poor health and sexual disturbances; women were prematurely old and ill; families were torn apart by repeated pregnancies; large families did suffer from crime, alcoholism, and disease; many women were irresponsible about sexual hygiene.

Sex reform prescriptions for the right kind of contraceptive, properly taught and used, augmented by knowledge about sexual technique, to prevent pregnancy and "marriage fatigue," did not always work. Effective use of a diaphragm necessitated privacy, running water, and detailed, patient explanation, yet frustrated physicians often blamed women for contraceptive failure. Doctors were especially annoyed when clients' sloppy habits and negligence about follow-up visits skewed research data or invited trouble with the abortion law. Dr. Elisabeth Prinz, clinic director in proletarian Berlin-Friedrichshain, bemoaned the "repeat offenders" who, pregnant once again and "using threats of suicide, . . . come begging for an illegal abortion."[92]

The social service institutions of the Weimar Republic—maternal and infant-care centers, school medical programs, and marriage and sex counseling centers—served not only to alleviate but above all to document with apparently "scientific" facts and figures a social misery that was not only material but also emotional and sexual. Doctors and social workers frequently perceived a dismal cycle of moral and physical degeneration in which a husband sought relief from his noisy, chaotic family and exhausted, resigned wife in the neighborhood bar where he would get drunk, succumb to the temptations of cinema, tobacco, alcohol, and casual sex, and take up with a prostitute who would infect him with venereal disease, which he would then pass on to his wife; she in turn would give birth to diseased children who would create more chaos for the household and perpetuate a depraved "culture of poverty." In another version of this vicious cycle, the housing crisis (*Wohnungsnot*) was connected to the sexual crisis (*Sexualnot*): overcrowded living conditions led to incest; early exposure to sexual activity; rape by boarders, stepfathers, and other relatives; teenage pregnancy; illegal abortions; venereal disease; prostitution; and a general brutalization of sexual and gender relations.[93]

Clinic doctors focused on the environmental causes of such "degeneration," but believed, despite the admitted paucity of scientific evidence, that, "the conditions inherent in the asocial behavior of parents can be transmitted to offspring."[94] Given such theoretical unclarity, the urgency of social crisis, and the lack of a clearly articulated socialist counterdiscourse to hereditarian thought, birth control and eugenic hygiene seemed sensible strategies. If fewer people were to be born, then they should be healthy and productive, and not burden the precarious national economy. In this view, order and discipline became eugenic measures in and of themselves.

Attempts to instill regular habits of contraceptive use and attention to sexual technique were also intended to stabilize chaotic proletarian lives plagued by unpredictable pregnancies as well as uncertain housing and employment. The key to reforming such a household was the wife and mother, who, whether or not she was also a wage earner, was held responsible for its health and stability. Like the working class, women were separated into those who managed and those who did not. Indeed, the general shift toward smaller families sharpened divisions between the disciplined (rationalized) working class and a "degenerate" or "asocial" "lumpenproletariat" unable or unwilling to rationalize its birth strategies and sexual behavior.

In that context, many committed sex reformers and birth controllers came to see sterilization as a positive social good and a cost-efficient method of reducing expensive "social ballast." Lotte Fink reported on the weary indifference of patients in her Frankfurt counseling center, noting flatly that, "Particularly with women from the lowest social strata, . . . peace and quiet could only be established after a tubal ligation."[95] The domino effect of dysgenic consequences seemed inexorable unless interrupted by birth control and, if necessary, sterilization. By the early 1930s, as the economic crisis deepened, the sterilization solution gained seductive power as a possible quick fix for the challenges of inculcating hygienic and rational habits in the urban poor.

Elite physicians and other scientists discerned in sterilization an opportunity for engineering perfection, and government bureaucrats saw an opportunity to save money. Sex reformers as well as government officials were fond of citing the costs of caring for the ill and crippled, as compared to the relatively minor expenditures necessary for sex and birth control education. Just as a nation with a steadily declining birth rate could not afford any part of that diminished number to be of poor quality, so a nation decimated by wartime death and casualties and hard hit by postwar inflation could not afford to support the unfit. Article after article in demographic, medical, and sex reform journals rehearsed the litany of alarming facts as a rationale for "procreation hygiene": 290,000 mentally ill, 95,000 epileptic, 390,000 alcoholic, 370,000 congenitally blind, 1,400,000 tubercular citizens, 73,000 minors in reform schools, and 58,000 children sentenced to prison.[96]

Lower-status female doctors and social workers, however, frequently aimed to relieve women's real misery as well as their own frustrations over how little they could affect either the economic situation or recalcitrant clients who would not be easily reformed. "Burnt out" by the pressures of their own helplessness in the face of shrinking services and growing despair, they envisioned benefits in permanent sterility for the poverty-stricken, the unemployed, and the disease-ridden. Voluntary sterilization based on informed understanding was desirable, but most medical proponents of legal abortion and access to contraception never completely ruled out the (still illegal) possibility of coercive measures against the "asocial." Hertha Riese, who worked with Lotte Fink in the Frankfurt BfM clinic, became convinced that, "these wretched victims become a burden to the family and everybody else, and even their offspring cannot become part of civilized life."[97] Riese reported that her sterilized patients emerged "rejuvenated and more eager to work."[98]

Sterilization was indeed enormously attractive to progressive doctors who already believed in the medical and social validity of eugenic judgments and in the potential of medical/technical solutions to mitigate social conditions. A relatively simple "clean" medical procedure that required no costly follow-up or patient cooperation, sterilization had the advantage of being quick and permanent. At the same time, and in contrast to abortion, it offered possibilities for medical ingenuity; doctors were experimenting with x-ray and radium-caused sterilizations as well as with the injection of hormone serums and immunization against semen. Since sterilization obviated (after the initial consent, which was—still—deemed necessary) the possibility for choice about procreation, it also seemed better to avoid the repeated dilemmas that arose with abortion and contraception over women's right to control their bodies, and generally about who made procreative decisions and on what grounds. It would certainly prevent the many repeat abortions that were decried by even the staunchest proponents of reforming paragraph 218. Doctors therefore generally agreed that women should be primary candidates for sterilization, although they acknowledged that male sterilization was considerably simpler and less dangerous; women, after all, were the ones to become pregnant, and even if a husband were sterilized, they could still be raped or seduced.[99]

Moreover, whereas the legalization of abortion and birth control access meant the medicalization of an already accepted and widespread practice, sterilization was a technique completely within the medical realm with no autonomous popular tradition in folk healing. It was, at least for Protestants, considered morally more palatable (*sittlich*) than abortions or even contraception since it lacked their long association with popular custom and sexual license. Hans Harmsen, who worked for the Protestant social welfare agency Inner Mission, remained opposed to liberalizing the abortion laws but zealously endorsed medical contraception and sterilization.[100]

On a continuum of expert intervention in reproduction—both in terms of the procedure itself and the designation of those eligible—sterilization clearly represented the most medicalized and eugenic extreme of sex reform population policy. It was conceived as a last resort, but one that might be appropriate for ever larger segments of an increasingly impoverished German working class. In fact, calls for the legalization of sterilization tended to be much less apologetic than demands for legal abortion, which always portrayed a necessary evil requiring regulation to assure its eventual demise and replacement by contraception.

Physicians and health insurance authorities operated with legal uncertainties in regard to sterilization as well as contraception and abortion. Sterilizations were generally interpreted as illegal under statutes prohibiting "bodily injury" while abortions and insurance prescription of contraception were specifically proscribed except in cases of medical necessity (itself an ambiguous category). Yet, like legally dubious therapeutic abortions, sterilizations were performed by physicians throughout the Weimar period. Furthermore, doctors were remarkably more open in announcing sterilization statistics than those for medical abortions; they rarely carried the same legal, moral, and professional stigma.

Dr. Harmsen reported in 1931 that 1,200 women had been sterilized for "social reasons" over a 12-year period at the Freiburg University gynecological clinic. Dr. Reiner Fetscher regularly approved sterilizations of minors or "incompetents" at his state-sponsored marriage counseling clinic in Dresden, provided their guardians consented.[101] Visiting the Frankfurt BfM birth control clinic that she helped support, a rather overwhelmed Margaret Sanger reported that Hertha Riese had ordered "75 of these major operations in one evening."[102] In the Dresden case and elsewhere, the health insurance authorities paid for the procedure, citing its cost effectiveness, whereas they resisted doing so for contraception or abortion.[103]

Whether clinic doctors believed that biology, social conditions, or—most often—a combination of both defined "degeneracy," sterilization was appealing because it seemed to attack both social and genetic causes: easing the burden on individual families and social services, and preventing defective genes from causing further damage. The concept of "differentiated welfare," which promoted a state "safety net" not for the "truly needy" but for the truly deserving, gained more currency in the early 1930s as state services were cut back and unemployment and welfare costs skyrocketed. In doctors' hierarchy of clients, the failure to rationalize family size by employing birth control could flag patients as "asocial"; hopelessness drove, as Riese suggested, people ever further away from the path of the "socially fit."[104]

Thus, political and economic definitions of "disorderly" or "disrespectable," derived from the ability and willingness to work, were conflated with medical definitions of deviance and health to create a new category of the "asocial," who were to be targets for sterilization. However—and these caveats are crucial in a history that is too often distorted as a straight line to National Socialist population policy—Riese also stressed that even when, "in extreme cases of absolute idiocy," compulsory action was considered, "we must always endeavor to employ whatever free will the person in question may yet show at the time." She proceeded to articulate the central dilemma with which sex reformers constantly grappled: the need to "reconcile the interests of the individual with those of the community and the race."[105]

Indeed, there were those like the liberal gynecologist Ludwig Fränkel and the socialist Dr. Käte Frankenthal who clearly recognized dangers in the enthusiasm voiced by some of their colleagues (and comrades). In his keynote address at the 1931 Gynecology Congress in Frankfurt, Fränkel argued powerfully that, "There must be other solutions to social need than an abdominal incision and a mutilation."[106] Rita Bardenheuer, a lay activist from the Bremen branch of the BfM and a Social Democratic member of the Bremen City Council, carefully noted a distinction that was all too often obscured in the idiom of "fit" and "unfit": the real reason sterilization might be necessary and desirable, she insisted, was not the inherent "inferiority" of the mother or the danger of "inferior" offspring but the clear social and medical fact that mothers were often so sickly and exhausted that they could not sustain the strain of further pregnancies.[107]

It is striking that so few sex reformers, even the most militant socialists, Communists, and feminists among them, chose to foreground that political argument. The drive toward medicalization, toward a taxonomy of "normal" and "abnormal," "healthy" and "unhealthy," "fit" and "unfit," blocked any serious left-wing critique of sterilization. Because socialists and Communists shared the broader fascination with the promise of science and technology, anticapitalist social criticism easily became entangled with eugenic and racial hygiene criteria. Marxism provided no equally persuasive and coherent countervailing analysis; certainly Marxism did not provide a theory of reproduction or sexuality or even a powerful enough approach to analyzing them. Indeed, its general explanatory framework that material conditions determine the quality of human life could be easily adapted to the apparently "material" facts of biology and the necessity of biological solutions. Moreover, sterilization's potential to remove the risk of contraceptive failure and to permanently prevent debilitating pregnancies and abortions lent it increasing appeal among those seeking to protect women.[108]

Reformers justified radical and wide-ranging projects such as the health insurance clinics and their prenatal care, birth control, and sex counseling programs within the rhetoric of the motherhood-eugenics consensus, positioning them as social welfare measures that would reduce the incidence of illegal and hazardous abortions as well as encourage healthy motherhood and discourage procreation of the sickly. In practice, however, sex reform doctors' energies remained focused on providing women with birth control services. And that daily clinical practice mattered intensely to women patients. It mattered whether one went to a state-sponsored eugenic counseling center and did not get birth control advice, or went to a sex reform–oriented center and walked home with a diaphragm or spermicidal suppositories, even if both those actions were justified in a similar language embedded in the motherhood-eugenics consensus. It is crucial to keep in mind that on a mass political level sex reform energy was always invested in the struggle for legal abortion and access to contraception, and not in any campaign for legal sterilization. Sex reform activists and clinic doctors saw sterilization as a medical tactic to be deployed when necessary, not a political demand uniting the working class and its professional allies.

## The Clinics and the Depression:
### Abortion Becomes the Central Issue

When the depression began to hit in 1929–1930, birth control clinics were more necessary and popular but also more threatened. Both the state and medical profession seized the opportunity offered by the economic crisis to chip away at the substantial empire built up by health insurance funds during the stabilization era. The emergency decrees of July, November, and December 1930 substantially cut back the autonomy of the health insurance system and introduced new financial burdens for the insured. Fees were charged for services and prescriptions; more supervisory doctors were installed to patrol the diagnoses of individual doctors, especially their judgments about a patient's fitness for work. The already limited accreditation of new insurance doctors was further cut, inflaming the animosity of younger physicians in large cities against established insurance physicians who were frequently socialists and Jews.

Under intense pressure to cut costs and personnel, the VKB's Kurt Bendix became an even more impassioned advocate of birth control as a cost-effective form of preventive medicine. After the spring of 1930, service reductions forced by the Brüning government's emergency decrees, mass unemployment, as well as the continuing impact of the 1928 insurance ruling limiting eligibility for clinic care, led to declines in the overall usage of health insurance services. However, the client load in both the prenatal and the sex counseling clinics steadily increased, even as the VKB had to reduce the number of prenatal clinics.

By the end of 1931, at the height of the depression and the public controversies about paragraph 218, the prenatal services provided 24,309 consultations (presumably including a good number of birth control clients) and the sex counseling centers 10,568 consultations annually at Berlin's 7 health insurance centers.[109] The VKB, neither completely public nor completely private, neither directly state controlled nor exclusively associated with any political party or group, offered the respectability and reassurance of medical expertise, as well as a holistic interest in patients' social welfare. By the end of 1931, the VKB ran 14 prenatal clinics (down from 18), 7 birth control and sex counseling centers, 10 clinics for orthopedic gymnastics, and one each for sports medicine, pediatric speech therapy, child psychiatry, and general pediatrics.[110]

The world economic crisis also undercut the American financial support that had been so critical to the development of birth control services in Berlin and Frankfurt, even as the German state was withdrawing resources. Already engaged in new birth control projects with the peripatetic Smedley, who had moved on to China, Sanger explained to her beneficiaries in Germany that even in the United States times were bad. Her second husband, Noah Slee, who for years had served as the financial angel of the birth control movement, needed to limit his commitments: "Conditions have never been like this in my lifetime. . . . The big men in Wall Street are scared."[111]

Without Smedley to mediate with the Berlin Communists, Sanger let her correspondence with Ruben-Wolf lapse. She renewed her contacts with the conservative birth controllers she had met in Geneva, especially Stützin and the ambitious young demographer Hans Harmsen, whom Ruben-Wolf had vainly tried to discredit as being "absolutely unknown in birth-control" and without any "masses behind" him."[112] Baffled and angered, but undaunted by Sanger's retreat from the Communists and Social Democrats she had supported in Berlin, Ruben-Wolf continued, with varying degrees of success, to solicit money from Sanger for various grand schemes, including the establishment of the Committee for Birth Control's own contraceptive laboratory and factory. This unrealized project was designed to earn money not only by the sale of birth control products but also by performing chemical analyses on the effectiveness and safety of other brands, which the committee would then guarantee with a seal of approval—for a fee, of course!

Once institutionalized, the growing number of marriage and sex counseling centers had quickly demonstrated both the urgency of the need and the inadequacy of the available resources—more so every day as the next decade began. Working in the clinics and counseling centers was itself a radicalizing experience, especially when it came to the struggles around paragraph 218.

Above all, birth control clinics were hampered by their inability to provide legally the one service that was still—despite all efforts—most required: safe, affordable abortions on demand.

In the final analysis, the major justification for medical sex reform and the establishment of counseling centers was the ever-rising number of illegal abortions. The struggle for a medical system based on social and preventive care, and for the spread of contraceptive knowledge among doctors and the general population, as pioneered in the clinics, could not be separated from the fight for abortion reform. This was what Sanger, in the United States, where access to contraception was not yet legal and diaphragms had to be smuggled into the country from Germany via Canada, was not willing to understand. She, Smedley, and their German allies Hans Harmsen and Kate Stützin hoped in vain to build a birth control movement that steered clear of the abortion issue.

Clinic doctors were constantly frustrated and embittered by their helplessness in the face of women's desperation. They were continually stymied by the fact that their hands were legally tied at precisely the moment when women were most in need and most likely to seek out lay and quack help. Alice Goldmann-Vollnhals's successor as director of prenatal care in the VKB remarked sadly:

> One question increasingly obsesses all concerned, especially the medical personnel: the question of abortion. . . . It is incredibly difficult for a doctor to maintain the trust of these women in oneself as doctor and caregiver, if one cannot always refer them for abortions. In some cases, it is impossible for us to persuade the women to remain in our care, after we have lost their trust on account of having been forced—with heavy heart—to deny their request, because of the lack of a medical indication, despite their usually miserable social situation.[113]

Goldmann-Vollnhals herself vividly described the not-untypical case of a pregnant 20-year-old mother of a year-old infant, whose plea had been rejected. She marched straight from the clinic to a quack who accidentally scraped out her bladder rather than her uterus; the young mother died.[114] Perhaps more than anyone else, doctors who served women patients sensed the explosiveness of the popular demand for access to safe legal abortions. Minna Flake, school physician in Prenzlauer Berg, clinic doctor, and VSA activist, spoke for many of her colleagues when she wrote in the socialist physicians journal:

> Especially the doctors who know most about the misery of the working masses must march at the head of the movement against the abortion paragraph.[115]

Indeed, it was the arrest of two physicians on charges of violating paragraph 218 that incited the mass campaign for abortion rights in the grim depression winter of 1931.

# — four —

# "Your Body Belongs to You"
## Abortion and the 1931 Campaign
## Against Paragraph 218

Oh, I am a valuable thing,
Everybody cares about me:
The church, state, doctors, judges—
For nine months,
But when those nine months are past . . .
Well, then I have to look out for myself.

KURT TUCHOLSKY[1]

If my economic circumstances permit me to have a child, then I shall
have one. If this is not the case, then I know what I have to do. Whatever the Pope proclaims does not concern us.

Letter in AIZ from F. FRANZISKA, age 28, metal worker[2]

On New Year's Eve, 1930, in Rome, Pope Pius XI issued an encyclical denounc-
ing birth control and abortion. A clear attack on the "new woman" and the
"new" smaller family of the 1920s, *Casti Connubii (On Christian Marriage)* insisted on women's subordinate position within the family and condemned
non-procreative sex and the false freedom of female emancipation. The pope
reminded states of their obligation to protect the weak and unborn, and specifically warned against the "pernicious practice" of eugenics.[3]

In Germany, the papal pronouncement provoked a swift reaction from the
Communist party and its allies in the sex reform and independent women's
movement, providing the initial catalyst for what would become a highly
visible and militant mass movement demanding women's right to abortion
and the repeal of paragraph 218. At a time when the Social Democratic and
Communist parties were attacking each other as the primary enemy and the
fragile fabric of Weimar democracy was rapidly unraveling, the movement
against paragraph 218 effected a brief and unparalleled alliance amongst liberal and radical lawyers, doctors, intellectuals, artists, Social Democrats, Com-

munists, and diverse constituencies of women. For several months an unprecendented mobilization of women on their own behalf occupied the attention of the German police and the Health and Interior ministries, and came close to forcing legislative action on a substantial reform of the sex crimes code, especially its most contested paragraphs: 218 and 184.3, which restricted access to contraception, and 175, which outlawed homosexuality.

The anti-218 campaign unfolded against a backdrop of mounting political and economic crisis, which momentarily brought feminist demands for reproductive rights to the forefront of a powerful movement for social and sexual reform, but also finally fractured the emerging diverse coalition of doctors, feminists, and leftists. "At certain times," Carroll Smith-Rosenberg has noted, "forces within a society catapult the issue of abortion to a position of political and moral centrality, transferring the acts of the bedroom and the doctor's office to the most public political arena."[4] This chapter describes one such potent historical moment, and tries to explain why it was so precarious and ephemeral.

In the spring of 1930, the SPD-led Müller government, which had presided over multiple social welfare and health initiatives between 1928 and 1930, collapsed, and Catholic Center politician Heinrich Brüning was appointed chancellor. The subsequent era of parliamentary paralysis and political polarization helped doom the republic. At the same time, it incited what Volker Berghahn has called a "massive politicization" of the population,[5] in which questions about women and reproduction moved to the center of a national debate on social priorities and entitlements.

Communist and especially National Socialist votes soared in the fateful elections of September 1930, leaving the Reichstag virtually paralyzed. Brüning then used Article 48 of the Weimar Constitution to establish an executive dictatorship. In the name of deflation and fiscal responsibility, he tried to dismantle the expansive welfare state, thus undermining the Weimar social compromise that had sought political and social stability through limited structural reform, broad social benefits, and large public expenditures. The papal encyclical appeared all the more menacing in the context of Brüning's draconian cuts to recent Weimar innovations in social and health insurance, including, of course, the rudimentary institutionalization of birth control and sex counseling in public health clinics. Official statistics of over four million unemployed and estimates of one million illegal abortions annually became the twin emblems of Germany's crisis of social policy and political legitimacy.

The KPD quickly dubbed Brüning the "hunger chancellor." Bitterly attacking the SPD for tolerating a national government of right-wing nationalists and Catholic conservatives, it interpreted the papal letter as a sign of the bourgeois system's turn toward fascism. Consistent with the Comintern line that predicted the emergence of ever more insupportable contradictions in capitalism, the KPD regarded the encyclical as part of a concerted effort by church and state to force the production of "cannon fodder" for an imperialist war against the Soviet Union, as well as a defensive reaction to capitalist crisis and working-class militancy.[6]

The Communist women's movement saw the encyclical as an attempt to legitimize the Brüning regime's emergency decrees that reduced social services while attacking married women's right to work and access to social insurance and unemployment benefits. Based on the Soviet model of organizing women as delegates to local, regional, and national conferences, a Committee of Working Women had developed from women's activism during the great Ruhr strike wave of 1927 to 1929.[7] At numerous conferences held from 1929 on, delegates, many describing themselves as "housewives," spoke out on their "personal" concerns about birth control, abortion, and feeding their families, developed a sense of community, and honed leadership skills.[8] Having strongly opposed paragraph 218 at the committee's first two national congresses in October 1929 and September 1930, conference delegates now in 1931 lost no time in warning that, "We women refuse to let ourselves be regarded as baby machines and then additionally to serve as slaves in the production process." Their "slogan," they insisted, was "not 'back into the family' but equal wages for equal work."[9]

On January 28, 1931, the Communist Committee of Working Women—now part of a growing delegate and conference movement—joined with representatives of the Bund für Mutterschutz (BfM) and the independent feminist Women's League for Peace and Freedom to plan strategy against the encyclical and its assault on women's rights. The remarkable campaign that developed depended on alliances that had been previously forged among the KPD, the broader Communist women's movement, parts of the feminist movement, the lay sex reform movement, and the birth control clinic network, and on the radicalization of those elements by the devastating economic crisis. Women physicians and other professionals had gained visibility and credibility in the sex reform movement while the Communist women's movement had wrested a good deal of autonomy from the party's central committee.[10] As we have seen, medical sex reform had been rather solidly institutionalized in muncipal and health insurance clinics. Now, mass unemployment was leading to the continued growth and radicalization of the lay leagues, and new challenges for sex reform physicians.

The two major lay organizations, the National League for Birth Control and Sexual Hygiene (RV) and the League for the Protection of Motherhood and Family Hygiene (*Liga*), grew rapidly, despite members' increasing difficulty in keeping up with dues and other organizational obligations. Spiraling unemployment forced a shift in the political arena of struggle from the workplace to the home and the community. Women therefore occupied an even more critical role in assuring economic survival and family stability, and the individual "reformist" solution of birth control seemed even more indisputably central to the class struggle. The lay leagues became both more militant and more interested in forming coalitions as ever more members (by 1931, 70 percent of RV members) were unemployed.[11] The RV, in particular, attracted strong support from socialist physicians.

In January 1930, representatives from the RV, the *Liga*, the Committee for Birth Control, the German branch of the World League for Sexual Reform (WLSR), and from several smaller groups scattered all over the country had established a Working Group of Sex Reform Leagues (*Arbeitsgemeinschaft der Verbände für Sexual Reform*). The rival RV and *Liga*, while still selling competing products and fighting for financial and organizational turf, agreed to cooperate. The Working Group asserted woman's right to control her own body and attacked "unjust sexual laws." Its members pledged to coordinate events, exchange speakers and information, jointly pressure contraceptive manufacturers to lower prices and improve safety, fight against commercial competition, establish a common press office and journal, and provide legal aid to victims of sex laws.[12]

Some of the participants in this new Working Group also attended the first meeting of a Center for Birth Control (*Arbeitszentrale für Geburtenregelung*), on January 23, 1931. The presence of some of the same doctors at these two meetings, one organized for the lay leagues, the other for medical birth controllers, demonstrates again the degree to which commitment to the cause of family limitation as well as professional solidarity among doctors, and common experiences in clinic practice, overrode even fierce political differences. The center's organizer was Kate Stützin, who used her connections with Margaret Sanger, and the spirit of cooperation produced at the Zurich birth control conference in September 1930, to get "together everybody, Communist, anti-Communist, people to the right and left."[13]

Touting its "purely scientific" character, the group vowed to encourage regulation of procreation and "responsible motherhood" under medical supervision, but distanced itself from the lay leagues supported by some of its members. Meeting monthly or biweekly, and held together by the dedicated laywoman (and doctor's wife) Stützin, the center offered doctors of disparate political persuasions—including Hans Harmsen, Max Hodann, Felix Theilhaber, Hertha Nathorff, and Anne-Marie Durand-Wever—a common forum for the exchange of research findings and clinical experiences. Its registry of physicians sympathetic to birth control provided crucial support for the anti-218 campaign and pressured the German Association of Gynecologists to make birth control a priority theme of its 1931 convention.[14]

Economic disaster and the increasing Nazi presence in parliament and the streets pushed many intellectuals and professionals closer to the KPD as the only party seriously committed to abortion reform, indeed as the only viable defense against fascism. Despite Helene Stöcker's ill health and the group's severe financial problems, the BfM celebrated its 25th anniversary in May 1930 with a speakout against paragraph 218.[15] The anniversary coincided with the opening of the film version of *Cyankali*, an anti-218 melodrama by Dr. Friedrich Wolf, which had been playing to full houses in Berlin's Lessing

Theater since 1929. Stöcker reminded her audience of the BfM's fundamental commitment to pacifism and to women's right to separate sexuality from procreation: "We are here not to hate but to love!"[16] With its firm stand for sex reform and its enthusiastic support for the Soviet Union, the BfM served as a kind of haven for "fellow-travelers," and the frequent references in Communist journals and speeches to Stöcker as a noted nonpartisan supporter indicate that the party was quite happy to be legitimated by the support of artists and intellectuals who did not carry membership cards.[17]

The International Workers Aid (IAH) also became an important gathering place for those who supported the drive against paragraph 218 and for sex reform but were unwilling to join the party itself. Founded in the early 1920s to organize famine relief for the young Soviet Union, it became, under Willi Münzenberg's charismatic leadership, a large umbrella organization, whose agenda encompassed such diverse causes as support for the "Scottsboro boys" jailed on lynching charges in the American South and running sex and birth control counseling centers in Germany.[18] Its International Central Committee boasted such luminaries as Albert Einstein and the French writer Henri Barbusse; the German Central Committee included Max Hodann, and Martha Arendsee of the party's social welfare arm ARSO.[19] Communist support for the anti-218 campaign also depended on the continued willingness of the Soviet Union (and the Comintern) to support sex reform initiatives outside its own borders at a time when the Bolshevik leadership and Soviet physicians were already raising serious questions about the effects of the Soviet legalization of abortion.[20] For Germany, the right to abortion was justified as a necessary response to a capitalist emergency.

Much to the frustration of sex reformers, all the years of parliamentary, legal, and agitational activity had not succeeded in making a fundamental dent in the criminalization of abortion. Indeed, the 1931 campaign was the climax of a decade of intense agitation on the issue. The birth of the Weimar Republic had initially raised hopes for penal code reform. The continuing persecution of women and their abortionists, especially in "monster trials" in southern Germany in 1922, as well as the severe economic pressures of the 1923 hyperinflation, had led to unsuccessful women's demonstrations for legalization. At least 19 left-wing motions for abortion reform were introduced in the Reichstag between 1919 and 1932. But since its codification in 1871, efforts at either piecemeal or comprehensive reform of sex crimes law were continually thwarted by war, change of regime, or government crises causing parliamentary dissolution and reconstitution.[21]

In 1926, the SPD had finally pushed through a limited reform that reduced abortion from a felony to a misdemeanor. Punishments ranged from one day to 5 years for the woman and her helper; if the abortion was performed for money or without consent, perpetrators faced sentences of no less than 3 months to 15 years. Passed with votes from Social Democratic, Democratic, Democratic People's, and Economic parties, and over the objections of the conservative Nationalist and Catholic Center parties, the 1926 revision gave Germany, as Cornelie Usborne has pointed out, the "most lenient" law in Western Europe.[22] It offered the possibility of limiting punishment to a symbolic level: minimum punishment was one day imprisonment or a 3-mark fine. But the principle that abortion was a crime was insistently preserved and supported by all parties except the Communists. Indeed, some hoped that reform would rationalize enforcement: by giving the presiding judge more latitude for "realistic" sentencing, convictions might be more likely. At the same time, paragraph 184.3, restricting the advertising and publicizing of contraceptives as "objects for indecent use," remained in effect, decreeing what the Communist party and many sex reformers termed a tyranny of forced childbearing (*Gebärzwang*).[23]

But whether the 1926 reform was, as Usborne insists, a "significant improvement" or not, by 1931, passions against the paragraph were aroused as never before. This "pragmatic" reform, confirmed by a 1927 Supreme Court ruling sanctioning "medical indications,"[24] could not contain the anger of women who perceived the class and gender injustice of a system that claimed to "protect" women but consigned proletarian women to "self-help" or the desperate search for a doctor or "quack" willing to "help," often for insupportable amounts of money and with danger to life and limb. Meanwhile, women with access to, and money for, sympathetic doctors could undergo "medically indicated" abortions in private clinics. Moreover, by 1931, it was abundantly clear that under the Brüning regime further reform was unlikely. The papal encyclical assured absolute Center party opposition to any reform at a time when the SPD, which had always supported reform if not decriminalization, increasingly saw a Catholic Center government as the only hope of saving the republic. That left the KPD as the only political party willing to fight for women's right to abortion and birth control, or, even for married women's right to employment.

## The 1931 People's Movement to Release Wolf and Kienle

Shortly after women's groups had begun to organize around the encyclical *On Christian Marriage*, the state of Württemberg presented the KPD with a situation tailor-made for Münzenberg's strategy (the so-called *Bündnispolitik*) of allying with special-interest groups, such as intellectuals, youth, or women, who were understood to be theoretically and organizationally marginal to the class struggle, but electorally useful.

On February 19, 1931, two physicians were arrested in Stuttgart. Friedrich Wolf was a KPD member and author of *Cyankali*; Else Kienle, a politically unaffiliated specialist in dermatology and venereal diseases, worked in an RV counseling center and frequently performed "medical" abortions in her private clinic. They were charged with seeking commercial gain by providing the required medical indication certificates for terminations of pregnancy and with having performed abortions on more than 100 women. These were the heaviest charges possible under the 1926 version of paragraph 218, carrying a potential sentence of 15 years of penal servitude. The timing of these arrests for what could easily have been deemed acceptable medical practice, and the enormous volume of police and government documentation, supports the Communist contention that the arrests were a direct response by state authorities unsettled by women's growing mobilization against the encyclical in a time of economic crisis.

Rather than breaking the momentum of the campaign, the arrests, especially of such a well-known Communist writer and activist, unleashed a storm of protest, spearheaded by the KPD's ARSO and its quickly constituted "Action Committee" (*Kampfausschuss*). Wolf's concluding call in *Cyankali*—"A law that turns 800,000 mothers into criminals every year is no longer a law"— became the battle cry of a growing movement.[25] The *Volkssturm* (People's Storm) against paragraph 218, as Wolf put it, shifted the focus of attention from Parliament and courtroom to the streets, and turned the prosecutors into the publicly accused.[26] Within a few days, the women's coalition, which had formed against the encyclical, was joined by a host of liberal, socialist, and Communist groups, all associated with the sex reform movement and the independent "homeless left"—from the League for Human Rights (SPD) to the Association of Socialist Physicians (VSA).[27]

A celebrities committee, which included Albert Einstein on its roster, met in the home of screenwriter Thea von Harbou and her husband, the film director Fritz Lang, and called on women "in secure stations in life" and their doctors to speak out about their own experiences with abortion.[28] The International Jurists' Union and the Committee for Birth Control sponsored a closed meeting for doctors, lawyers, and journalists, who jointly declared that the paragraph no longer reflected popular opinion and should at least be reworked to allow for social as well as medical indications. Communist Friedrich Wolf, the Social Democrat Dr. Carl Credé, who had also been imprisoned on abortion charges, Dr. Emil Roesle from the national Department of Health (RGA), and Kienle's lawyer Alfred Apfel, all shared the platform—an astonishingly eclectic range of political affiliations at a time of ever-increasing bitterness within the left.[29]

Newspapers announced open readers' forums and sponsored rallies, providing women with an opportunity to speak out about their personal experiences. When the *Berliner Volkszeitung* polled its readers about keeping, abolishing, or reforming the law, 45,000 responses, most of them from working-class women, poured in within a few days. Only 150 favored keeping paragraph 218.[30] The Münzenberg daily *Die Welt am Abend* printed life stories in a public "Indictment," in which women recounted their painful odysseys through doctors' rejections and quacks' dangers. A 20-year-old pieceworker turned away by her doctor could not afford the 60 marks charged by the local "angelmaker" and therefore resorted to "stinking pills, . . . bitter medicine by the bottle, . . . hot and cold baths, . . . jump[ing] down the stairs," and finally a "burning solution" of Lysol, which she injected into her "abdomen every two hours with a borrowed syringe." In the end her efforts resulted in probable sterility: "A severely tipped uterus remains as a consequence of my self-help."[31] The liberal bourgeois *Vossische Zeitung* reported that the arrests had pushed the abortion struggle to an "acute, virtually sensational stage."[32]

Kate Stützin of the Center for Birth Control, herself an opponent of abortion reform, reported to her friend Margaret Sanger, "You cannot imagine the excitement."[33] In the winter and spring of 1931 it was virtually impossible—at least in Berlin—to go to the theater, cinema, or cabaret, listen to popular music, or read newspapers, magazines, or novels without being confronted with the passions surrounding "this most cursed paragraph of our penal code."[34] Performances of *Cyankali* were transformed into spontaneous demonstrations.[35] Ernst Piscator's socialist drama collective went on nationwide tour with a play adapted from the book *Volk in Not* by Dr. Carl Credé, written when he was jailed as an abortionist in 1926.[36] Erich Weinert, Kurt Tucholsky, and Bertolt Brecht were inspired to publish new poems.[37] Brecht's verse sarcastically addressed women:

> You're going to be a lovely little mother
> You're going to make a bunch of cannonfodder
> That's what your belly's for
> And that's no news to you
> And now do not squall
> You're having a baby, that's all.[38]

The Red-One-Mark-Series, the KPD's version of the penny novel, published Franz Krey's lurid small-town melodrama *Maria and the Paragraph* about the consequences of a stenotypist's botched abortion. It was serialized to great success in Münzenberg's mass circulation *Arbeiter Illustrierte Zeitung (Workers Illustrated Newspaper, AIZ)*.[39] Appealing to women workers, who were presumably accustomed to a literary diet of romance, crime, and tragedy, it invoked every conceivable stereotype in order to arrive at the inevitable conclusion that only the KPD could wage an honest struggle against the abortion paragraph. Maria, pregnant and unmarried, turns to a "wise woman" who drives her into a ghastly world of crime. By the end, Maria has been accused of murdering a cleaning woman who tried to blackmail her, survived the delirium of childbed fever, participated in a show trial of the quack's patients, and joined (together with a liberal journalist, a feminist, and a sympathetic doctor) the movement to abolish paragraph 218. She has demonstrated, received a reduced sentence for her crimes (on grounds of her "mental condition"), and confronted both the timidity of the SPD and the anti-Semitism of the local "patriotic" women's association. She also becomes involved with a kindly widower whose wife was killed by a botched abortion and who needs a sexual partner and mother for his children.

In the spirit of "alliance politics," the story ends not with the victory of the working-class movement in toppling the law but with the young doctor's conversion to the cause of legal abortion and sex reform. He will presumably go on to open a medically supervised birth control and sex counseling center in town and thus help to combat the twin dangers of quack abortions and police repression by rational application of contraception. *Maria* supposedly garnered 6,000 new members for the KPD and numerous subscriptions to the *AIZ*.[40] The film *Kuhle Wampe*, produced by the Communist Prometheus film company in the summer of 1931, juxtaposed images of men scurrying around town on bicycles looking for work with those of young women frantically rushing through city streets searching for safe abortions: as dual emblems of capitalist crisis.[41]

In Berlin, a prestigious art show dedicated to representations of "Women in Need" (*Frauen in Not*) presented woman as the ultimate victim of the depression and bourgeois morality: "She stands with her body in awful battle against the laws and ideas of a collapsing social order and an outmoded morality."[42] Women's "biological tragedy" was stylized into the most visible manifestation of a general social catastrophe. But some of the images shown defied the pervasive coding of women as victim and reflected the power of the 1931 mobilization. Alice Lex-Nerlinger's painting, for example, presented a group of active, strong, and united women pushing collectively with all their might against a paragraph 218 carved on an enormous cross, while the conventional icon of the long-suffering solitary woman, with kerchief and big belly, recedes pale and faceless into the background.[43] The 1931 image stood in stark contrast to Käthe Kollwitz's "Down with the Abortion Paragraph" poster, produced in cooperation with the KPD in 1924, which depicted the classic figure of the "desperate woman" (*Frau in Not*), a proletarian woman in misery and despair clutching her hungry children to her pregnant belly.

On International Women's Day, March 8, 1931, the campaign moved from speeches and propaganda into the streets, as over 1,500 rallies and demonstrations were held throughout Germany. Three thousand women defied an emergency decree banning outdoor demonstrations and marched through the streets of Berlin shouting, "Down with the Brüning dictatorship; down with paragraph 218; we want bread and peace!" Thousands of women throughout Germany called for equal pay for equal work, social protection for mothers and children, and an immediate stop to the prosecution of Wolf and Kienle. At numerous regional conferences of the Communist women's movement, delegates bore witness to their personal experiences with unwanted pregnancies and illegal abortions.[44]

The International Women's League for Peace and Freedom, led by radical feminists Anita Augspurg and Lida Gustava Heymann, held a meeting of

1,000 people in the Schöneberger Rathaus. It turned into a raucous debate between anti-218 doctors, including Martha Ruben-Wolf, and religious Christian women doctors who warned of the medical dangers of abortion and were, in turn, shouted down as childless moralists. The entire event was finally disrupted by Nazi youth whose shouted anti-Semitic slogans produced a "pogromlike mood."[45]

On March 16, a huge gathering of women professionals sponsored by the Berlin League of Women Doctors (BDÄ) supported abolition of paragraph 218 as a matter of medical privilege, social health, and women's rights. The women's rally was a great success; hundreds stood outside when the hall overflowed beyond its 4,000-person capacity. The meeting enthusiastically endorsed all the standard sex reform demands, from mass sex and birth control education, to free distribution of state-licensed contraceptives by health insurance and welfare agencies, to comprehensive social welfare measures for social health and family stability. A long list of distinguished women doctors, lawyers, politicians, and writers, including Democratic party Reichstag deputy Katharina von Kardorff and *Metropolis* scriptwriter Thea von Harbou, addressed the crowd. Paragraph 218 was damned as inconsistent with the "dignity of human rights and the position of women within the state" as well as with "a high-quality offspring and the preservation and encouragement of the ethical power of the family to preserve the state." Thus, arguments framed within the dominant motherhood-eugenics consensus converged with a commitment to women's public equality. Foregrounding gender rather than class politics, the rally specifically demanded that "women participate to the greatest degree possible in the formulation" of a new reformed abortion law.[46]

## Feminism and the Politics of Abortion

No one illustrated the complexities and ambiguities of these positions better than the defendant Else Kienle. She had been radicalized during her medical training when, working with prostitutes in a venereal disease ward, she saw the callousness with which male doctors treated their disreputable patients. Unlike Wolf, she was not a member of the KPD prior to her arrest; indeed she seems to have had social connections with Nazis through her wealthy and rather mysterious husband, who also supported her private clinic "Edenhall."[47]

Defiantly unrepentant, Kienle insisted that she performed abortions only on truly needy women. She voluntarily surrendered her incriminating medical records; indeed Kienle had always been careful to obtain the requisite second opinion, in many cases from her colleague Friedrich Wolf. According to her own account, published in the independent left journal *Die Weltbühne*, she was arrested just after giving a lecture on the evils of paragraph 218 at a meeting of the (Communist-associated) Freethinkers League. Because she was unknown and unprotected by the KPD, which obtained Wolf's speedy release on bail, Kienle was kept in pretrial detention and steadily interrogated for one and a half months. She gained support from the sex reform and Communist women's movements only after she engaged in a bitter hunger strike that brought her near death and won her release on March 28.[48]

Although she went on speaking tours for the KPD, reportedly joined the party after her release, and then toured the Soviet Union, the conspicuously unproletarian Kienle was an uncomfortable heroine for the Communists. She took pains to define the necessity for abortion in terms of "need," and like many reformers, she asserted that the so-called social (rather than strictly medical) indication for abortion was a given for any working-class woman "anno 1931."[49] But unlike Communist sex reformers, she subscribed to a maternalist feminism that stressed women's essential difference from men, while insisting on equality in the public sphere. In common with many women doctors, Kienle assumed that female nature could truly be fulfilled only in motherhood; but she nevertheless claimed women's right to sexual pleasure and control over their own bodies. In her impassioned prison diary, she reflected:

> As a woman, I stand against the man; as a woman, I must defend women's cause against the law, against the court of men. . . . Our present legal system is in every detail and particularly in this respect, a male system. The woman senses that very precisely. She resists in her own way: She circumvents male law, which she cannot recognize as binding, just, or natural for her.[50]

In a challenge to the mainstream bourgeois feminism of the Federation of German Women's Associations (BDF), which also focused on maternalism and difference but ignored sexuality and reproductive rights, Kienle asked, "Of what use is suffrage to woman if she is still to remain a helpless baby machine?[51] She explicitly defined herself as a "new woman" who:

> claims above all the right to her own body, in full consciousness of her responsibility. . . . The time for motherhood must no longer be simply determined by the man. Precisely because she is conscious of her great calling, she demands the right to decide about the most important hour of her life. . . . This point is decisive for women's struggle: the conquest of the right to her own body. . . . Only a comprehensive, open and sincere clarification of real equality between the sexes, also in terms of the body, the erotic, and sexuality, will create a new sexual morality.[52]

Kienle's self-consciously feminist arguments for women's bodily integrity were widely echoed during the anti-218 campaign. At a Mother's Day rally on May 10, sponsored by the left-wing *Berliner Volkszeitung*, 2,000 angry participants heckled a representative of the Berlin Archdiocese defending the church's views on abortion, and listened to von Harbou articulate an explicitly feminist position. She envisioned "a new form of preventing pregnancy" that would "make the entire paragraph 218 unnecessary." In the meantime, however, paragraph 218 was "no longer a law," not only because it was unenforceable and socially discriminatory but because it was "no longer morally recognized by women." Legal and constitutional equality, even equality in education and employment, was a sham if women were victimized by "constitutional inferiority" and could not control their own bodies.[53]

Despite the cross-class appeal of the anti-218 movement and the conspicuous involvement of professional "new women," as well as proletarian housewives and workers, the BDF and its journal *Die Frau* held themselves studiously aloof. As a broad umbrella organization that included conservative housewives and Protestant women's groups, as well as professional leagues like the BDÄ, the BDF occupied a lowest-common-denominator position, claiming that the abortion issue could only be resolved as part of a general program for family health and stability.[54] Indeed, *Die Schaffende Frau (The Active Woman)*, a journal directed at the "new" married professional women, which regularly featured photographs of successful career women, their husbands, and children on its covers, angrily accused the women's movement of treating violators of the paragraph as victims, not only of predatory men but of their own lustful desires.[55]

As more and more members of her Center for Birth Control became preoccupied with the paragraph 218 crisis, Kate Stützin, too, wished the issue would go away. Asking whether Sanger considered her position "narrow-minded," she lamented:

It is so difficult that in Germany they . . . consider abortion as a part of B.C. . . . I refuse any discussion about abortion. . . . The public opinion must know clearly that my name is only connected with Birth Control in the real meaning and has nothing to do with abortion. . . . I personally and privately am *not* in favour of abolishing the law (because it protects women in some way), only for changing it.[56]

Stützin's stance, which she shared with Hans Harmen, set her apart from all the most visible sex reform activists: the Communists, the leftist doctors in the VSA, and the women of the Berlin BDÄ. Women physicians had a special stake in the abortion controversies due to their focus on treating women and children and their work in clinics that served the poor and the working class. They generally vigorously disapproved of abortion as a regular method of birth control but were daily exposed to desperate stories of unwanted pregnancies and unsatisfying sex from patients who frequently expected special understanding from women doctors.[57]

Dr. Käte Frankenthal, municipal physician in Neukölln and a Social Democratic city councilwoman who advocated full abolition of paragraph 218 and eventually broke with the SPD on the issue, recalled in her memoirs:

Hardly a day went by that some weeping woman or girl did not appear in my office and accuse me: "If you don't help . . . after all you have said and written that the law is bad."[58]

Henriette Magnus Necheles, an avowedly apolitical general practitioner, had similar memories:

. . . no method of birth control was too dangerous. . . . I had hardly any adult women patients who had not had at least one abortion. . . . It was useless to argue with my patients. "Only idiots have many children," was the answer, and unfortunately they were right.[59]

Female physicians knew only too well that criminalization did not prevent abortions, but simply made them more expensive, more dangerous, and more unequally available. Dr. Alice Goldmann-Vollnhals, head of the Health Insurance League's (VKB) prenatal services, starkly stated:

On the basis of our experience we must say: if a woman sees her pregnancy as undesirable and wants to be freed from it, she will know how to do it by all and any means necessary, even if she pays for it with her life. All threats of legal punishment are illusory in the context of the terrible economic situation, and do not stop anyone from having an abortion. This cannot be stressed strongly enough.[60]

Dr. Elisabeth Prinz, director of a BfM counseling center in Berlin, spoke for many of her colleagues when she said that for anyone who experienced women's "desperation," terms such as "immorality and godlessness became empty concepts."[61] Goldmann-Vollnhals entitled an article published during the 1931 campaign "Paragraph 218: Horrendous Facts"; she reported that in the VKB's prenatal clinics, 78.7 percent of all confirmed pregnancies led to "miscarriages, 99 percent of them illegal abortions."[62]

These experiences fostered a remarkable level of political and professional activism. In May 1930, as economic crisis intensified, 356 of the 476 women doctors organized in the League of Women Doctors' Berlin branch submitted a highly publicized petition to the Criminal Justice Committee of the Reichstag, demanding the legalization of abortions certified as necessary on medical, eugenic, and social grounds. Basing their credibility on their clinical practice, they stated the obvious: Paragraph 218 not only did not reflect popular opinion but it in no way "achieve[d] its goal." It was "useless in practical terms since it protects neither the mother nor the fetus" but only perpetrated class injustice and jeopardized the life and health of countless women. Referring to the other great social scourge, they concluded: "No illness, not even tuberculosis, causes so much human sacrifice."[63]

Berlin women doctors thereby clearly broke ranks with the majority of their profession, which had confirmed at the Leipzig medical convention in

1925 its opposition to all except strictly medically necessary abortions. They also went considerably further than the Berlin Medical Society which, despite massive pressure from its VSA members and vocal KPD minority, had agreed in December 1928 to only limited consideration of social conditions but broad acceptance of eugenic indications when there was a danger of hereditary disease.[64]

A close reading of the demands for reform of paragraph 218 underscores, however, that even among those women doctors who agitated most determinedly for women's right to reproductive choice, the paramount goal was not to assure individual women's inalienable right to control their own bodies but to "strengthen the will for a child, ease the burdens of motherhood and achieve healthy offspring."[65] Mobilized by their repeated experiences with "mortality, illness and infertility" caused by illegal abortions, the 356 Berliners stated:

> We certainly do not condone frivolous abortions. We do believe that the will to motherhood cannot be coerced through legal paragraphs and threats of punishment, but is rather a natural female instinct which can be temporarily repressed by worry and despair, but which will naturally reassert itself when conditions have improved.[66]

Yet, despite the reassuring comments about women's inherent maternal proclivities, the Berlin women doctors' interpretation of "adverse conditions" and "social indication" was so broad that they were de facto advocating decriminalization. Already in 1929 at the London WLSR meeting, Dr. Hertha Riese unabashedly asserted that any absolute right to life for the fetus was illusory since virtually everyone agreed on the validity of medical indications. Therefore it was only proper to privilege the right of a woman, "the consciously living and suffering human being, over the unborn human life that is still unconscious."[67]

Of course, not all women doctors agreed, although virtually all presumed a special gender-based authority in discussing the issue. Shortly after the Berlin BDÄ local submitted its petition to the Reichstag, a group of mostly Catholic rural practitioners angrily disassociated themselves from their metropolitan sisters, arguing that, "Economic and social conflicts cannot be solved through killing but only through alleviation of the economic crisis and appropriate welfare measures." Asserting an unusually rigid "right-to-life" position that went beyond even the restrictive policy of the national medical association, they denied the legitimacy of medical indications, insisting that, "Even the most careful medical abortion remains a serious procedure with often unpredictable consequences."[68]

Like many conservatives and quite a few feminists who saw paragraph 218 as a protection against men's sexual exploitation of women, they also worried about the moral impact of legalizing abortion at a time when so many ethical principles seemed to be in disarray. For the Berlin petitioners, of course, the greater danger to women came from illegal and risky abortions. As the young physician Barbara von Renthe Fink argued in *Sexual-Hygiene (SH)*, religious convictions against abortion were personal matters that must be respected but not imposed on others.[69]

In general, the militance and momentum of the campaign, the attention from the media, and the broad appeal to women of all classes provided a space for highly public and pointedly feminist interventions unique in the history of Weimar sex reform. Despite the repeated assurances that "women would gladly return to motherhood" when conditions improved, the intense campaign left space for women to call for a new female-defined morality and justice that could incorporate women's right to self-determination over her body and her life. The politics of "Your Body Belongs to You" (*Dein Körper Gehört Dir*), which had not been a standard part of political, medical, or eugenic arguments for abortion, slipped into the struggle in 1931 and managed temporarily to disrupt, if not displace, the dominance of class-struggle politics and the motherhood-eugenics consensus in sex reform discourse. Thus, the KPD rather inadvertently found itself in the vanguard of a movement that linked woman's economic and political emancipation with the right to control her own body and that spoke for all women, not just the most oppressed and downtrodden.[70]

## Communism and Abortion Politics

The high point of popular agitation came on April 15, when over 15,000 people gathered in the Berlin Sportpalast for a mass protest rally. A police report described a packed hall, walls and galleries draped with posters and banners, and noted with particular consternation that, "Among the female guests, there were numerous well dressed and even elegantly dressed women and girls."[71] Wolf and Kienle (who had just been released from prison in the wake of her hunger strike) reiterated the KPD's carefully crafted defense of "abortion as the ultima ratio, the last resort when birth control fails."[72]

Rather astounded by the militant women's movement it had encouraged, and clearly discomfited by the recurrent challenges to the primacy of its economic analysis, the KPD trod a delicate line between feminist and class politics. It tried desperately both to sustain a commitment to abortion rights and to subsume that commitment within a larger and primary class struggle. The Communist party's categorical demand for the abolition of paragraph 218 and decriminalization of all adult consensual sexual behavior was a clearly radical gesture, as was its call for public funding of sex education and counseling, as well as of abortions and contraception.

Communist population and sexual policies nonetheless remained limited and ambivalent. The slogan "Your Body Belongs to You" was adopted by the left, with as little critical self-reflection as the eugenic politics of race hygiene and race betterment had received; it was an ad-hoc response to crisis. Moreover, while the KPD supported complete decriminalization, the Soviet Union was considering recriminalization, a fact that was not lost on opponents of reform who enjoyed pointing to doubts within the "socialist paradise" about legalized abortion.[73] Within Germany, however, Bolshevik Russia continued to serve as a model society where legalized medical abortions, coupled with a comprehensive program of protection for mothers, working women, and children, assured population growth. Socialist achievements in female emancipation, social welfare, and the encouragement of motherhood were contrasted to both "sterile" Germany, and Mussolini's Fascist Italy, where attempts to remove women from the work force and return them to their "natural" roles as wives and mothers had produced only a minimal upturn in the birth rate.[74]

Like every other political group across the Weimar spectrum, the KPD touted the magic of motherhood and demanded improved benefits for mothers and children. Perhaps trying to reassure himself as much as his audience, Friedrich Wolf confidently declared that, "Every healthy German woman has the desire for a child."[75] Communists assumed that a socialist society on the Soviet model would ultimately render abortion unnecessary by providing the adequate welfare and socialized housework that were preconditions for joyous and carefree childbearing. The "triple reproductive burden" of childbearing, childrearing, and housework would be lightened by a technological solution to the "petty slavery of housework" in communal kitchens or laundries, or at least by greater efficiency in individual housework. But women remained responsible for childbearing and childrearing—therefore, of course, also for abortion and birth control. The KPD's primary target was not the family or the sexual division of labor within the family but the hypocrisy of bourgeois morality and the social and economic conditions that threatened the well-being of the proletarian family. At rallies, the recently freed Kienle joined Wolf in proclaiming, "We know that our women and girls will once again joyfully give the gift of life to children, even in Germany . . . but in a free socialist Germany."[76]

Ideological ambivalence notwithstanding, it was the organization and resources of the KPD that made sex reform issues public as never before. And it remains a noteworthy political fact that the one instance in its history when the KPD successfully attracted and mobilized masses of usually skeptical women came with a campaign for abortion rights: the topic that so many Communist and socialist parties and reform groups have been wary of, for fear of alienating the "masses." With its analysis of women's dual oppression in production and reproduction (the latter divided into the "triple burden") the KPD recognized that a woman's ability to control her own body was at least as crucial to her active participation in the class struggle as was her integration into the social process of production. In the words of KPD Reichstag deputy and population policy spokesman Emil Höllein, abortion was "at the very center of proletarian struggle."[77]

————Party leaders unabashedly used the issue to recruit women. Continually frustrated by a persistent gender differential at the polls, which was considerably higher than for other parties and frequently over 20 percent, the KPD was in dire need of female voters.[78] Officially the Central Committee remained primarily interested in organizing women workers, preferably in industry. The considerable latitude given to Münzenberg and his "mass" groups and media in appealing to women beyond that narrow range was, however, a tacit acknowledgment that for the KPD, as for the SPD, the most active female support came from housewives. Attention to women's "personal" problems might neutralize opposition especially from housewives and white-collar workers, and counteract their impression of Communists as "barbarian cannibals" (*Menschenfresser*).[79]

The creation of a highly visible coalition against paragraph 218, and for the defense of Wolf and Kienle, was consistent with the current party line of "Go to the People" (*Heran an die Massen*). It offered a rare opportunity to employ the "united front from below" strategy ordered by the Sixth Comintern Congress in 1928, which had declared Social Democracy "social fascist" but had also urged alliances with the working-class base of the SPD. By unequivocally calling for abolition of paragraph 218, the KPD scored propaganda points over the SPD, which insisted on keeping an abortion law on the books—if only to protect women against irresponsible men trying to escape their paternal obligations—while allowing for all kinds of exceptions and extenuating circumstances.[80]

By raising the slogan, "Your Body Belongs to You" and by waging a lonely battle in the Reichstag for complete decriminalization of abortion, the KPD broke the bounds of its own class analysis. Implicitly, if rather nervously, it defended even a bourgeois woman's right to choose abortion for personal reasons not directly connected to dire material need. According to the psychologist and writer Manes Sperber, it was the party's strong stance on the abortion issue that gave many social reformers and intellectuals within the Communist left "the feeling that we were on the right side."[81]

Abortion politics also offered female leadership an opportunity to gain importance and visibility beyond the confines of the separate women's conference movement. Helene Overlach, a veteran party organizer, who had first viewed her assignment to organize women as a demotion, and complained that, "Again and again, for weeks, months, years, until it made us retch, we did the abortion paragraph,"[82] experienced some of her proudest moments during the campaign. Five months pregnant, she fought for the right to be the party's main speaker at the huge April 15 rally. "This is, after all, a women's question; I can do this better than a male comrade," she insisted, and won her point.[83] Orthodox cadres worried about possible dilution of class politics soon reasserted their power, but in the winter of 1931, the majority seized the chance to humanize the party by addressing women both as mothers and as "new women."

Still, in the final analysis, a coherent politics of reproduction was never adequately integrated into Communist ideology, and the argument for abortion remained a remarkably contingent one. It was made only more conditional by the supposedly "special" emergency conditions of the economic crisis. Economic arguments were collapsed with biological assumptions about the ultimate "naturalness" of women's mothering, which was only temporarily and tragically repressed by social conditions. In a curious way, the law was both challenged and defended in the same terms: the obligation of society (and the state) to protect and provide for the family. Despite the slippage into rights rhetoric, for most sex reformers, the right to choice in sexual and reproductive matters was never inalienable. It was generally not framed in terms of rights, either of the woman to control her own body or of the fetus to life.[84] In a needs-based discourse of collective welfare, whether of class, *Volk,* or nation, sex reformers managed to argue that legalization combined with widespread contraception would ultimately reduce not only the number of unwanted and unfit babies but also the number of abortions.

Abortion therefore served multiple symbolic purposes and was usefully overdetermined. It could be defended while still being acknowledged as an evil. Indeed, its legalization could plausibly be presented as the best way to attain its elimination. Moreover, the specter of rampant unregulated abortion could be used to justify sex education, birth control, and the establishment of sex and marriage counseling centers. In the Marxist terms familiar to many reformers, a regime of legalized abortion would eventually lead to its withering away, just as the establishment of a socialist state would lead to the withering away of the need for abortion. This reasoning was very effective in galvanizing a broad coalition of forces for legalization. But it embraced troubling assumptions. As the lay journal *Ideal Lebensbund* wrote:

> If only the living standard will be raised again, ensuring healthy and adequate conditions, then women will all on their own return to their natural task— motherhood; because to enjoy bringing forth children, a woman must first of all be healthy in mind and body . . . not oppressed by economic worries.[85]

According to this analysis, if and when a state were adequately to fulfill its social welfare promises, it would then have the right to regulate childbearing, a proposition that would quickly be borne out in the Soviet Union by the Stalinist recriminalization of abortion in 1936, by the social health claims of the National Socialists in Germany, and even by the shifting abortion policy later followed by the East German state. This gulf between a projected socialist future where abortion would presumably be unnecessary, and a highly contested present where Communists and sex reformers fought hard for women's access to abortion, gave at times a curiously unreal quality to anti-218 propaganda.

### Doctors and Abortion Politics

The contradictions of KPD policy were illustrated most clearly by the conflicts facing sex reform physicians. The dilemma of wanting to "help" but being unable to do so legally was especially acute for leftist sex reform physicians who had taken public stands in favor of abolishing or reforming the paragraph. Like virtually all women doctors, they were deluged with pleas from women who expected them to back up their political position with concrete aid in the consultation room. Few activist physicians managed to turn their patients away with the politically correct finesse recommended in Max Hodann's popular sex manual *Geschlecht und Liebe (Sex and Love)*, produced at the height of the abortion campaign. In a chapter entitled "Only a Formality," he tried to impress upon his working-class readers that fundamental political change was necessary before they could expect their doctors to rescue them from unintended pregnancies.

As in most of Hodann's books, the chapter was written in the informal style of a conversation between doctor and patient, asserting the avuncular authority of the white-coated professional. A young man asks for help; his girlfriend's period is late. Kindly, but condescending and controlling, Hodann orders the young woman to come in and speak for herself, and then asks, "Well, little girl, what's the matter?" Having heard that obtaining a certificate for a "therapeutic" abortion would be "only a formality," the couple is shocked when comrade Dr. Hodann turns them down with a lecture on narrow medical indications (severe thyroid, heart, or kidney disorders or tuberculosis) and broad political principles. An individual physician, Hodann submits, cannot challenge an unjust law; that can only be done through a mass political movement, which his young patients should join. When the desperate boyfriend asks once again what can be done, the doctor replies in all seriousness:

> At this moment my answer will be of little use to you. Come the next elections for the Reichstag, vote for the representatives of the proletariat. . . . Then perhaps the situation which keeps my hands tied today will change. Please think of this, both of you, at election time.

He adds a special chastising note for women who continued to resist the only political party that supported the decriminalization of abortion:

> Unfortunately, it is mainly women who, as soon as their misery is over for the moment, mostly forget far too fast how they had suffered and to whom in the Reichstag their thanks should go.

Committed to opening up honest communication between the generations, Hodann promises to write to the girl's mother, asking her to come and speak to him, and sends the young couple off with a referral to a woman obstetrician. But for all of his strict but jolly manner, and his faith in political rather than individual solutions, he does not want to present his readers with a "happy end." Hodann concludes his political morality tale, under the heading

"Does this have to be . . . ?" with a typically tragic denouement and another staple of left-wing iconography: "Suicide. This morning the body of a young girl was fished from the Spree."[86]

A story in the KPD women's magazine *Die Kämpferin*, repeated at KPD women's conferences, underscored this continual conflict between the desire to provide alternative services in an emergency situation and resistance to individual solutions of social problems. A delegate to the second National Committee of Working Women Conference in Berlin in November 1930 joined a woman's delegation to the Soviet Union that December. She came home extremely impressed by Soviet achievements in birth control and protection of mothers and children, and reported:

> I asked a doctor if he could not recommend a suitable birth control method to take home to the proletarian women in Germany, where thousands of women are destroyed by the Paragraph and many hundreds of thousands physically harmed. The doctor gave me the following reply, "Yes, comrade, I can tell you one sure-fire method. Make a revolution in Germany like we made in Russia in 1917 . . . then you too will be able to bear healthy children with the aid of expert medical attention."[87]

In fact, many women did not bleed to death or commit suicide but survived reasonably safe abortions performed by doctors or competent "quacks."[88] There was often a divergence between the public position—either pro or contra reform—of doctors and what they actually did or recommended in the privacy of their consultation rooms and clinics. Doctors, especially doctors active in the anti-218 movement, certainly had compelling cause not to advertise their willingess to help, and counseling centers for birth control and sex advice were generally scrupulous about not recommending abortions except in clearly indicated cases. On the other hand, many reputable doctors would quietly refer or even perform abortions.[89]

Hertha Nathorff, who prided herself on never doing abortions, nevertheless occasionally whispered to a particularly needy patient that there were "Communist doctors who do such things"; these actions earned her arrest on abortion charges after the Nazis came to power.[90] Even the circumspect Hodann himself was rumored to have performed abortions for comrades. Indeed, access to sympathetic physicians was clearly considered one of the advantages of participation in the sex reform or Communist movement. As one Berlin activist remembered:

> We found a doctor: Dr. Max Beer. He was a Communist and risked his livelihood, his freedom. Later also his head, which the Nazis took from him. But he helped and didn't take a penny. I was admitted to a women's clinic.[91]

An extraordinary example of this split between rhetoric and experience is a letter written to Friedrich Wolf by Renee Strobowa, the actress who played the tragic young heroine Hete on the national tour of his anti–paragraph 218 play *Cyankali*. Every evening on stage she played the hapless Hete who cried out her pain: "We working women know much too little of those things that we should know. Every day they hit us. And then no one will help us." Desperately, the young white-collar worker (a stock figure of Weimar fiction), in love with a good but unemployed comrade who cannot afford to start a family, searches for an abortionist. She is turned down by everyone, from doctor to midwife; even the quack is too expensive. In the familiar scenario of the futile quest for a safe and affordable abortion, Hete finally resorts to the most dangerous solution: self-help. Her own loving mother feeds her the poison pills (*Cyankali*), procured from an unscrupulous "angelmaker," which agonizingly and slowly kill Hete before the helpless eyes of her mother and her lover. At the end, the dying Hete cries out the message that defined the movement: "A law that turns 800,000 mothers into criminals every year is no longer a law."[92]

Off-stage, Renee the actress was playing out a different drama:

Dear Wolf: We need your advice, we urgently need your help. Why must you write such plays, it rubs off. Ilse Fürstenberg [another member of the company] has met with the unhappy fate of your Hete. It [her period] didn't come. Now she is completely in despair because she is on tour and has no idea how to help herself. The group naturally knows nothing, only I, and they mustn't suspect anything. . . . Do you know of anyone here or in Cologne, a trustworthy doctor to whom she could turn. It is all so stupid because she cannot stay away in the evening . . . she hopes that she could appear on stage at night in spite of such an operation. Please, dear Wolf, write to me by return mail what one could do, the poor thing is so desperate. Of course, it would have to be a doctor who doesn't take Paragraph 218 too seriously. Otherwise we are fine.[93]

This letter, found amidst Friedrich Wolf's papers on *Cyankali* and the public campaign against paragraph 218, is an astonishing document because it so clearly points to the multiple contradictions within Weimar left sexual and reproductive politics. Ironically, Ilse (and Renee) are afraid to discuss her (their) predicament with their comrades in a collective of avowedly leftist actors touring in a play designed to agitate about the evils of paragraph 218. At the same time, they firmly assume that there is a network of trustworthy doctors who will help quickly and safely. But it must be done discreetly, in secret; unlike Hete's story, this is not the kind of abortion case with which the KPD would have mounted the barricades. Ilse is neither a victimized and self-sacrificing wife and mother, nor an oppressed worker, but a "new woman," unwilling to bear a child because she wants to get on with her career and her political work. She feels herself unable even to take one evening off to have an abortion, much less to carry and rear a child; one can hardly imagine her considering the possibility so urgently suggested in Hodann's manual: to resign herself to her fate and get married.

## Abortion and Representation: Popular Culture and the War of Images

Thus, while anti–218 propaganda unremittingly presented women as hapless victims of cruel laws that left them at the mercy of their bodies, official statistics and mass culture increasingly presented a different kind of aborter: closer to Ilse than to Hete and her mother. Historians of changing attitudes toward abortion in the nineteenth and twentieth centuries have noted that panic about abortion "epidemics" was driven not only by the professionalizing ambitions of physicians but by the changing profile of the "aborting woman."[94]

In Germany, it was only after the First World War that the tropes beloved by left-wing campaigners for reform—the exhausted proletarian mother with a baby at her breast, toddlers tugging at her skirts and pregnant again, both heroic and pitiable, or young girls raped by brutal stepfathers—did not clearly mesh with the "real" women seeking abortion. Neither did they fit middle- or working-class women who were limiting their families—or young women of all classes who just wanted to get on with their lives and loves without disruption by a baby. In a context where average working-class family size had shrunk to about four, and the "two-child system" had become the norm, women were redefining the meaning of "need" or "hardship" requiring prevention or termination of pregnancy.

Moreover, the declining birth rate differential between city and country signaled that both abortion and contraception practices were well entrenched in small towns and countryside as well as cities. There also seemed to be a rise in abortions among young married "new women," who sought to postpone childbearing and limit family size to one or two children. But the significant fact about abortions in the Weimar era was not their absolute increase but a shift in who was having them, when, and with what kind of visibility. Women were starting to abort at a younger age and tended to have more abortions over a lifetime.[95]

The emergence of abortion as a public, political issue and, in Carroll Smith-Rosenberg's terms, as a "political code" for broad social changes,[96] therefore had its roots in structural changes: just as the birth rate decline began to cause extreme concern after the war, when it seemed to affect the working class as a mass phenomenon, so the abortion rate began to provoke grave anxiety when it affected younger women who had not already borne many children. In fact, the "abortion scourge" may have been so disturbing precisely because many younger women were using abortion to delay or space childbearing. But "new women" like Ilse presumably came too close to the antiabortion stereotype of frivolous women making decisions out of "convenience" to evoke much sympathy as propaganda images.

Popular culture, more clearly than left-wing sex reform propaganda, reflected women's dilemmas as they experimented with sexual freedom and coped with the consequences: caught between the oft-intoned "rational" commitment to sex as a natural and healthy activity, and quite "irrational" panic about becoming pregnant. The often desperate search—the attempt to seek out sympathetic physicians, the bitter awareness that safe "therapeutic" abortions could be obtained from many doctors for a price, the anxious routes to quacks—was inscribed in commercial culture, in films, plays, newspapers, popular novels, even in cabaret hit songs, as well as in scientific and sociological documents. In Claire Waldorff's cabaret chanson, *"Die Grosstadt-pflanze"* (*"The City Slicker"*), a Berlin moll is impregnated and deserted in the fancy West End and comes home for her abortion to working-class northern Berlin: "I went to see Mrs. Schapke, Mühlenstrasse 5. Knock hard, for a certain reason. And then it was gone."[97]

In Irmgard Keun's popular novel *Gilgi, Eine von uns* (*One of Us*), the tough young white-collar worker Gilgi minces no words confronting a patronizing doctor who counsels her to get married:

> Quit this grandpa manner—I don't want a child. . . . I wouldn't mind at all bringing five illegitimate children into the world, if I could care for them. But I can't. I have no money, my boyfriend has no money. . . . Listen, doctor, it is definitely the most immoral, the most unhygienic and the most absurd thing there is to let a woman bring a child into the world which she can't support. Quite apart from this, it is altogether the most immoral, the most absurd thing imaginable to let a woman bear a child she does not want.[98]

The contradictions between independence and maternalism are finally resolved when the unmarried Gilgi resolves to flout convention and have the child on her own.[99]

Another successful Weimar novel, Vicki Baum's *Stud. Chem. Helene Willfuer*, published in 1928, portrayed these same tensions. The young chemistry student, seeking both a career and a sex life, tries in a famous scene to solve her problem with a steep belly flop from a diving board. Desperately she searches for information about the body that has become her enemy. She tries to use her expertise to concoct an abortifacient in a big pot borrowed from her sympathetic landlady: "It is a free composition by cand. chem. Willfuer, indeed, so to speak, her first independent production."[100]

Helene Willfuer also struggles to reconcile her acceptance of sex with her terror of getting pregnant: the dilemma of the 1920s "new woman":

> There was one immutable fact: one must not have a child. Though one is accountable only to oneself, possesses every freedom, is not touched by the narrow-minded notions of earlier times, has morally nothing, absolutely nothing, against unwed mothers: but one does not have a baby if one studies chemistry and aspires to the doctorate.[101]

In the waiting room of an "ample, resolute and kind" woman doctor, Helene is introduced to a sorority of suffering. The older professional woman hates "our ominous paragraph" but resolutely refuses to flout the law.[102] She can only offer the solutions of her older generation of "new women": either get married as soon as possible, or if that is not possible, see it through and have the courage to be a single mother; after all, the women's movement had gained certain benefits for unwed mothers and illegitimate children. Baum's melodrama continued to a predictable end: Having reneged on a mutual suicide pact with the father of the fetus, Helene finally resigns herself to her condition, marries her professor, resolves to be his wife and assistant, and to relinquish her dreams of herself one day becoming a professor—a female fate, marked by the failed search for an abortion and the acceptance of motherhood.

In the codes of popular and political representation, women appeared as victims of paragraph 218, either as helpless figures, victimized by lack of knowledge, male pressure, and poverty; or as tough young women, unrepentant about their sexuality and cynical about maternity—threats to the established moral code, but nevertheless finally driven into submission to motherhood and/or death and disease by bourgeois law and morality. Interestingly, women doctors were often used to represent the tired voice of reason; sympathetic but ultimately also helpless, they were caught between protecting their professional status and trying to aid other women.[103] In practice, however, doctors frequently faced active agents who felt not only entitled to abortion but also convinced that they had a right not to die or go broke in the process. Furthermore, in a disturbing counterpoint to the reform argument that "prevention" would avoid abortions, as contraceptive use and knowledge increased, so ironically did abortion. Having made the "modern" decision to limit births, people were less willing to accept failure. Heightened health education, broader access to contraception, and the influence of sex reform agitation had only reinforced women's traditional predisposition to claim abortion as their natural right.[104]

### Abortion and Representation: Reform and the War of Numbers

Since paragraph 218 obviously could not be properly enforced, government officials in the national Department of Health (RGA) and local authorities were reduced to bemoaning the situation, coordinating pronatalist propaganda, and, most importantly, tracking abortion statistics: total number, legal and criminal, where performed, and by whom. The RGA diligently collected data from hospitals, midwives, and local health officials, and also kept careful tabs on anti-218 campaigns. RGA files, filled with clippings on the abortion controversy, grew steadily thicker over time.[105]

Estimated statistics thus became elements in the abortion battles. Not surprisingly, the drive to collect data only confirmed the unreliability of statistics on an illegal or semilegal procedure. By the peak of the campaign in 1931, many on both sides agreed that approximately one million (out of a total

female population of 31.2 million) German women underwent abortions annually.[106] Official statistics were in any case notoriously biased and inaccu-
rate.[107] Obviously, hospital statistics, even if scrupulously reported, could only
encompass the minority of botched cases that actually ended up there, and
therefore tended to exaggerate the degree to which illegal abortions resulted
in death or "severe health complications."[108]

Much statistical evidence was essentially anecdotal, publicized by sensational trials or publications. At a widely watched trial in May 1927, the pharmacist Paul Heiser proudly confessed to having interrupted 11,000 pregnancies in four years.[109] Testifying in his defense, the Berlin gynecologist Dührssen
noted that if the law were strictly applied, then "no doubt the greater part of
all German wives would have to march into prison."[110]

Probably the best publicized documentation of medical abortion practice
was published by Alfred Grotjahn, the Social Democratic professor of social
hygiene, at the height of the paragraph 218 controversy in 1931. Mysteriously
delivered, the so-called Grotjahn File (*Kartothek*) purported to contain the 1927
medical records of an anonymous deceased doctor in a town with a population
of about 25,000. Of 556 patient consultations related to abortion, he rejected
127 requests and performed 426 (sic) abortions. The good doctor apparently
preferred to maintain control (and good business) by performing repeated
abortions, up to 7 a day (consistent with Heiser's 11,000 in four years), without educating his patients about contraception.[111]

Grotjahn, of course, opposed reform and was interested in demonstrating
exploitative practices. Indeed, both opponents and defenders of the paragraph
had an interest in maximizing the possible dangers resulting from illegal abortions. Both sides strove to present women as victims. Pro-legalization forces
wanted to prove that illegal abortions jeopardized national health and fertility,
while minimizing the complications from legal therapeutic abortions; antiabortion forces sought to show that abortion was dangerous and harzardous
under all circumstances.

The RGA, as a defender of the status quo, estimated a relatively low 4,000
deaths annually, while Communists usually estimated 10,000–12,000 (although
on occasion up to 40,000) fatalities, with 50,000 cases of health complications—
their high figures matched those offered by abortion opponents.[112] Legal prosecutions for illegal abortions of course also offered a distorted statistical view,
since they always constituted only a tiny percentage of the actual cases. Still,
convictions rose sixfold from 1910 to 1925, reaching a peak in 1925 just before
the reform was legislated.[113]

Doctors in particular were anxious for clarity on the abortion law because
the ambiguities of the strict medical indication provisions clouded the precise definition of a "legal" abortion. The most current German Supreme Court
verdict of March 11, 1927, pronounced abortions legal "if the danger to the
pregnant woman could not be dealt with any other way," an apparent step
toward the acceptance of social conditions as a factor in determining medi-

cal necessity. Yet German physicians' 1925 national convention in Leipzig had reaffirmed that pregnancies should be terminated only if the mother's life was in danger. This restriction to medical indications represented something of a trap for doctors, since improvements in medical treatment and in general health meant there were fewer legitimate grounds for abortion. Obstetricians, especially, sometimes felt professionally challenged to prove that pregnancies could be sustained even under adverse conditions requiring significant medical intervention.

As Barbara Brookes has astutely noted for interwar England, "Doctors had less reason to induce abortion while women apparently found more."[114] Other physicians clearly were content, as Margaret Sanger had noted during her 1928 visit, to keep abortion illegal and contraception mysterious in order to preserve medical omnipotence: "With abortions, it is in our hands; we make the decisions and they must come to us."[115] In general, as we have seen, interpretations of medical necessity depended on a physician's political sympathies or the amount of money a patient was willing to pay.

By the time of the Wolf/Kienle arrests, however, an increasingly vocal minority of doctors had became convinced that only legalization could clarify their own practice and rationalize a procedure that was shrouded in the protective secrecy of informal women's networks. Increasingly, there were professional reasons to support further reform. Doctors wanted to protect themselves both from the intense pressure applied by women determined to procure safe if illegal abortions, and from official complaints that discerned a "shameless abortion epidemic among physicians." Health officials concerned about the "abortion mania" charged that, "It seems there is no illness left which does not first require inducement of a miscarriage."[116]

Such reports indicated the degree to which doctors were questioning the medical and ethical legitimacy of paragraph 218, especially after the 1926 reform and the 1927 court ruling had further confused the legal situation and emboldened women to demand "legal" medical indications. Even as the 30,000-strong Hartmann Bund remained adamantly opposed to any change, doctors in growing numbers resented a law that arbitarily and unpredictably infringed on their professional practices.[117] A questionnaire distributed to Hamburg-area physicians in late 1930 indicated overwhelming desire for clarity and reform that would both protect and further empower doctors. While fewer than 10 percent of the respondents supported complete decriminalization or abortion on demand, virtually all favored some kind of liberalizing change in the law, with about 80 percent favoring a broader range of medical and social indications.[118] As became clear in the 1931 campaign, a significant number of physicians were now willing to assert, as they had already begun to do with contraception and sex counseling, control over the domain of female reproduction and to demand reasonable professional guidelines for performing abortions.

But unlike sex reform efforts to promote contraception and the establishment of clinics, abortion could not be contained as a medical issue. The cruel inefficacy of the abortion paragraph symbolized the bankruptcy of Weimar democracy and its promises of civil equality for the sexes and social justice and protection for the family. Women's determined resort to abortion signaled the state's inability to establish its most basic legitimacy; it provided visible evidence of the failure of the Weimar welfare state to either help or control its citizens. Still the campaign to change the law failed.

The embattled Weimar Republic insisted on maintaining on the books a law that was highly unpopular and persistently flouted. Hardly anyone believed that the law could substantially prevent abortions, and most policymakers doubted that, at least at a time of economic crisis, government intervention could really influence reproductive decisions. Yet, except for the KPD, all political parties supported some form of criminalization as a sign of the government's commitment to raise the birth rate and police sexual morality, at a time when conventions in those areas seemed to be collapsing. For critics on the right, abortion represented the decadence and degeneracy of a modern society dedicated to individualism and materialism, where women's egocentrism precluded altruism toward the family. For the KPD, as we have seen, the abortion issue dramatized the failure of bourgeois society. It—for once—allowed the KPD to present itself as an ethical voice. Both opponents and supporters of antiabortion legislation stressed that the massive violations of the statute encouraged general disrespect for the law and the government, especially threatening in a time of political instability and economic disorder.

As the depression dragged on, unemployment rose, and the social welfare system tottered, the political and moral, as well as fiscal, bankruptcy of government social policy became ever more apparent. Right-wingers and Social Democrats alike were left with little more than sentimental and patriotic appeals to the solidarity of the *Volk*, and the self-sacrifice and maternal instinct of German women. Yet, just this appeal was apparently rejected as German women resorted in ever greater numbers to abortion. Because motherhood was not a private matter, impinging as it did on the welfare of the family, and by extension the state, the birth rate was stylized into an index of Germany's economic and political future.[119]

New sociological-psychological studies stressed the indispensable role of the mother in making ends meet, soothing conflict, and holding the family together during times of economic uncertainty.[120] Conversely, women's resistance to that role, allegedly measured by reduced family size, and most dramatically by resort to illegal, hazardous, and potentially fatal abortions, took on an even more subversive cast. Government, church, and political officials assigned political meaning to women's procreative behavior. While not consciously "on strike," women did desperately try to limit births when forced simultaneously to cope with the pressures of their own and their men's unemployment, as well as to pick up the slack for reproductive work that social service cutbacks were returning to the family.

The search for reliable birth control and recourse to abortion functioned as tactics in a reproductive strategy that insured the survival of both the woman herself and the family within which she defined her identity and organized subsistence. But for anxious observers, the high abortion rates raised the specter of women as selfish, individualistic, materialistic, and heartless (as well as "frigid"), all characteristics associated with the "new woman" and the rationalization of everyday life—and just at the moment when women's nurturing qualities were deemed most necessary.[121] In this sense, the abortion controversy was only the most visible part of the larger debate about values, ethics, and a "new morality" associated with the emergence of a "new woman."

An expert National Committee for Population Policy Questions, led by Prussian Interior Minister Severing, had been convened in January 1930 to consider the birth rate decline and "how to combat it." It labeled abortion the primary "national scourge," debated how to encourage the fading "will to a child," and gloomily raised the specter of a degenerate nation deprived of replacement numbers. Three commissions, including representatives from the Berlin VKB, the Federation of Large Families (*Bund der Kinderreichen*), as well as midwives and obstetricians, called for financial incentives to entice women out of the work force, improved prenatal care, better training for obstetrician-gynecologists, and stricter regulation of midwives. But they were confounded by the quandary of how to encourage childbearing in the absence of material benefits or better living conditions.[122]

The only solutions politicians could imagine were unworkable: either unenforceable laws disdained by the citizenry or expansive public welfare and tax schemes that became ever more illusory after 1930. Finally, even the staunchly pronatalist Social Democratic population expert Dr. Alfred Grotjahn, together with his colleague, Prussian medical official Dr. Adolf Gottstein, resigned from the commission, stating that: "In view of the recently passed emergency decree, . . . within the forseeable future a fruitful continuation of the work is not possible."[123]

With resignation, government officials noted that a total prohibition on abortion was virtually impossible, since one would then have to ban irrigators and douches, hairpins and knitting needles, pencils, pens, catheters, ear spoons, and all manner of objects that women used to abort; furthermore, one would have to forbid pregnant women from taking hot baths, jumping up and down, and performing any number of other normal activities. The gynecologist Max Hirsch dourly reported to the Prussian Welfare Ministry that women were "perfectly capable of inserting syringes . . . knitting needles and other similar objects through the cervix into the uterus . . . without doing themselves any harm." With evident amazement, he noted that women seemed to feel that the fetus was a part of the female body, "with which the carrier could do whatever she wanted."[124]

In the final analysis, women did control their own bodies (even if not under conditions of their own choosing). They found abortions "through an odd kind of secret service for women, with rarely any news of the goings-on leaking to the outside." Neither criminal laws nor religious belief inhibited abortion; women believed that "the state doesn't care a hoot about their personal distress and God in Heaven no doubt will understand."[125] Indeed, illegal abortions were "just as common in Catholic as in Protestant areas."[126] And as one Weimar intellectual recalled, in a city like Berlin it was easy to assume that abortions were "almost legal."[127]

But the Weimar Republic clung stubbornly to the abortion paragraph. If anything, the flood of data about declining birth and rising abortion rates provoked an increasingly unbending and pessimistic mood among government population and health experts. Official pronouncements took on an ominous tone as the economic situation worsened; a 1931 Memorandum on the State of the National Health warned that the birth rate decline could only be reversed by "a strong nationalistically-motivated inner revolt against certain mutilation of our people and too many foreign elements."[128] Such pronouncements could offer no realistic solutions but surely helped to legitimate and make plausible the slogans and appeals of the one party that most loudly promised the protection of motherhood, the encouragement of childbearing, and the removal of women from the work force: the National Socialists.

The KPD, which had so successfully launched the 1931 mobilization, was also unable to offer realistic alternatives. Nor could it maintain its role as catalyst for mass broad-based protests. With the release of Wolf and Kienle from prison and the calming of public protest, the KPD was increasingly on the defensive, more and more divided between a rigid cadre politics and a mass-propaganda effort directed by Willi Münzenberg, as well as more and more trapped in conflict with the SPD. Increasingly a party of the marginal and unemployed, it was reduced to helplessly if angrily protesting the dismantling of the Weimar Republic and its Social Democratic reforms, and providing small-scale if sometimes imaginative alternative services. Furthermore, it lacked a theory that could explain the importance of the issue around which it had so effectively mobilized. Inasmuch as the anti-218 campaign was part of the general working-class movement, it shared its fate and was destroyed by the combined pressures of economic collapse, growing National Socialist strength, the disunity of the left, and intensifying political repression.

The emergency decree of March 1931 severely restricted the right to outdoor demonstrations, and *Die Kämpferin* was banned in May 1931 for publishing an anticlerical series.[129] As the Wolf/Kienle campaign slowly petered out by the early summer of 1931, the police noted with relief that there was a marked reduction in activity around paragraph 218.[130] In a society increasingly marked by political paralysis and civil disorder, sex reform activity returned to the level of self-help and service provision. Nevertheless, at virtually the last minute during the republic's final year and a half, the Weimar sex reform movement was, if in many ways most divided, also most radical.

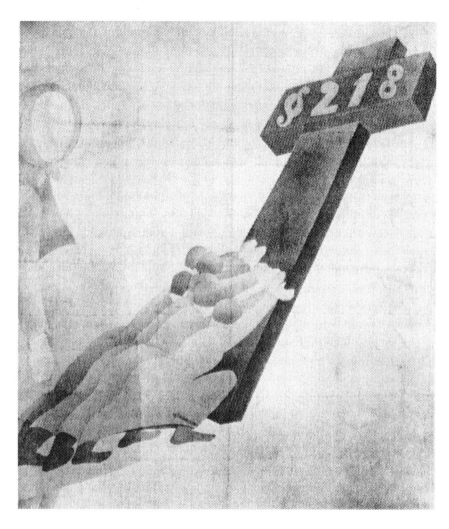

*Paragraph 218*. Painting by Alice Lex-Nerlinger, 1931 (Märkisches Museum, Berlin).

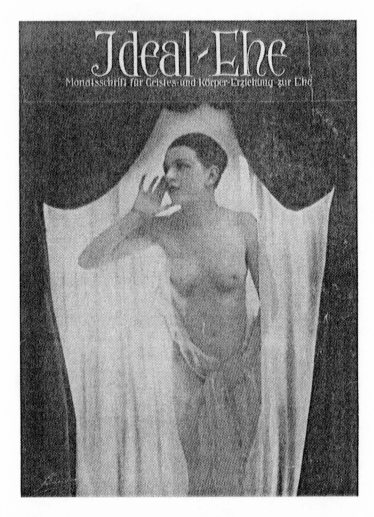

*Ideal Marriage. Monthly for Spiritual and Physical Marriage Education*, Berlin, December 1927 (Staatsbibliothek zu Berlin-Preussischer Kulturbesitz).

*Ideal Life-Companionship.* Weekend and Marriage, Berlin, July 1928 (Staatsbibliothek zu Berlin-Preussischer Kulturbesitz).

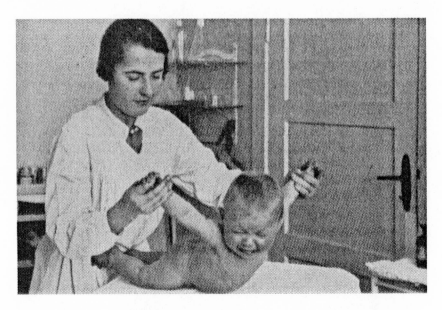

Infant gymnastics in Health Insurance League clinic, Berlin. *Jahrbuch der Ambulatorien des Verbandes der Krankenkassen Berlins 1928/29* (Staatsbibliothek zu Berlin-Preussischer Kulturbesitz).

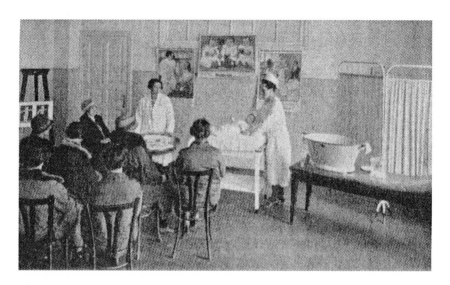

Infant-care course, prenatal clinic, Berlin. *Jahrbuch der Ambulatorien des Verbandes der Krankenkassen Berlins 1928/29* (Staatsbibliothek zu Berlin-Preussischer Kulturbesitz).

Orthopedic gymnastics for children, Health Insurance League clinic, Berlin. *Jahrbuch der Ambulatorien des Verbandes der Krankenkassen Berlins 1928/29* (Staatsbibliothek zu Berlin-Preussischer Kulturbesitz).

One of five waiting rooms, Health Insurance League clinic, Alexanderplatz, Berlin. *Jahrbuch der Ambulatorien des Verbandes der Krankenkassen Berlins 1928/29* (Staatsbibliothek zu Berlin-Preussischer Kulturbesitz).

"Women in Need," *Eulenspiegel* 4:10 (October 15, 1931) (BArchK).

Dr. Else Kienle addresses anti-218 rally at Sportpalast, April 15, 1931 (Sapmo-BArch).

Red Women and Girls League march, Königsberg, 1927 (Sapmo-BArch).

"Between the Walls of the Law," *Arbeiter Kalender*, February 1931 (BArchK).

"Collective Life—Collective Struggle!" *Arbeiter Kalender*, January 1931 (BArchK).

Dr. Friedrich Wolf, c. 1948 (Sapmo-BArch).

First Women's Club, Democratic Women's League of Germany, Berlin 1947
(Sapmo-BArch).

— five —

# Forbidden Love
## Sex Reform and the Crisis
## of the Republic, 1931 to 1933

We have emergency decrees in the purest sense of the word, for they
decree a social emergency and escalate the state of emergency that
already exists.

CLARA ZETKIN,
in her final address to the Reichstag
on August 30, 1932[1]

The abortion campaign wound down as the Weimar Republic lurched toward
its chaotic final year. Weakened by spiraling unemployment and the bitter
divisions between Communists and Social Democrats, the working-class
movement with which sex reform was so tightly linked fragmented further,
even as some urban neighborhoods settled into a state of virtual civil war
between Nazis and Communists.[2] The social welfare institutions, which were
the focus of so much sex reform effort and ire, unraveled while trying to cope
with mounting social and economic tensions. Paradoxically, the breakdown
of traditional working-class and family structures and the extreme precarious-
ness of the Weimar welfare state created space for radical innovation by the
left and sex reform, especially in the "sexual struggles" of youth and women.
Conventional politics seemed increasingly out of control as the republic endured no fewer than five major electoral campaigns in 1932. A divided and
angry left saw the Nazis exploit a virtually unbroken stream of public exposure and activity.

Yet Berlin became even more "red." With the Social Democrats firmly
ensconced in the Prussian state government (until the July 1932 Papen coup),
the Communists were the strongest party in the capital. In the last Weimar
election in November 1932, nearly one-third of the Berlin electorate voted
Communist, and the KPD gained a majority in nine proletarian districts that
were also centers of sex reform activity (Wedding, Friedrichshain, Neukölln,

Mitte, Prenzlauer Berg, Kreuzberg, and the suburbs of Lichtenberg, Reinick-endorf, and Weissensee).[3] The feud between Social Democrats and Commu-nists, basically unbridgeable since "Bloody May Day 1929," when a Social Democratic police commissioner had ordered attacks on Communist dem-onstrators, was exacerbated by the KPD's struggle to adhere to rigid Com-intern directives.

At the same time, the party's appeal to antifascist intellectuals and profes-sionals and Willi Münzenberg's broadly based "front" organizations fostered a vibrant Communist counterculture.[4] As municipal and health insurance clin-ics struggled to meet increased demand with decreased resources, the anti-218 coalition crumbled, and many physicians embraced National Socialism. The sex reform movement in the last year and a half of the republic became more and more tightly linked with the KPD and its increasingly radicalized sexual politics—a trend that later came (misleadingly, as we shall see) to be associated with Wilhelm Reich and the term *Sexpol*.

The KPD turned to neighborhood and "social issue"–oriented politics such as abortion when workplace organizing—still granted rhetorical primacy by many cadre—was undermined by mass unemployment. But although the United Front strategy did temporarily attract masses of women to the anti-218 campaign, it failed to snatch organized workers from the "social fascist" SPD. After the waning of the abortion struggle in early summer 1931, the KPD began to search for new recruits among the restless "lost generation" of de-pression youth, especially youngsters in foster care or reformatories or in trouble with youth welfare authorities. The party tried to appeal to young people (especially young men) on the wrong side of the law, in the "cliques" that competed with organized youth movement activity, even to those with ties to the underworld, and to the streetfighters associated with the SA and the Communist Red Front.[5] Unlike the SPD, the KPD was willing to engage in illegal acts such as forcible prevention of evictions, armed self-defense, the protection of runaway adolescents, and referrals for illegal abortions.[6]

As part of its effort to reach beyond its primary constituency of workers, the KPD experimented with both new sexual ethics and utopian visions of "new women" and "new men." Contending with the vaunted Weimar "gen-eration gap" as well as working-class attraction to mass consumer culture, Communist youth groups and their doctor and lawyer advisers sought support by engaging the "sexual struggle of youth" and concretely meeting urban young people's need for sex advice, contraceptives, abortion, and protection from repressive parents and state agencies.

## The KPD Women's Movement and Its Failures

The new focus on youth and sexuality followed the collapse of the 218 cam-paign, in certain ways substituting for further mass organizing of women. Unable (and unwilling) to sustain the momentum and promise of the movement to free Wolf and Kienle, the KPD was nonetheless still impressed by the continuing appeal of the lay leagues and the powerful resonance of the abortion issue. The party recognized that much of its core constituency was now unemployed, spending time waiting on line at welfare and unemployment offices rather than working on the production line, where Communist organizing was theoretically supposed to happen. Moreover, the campaign's demonstrated potential for a powerful mass women's movement posed a fundamental and ultimately insoluble problem for the KPD. Always leery of women's separatism and its association with "bourgeois" feminism, the party leadership feared losing control over the strong, broad-based, and potentially autonomous women's movement that its support of "alliance politics" had helped to create.

Communist activists like Helene Overlach had set into motion masses of women with no long-term strategy for organizing them and no structures into which they could be absorbed. The move into party cadre, where reproductive issues were again subordinated, was too long a leap for most new recruits. The women's delegate and conference movement, which had been so central to the anti-218 campaign and might have provided a political home for women politicized by the abortion struggle, was slowly disintegrating, partly because Overlach, its designated leader, became ill and partly because the party was withdrawing support.

Party policy on women's role had of course been conflicted from the outset. Already in 1920, "Guidelines for the Communist Women's Movement" ordained the principles of the separation between the bourgeois and the proletarian women's movement, and the partial nature of women's struggle within the general class struggle, but also reluctantly affirmed the necessity for separate women's organizing.[7] Throughout the Weimar years then, both the central committee and party women's and social welfare organizations continually stumbled, practically and theoretically, as they tried simultaneously to organize women as a distinct constituency and subordinate their issues to the larger (and more important) class struggle.

The failure of KPD revolutionary strategy after 1923 and shifts in party politics starting in 1925 nonetheless gave new organizational importance and visibility to women's and social welfare issues. The Bolshevization program pushed by the Comintern at the 1925 party congress in Frankfurt tried to focus on "point of production" organizing.[8] Yet, while stressing workplace organizing for party cadre, Bolshevization also encouraged the development of "mass" organizations, one of which was the KPD's first separate women's organization, the Red Girls' and Women's League (*Rote Frauen und Mädchen Bund*, RFMB), established in Berlin in November 1925 as a counterpart or auxiliary to the self-defense organization Red Front-Fighters League (*Rote Frontkämpfer Bund*, RFB). The "Front Fighters" wanted to preserve their paramilitary image from increasing infiltration by young female militants, and the party agreed that the RFB was an unsuitable vehicle for attracting working women and working-class housewives. Although some women resisted re-linquishing the uniformed glamour of the RFB, RFB and KPD wives as well as some previously unaffiliated women were instead recruited into the RFMB.[9]

The twists and turns of the KPD's politics on women and reproduction are well illustrated by the shifting fortunes and convictions of Helene Over-lach, who was chosen by Ernst Thälmann, the party's leader and 1925 presi-dential candidate, to take over leadership of the RFMB. Overlach, who re-jected "the formation of a women's movement since women belonged in the party on equal terms," initially resented her new assignment for pulling her away from the "real" politics of wages and work conditions, war and peace.[10] The RFMB's mission was to use "personal" issues such as motherhood, sexu-ality, abortion, and food prices to move women toward the general (and al-ways primary) class struggle, thus eventually pulling them away from the immediate concerns that had first mobilized them.

Having yielded to party discipline, Overlach dutifully organized women's and children's meetings where previously "indifferent" women sang, read poems and stories, and were gently introduced to political themes in 30-minute question and discussion periods, while their children ate sweets and were entertained by a "red marionette puppet." But she remained frustrated in the "women and children's" realm, complaining that it would be more impor-tant to organize the large numbers of women working in the crucial chemi-cal and electrotechnical industries.[11] With the imposition of the "united front from below" strategy by the Comintern in 1928, the place of women's and social issues within party strategy changed again and Overlach was rewarded by a prominent place on the list of KPD parliamentary candidates. Elected to the Reichstag, she assumed leadership of the National Committee of Work-ing Women whose delegate and conference movement would be central to the movement against paragraph 219 and the 1931 papal encyclical.

In keeping with the party's new "mass" line, the new women's movement was designed to replace a wilting, still mostly cadre-oriented RFMB and to track "unorganized" wives and mothers as well as women workers into the KPD—or at least one of its mass organizations such as the International Work-ers Aid (IAH) or the Red Aid (*Rote Hilfe*) for political prisoners and their fami-lies. Much as the party tried to downplay its leadership role, the new groups probably also drew primarily women who were themselves already close to the party, or whose family members were. Still, unlike the RFMB, which was ordered into existence as a foil to the RFB, this women's movement arose independently through women's activism during the Ruhr and Silesian strikes of the late 1920s. Its regular conferences also offered delegates a rare opportunity to escape their families and develop their own political con-sciousness, whether debating resolutions, touring the big city, or hiking in the woods.[12]

Overlach slowly developed into an ardent advocate of separate organizing for women within the party. She defended the "coffee and cake" after-noons, where women talked, sang, or read poetry, against party leaders who mistrusted such get-togethers as petty bourgeois, SPD deviationism, or sim-ply a waste of time. Carrying her guitar, she canvassed the dark courtyards of working-class Berlin with homemade brochures because she considered the official ones unsatisfactory. Overlach was keenly aware of the tension between the tactics useful for first attracting women and those required for the more difficult job of organizing them and containing their energy once they had been mobilized. "One has to hang on to them, after all," she fret-ted, as she continually faced the dilemma of simultaneously taking women's daily struggles seriously and suggesting they were not really so important. While she could pull women to an abortion rights or International Women's Day demonstration, she could not produce enough disciplined cadre, and Wilhelm Pieck, her direct superior, criticized her nonauthoritarian approach as indecisive.[13]

At the same time, any considerable success at mobilizing women—espe-cially nonworkers—provoked ambivalence in the KPD leadership. Rosa Meyer-Leviné, the wife of a central committee member, recalled:

> Once I was carried away by the sight of a large demonstration. "Too many housewives, women, youngsters," Ernst coolly remarked. "What is wrong with women and youngsters," I asked slightly piqued. "Nothing. But for the revolu-tion we need factory workers, organized in a party or at least in trade unions."[14]

Certainly, women's political activism sometimes led to a sense of empower-ment that was perhaps not quite what the KPD had hoped to achieve. As one woman reported in *Die Kämpferin*:

> I had fights with my husband about whether I would go to this congress or not. He told me not to go (of course, he was in the SPD!). And I said, yes, I am going, and even if you have to pick me up in three months from Moabit [prison in Berlin], I am going to go. I am telling you comrades, we do not have to beg, we must demand.

Organizer Overlach was hard-pressed to resolve the contradictions be-tween the "personal and the political" in her own life. Determined to have a child, she finally became pregnant at age 37, just as the abortion campaign was heating up. Unmarried and deeply involved in her political work, she was nonetheless convinced that as a mother she would be better able to reach her constituency of working-class women. But in fact she became so ill dur-ing her difficult pregnancy that she was forced to withdraw from her leader-ship position after the big April 15 rally. Later, Overlach blamed the dissipa-tion of the anti-218 movement on her illness: "Unfortunately, because I had a baby, the work did not progress," she remembered, barely aware of the irony implied by her words.[15] Indeed, it was surely no accident that the Central Com-

mittee packed this most visible women's leader off to Moscow to work for
the Comintern just at the moment in summer 1931 when the women's committees might have invigorated the faltering abortion campaign.

Loyal as always, Overlach went to the Soviet Union, still recovering from
her pregnancy, with a two-month-old infant, and speaking not a word of Russian.[16] Meanwhile, Friedrich Wolf and Else Kienle, the catalysts and symbols
of the campaign, also conveniently embarked on a tour of the USSR and were
unavailable for further agitation. The journey seems to have ended Kienle's
very brief career as a Communist: her glimpse of Soviet life "killed any spark
of sympathy I might have had."[17]

The collapse of the KPD anti-218 women's movement and its replacement
by IAH and ARSO efforts to influence and dominate the sex reform movement must therefore be understood in the context of the party's ambivalence
toward women's politics. That ARSO and its Action Committee, rather than
the delegate and conference women's movement, was assigned major responsibility for the Wolf/Kienle campaign was consistent with this attitude: while
women's rights had long been party planks, and Marxist analysis identified
women as a particularly oppressed group, in practice, women, especially
housewives, were distrusted as unreliable voters and conservative influences
on their Communist husbands. Somewhat like the *Lumpenproletariat*, women
were suspect as an overly spontaneous, undisciplined, potentially dangerous
anarchic mass that had to be organized and disciplined. The National Committees of Working Women in the delegate and conference movement fell
victim to this anxiety.

## The Politics of Economic Crisis and the KPD

Rather than nurture the delegate movement or the anti-218 coalition, the KPD
Reichstag faction introduced at the height of depression retrenchments in
October 1931, an ambitious but utterly unrealistic "Protective Program for the
Working Woman." Radically extending the demands of the abortion campaign, it called for women's complete economic, social, cultural, and political equality; equal pay for equal work; no employment discrimination against
married women or mothers; full social insurance for all working women; no
dismissals up to one year after childbirth; full legal rights for married women,
with equal parental control over children; equal rights for illegitimate children and unwed mothers; the right to be called *"Frau,"* regardless of marital
status; and finally, state funding for medical abortions and the abolition of
paragraph 218 with amnesty for all those previously convicted.

While the program was nominally aimed at working women, it contained
numerous demands that applied to all women, thus acknowledging their special status as social glue and casual breadwinners at a time of skyrocketing
unemployment. In its calls for protection of women's employment and insurance rights, the KPD also recognized that women, especially married

"double earners," were particularly victimized by employer and state responses to the economic crisis. Far from benefiting at the expense of unemployed male workers—as a wide spectrum of political opinion insisted—women suffered multiple blows; their already low wages were lowered further, they were more likely to lose benefits, and their domestic work increased.[18]

Indeed, Brüning's deflationary program had not halted the pace of unemployment. The pioneering comprehensive unemployment insurance program passed in July 1927, which provided for 26 weeks of compensation plus health benefits and then moved workers onto the relief rolls (*Krisenfürsorge*), was sorely unprepared for the massive demands suddenly placed upon it.[19] Employed wives were the first casualties, when their newly gained right to unemployment compensation was converted back into a needs-based welfare benefit. The state-orchestrated campaign against working wives was fueled by insurance and trade union statistics showing a lower unemployment rate for women than for men; these figures, however, omitted large categories of women workers and obscured both women's hidden unemployment and their hidden employment when forced into uninsured occupations in order to support themselves and their families. The (futile) attempts to combat male unemployment by pushing women out of a tightly sex-segregated labor market worked less to eliminate women workers than to deny them the benefits accorded "full" workers.[20]

In a clear attack on the "double earner," a June 5, 1931 emergency decree required married women workers to prove "need" before they could be compensated for unemployment—turning right into privilege and insurance into welfare. A wife's wages were also deducted from a husband's unemployment payment—a new disincentive to seek insured work. Within two weeks, the number of women drawing unemployment compensation dropped precipitously. Moreover, an October 6, 1931 amendment sanctioned the so-called Krumper system, which allowed employers to replace senior workers entitled to fringe benefits with temporary workers or new hires who did not qualify for unemployment insurance or relief, thereby relieving employer and state treasuries. Further wage and benefit cuts followed in December 1931 and throughout 1932.[21]

As regular sources of income dwindled, family survival required more management and ingenuity. As Marie Jahoda and Paul Lazarsfeld demonstrated in their pioneering study of Marienthal in Austria, unemployment meant less work for men but more work for women, regardless of whether they were working for a wage.[22] Women were responsible for maintaining a precarious family "subeconomy," which might include taking in boarders, raising rabbits on the roof and foodstuffs in the family garden, working off the books, negotiating the welfare system, and finding bargains through community gossip networks.[23] By February 1932, over six million people were officially counted as unemployed: there was barely a working-class family that was not somehow affected.

The KPD's legislative response to these hardships had of course no chance of enactment, but the party's eagerness to take advantage of the intense crisis did provoke a more intensive focus on household and reproductive issues in both propaganda and activity. Münzenberg's *Weg der Frau* and *AIZ* offered recipes for nutritious and economical meals, patterns for sewing one's own clothes, tips on home repairs and how to do housework without expensive appliances, accompanied by the inevitable comparisons with happy workers' families in the Soviet Union.[24] ARSO officials urged *Weg der Frau* editor Marianne Gundermann to institute a medical advice column since health insurance cutbacks had made mothers less likely to take their children to the doctor. Women were expected not only to compensate with home remedies and nursing care but to handle the nervous tensions afflicting the families of the unemployed.[25]

Communist journals prodded husbands with time on their hands to pitch in with the housework so their wives would also have some time for political activity. Such comradely help did not, of course, fundamentally alter the sexual division of labor within the family, as illustrated in a typical plot line for "A Day in the Life" of a proletarian Berlin family. The husband leaves home for meetings of the Communist trade union opposition, while his wife's political involvement begins when, after "mending everybody's stockings, . . . she has a short hour's rest and is glad that she can finally sit still a little after all the day's drudgery," and read "the great women's magazine *Weg der Frau*, which every working-class woman must read." If she later, the article adds, "talks to the other tenants about a way out of the misery of the proletarian life, she too contributes her share in the struggle against the oppressors."[26] Another classic example of Communist notions of companionate marriage was an entry in the 1932 *Workers Calendar:* "Common Life, Common Struggle" captioned a photo of a man sitting at a kitchen table reading the KPD daily *Rote Fahne (Red Flag)*, while a woman wearing an apron stands at the stove, stirring a pot, and glancing over at him and his newspaper![27]

Such examples from working-class movements have by now been documented and commented on so often as to become trite and expected.[28] Nevertheless, they provide context for KPD sex reform politics. Communists perceived the political implications of the double burden and women's heavy responsibility for family survival. But they resisted any basic reconceptualization of the family or gender relations. As with birth control, abortion, and sexual techniques, the proposed solution was mechanistic. The alternative to the double day was not to push women out of the work force and "back into the home" but to ease their "burden as housewife and mother by shifting to communal and technically advanced living and household conditions." Especially necessary, of course, was "rational birth control."[29] The party never retreated from defending women's right to work, but it also never questioned women's primary responsibility as mother and housewife. The "new" Bolshevik woman presented in a play titled *Nora 1932* would be "A new type . . .

that will have nothing in common with either the emancipated woman or the comely little housewife," and who could appreciate technology's potential to lighten traditional tasks and stabilize daily life.[30]

Unlike the women's delegate movement, which the KPD had been reluctant to support, social welfare groups such as the ARSO and IAH that addressed sex reform issues were not exclusively female. Thus, attention to sex reform enabled the KPD to address women's concerns without having to contend with a women's movement. Rather than continuing the attempt to build separate Communist women's organizing, the KPD focused on ARSO and IAH efforts to take over and politicize the lay sex reform movement and its medical allies.

After the demise of the delegate and conference movement, the International Workers Aid (IAH) became the most important women's space connected to the KPD. With a total membership of 55,635 in 1931 (many of them women), the IAH functioned as a kind of KPD auxiliary for intellectuals and a broad range of women uncomfortable with party discipline and rigidity.[31] Indeed, a disillusioned Clara Zetkin—still an important figurehead for the KPD—wrote from Moscow to her young protegée Maria Reese (that prized commodity, a convert from the SPD), urging her to join the Women's Committee (*Frauenrat*) of the IAH as a more congenial alternative to the party itself.[32] Like the lay sex reform leagues, the IAH discovered that women were more comfortable talking amongst themselves and instituted so-called "sewing circles" for regular lectures and discussion. IAH women also did important strike-support work and helped to run the sex and birth control counseling centers. The IAH, therefore, simultaneously offered women a "room of their own" within the KPD, and contributed to their continuing marginalization—only briefly challenged by the anti-218 campaign—into social welfare and domestic arenas.

As an outgrowth of the abortion campaign, the IAH established two subgroupings designed to attract middle-class professionals: Clubs of Intellectual Workers and a medical section. IAH physicians provided first aid at demonstrations and staff for counseling centers; they also conducted propaganda actions such as free examinations for over 1,000 working-class youngsters during International Children's Week in October 1932.[33] As late as January 1933, ARSO and IAH members organized highly publicized medical exams of tenants in buildings on rent strike, both to gain support for the action and to dramatize the terrible health and hygiene effects of the desperate housing situation.[34]

ARSO (Working Group of Social Political Organizations), whose membership partially overlapped with the broader support group IAH, was the KPD organization explicitly responsible for contacts with the lay sex reform movement, as it had been for party agitation during the anti-218 campaign. Since its formation in 1928, ARSO worked to infiltrate, win over, and politicize, on Communist terms, the mass lay movement that it repeatedly accused of a

single-minded neo-Malthusian focus: "The tasks of the population political
organizations are not fulfilled in that they distribute cheap contraceptives to
their members."[35] ARSO members also tried to woo members of the pronatalist Federation of Large Families (BKR), recognizing that "the parties of
the left did not show enough concern" about "child-rich" families who might
prefer birth control information to glorification—a fact that the BKR had
already registered when its members began showing up at *Liga* meetings![36]

As the crisis deepened and welfare benefits became ever more precarious,
ARSO increasingly—and much to the distress of city administrators—advo-
cated for clients as if it were a recognized social welfare organization, like the
Catholic Caritas, Protestant Inner Mission, Jewish Welfare, or the Social
Democratic Workers Welfare (ARWO). An ARSO subgroup, the Working
Group of Marxist Social Workers (*Arbeitsgemeinschaft Marxistischer Sozial-
arbeiter*, AMSO), drew heavily from psychologists and social workers involved
with education and sex reform, especially those influenced by the theories of
Alfred Adler and his Society for Individual Psychology.[37]

## From Sex Reform to Sexual Radicalism: EpS, KPD, and RV

But neither the alliances forged in the anti-218 campaign nor the numerous
efforts to win over lay groups succeeded in gaining large numbers of converts
to Communism; most of the working class, it seemed, was unwilling to relinquish its "false consciousness." These failures pushed the KPD toward a
separatist policy of establishing its own politically reliable sex-political organization, which would then try to assert leadership within the larger movement. ARSO was assigned to organize the separate Communist sex-political
organization, the Unity League for Proletarian Sexual Reform (*Einheits
Verband für proletarische Sexual Reform*, EpS).[38]

The EpS made its public debut at a sex reform "unity" conference held in
Berlin in June 1931. Initially planned at a preparatory meeting of sex reform
groups in January 1930, and often postponed, the meeting finally took place
after a period of apparent success: the support provided by physicians in the
Center for Birth Control (*Arbeitszentrale*) organized by Kate Stützin after the
Zurich birth congress, the priority accorded to birth control at the May 1931
conventions of both the Association of Socialist Physicians (VSA) and German
Gynecological Society, and the momentum of the anti-218 campaign. During the long gestation period, however, the dominance of the RV (National
League for Birth Control and Sexual Hygiene) and the *Liga* (for Protection
of Mothers and Social Family Hygiene) in the lay movement had been somewhat eclipsed by KPD leadership in orchestrating the abortion rights struggle.
Nonetheless, the lay sex reform organizations clung tenaciously to their primary role as birth control and sex advice providers and their non-party-po-
litical identity. The entrance of the EpS further complicated an already deli-

cate balance between RV, *Liga*, and KPD, ultimately helping to turn the "unity" gathering into a "fiasco."[39]

Fifty-five delegates representing over 55,000 members from the *Liga*, RV, and various smaller groups spent a day and a half in continual haggling and frustration. The congress, which had intended to mediate the competition between the RV and *Liga*, was instead dominated by the unexpected and disruptive appearance of the entirely new EpS. The EpS had been formally established only one week before, as the KPD's main vehicle for attempting the consolidation of all lay sex reform organizations under its disciplined classconscious leadership.

Claiming to represent 10,000 members in the lower Rhine and Ruhr regions, the EpS was outraged that the conference recognized only three of its delegates. The mass lay leagues, for their part, were infuriated by the upstart organization, whose members they counted at no more than 3,000, which invaded their long-planned conference and demanded its dissolution into a new Communist-dominated organization. The lay leagues had supported the KPD-led struggle to free Wolf and Kienle and abolish paragraph 218, but their major concern remained the provision to their members of effective and affordable contraception and sex counseling. Their response to the EpS "invasion" focused on its tactics, not its program, and reflected the anger and resentment KPD politicization maneuvers often provoked. The RV's deeply disappointed Dr. Hans Lehfeldt remembered that although he personally liked and respected many KPD activists, they were often hard to work with because, "The Communists always thought that the others didn't do enough, that they had all the wisdom *(Stein der Weisen)*."[40]

Indeed, ignoring their own contribution to divisiveness, EpS representatives complained that unity was impossible to achieve among "pettybourgeois, reformist and anarcho-syndicalist leadership cliques," obsessed with petty organizational rivalries ("horse-trading"), and more interested in maintaining the Social Democratic compromise with Brüning's Catholic Center government than the needs of the proletarian masses.[41] Charging "SPD betrayal," EpS accused the other groups of being fronts for birth control manufacturers and indiscriminate dispensers of contraceptives in a situation where "pills alone could not cure."[42] From the lay leagues' perspective, however, the EpS was sabotaging years of hard practical work with which it had not been involved for the sake of abstract political rhetoric.

Much of the conflict stemmed from differences about the consequences of party affiliation. The EpS asserted that only KPD leadership could assure a class-conscious independent movement; the RV insisted on a generally socialist but explicitly nonparty position. In the face of the devastating effects of the SPD/KPD split on working-class politics, the lay movement, with its mixed Social Democratic, Communist, anarchist, and independent membership, was determined to continue its record of dodging many of those splits.

At the same time, as the KPD charged, the avoidance of party identification was connected to—and probably increased—sex reform dependence on
physicians who were in fact wedded more to medicalization of birth control
and social hygiene than social revolution. Open affiliation, certainly with the
KPD, would have scared away many physicians whose services had become
crucial to the whole movement, as well as presumably made it more difficult
to acquire the donated samples from manufacturers that the lay leagues willingly used. Finally, it was abundantly clear to most organizers that clients
sought primarily a service and not a political education. The RV and other
lay groups justifiably suspected that an envious KPD wanted to exploit their
access to large numbers of working-class people for its own broader political
ends.

The June congress finally fell apart on the apparently trivial issue of
whether local groups should pay monthly dues of 10, 13, or 15 Pfennig to a
proposed central organization. When delegates agreed on the higher levy,
thereby undermining local jurisdiction and tying the local groups more tightly
to a central office, the RV walked out, leaving behind an impotent rump and
an accusatory EpS. The RV's GESEX (Society for Sexual Reform) faction, however, to which Lehfeldt and many other doctors belonged, continued to press
for unity. Angered by the walkout, the GESEX finally split off from the RV
and joined with a smaller group (Workers Association for Birth Control, AfG)
originally established by the pharmacist and abortionist Paul Heiser in 1925.
Thus the long awaited unity conference not only failed to unify but led to
the breakup of the RV/GESEX, which had been the most organized and
sophisticated of the national groups.

The withdrawal of many doctors and intellectuals in the GESEX, and the
heightened economic and political crisis, pushed the RV to a more uncom-
promisingly radical but still anti-KPD stand. Its revised 1932 RV program was
more explicitly political and anticapitalist than the 1928 version. It asserted
that "as long as" hunger, unemployment, inadequate housing, and abortions
forced by economic need turned hapless proletarians into "despondent" victims, birth control and sex counseling was necessary to alleviate "the present
times of almost unbearable misery and economic hardships" and to prevent
the birth of children "doomed to a life of hunger, misery and disease."[43] As
the contingent formulation, "as long as," suggested, a real cure would of course
require fashioning a vaguely envisioned new society where birth control and
incentives for motherhood would once again make women's natural calling
both a happy personal experience and a social contribution. Arguably, this
lack of political clarity in sex reform about the proper place of either socialism or eugenics, reform or revolution, as well as constant pressure from the
KPD, contributed to an intense sectarianism in which the drive for the currently "correct line" sabotaged effective organizing.

The formation of the EpS signaled that having won its immediate battle
for the release of Wolf and Kienle, and having lost the effort to control the

lay movement, the KPD was extending the strategy that had led it to withdraw from the SPD-dominated trade unions and establish its own Revolutionary Trade Union Opposition (*Revolutionäre Gewerkschaftsopposition*, RGO) to
the sex reform movement: it withdrew from the mass base of the movement—
one that it had helped to mobilize during the anti-218 campaign—and created
its own separate opposition organization.[44] ARSO proceeded to build a small
EpS group based in Düsseldorf into a national organization responsible for
carrying out mass protests against paragraph 218, the double standard, and
the "sexual disenfranchisement of the poor."[45] The KPD was determined to
politicize the movement even if it meant splitting it. Hopes for a mass unified
sex reform movement that would continue to push for abolition of paragraph
218 fell victim to the ever-increasing polarization between SPD and KPD.
Indeed, the 1931 anti-218 struggle may have marked the last time that Communists and Social Democrats publicly agitated together on the same platform.

Yet, this dire picture of division and disunity is not the whole story. At
almost the last minute in late 1931 and 1932, the sex reform movement's commitment to self-help also fostered new initiatives. Precisely the "apolitical"
service aspect of sex reform, so vehemently criticized by the KPD, accounted
for its broad appeal and enabled it somewhat to circumvent the political divisions ripping apart the working-class movement. Despite the failure of the
June conference, lay groups continued to grow until the very end of the
Weimar Republic; indeed the very success of those activities fortified the RV's
insistence on autonomy and ironically contributed to the June "fiasco."

On the local level, there was also more cooperation and overlap than
the rifts among leaders might suggest. Moreover, doctors and intellectuals
who belonged to or were close to the KPD continued to work in a variety
of social medicine and sex reform areas. For example, starting in April 1931,
Dr. Max Hodann, head of the German-Soviet Friendship Society and often
identified with the KPD, contributed a regular advice column to the RV's
*SH*. The multiple connections among sex reform physicians of differing
political persuasions were particularly striking at a time of overt and fierce
KPD and SPD hostility.

As noted before, the circle of doctors willing to fight for birth control and
abortion reform was so small that common background and professional training as well as mutual respect and commitment to the cause often overrode
factional differences. This tolerance, as the June conference showed, did not
generally extend to lay functionaries. Cross-party solidarity among doctors
raises interesting questions about the privileged position of professionals and
intellectuals, particularly doctors, within the working-class and sex reform
movement, and about the relationship between professional and political
identification. In late 1931, the staunchly Social Democratic Dr. Elkan from
the Hamburg RV, wrote to an English birth control activist about his comradeship with the more radical Hodann:

If this economical crisis continues, we will surely get a revolution and a national socialist government. That means: back into the Middle Ages and death, prison and fire for everybody with our ideas. My only help in these black days is Max Hodann who really is a good and able companion. The doctors here all already hide in their holes for fear of being made responsible as "population traitors" or how they will call us. (sic)[46]

Given that working-class members of sex reform leagues were themselves most interested in access to birth control information and products, regional variations depending on local leadership and alliances may have been at least as important as ideological lines in determining organizational success. EpS organized most successfully in the industrial Ruhr; the RV in the eastern provinces of Saxony and Thuringia as well as Hamburg and Bremen; other smaller groups flourished in Kassel and Hanover; Berlin, as we have seen, was well served by a wide variety of clinics and groups. And despite its self-presentation as the genuinely proletarian revolutionary vanguard of sex reform, EpS demands for public provision and medical supervision of abortion, contraception, and sex counseling, and for extensive maternal and infant benefits, differed little from the RV and WLSR programs. They all relied on the Soviet model, and struggled to reconcile a radical vision of transformed social and sexual relations with an immediate mission to provide practical aid.[47]

The EpS long-range program did, however, engage issues that other lay and medical groups had avoided. Its cover styled like a movie poster—a blond woman gazes lovingly at the strong male worker towering over her—*Liebe Verboten (Forbidden Love)*, the 1931 EpS manifesto, expressly and unabashedly supported "sexual desire" as "one of the few pleasures left to these oppressed people."[48] Written by activists in Düsseldorf and published in Berlin, its sex political program was indeed more far-reaching than any previously offered by lay or KPD groups: the persecution of pimps, not prostitutes; the abolition of "bourgeois" marriage and divorce laws; a halt to punishment for sexual deviations; amnesty and psychiatric care for sexual criminals; sex education in science courses and in the popular media; sexual science training for medical students; support for collective childrearing; research on prevention of sexual neuroses and dysfunction; and, finally, free treatment for sexual disturbances caused by capitalism and the bourgeois family![49]

*Forbidden Love* angrily argued, as Wilhelm Reich had done at the Vienna WLSR Congress in 1930, that social conditions reduced working-class sexuality to a sexual misery (*Sexualnot*) defined not only—as most sex reformers posited—by inadequate sex education, birth control, privacy, sanitation, and leisure, but also by ideological socialization for sexual repression in the service of "bourgeois monogamy." According to the EpS analysis, women in particular suffered in the "desolate graveyard of human happiness, a jail filled with mutual deceit and bitterness," which was "lifelong monogamy."[50]

Thus, the continuing devastation of the welfare state in late 1931 and 1932 and the failure to achieve a popular front of sex reform organizations provided KPD-sponsored groups with a space in which they began to articulate a more radical, but also more isolated, sexual politics. EpS and ARSO propaganda mercilessly denounced the cynicism and hypocrisy that characterized late Weimar's "sickbed of democracy":[51] millions were made available for the army and police, while social services were drastically reduced to little more than the symbolic porcelain cup with which the Prussian government rewarded the birth of a twelfth child, provided that the other eleven were still alive![52] Such critiques of course were linked to glorification of the Soviet Union as the "only" nation to have begun to "solve the sexual problem."[53]

As in the struggles for the establishment of birth control and sex counseling clinics in the 1920s, the KPD's agenda for politicization of lay sex reform, its attacks on "profiteering" and calls for state control of the contraceptive industry, dovetailed curiously well with physicians' campaigns for medicalization. By demanding state financing and supervision of birth control even from the existing bourgeois state, by attacking other lay organizations as both insufficiently political and dangerously unscientific, and by insisting on medical control of its own EpS-run clinics, the KPD signaled once again the extraordinary faith in both science and the state exhibited by progressives in the period between the wars.

## EpS and Sex Counseling

The EpS counseling centers that opened in Cologne and Düsseldorf in 1931 expressly advertised that they would admit no homeopaths or nonacademically trained doctors as consultants. They promised to provide a medically vetted contraceptive—guaranteed harmless—that was best suited to women's individual needs. Still, the 1931 EpS "Winter Work Schedule" was directed at lay female cadre and focused more on class politics than health or eugenics. Rather different than comparable RV or *Liga* programs, it announced courses on "Means and Methods of Contraception," "Sexual Oppression in the Capitalist Economic System," "The Woman in the Soviet Union," "Why Coercive Childbearing?" and "An Introduction to the Laws of Capitalist Economic Policy."[54]

It is, of course, unclear how much political education was absorbed by women who came to clinics for practical aid. However, unlike patients in RV or health insurance centers who were often drawn from the surrounding neighborhood, most EpS clients were probably already members of, or closely connected to, the party mass organizations.[55] In any case, the EpS centers did not have the facilities, and certainly not the medical personnel, to serve masses of women. Despite the assurance of expert medical attention, the EpS center in Düsseldorf relied on a rotating staff of volunteer physicians, while party members' wives provided the regular counseling.[56]

The alternative services provided by an EpS or RV center became more and more crucial as established social welfare offices increasingly became the "besieged outposts" of a beleaguered welfare structure that could not cope with the force of the crisis. Indeed, the EpS office on Düsseldorf's Immermann Strasse was located in the same street as the city's totally overwhelmed and overcrowded welfare office, where social workers could barely "prevent riots breaking out" and one official reported having to "jump out of the window onto the street" in order to escape the crush of desperate clients.[57]

With over 4.5 million officially counted unemployed, equaling "33.7 percent of trade union members, or almost 22 percent of the registered work force,"[58] and over half a million young people unemployed by the summer of 1931,[59] it is no surprise that authorities monitoring the EpS in the industrial Ruhr resignedly concluded that, "Considering the bad economic situation of the working population, we must expect an increase in membership."[60] In January 1932, with the unemployment count soaring over six million, the police counted 32 local groups with 3,850 members. By April 15, there were already 6,010.[61]

The EpS journal *Die Warte* (*The Look-out: The voice of struggle in the fight for proletarian sexual reform and protection of mothers*) was published in Düsseldorf for one year, from January 1932 to January 1933. Modeled on the RV journal *Sexual-Hygiene*, but much less polished (for example, it used old-style German print rather than the clean Bauhaus-style font favored by the *SH*), *Die Warte* presented experts' advice on sexual technique and contraception, as well as standard cautionary tales of suicides, infanticides, and deaths caused by unwanted pregnancies and quack abortions—all in predictable contrast to conditions in the Soviet paradise ("The Healthiest Country in the World").

But a report on the future of "Love in the Third Reich" was unusual in its explicit warnings about Nazi racial hygiene and sexual repression. *Die Warte* offered a dark vision of the National Socialist future, forecasting not only "monstrous pressure for coercive child bearing" but also total "police surveillance" of "people's love-life." Moreover, "everybody who wants to get married, will first have to go to a marriage counseling center to secure a marriage permit—which will only be granted if he fulfills all the Nazis' requirements with regard to racial purity etc," and, "given rumors that even gratification of sexual desire cannot be allowed for everybody, . . . all those who have intercourse without the permission of the counseling centers will be prosecuted and put in jail."[62]

At the same time, *Die Warte* continued EpS assaults on non-Communist sex reform organizations. Echoing the overheated rhetoric of KPD attacks on the "social fascist" SPD, it accused the rival lay journal *Weckruf* of "insulting" Berlin youth as "immoral" for "necking in the hallways," instead of assailing the "sexual misery" that forced young women and men "to satisfy their sexual needs in hallways and basements" and the "massive unemployment" that drove proletarians "who have no home and are tormented by hunger" to "sell their bodies for a piece of bread and margarine." Accompanying the warnings about National Socialism were equally dramatic accusations that "wretched reactionary" Social Democratic leaders were responsible for turning a lay group, supposedly "working for birth control and sexual hygiene," into a "handmaiden of fascism."[63]

On a more pragmatic note, a section entitled "From the Counseling Centers" offered sex advice seasoned with political education. In one sample case history, similar to the scenarios in Max Hodann's advice manuals, a young male worker comes to the center with an apparently straightforward question about the efficacy of contraceptive sponges and emerges with a rather complete sexual and political education. He is advised that sponges are not reliable and that his girlfriend should use a diaphragm with spermicide, but he is also questioned about the quality of their sex life and her absence at the session. The 24-year-old confesses that his seamstress girlfriend would never dare approach a doctor with such questions, and that their erotic life was limited to anxious encounters once a month in a borrowed room; furthermore, his girlfriend lies quietly, while he "comes on" very fast. The doctor insists that the young woman come speak for herself, and a quick course of sex therapy is initiated; along with useful birth control tips, the couple learns that both partners must make movements toward each other during intercourse, that the girl must spread her legs, and that there is nothing shameful about moaning and otherwise openly expressing sexual arousal.

That the young woman might be anxious and unsure about the relationship itself, or whether she wanted to have intercourse, a question often raised by women doctors in counseling centers, was not even considered. Her "frigidity" was attributed to "nervous fear" of pregnancy and contraception, the misguided "petty bourgeois morality" of her factory-worker father who refused to allow the young couple to make love in his home, and the unemployment and housing shortages caused by capitalism. Yet, even if a full resolution to proletarian "sexual misery" had to await the overthrow of capitalism, a medical model of sexuality in which a certain kind and frequency of sexual contact was considered "healthy" could offer intermediate relief. Emboldened by their counseling sessions, the couple finds better quarters for more regular lovemaking; within two weeks, readers were told, the young woman's condition greatly improved.[64]

In a sentimental short story in the same issue of *Die Warte*, "healthy" but besieged working-class sexuality confronted bourgeois hypocrisy. Minna, the maid, is discovered *in flagrante* by her employers and promptly dismissed; she summons her best Berlin dialect to fire back, "I don't have no money for rooms by the hour, like your Fräulein and her fancy lawyer." Her upright class-conscious lover spirits her away to the welcoming home of comrades who can provide no new job but understand "that two young healthy people need to make love sometimes, because proletarians aren't pigs who always think nature isn't natural when they aren't doing it themselves."[65] In this left-wing

version of medicalized discourses about sexuality, sex was a natural and normal—healthy—need while repression was unnatural, perverse, and perhaps
worst of all, "petty-bourgeois." Health, if not next to godliness, was certainly
next to class consciousness!

### EpS, Wilhelm Reich, and the Myth of Sexpol

Clearly, the EpS program and rhetoric reflected the radical sex-political ideas
that have come to be identified with Wilhelm Reich. Indeed, especially in his
book *People in Trouble*, Reich later claimed credit for EpS activities and the
program published in *Forbidden Love*.[66] It is therefore necessary at this point
to interject a brief critical discussion of Reich's actual historical role—as best
as it can be reconstructed—in EpS, in KPD population and sexual politics, and
in the sex reform movement as a whole. This *Exkurs* is all the more necessary, because the myth of *Sexpol* and Weimar sexual radicalism was trans-
ported into the collective consciousness of the 1960s student movement from
Paris to Berlin to New York to Berkeley. New left notions of sexual radicalism—many of them so thoroughly questioned by the subsequent feminist and
gay liberation movements that they themselves now appear antiquarian—
were powerfully influenced by Reich's copious and often self-serving writings.

Not only Reich's loyal followers but also scholars who have researched
his life and work have tended to take on faith his version of a movement called
*Sexpol*. They present Reich—as he presented himself—as a lonely pioneer
in an inhospitable German Communist party, the champion of a united front
of sexual reform groups (whose membership he estimated at 350,000) at a time
when no one else was interested in unity, and as the sole author of the Communist sex political platform adopted by EpS in Düsseldorf (and proposed at
the June "unity" conference).[67] Yet, in this detailed discussion of the German
sex reform movement and its relationship to the KPD, there has been remarkably little mention of Reich, and nothing to substantiate his grandiose claims
of leadership in the EpS. Party sources, which might be suspected of having
minimized his role, barely mention him, but neither do police documents that
reflect careful monitoring of sex reform activities, particularly as they intersected with the KPD, and would have had no reason to ignore him. He was
not reported as active in any of the myriad events connected to the Wolf/
Kienle campaign in 1931, extremely well documented though it was by officials and the media.

Surviving copies of the journal published by the organization that Reich
claimed to have established never mention him, and he never seems to have
mentioned *Die Warte*. Surviving sex reform activists interviewed for this study
also minimized or disparaged his role, stressing the much greater importance
and visibility of a Max Hodann, Kurt Bendix, or Martha Ruben-Wolf. He was
remembered as a psychoanalyst rather than a political figure,[68] or as a diffi-

cult, argumentative, "crazy" colleague.[69] Max Hodann especially was much better known and beloved among socialist, anarchist, and Communist youth groups for his lectures and popular sex education pamphlets, which provided a carefully mixed diet of political propaganda, basic physiology and biology instruction, and birth control and sex advice.[70]

This is not to deny that Reich had an important theoretical influence on at least some members of the sex reform movement. The pamphlets he helped to publish, particularly his wife Annie Reich's *Das Kreidedreieck* (*The Chalk Triangle*),[71] which discussed in story form the sexual education and miseducation of children, and his *Sexual Struggle of Youth*, defending young people's right to sexual expression, did exercise a certain influence, particularly in the Communist youth movement (*Kommunistischer Jugend Verband Deutschlands*, KJVD).[72] Reich was also a radical voice at some sex reform gatherings, particularly the WLSR Congress in Vienna in 1930.[73] Reich's practical impact was most visible in Berlin, where he offered birth control and sex advice to adolescents at the EpS clinic, and lectured on the politics of sexuality at the Marxist Evening School (*Marxistische Arbeiter Schulung* MASCH).[74] Unlike more activist comrades, Reich produced serious theoretical work on sexuality. He may have been more far-seeing on the importance of winning over youth and the seriousness of the issues surrounding adolescent sexuality.

There was, however, no organization known as *Sexpol*. EpS functioned as the organizational embodiment of *Sexpol* ideas, and those were not the exclusive property of Wilhelm Reich. The KPD, after all, had an ongoing commitment to sex reform that dated back to prewar debates on abortion and birth control within the SPD. Early KPD platforms consistently called for the abolition of paragraph 218. Sex reform ideas attained organizational form in ARSO by 1928, and were expressed most dramatically in the 1931 paragraph 218 campaign. Reich's claim that, "Until that time [EpS] the Communist party had had no organizations for sexual reform, and also had taken no stand on sex-politics, except toward Soviet legislation," is, as has been amply shown, a considerable distortion.[75]

Indeed, it seems likely that Reich moved to Berlin from Vienna in 1930, not only because, as he noted, the psychoanalytic community there was more hospitable to Marxism, and further removed from Freud's dominating presence, but because the city already offered a network of health and sex reform activists, both within and without the KPD. Far from initiating workers' sexual counseling centers, Reich participated, albeit not without controversy, in an ongoing project. By 1931, when he opened an EpS counseling center, the workers' sexual counseling centers, which he had started as an experiment in Vienna, were already, as we have seen, an institutionalized reality in Berlin, sponsored by municipal and health insurance authorities and the *Bund für Mutterschutz* (BfM).[76] As Reich himself acknowledged, "Berlin now offered me splendid opportunities."[77]

Reich's EpS clinic did substantially differ from other Berlin birth control and sex counseling centers in its open support for the "sexual struggle of youth," its use of psychoanalytic language, and its willingness to train working-class youth in peer-counseling techniques. Reich insisted on handling all questions about abortion and venereal disease as well as fittings for diaphragms, but consistent with the EpS's dual commitment to medical control and sexual radicalism, young volunteer workers were free to advise clients about birth control and sexual anxieties, handing out "mountains" of free condoms and vaginal jellies. Like Max Hodann and other left-wing sex reformers who prided themselves on their "rational" and "matter-of-fact" sex-enlightenment work with adolescents, Reich was preoccupied with simultaneously reducing guilt about masturbation and seeking to explain it as an unfortunate effect of sexual repression. Ernst Bornemann, who worked in the clinic Tuesday and Thursday afternoons, remembered reassuring clients that everyone, including Wilhelm Reich himself, had masturbated in their youth. It was nothing to worry about provided it did not substitute for "normal" sexual relations and lead to disappointment in the "real thing" which, even at a relatively young age, was "healthier" than masturbation or homosexual relations: "Whoever makes a habit of masturbation, he used to say, will also expect his dinner to be handed to him on a silver platter."[78]

Hodann, while more cautious about adolescent sexual activity, also urged the young people who came to his lectures and read his pamphlets to "overcome the habit as fast as possible."[79] For both men, intervention by a tolerant and omniscient medical authority was crucial; as Bornemann recalled: "True, we had fewer problems with our sexuality than the bourgeois children, but still there were questions which only a doctor could answer."[80] Despite some unorthodox practices, on the issue of medical supervision, Reich was more in tune with, than in rebellion against, the mainstream of Communist and left-wing sexual reform. Even in the most radical outpost of the organized sex reform movement, physicians and party leaders alike were intent on bringing sex reform under direct medical supervision in established clinics.

It is only in retrospect, when we had lost the history of the entire sex reform movement, yet maintained access to the writings of Wilhelm Reich, that he appeared as such a singular and radical figure; in fact, he was one part of a large movement. His allegiance to Freudianism was unusual in a movement more attracted to the immediate social relevance of Adler's "Individual Psychology,"[81] and it earned him the suspicion of both Communists and sex reformers. But Reich's actual clinic practice was not so different from other centers throughout Berlin. If anything, Reich's description in *People in Trouble* of women who came to him for abortions was harsher than the eugenics and social health discourse used by sex reformers and certainly more derogatory than the maternalist vocabulary of most women clinic doctors. Patients "who had become pregnant through clumsiness or ignorance" were referred to "the city birth control clinics," but not before "we ourselves instructed them in the use of contraception and in physiological function of the genital embrace." Reich confidently stated that:

> Among them there was not a single case where advocating a continuation of pregnancy would not have been inhumane, unethical, base and cowardly. Literally, *not one* of these women and girls should have been *allowed* [his italics] to bring a child into the world . . . even if material provisions were made, and for some women they were at hand, these women . . . simply should not have children. These mothers and women and girls, were able to bear a child but incapable of rearing it, caring for it, or keeping it alive. All of them . . . were seriously neurotic and had a very poor relationship with their husbands, if any relationship at all. They were frigid, careworn, covertly sadistic or overtly masochistic . . . latent schizophrenics, or morbid depressives, vain little women, or wretched, disinterested work animals.[82]

Such views led him to assert, without apology, "the unquestionable right of every woman to have an abortion, with or without all the various indications. . . . I knew exactly what I was doing and considered it a matter of course to assume the risk."[83]

## Youth Counsels Youth

The sexual rights and problems of youth had long been a major focus of anarchist youth groups. In late Weimar, despite much antagonism, they strongly influenced the Communist and sections of the Social Democratic youth movements as well as leftist social workers and educational reformers. In group meetings and counseling sessions, youth of both sexes expressed their worries about masturbation, venereal disease, birth control, and satisfying themselves and their partners. Right-wing and church groups considered such adolescent sexual activity a sign of "decadence," encouraged by the "free-love" and pro-abortion propaganda of the left and working-class press.[84] They conjured up frightful images of the Soviet *Besprisony*, the wild youth who roamed revolutionary Russia, deserted by their parents in the wake of war, revolution, and a reformed family code that facilitated divorce and fathers' evasion of family responsibility.[85] Leftist reformers also professed disapproval of sexual licentiousness, but in different terms (on which they hardly agreed). Far from seeing in organized youth groups a haven for immorality, they welcomed their emphasis on physical fitness and "comradely" relations between the sexes as an antidote to the "wild cliques" of unorganized urban youth culture and the turmoil of adolescence.[86]

The official KPD position was, of course, influenced by Lenin's famous conversation with Clara Zetkin in which he urged her to use the maternal influence of the women's movement to assure that Communist youth spent their time swimming, hiking, and doing gymnastics rather than expending energy discussing or engaging in sex.[87] Lenin surely would have included Wilhelm Reich in his critique of sex-political organizing among women and youth as a fad being pushed by bourgeois party intellectuals trying to justify their own "overheated sexuality."[88] By the early 1930s, however, sex reformers in, or close to, the KPD were stretching the definitions of healthy and natural to include adolescent sexual activity among adolescents as preferable to masturbation or initiation by prostitutes, and indeed as useful for building satisfying companionate adult relationships.[89] In terms not so different from those espoused by Lenin, even Reich, the supposed apostle of sexual radicalism, contended that a liberated orgasmic (genital, heterosexual) sexuality would create a better socialized and disciplined human being and comrade.[90] In the radical sex reform discourse, sexual satisfaction promised not only to produce a better, more stable, and disciplined worker and family member but also a better comrade.

The institutionalization of the concept "youth counsels youth," which suggested that, like women, young people might be best served by discussing sexual problems with understanding peers, was lent urgency by a widely reported scandal purportedly highlighting the dangers of repressed adolescent sexuality. In the notorious 1929 "Krantz case" (or "Steglitz Pupils' Tragedy") a middle-class girl, her boyfriend, her brother, and his lower-class friend Paul Krantz were involved in a drunken shoot-out during which the girl's brother shot her boyfriend and himself with Krantz's revolver (an accoutrement of his membership in a right-wing youth group). Star defense attorney Erich Frey took on the sensational case and succeeded in acquitting Krantz, who was then, with much fanfare, hustled off to the progressive Odenwald boarding school, where he did indeed reform, both politically and psychologically, and eventually developed into a minor literary figure.[91]

However, in some cases, the "help" in the "sexual struggle" offered by radical youth groups had not come without a price. At least one member of the youth movement, that had received free contraceptives and abortions from the pharmacist and lay league leader Paul Heiser reported that the prosecution may have been correct in accusing Heiser of "erotic" motives in the 1927 trial for illegal abortions performed in his Beauty Institute Mutabor in Berlin. The young activist remembered that Heiser tried to rape a young woman from the provinces who had sought help at an anarchist youth club in eastern Berlin, and then botched the abortion so badly that a physician had to be called in the middle of the night to finish the job.[92]

The Krantz affair moved sex reformers like Helene Stöcker, Magnus Hirschfeld, and Max Hodann to support the establishment in 1929 of a pioneering youth center that operated three afternoons a week out of the law office of Alfred Apfel (who would defend Else Kienle during the paragraph 218 trial) and Kurt Beck.[93] Max Fürst, one of the young therapists, lived with his (initially 14-year-old) girlfriend in a commune in the Scheunenviertel, the old ghetto in eastern Berlin where Eastern European Jews lived side by side with gypsies, pimps and prostitutes, petty criminals, and leftist refugees from bourgeois respectability. In a wonderful memoir, he described his struggle to understand that even he as a rebel needed to learn "not to be surprised at anything" and "not to judge but to help." The most common question young women asked was, "How can I sleep with my boyfriend and not have a baby right away?"[94] Abortions, Fürst insisted, were not hard to procure, despite the fear of informers:

> The problem was not the physicians, nor even money. There were enough doctors who were willing to help, confident they could earn enough in their private practices to be able to work for our friends for free. A letter from me or a call were all that was needed.[95]

The lay therapists—all required to be 25 or younger—provided concrete aid: shelter for runaways, advice on family and job problems, and arrangements for abortions. They offered a sympathetic ear to their clientele of young workers and apprentices, and determined whether or not professional help was indicated. In emergencies, they sometimes took homeless runaways or those in flight from the authorities into their own homes. Contemptuous of the official municipal youth services, these counselors nonetheless relied on the help of sex reformers like Hodann who were ensconced in the municipal social welfare system, or activists like Stöcker who ran homes for unwed mothers and abused girls. Their activities, many of them illegal, depended on the existence of an extensive and developed support network that included doctors, lawyers, social workers, psychologists, and psychiatrists willing to provide free space, money, expert counsel, and services.

Acting independently of official agencies (regardless of whether they also worked in them), adult sex reformers respected, if not without skepticism, the aggressively independent culture of the Weimar youth movement, which valorized the newly defined generation gap and insisted that young people could trust only their "age-comrades" and certainly not any state or church institution. Youth centers run by the IAH, EpS, BfM, and ARSO consciously avoided representing police or social welfare authority; indeed, counselors made a point of serving as advocates, running interference with officialdom for their clients, accompanying them to agencies, helping fill out necessary forms, and interceding with parents, employers, teachers, and caseworkers. Nevertheless, inspired by their adult collaborators and painfully aware of the short-term, palliative nature of their own work, some lay counselors went on to train as professional psychologists and social workers; most of them eventually emigrated.[96]

By the time Reich opened his EpS clinic in 1931, both the IAH and the *Bund für Mutterschutz* were offering youth counseling services in Berlin. The BfM reported that 667 youngsters (419 male and 248 female) had come for help in 1929; a year later, 987 (624 male and 363 female) young workers and ap-

prentices had come for advice on a wide range of problems, including teenage pregnancy, applications for child support, sex counseling and birth control,
negotiations with guardians and child welfare authorities, and most frequently, the search for employment and housing.[97] The IAH offered youth
counseling one day a week for two hours each at several Berlin locations, in
addition to its birth control clinic in Neukölln. ARSO maintained five offices
that offered guidance in navigating the maze of social service bureaucracy.
The alternative Red Welfare Service (*Rote Wohlfahrt*) had 20 outlets which
handled roughly 25 cases daily. Such offices primarily served party members
and their families, or members of the KPD's mass organizations; they very
clearly constituted a fringe benefit of party affiliation.[98]

Sex, legal, and welfare advice clinics helped clients to avoid moralizing religious charities and to maintain autonomy while taking fullest advantage of
services still offered by the Social Democratic and Communist-dominated
municipal government. They not only helped members organize welfare and
unemployment claims but also provided guidance on handling party responsibilities, particularly how to achieve the proper balance between personal
desire and party discipline. At the IAH's Proletarian Youth and Education
Counseling Center, young people were advised on "proper proletarian behavior," so that unresolved sexual and emotional difficulties (such as jealousy)
would not thwart the development of sturdy and committed comrades.[99]
Activists like Hodann complemented the centers' work with special lecture
series directed toward youth; Hodann, Friedrich Wolf, and Magnus
Hirschfeld's Institute for Sexual Science also ran sessions in which written
questions about sexuality and reproduction would be anonymously answered.
These encounters then formed the basis for advice manuals such as Hodann's
*Geschlecht und Liebe* (*Sex and Love*).[100]

Even with a backup network of sympathetic professionals, such centers,
with their limited hours and personnel, could not match the comprehensive
services provided by municipal and state agencies, even under the duress of
economic crisis. Rather, they served a dual political function: like all alternative service institutions, they simultaneously provided that which the state
was unable or unwilling to provide—such as abortion referrals—and also, by
the very limited scope of what they could offer, demonstrated the urgency
of demanding such services from the state. Located in offices or storefronts
of other organizations and open only a few hours a week, such "counseling
centers," deserved their title perhaps more in emblematic than concrete terms.
They served as consciousness-raising tools that could denounce present conditions and present a glimpse of a revolutionized future. The left press, in particular, promoted the centers as symbols of the movement's ability to provide real services for its adherents. But the practical benefits they offered
young clients were especially crucial as the depression deepened and more
and more unemployed workers and their families lost access to insurance
benefits.

## The End of Weimar and the Final Months of Sex Reform

Wilhelm Reich's retrospective critique of the lay sex reform movement was completely in accord with KPD or RV analyses. His analysis of the failed if frantic unity efforts of the final Weimar years was also substantially on target, although he never acknowledged his own participation in those splits. He conceded the "self-sacrificing efforts of people like Helene Stöcker" in building "a network of birth control centers" and defending "those accused in abortion trials." He lamented that the movement "did not reach even a tenth of the population," that the information provided was "often incorrect and overburdened with questions of eugenics and population politics," and that, "The dealers, who infiltrated the groups and made their profits from the demand for contraceptives, constituted one of the greatest evils."[101] In an interesting reflection on the true "service" of the lay leagues, he noted: "They tried to protect marriage more than did the bourgeoisie themselves."[102]

The tension between providing immediate necessary services and positing a radicalized vision of the future, between offering first aid and making impossible demands, always marked the work of the KPD and its affiliated groups. Radical sex reformers recognized, and were intensely frustrated by, the limitations of their practical work and their relatively small constituency. In Reich's words, "The people simply wanted practical advice and help with their marital and childraising problems, their sexual disturbances and their moral pangs of conscience."[103] But time was running out for the reformers of the Weimar Republic. In the face of intense economic and political crisis, leftist social welfare groups were too pressed to work out political questions or develop and expand their pioneering institutions. As Reich explained years later:

> But the rush of demands was overpowering and there was simply no time for quiet, thorough work. Meanwhile, the nervousness of the untrained functionaries increased with the growing strength of the movement. . . . The movement for a unified group became deadlocked in discussions on fundamental politics and organization. In addition to this, the police began to intervene.[104]

In the last stages of the Weimar Republic, neither KPD nor SPD nor the working-class movement in general were able to defend existing social welfare services, much less successfully press for new ones or fully develop radical sexual politics. The third and last Congress of Working Women met in Berlin in the spring of 1932 after several postponements, under the banner "Against Hunger, Fascism, War." By this time, the recruiting successes the KPD had scored among women during and just after the anti-218 campaign had faded again.[105]

As the sex reform movement split after the failure of unification efforts, KPD sex-political, social welfare, and women's organizations were reduced to documenting and minimally alleviating the devastation of economic crisis and the emergency decrees that only exacerbated its impact. No matter how inadequate, how reformist, how heavily criticized, the social service programs initiated by Social Democracy had at least provided a structure within which to organize for further reform; now they were on the verge of extinction. And in terms of the KPD's self-understanding, to offer the working class diaphragms rather than revolutionary activity represented a kind of political failure. By May 1932, with the Brüning regime close to collapse, the police were breaking up and closing down EpS meetings while other lay groups were attempting a last stab at unification.[106]

The summer of 1932 was punctuated by the July 20 coup that deposed the SPD–Center coalition that had ruled Germany's most important province and installed von Papen as *Reichskommissar* for Prussia. For the sex reform movement, the last months of the Weimar Republic brought feverish activity; for many young activists it was even an exhilarating and intense period when they saw themselves constructing in microcosm a brave new world of social and sexual liberation. It was also a time of continuing and disastrous polarization between the SPD and the KPD. Nevertheless, that final summer, fall, and winter witnessed renewed attempts at establishing a unified sex reform movement, notably overtures toward reconciliation between the EpS, the IAH, *Liga*, and RV.[107] In January 1932 the RV and the *Liga* had again joined medical sex reformers in a Central Working Group for Birth Control.[108] In March, the GESEX and AfG rejoined an enlarged RV based in Berlin-Brandenburg.[109] In August, the ARSO journal acknowledged with a bit of rueful surprise: "We have here in Germany a broad, population-political movement which up to now we have underestimated."[110]

EpS chapters in the Ruhr, where the organization had originated, also continued to grow. A regional conference in Essen, in April 1932, reported 32 locals with a membership of 3,850 by the end of January 1932 and an increase to 6,010 members by mid-April.[111] In May, Berlin police disrupted a so-called "Unity Congress of the Sex Leagues" that featured Martha Ruben-Wolf as the main speaker and attracted approximately 100 participants, many of them women party or mass organization members.[112] A few days later, EpS and IAH representatives met in Berlin to negotiate further with the *Liga* and several smaller lay leagues; again the large proportion of women present (25 of 80) struck the police reporter.[113]

As the KPD persisted in seeking influence in the larger sex reform movement, it also debated the question of sexual politics within its own ranks. Reich's theoretical impact was perhaps slowly being felt. In late 1932 and early 1933, he participated in a well-attended series of debates on "The Sexual Question in Bourgeois Society." His opponent was the young Marxist Adlerian psychologist Manes Sperber. The meetings were held on December 8, January 11, and January 18, 1933, just days before Adolf Hitler became chancellor.

They were sponsored by AMSO, the ARSO subgroup for social workers and psychologists, and drew considerable audiences of students and professionals.

Both Reich and Sperber spoke as mental health professionals confronting the relationship between Marxism and Freudianism. Each was determined to prove himself the better and more correct Marxist, but they vehemently disagreed on whether psychoanalysis could significantly enrich Marxist theory and practice. Reich argued affirmatively; Sperber, in accord with Adler's view that sexual problems were social in origin, disputed the Freudians' emphasis on individual etiology and general overemphasis on sexuality.[114] Sperber later recalled his arguments with Reich before the open meetings:

> In the end I said, "Willi [Reich], if you wish to politicize sexuality, go right ahead. Whatever this may mean, it cannot hurt our struggle, it can only help. If, however, you intend to sexualize politics, you are making a dual mistake, a psychological and a political one."[115]

Many meetings held by sex reformers toward the very end of the republic concerned remarkably innocuous topics—the police monitored Dr. Käte Frankenthal lecturing on infantile paralysis to 11 men and 20 women at a *Liga* meeting in October 1932,[116] and on January 19, 1933, Dr. Annie Reich spoke at a Berlin EpS gathering on "How to Avoid VD."[117] Organizers were clearly preoccupied not only with building cooperation among the various groups but with avoiding police repression. When the *Liga* planned its lecture series to also include talks on "families in crisis" by an RV member, on "the double standard and its consequences" by Dr. Leo Klauber of the KPD Proletarian Health Service, and on gymnastics by nudist colony director Adolf Koch, it defensively pleaded with the police for guidelines because, "We wish to avoid under all circumstances that the evening has to be broken up."[118] *Liga* concern was well founded: as of October 31, 1932, the police closed Koch's "Body School" at the urging of National Socialists and right-wing nationalists who claimed it allowed "hundreds to satisfy their sexual lust."[119]

The exclusively medical birth control committees, on the other hand, seem to have retreated from public activity already in the spring of 1932. In a letter to one-time benefactor Margaret Sanger, Kate Stützin—organizer of the Center for Birth Control, which had brought together physician sex reformers of varying political stripes—reported that the lack of funds was causing her to shut down her work. She added that she would have to shelve her plans to find a German publisher for Sanger's memoirs: no one was willing to risk publishing the American birth controller's book at this time.[120] Sanger met Stützin's request to continue her already reduced financial support with sympathetic rejections, along with promises to "beg, borrow or steal funds," as soon as her husband's finances stabilized.[121] Nonetheless, the irrepressible Stützin found a silver lining in the crisis: "Circumstances" were "so bad" that "nobody has money to spend for dinner parties! I am sorry about the bad situation but not sorry about the lack of dinner parties!"[122]

A sex reform movement that united doctors, intellectuals, and working-class lay members began to develop by 1928; its greatest popular success coincided with the height of the depression in 1931 and 1932. The Weimar era in general, and the four years from 1928 to 1933 in particular, were a painfully brief period of momentum and experimentation, abruptly and brutally cut off by the National Socialist seizure of power. We cannot know how the movement might have developed under more benign historical conditions.

In his 1932 report on the lay movement, Dr. Hans Lehfeldt noted that the three most important lay journals had reached new peaks in circulation: 60,000 for the *Liga*'s *Liebe und Leben*; 30,000 for *Weckruf* (Volksbund für Mutterschutz und Sexualhygiene); and 21,000 for the RV's *Sexual-Hygiene*. Moreover, those figures only reflected part of the huge movement.[123] An article in the *American Journal of Obstetrics and Gynecology* estimated that by 1933 there were about 1,000 counseling centers in Germany, most of them supported by lay organizations and staffed by physicians and "functionaries." The BfM had over 100 affiliated centers: doctors were in charge in Berlin, Frankfurt, and Hamburg; elsewhere, trained social workers did most of the counseling and referring. The *Liga* boasted over 500 birth control outlets, of which only 3 were directed by a physician. The RV had 230 affiliated local groups, each with a birth control center; in Berlin, Hamburg and Nuremberg, they were supervised by doctors.[124] The March 1932 newsletter of the Central Working Group for Birth Control's Information Office, edited by Max Hodann, featured a masthead that included Helene Stöcker, Friedrich Wolf, Rudolf Elkan, and Ernst Gräfenberg. It listed 34 clinics in Berlin offering birth control, plus an extensive list of sympathetic doctors in 81 German towns.[125]

But the growing Nazi presence shadowed the movement. On July 30, ten days after the overthrow of the Prussian Social Democrats, Dr. Rudolf Elkan of the Hamburg RV had dispatched a gloomily prescient letter to a birth control activist in England:

> And if later on you never get any letter from me again you may know that all friends of the birth control movements have been slain or imprisoned by the damned National Socialists. . . . (Don't mind this political remark; times are too bad here today.)[126]

In September 1932, the WLSR held a last congress in Brunn, Czechoslovakia. Magnus Hirschfeld, who had been on a world tour since March 1931 and would never return to Germany, presided one more time over a congress whose agenda covered the usual topics of eugenics, sex education, and sex research. If anything, the themes were less overtly political and sometimes more esoteric: a lecture on the steady increase in male impotence, but also a slide show on sex-change operations. Certainly they lacked the energetic and controversial tone of the Vienna conference. The most controversial moment came when Dr. Elkan questioned whether women had a "right" to orgasm equal to that of men, since orgasm supposedly did not exist in female animals.[127]

Plans were made for the next congress, finally to be held in Moscow. And as if in response to the Elkan controversy in Brunn, in November 1932, the RV journal initiated a survey among its readers on the incidence and experience of frigidity among women. Influenced by Freudian tenets, *SH* identified frigidity as a psychological problem with deep-seated causes; at the same time it reported on sexual techniques to overcome it. A reader identified only as F. responded skeptically: "In my opinion, it is impossible to get a correct view and explanation of frigidity from a man."[128]

The Moscow conference was never held; by then Hirschfeld was in exile, the WLSR was falling apart over political squabbles, and the library of Hirschfeld's Institute for Sexual Science in Berlin, the world headquarters of the sex reform movement, had been burned and sacked by Nazi gangs. The irony of the frustrated and doomed quest for unity among the various sex-political groups was that they had much more in common than they were sometimes willing to admit. The actual practice in an EpS, or an RV, or even a municipal or health insurance center, was not so very different: all distributed contraceptives and offered sex counseling. As someone asked Wilhelm Reich at an EpS meeting in February 1932: "Can you tell me the difference between a Social Democratic and a Communist uterus?"[129] Certainly, the Nazis made no such fine distinctions when they systematically dissolved all sex reform groups and arrested any leaders they could find in the spring of 1933.

# six

# Continuity and Discontinuity
## Gleichschaltung *and the Destruction of the Sex Reform Movement*

If we really get a national socialistic government, help God us [sic] German Jews and German socialists.

DR. RUDOLF ELKAN,
July 30, 1932[1]

The National Socialist triumph in 1933 ended the hopeful and problematical experiment that had been Weimar sex reform. The National Socialists destroyed sex reform leagues, closed birth control clinics, and arrested and forced the emigration of many movement doctors and activists. At the same time they expropriated many of the movement's social health and public hygiene goals in the name of *Volksgesundheit*, placing them in the service of an ultimately genocidal racial hygiene program. As we have seen throughout this study, the language and concepts of eugenics and racial hygiene were deeply rooted in even the most "progressive" Weimar social health and welfare initiatives. Nonetheless, in this chapter I argue that sex reform and social medicine underwent a definitive and irrevocable break in 1933.

If Nazi social health policy in many ways continued the harsh fiscal rationalization and extensive state intervention intermittently imposed during both the stabilization and depression periods, it also represented a profound change: fiscal rationalization was now combined with racial and political purification. The goals of urban social hygiene shifted from the regulation and treatment of the sick, needy, and dependent to the coercive elimination of the "unfit" and mobilization of the "fit." The new emphasis on "blood, race, heredity, selection, family as the germ cell of kin and *Volk*,"[2] together with the massive firing of racially and politically undesirable personnel, had immediate and concrete institutional consequences. Berlin's Treptow district, for example, reported:

In line with the National Socialist spirit, the exaggerated solicitude for the inferior and the asocial was terminated, the facilities for psychopaths and the retarded closed and the further supervision of disturbed children handed over to the responsible school physicians. Marriage and sex counseling, alcoholism treatment, and sports medicine programs as they had been previously organized also contradicted the National Socialist *Weltanschauung* and required fundamental restructuring.[3]

Many of the pioneering and always precarious Weimar innovations in sex and birth control counseling, addiction and alcoholism therapies, venereal disease, tuberculosis and psychiatric treatment, child and youth welfare were destroyed while still in the pilot project stage. They had only been established between 1927 and 1929, as the fiscal discipline of the early stabilization period yielded to extensive social welfare legislation and public works construction. The Berlin-centered experiments in family planning and social medicine had then been dealt heavy but bitterly contested blows with the collapse of the short-lived national Social Democratic coalition government and the imposition of Brüning's rule by emergency decrees in the spring of 1930.

The "zero hour" for sex reform, however, came not with the simultaneously debilitating and radicalizing effects of economic and political crisis but with Nazi *Gleichschaltung*—the smashing of working-class and sex reform organizations in the winter and spring of 1933, and the cumulative effects of anti-Semitic and racial hygiene legislation from 1933 to 1935.[4] The Nazi regime denounced the bold Weimar social welfare experiments, such as the health insurance and municipal clinics, as profligate purveyors of fiscal waste, sexual immorality, and eugenic irresponsibility, which disproportionately benefited the "unfit" and "asocial" at the expense of "worthy" healthy citizens.

The government closed birth control and sexual advice clinics and retooled them as centers for "hereditary and racial welfare" (*Erb-und-Rassenpflege*). It sanctioned coercive sterilization and also began stricter enforcement of restrictions on abortion procedures and birth control advertising, on the books since 1871 but only loosely and irregularly applied during the Weimar years. Physicians associated with birth control and sex reform, especially Jews, Communists, and women (considered particularly susceptible to the desperate pleas of their sisters), were accused and arrested as abortionists. Kate Stützin, director of the Center for Birth Control, penned a handwritten note to her friend and supporter Margaret Sanger on April 21, 1933, which simply stated, "Heaps of things have happened since I have written you. . . . B.C work is not to be done now." Sanger responded in equally stark but naive terms, "I think it best that I do not write her further until conditions are more normal."[5]

## The Destruction of Social Medicine

The impact of the Nazi takeover (*Gleichschaltung*) on health and welfare can be seen clearly on the local level in Berlin. Berlin was surely not typical, but it was exemplary. An international center of sex reform and social medicine, it was the showcase of the Weimar innovations that the Nazis condemned both as degenerate Jewish ventures in cultural Bolshevism and as the false prosperity (*Scheinblüte*) of benefits squandered on the "unworthy." The Nazis rapidly consolidated their control in 1933 through purges of public employees and the elimination of working-class political party dominance in municipal administration.[6]

The April 1933 Law for the Restoration of the Civil Service and a broad range of other restrictive regulations promulgated in the spring of 1933 fundamentally transformed the landscape of medical practice in Germany. Politically suspect, "non-Aryan," and "double-earning" employees were dismissed from the municipal and communal health systems in which they had been so active. They were also denied access to health insurance eligibility and other money-making work such as Sunday and nighttime housecalls, thus cutting off a major source of their livelihood. A whole generation of established and highly qualified physicians was expelled, and the careers of a significant number of women doctors, many of whom had just begun their work, were suddenly cut off.[7]

An extremely high proportion of the physicians working in urban social health services were Jewish and/or on the political left. Well over 50 percent of all municipal hospital doctors and even more in the public clinics were Jewish.[8] In the proletarian "red Wedding" district, 80 percent of the doctors in the children's hospital were Jewish, as were 80 percent of the public welfare doctors, five of the six school physicians, three of the six school dentists, and the directors of the infant and children's, prenatal care, and marriage counseling services.[9] A disproportionate number of those doctors were women who had found congenial employment opportunities in the muncipal and health insurance system. Many of them fell victim to *Gleichschaltung* not only as Jews, socialists, or Communists but also specifically as women, as "double earners" or spouses of Jews, frequently in several of these categories. One central Berlin district reported laconically (and without great enthusiasm for the national renewal) that after the April 1933 decrees:

> The great majority of the medical personnel in the infant and children's services, as well as a school physician, disappeared. Their replacement has proved to be extremely difficult given the shortage of properly trained physicians willing to take over, and this has had a good many ill effects on the fulfillment of our duties. A good number of social workers also had to depart for the same reasons.[10]

On the other hand, the new authorities reported with relief that elimination of the "red" employees had restored peace and quiet to muncipal agencies. No longer did riot police have to respond to agitated crowds in overcrowded waiting rooms, bullhorns trumpeting inflammatory speeches, the sudden singing of the "International," damage to furnishings and files, or insults and physical assaults on staff. Equally important, there was no more "totally inappropriate compassion" from Communist and socialist employees who sometimes appeared to have cast their loyalties with their supplicants rather than with the cost-cutting authorities.[11] Even the physical environment changed as new posters with hereditary health messages were mounted on the walls.

*Gleichschaltung* and Aryanization brought general cutbacks and centralization in personnel and services. In large cities like Berlin the purges decimated hospital and clinic staffs. At the same time, new hereditary health regulations increased demands on smaller staffs but also offered numerous career opportunities for younger "Aryan" doctors anxious to enter the secure world of state-supported insurance and public health practice. Novice physicians, some of them women, found a niche in the gigantic project of certifying marital and procreative fitness and targeting sterilization candidates.

Despite National Socialism's appropriation and embrace of technology and technocrats, much of its rhetoric was devoted to attacking the soulless materialism and leveling anonymity of the bureaucratic welfare state. The destruction of Social Democratic and Communist-dominated clinics and health insurance services was presented as a triumph for the restoration of trust in the doctor-patient relationship and a wholistic, "organic" approach to medicine. Nazi doctors deplored the specialization and the decline of the "art of healing" that had led to a mass-oriented and impersonal social medicine.[12]

The introduction of "free choice of doctors" on November 1, 1933, undermined the power of municipal and insurance health officials and thereby satisfied long-standing grievances against the clinic system held by the conservative majority of the medical profession. The entire network of decentralized local health offices (*Gesundheitsämter*), which had offered such opportunities to KPD and SPD reformers, fell victim to the 1933 purges and the 1934 law on the reorganization of health services. Services were centralized and combined, and local health officials turned into official agents of the state (*Amtsärzte*), more committed to policing than treating.[13] Certainly they no longer were bearers of socialist and Communist political messages, as some doctors and social workers had been during the Weimar years.

The process of "liquidating useless and politically unreliable employees and replacing them with staff above suspicion" was therefore eminently economic as well as ideological, fulfilling multiple and overlapping functions of racial purification, political stabilization, professional elitism, and fiscal rationalization (*Sanierung*).[14] It offered the new authorities a way to restore political order, trim the supposedly bloated budget of an overextended and "abused" welfare state, reduce municipal indebtedness, cut back the total number of employees, and fulfill depression campaign promises to remove married women from public employment, as well as purge "non-Aryans."

According to the Nazis, the error of the Weimar health system had been to provide care, however limited, on the basis of individual need rather than the priorities of the racially defined collective welfare (*Volkskörper*). One district mayor noted:

> Beginning and end of all initiatives in preventive medicine and health care today
> is hereditary and racial welfare, a concept that was treated with suspicion and
> enmity by the previous Marxist administration. Certainly the red authorities
> (*rote Herrschaft*) practiced social hygiene and preventive medicine. But their insti-
> tutions indiscriminately benefited everyone who needed them, according to
> the dictates of that time.[15]

Under National Socialism, collective welfare clearly meant transferring resources from care and regulation of the dependent and ill to maintenance and reward of the healthy and strong. Preaching "that the National Socialist state is not there to relieve you of responsibility for your children,"[16] party and state officials attempted to inculcate a new attitude toward welfare that demanded less government expenditure and more work from individual families, especially mothers. Authorities proudly reported declines in the number of welfare cases and hospital patients due to better health associated with the economic and political upturn. In fact, political, racial, and economic eligibility requirements for welfare had been tightened; hospitals now admitted only the most gravely ill and then for shorter periods of time.[17] In the name of national renewal, fiscal accountability, and opportunity for "Aryan" doctors, patients entered and left hospitals sicker, mortality rose, and standards of care declined.[18]

The state rapidly relinquished the costly responsibility for care of the needy and "worthless." Programs to treat drug addiction, alcoholism, mental illness, and venereal disease as well as to care for handicapped and poor children were initially handed over to private or church charitable organizations or private doctors. The innovative social welfare offerings still available in late Weimar Berlin, such as sex education lectures, speech therapy, swimming, and even ski instruction for needy schoolchildren, were eliminated. In October 1933 a decree by the chief mayor mandated that all municipal crèches be closed and their charges handed over to private charities; infants who had been cared for in district 24-hour child-care centers were transferred to local hospital wards.[19] Venereal disease control, as provided for in the 1927 law (which had itself been roundly criticized from the left as repressive), shifted from education and treatment to research on "sources of infection," that is, to surveillance and punishment of prostitutes.[20]

Far from being "precursors of the Nazi clinics for *Erb-und Rassenpflege*,"[21] birth control, prenatal-, and maternal-care clinics that had "worked in the spirit of Van de Velde and against paragraph 218 [were] immediately closed after the seizure of power."[22] In their place, a March 1934 mayoral decree for the "Repopulation of Berlin" mandated the establishment in all districts of counseling centers for hereditary and racial welfare (*Beratungsstellen für Erb-und Rassenpflege*), charged with changing Berlin's status as Europe's most "sterile city," and taking over—in keeping with new racial hygiene principles—marriage counseling, and prenatal-, infant-, and child-care services.[23]

The following month the city of Berlin published its new and rather miserly guidelines for the provision of baby bonuses (*Ehrenpatentschaften*). "Biologically high quality" parents (with no criminal record other than any earned in the struggle for National Socialism) of legitimate children were promised 30 RM ($12) a month in the first year of life for each third or fourth child, and 20 RM ($8) monthly from the first through the fourteenth birthday, provided the child stayed alive. All city agencies were ordered to give preferential treatment to these "child-rich" families.[24]

The retooled counseling centers no longer advised and treated, but observed, judged, and evaluated. Fully in place by 1935, they conducted marriage counseling according to the dictates of the Marital Health and Nuremberg laws, targeted candidates for sterilization according to the Law for the Prevention of Hereditarily Diseased Offspring, and examined applicants for baby bonuses and marriage loans.[25] Like their predecessors, they promised "marriage, prenatal, and pediatric counseling" but on quite different terms. For all the rhetorical stress on fitness and strengthening women's "will to a child," marriage counseling in Weimar Berlin had in fact mostly provided contraceptives and sex advice.

Now the priorities in maternal and infant care and marriage counseling veered from an emphasis on birth control and the combating of infant mortality to the encouragement of large "fit" families and the advancement of genealogical research. Limited support for the "fit" family, education for eugenic self-discipline, and sterilization for the "unfit" was certainly less burdensome than actually providing services for the dependent and undesirable. The Nazis rationalized the health system both by narrowing eligibility for benefits by racial, social, political, and physical criteria, and by restricting the benefits available even for the "fit."[26]

This was indeed a rather different concept of social welfare than had been practiced before 1933, as patronizing, disciplinary, and intrusive as the essentially Social Democratic Weimar model may have been. It was also something quite different from the severe cutbacks imposed during the depression. Despite insistent invocations of the insupportable costs of maintaining the "asocial" and physically or mentally "unfit," cutbacks then had been across the board, not calibrated by criteria of racial or hereditary worth. Furthermore, the extent of the closings carried out by the Nazis demonstrated that a surprising number of initiatives had survived and even flourished until the very end of the republic.

## The Destruction of the Health Insurance Clinics

In 1933, the 38 Health Insurance League (VKB) clinics (*Ambulatorien*) in Berlin were forcibly closed, fulfilling Goebbels' promise to rid Germany of the "pigsty

of the red local insurance associations."[27] On March 1, 1933, a month before
the civil service laws were promulgated, a "First Decree for the Restructuring of Health Insurance" empowered the Reich minister of labor to take over
the health insurance system and install his own commissars. On March 23,
the SA swept through the clinics in a "cleansing action," confiscating medical records and searching for staff physicians. Some were beaten and arrested.
Kurt Bendix, the chief of clinic services who had instituted the VKB's sex
counseling program, was arrested; released a few days later, he attempted to
return to work, where he was apparently welcomed back by a loyal "Marxist" secretary. He was finally removed on Boycott Day, April 1; little is known
about his fate thereafter except that in 1942, like many Jews remaining in Berlin
and in fear of deportation, he committed suicide.

Julius Cohn, the director of the entire Berlin insurance system, just managed to escape arrest on March 23 and immediately left the country with his
family, beginning his emigration to Palestine. Julius Moses, the SPD health
insurance and population policy expert, also remained in Berlin until he was
deported to Theresienstadt, where he died in 1942.[28] After the April civil service laws had removed all but 40 of about 200 VKB doctors, several clinics
closed immediately for lack of personnel. Those remaining shut their doors
on December 31, 1933.[29]

After the clinics were shut down and their doctors arrested and exiled, the
voluminous records so scrupulously collected by the champions of this comprehensive system of social and preventive medicine were left behind. About
1.75 million patient files were handed over to the section for hereditary and
racial welfare of the newly nazified VKB to use in enforcing the sterilization
law.[30] Records of the mental health, prenatal, and marriage and sex counseling clinics were especially useful to the hereditary health courts in identifying sterilization targets, particularly those classified as "feebleminded"—the
largest category of candidates—and also in providing evidence against those
who tried to deny their "disabilities." The community health projects of the
Berlin VKB unwittingly performed this function of corralling victims for Nazi
population policy.

Numerous historians have pointed to the surveillance and registration
function of Weimar social welfare, as evidenced, for example, by its interest
in "psychopathic" or tubercular youth. Certainly Weimar reformers had been
enamored of the virtues of accurate and large-scale record keeping for purposes of research, for making eugenically appropriate decisions about marriage and reproduction, and also in order to better serve their individual patients. Certainly the expansion of public health facilities, and the broadening
of medical competencies to include ever-larger sectors of the (still) "healthy"
population during the Weimar years, facilitated the information gathering
and medicalized intervention necessary to the National Socialist racial hygiene
project.[31] But it is important to note how loudly and specifically the Nazi

authorities complained about the "total neglect of eugenic factors" in the work of VKB marriage and sex counseling clinics.[32] The coercive exploitation of the detailed records kept by Berlin health officials and insurance clinics cannot be equated with any "seamless" continuity of medicalized social control from Weimar to Third Reich.[33]

## *The Enforcement of Sterilization*

Clearly, enthusiasm for reducing the burden of caring for the unfit by providing "selective welfare" (*differenzierte Fürsorge*), which privileged the potentially productive and prevented the reproduction of the "unfit," was not new. The familiar language of motherhood, eugenics, and social hygiene, as well as the ill-concealed longing for some kind of coercive alternative when eugenic education failed, surely lent credibility and legitimacy to National Socialist promises to promote the health of the *Volk*. Particularly those who were not committed Nazis or racists may not have fully grasped the changed meanings.

As has been amply demonstrated—in this book and numerous others—the Weimar years had seen a considerable interest in sterilization—including compulsory sterilization—across a broad spectrum of scientific, political, and popular opinion.[34] Already in 1922, the national Department of Health (RGA) had urged the establishment of a national Institute for the Study of Human Heredity and Population.[35] In 1926, the RGA had officially affiliated with the moderate German Federation for Racial Improvement and the Study of Heredity (*Deutscher Bund für Volksaufartung und Erbkunde*);[36] in 1927, it had sponsored an exhibition on heredity and eugenics together with the German Museum of Hygiene and the German Society for Racial Hygiene (*Deutsche Gesellschaft für Rassenhygiene*).[37]

Starting in the optimistic year 1928, ministry officials began holding secret sessions with guests from the more *völkisch* Society for Racial Hygiene and the Kaiser Wilhelm Institute, home of some of the most prominent racial thinkers in Germany, in which they entertained the possibility not only of forced sterilization but of killing the severely mentally disabled (*Tötung der Vollidioten*).[38] But scientists and public health officials remained cautious. They were held back by legal constraints as well as a fear of public opinion and the recognition that current scientific knowledge about heredity did not justify the more drastic measures they might have wished to undertake. Moderate eugenicists still stressed the importance of education and consent.

With the onset of the depression, some of these interim restraints began to evaporate, and government officials were increasingly attracted to sterilization as a feasible form of cost-effective crisis management; indeed, as we have seen, in some cases, Weimar health insurance or municipal funds paid for these semi-illegal procedures. By the end of 1929, the minutes of the committee on sterilization of the "inferior" were no longer stamped "confidential." But the numerous discussions produced only vague hopes for tax or insurance reforms to privilege large and healthy families, a greater acceptance of voluntary sterilization of certain criminals, and pressure to legalize medically approved sterilizations.[39] In 1931, the Prussian State Council (*Staatsrat*) inquired—despite the continuing and virtually ritualistic calls for more children—"Do we not already have far too many inferior people who daily swell the army of welfare applicants?"[40]

But not until 1932 did a full-scale debate specifically on the issue of eugenics and sterilization erupt in the Prussian State Health Council (*Landesgesundheitsrat*). The discussion unabashedly mixed judgments about the differential value of human lives with fiscal arguments, suggesting that, "Mankind would be spared an enormous amount of suffering if many of these people were never even born," as well as, "If we could get rid of them, the social burden could be considerably lessened."[41] Still, the landmark 1932 Prussian debates centered around the eventual economic benefits of preventing the reproduction of social "ballast," not the creation of a perfect race.[42] And in the simple and didactic tone characteristic of most lay journals, the January 1933 issue of *Volksgesundheit*, for example, cited the (in)famous American example of Ada Jukes and her 2,820 descendants, who collectively cost the state a minimum of $2.5 million. In an article entitled "Does Every Person Have a Right to Procreate?" the journal reassured its readers:

> Of course, it is not extermination of people that is to be recommended, but only the prevention of procreation, which on the basis of hereditary factors might be expected to lead to inferior offspring.[43]

Despite the escalating rhetoric, in 1932, there was still intense debate on whether or not coercive measures were justifiable or desirable. Dr. F. K. Scheumann, whose state counseling center in Dresden was renowned for its active sterilization practice, pointed out that among 3,000 cases, he had recommended only 184 sterilizations, otherwise preferring the less extreme methods of contraception and abortion.[44]

Even the Prussian draft sterilization law presented in September 1932, after Papen's July 20 coup against the state's longtime SPD government, plainly provided for at least formal consent by the patient. Article 12 of the Law to Prevent Hereditarily Diseased Offspring, promulgated by the young National Socialist regime on July 14, 1933, however, explicitly invoked police power if the sterilisand resisted his or her fate.[45] It therefore seems at least questionable to argue that because the distinction between voluntary and compulsory sterilization was "blurred" during Weimar, it "seems legitimate to regard the 1933 Nazi law of compulsory sterilisation . . . as a natural progression from the 1932 Prussian bill of voluntary eugenic sterilisation."[46] Some non-Nazi participants in the Prussian discussions were indeed outraged that the new government claimed the July law as its own contribution to the health of the *Volk*, when the way had been fruitfully paved before January 1933. But it is crucial to note that even at the end, Weimar sterilization discourse and practice, indeed health and population policy in general, never carried with it the force of state power it acquired in 1933.[47]

To talk of sterilization, even to perform the procedure, or to consider the possibility of coercive sterilization, was not the same as to practice it with all the combined forces of medical, police, and legal powers in a terrorist state. As Magnus Hirschfeld wrote from exile to his old friend, the German apologist George Sylvester Viereck:

> No doubt the purification process which is now being carried out in Germany is in many respects just what we had wanted for a long time, but the costs of this procedure, the violent behavior and particularly the intolerance, are too high a price to pay.[48]

## The Destruction of Sex Reform Organizations

Throughout 1933 as the Nazis were dismantling the social welfare system, purging the public service sector, and instituting racial hygiene programs, they also smashed the lay sex reform movement, along with its affiliates in the Communist and Social Democratic parties. A Gestapo file entitled "Liquidation" (*Auflösung*) documented the destruction of sex reform. One by one, between February and June, the headquarters of sex reform organizations were searched and closed. Their leaders were arrested and interrogated or listed as "wanted" if they had succeeded in fleeing; funds and literature were confiscated. A huge library of sexology and sex reform writings (virtually every text or journal cited in this book) was strewn about in police stations throughout Germany, even as the authors and league leaders, many of them additionally suspect as Jews and/or Communists, were arrested, committed suicide, went underground or into exile.[49]

On May 30, 1933, the Gestapo "dissolved" the GESEX/RV and two smaller workers' birth control groups "because it is to be expected that the aforesaid organizations will in future also serve cultural-bolshevistic, and thus subversive aims." Felix Theilhaber was jailed for two months, together with some 50 other (mostly physician) RV/GESEX and VSA members, in Plötzensee Prison in Berlin.[50] Only the *Liga*, which touted its anti-Communism more loudly than the overtly leftist GESEX/RV, survived until June by changing its name yet again and claiming to be an emergency fund for death benefits. But it, too, was liquidated when its leader Hans Hexel finally admitted to having once been a member of the KPD. Security forces professed particular outrage at the participation of adolescents in actions against paragraph 218.[51] The antimodernist drive of the National Socialists—sometimes in danger of

being submerged by the recent focus on the regime's destructive and "pathological" modernity[52]—was dramatically foregrounded in the repression of sex
reform, as expressed in this 1933 Gestapo report:

> It is especially important to demonstrate the connections between the Jewish-
> Marxist spirit and the signs of decay so present under the previous system in
> the areas of sexual science (sex reform efforts, such as Magnus Hirschfeld's
> Institute, the campaign against paragraph 218, pornography, Communist work-
> ers sexual journals, plus modern art and pedagogy).[53]

On May 6, 1933, over 10,000 volumes gathered from the Institute of Sexual
Science as well as a bust of Magnus Hirschfeld were burned in Berlin's Opera
Square. To the accompaniment of a brass band, students and storm troopers
vandalized the buildings near the Tiergarten that had housed Berlin's first sex
counseling center and had become the symbol of an international sexological
and sex reform movement. Students, recruited from the Institute for Physical
Fitness, poured ink over books and manuscripts, and played soccer with books,
posters, and photographs of "deviants." The Nazi newspaper *Der Angriff* (*The
Assault*) described "Energetic Action Against a Poison Shop" of "dirt and filth,"
as "German students fumigate the 'Sexual Science Institute,'" which had been
"controlled by the Jew Magnus Hirschfeld . . . and . . . protected during the
14 years of Marxist rule by the authorities."[54] Magnus Hirschfeld himself had
embarked in late 1930 on a "World Journey of a Sexologist," which took him
through the United States, Japan, China, the South Sea Islands, India, Egypt,
and Palestine. He observed developments in his homeland from afar, drew
his conclusions, and never returned to Germany.[55]

Following the final World League of Sex Reform conference in Brunn,
Czechoslovakia in September 1932, Hirschfeld settled in Paris where he unsuccessfully tried to continue the WLSR's work. Finally, like so many German
artists and intellectuals, he took refuge in Nice in the south of France, where
he died suddenly on May 14, 1935, his 67th birthday. His colleague and longtime companion Karl Giese eulogized him as a "gentle fanatic."[56] The often
controversial force of "this eager little man, with a shock of wild grey hair,
dashing hither and thither, consumed with glowing enthusiasm for his ideals"[57] and his faith in the indivisibility of science and social justice, had held
the WLSR together.

Without Germany as its center, the international sex reform movement,
riven by tensions between those (mostly Anglo-American) who focused primarily on birth control and sexology, and those (mostly German, Austrian,
Scandinavian, and Soviet) who were committed to a new sexual ethics in the
context of social revolution, could not survive. As Hans Leunbach, Norman
Haire's Danish co-chairman, had written to Sanger in May 1934, "For the
WLSR, the German overturning has been a mortal wound and it is doubtful
whether it will be able to arise again."[58]

Helene Stöcker, Hirschfeld's colleague in the WLSR and longtime head of the *Bund für Mutterschutz*, was by 1933 physically ailing, financially strapped, and emotionally drained by her difficult relationship with the eugenicist Bruno Springer, who had apparently committed suicide in 1931. She had spent long periods of time in Czech sanitoria and returned briefly to Berlin in March 1933 to gather some papers and prepare her final emigration. Then, like so many of her comrades, she took the train to Switzerland. In the meantime, in a cruel irony, the remnants of her BfM (complete with its savings account) were taken over by the Nazis in March, renamed *Deutscher Bund für Mutterschutz* and mobilized for the protection of "fit" unwed mothers and the sterilization of the "unfit."

In utterly cynical fashion, the retooled organization referred to the BfM's long honorable history of maternal aid when requesting more funds for unwed mothers, because, "the demands placed on us are constantly growing greater since the happy rise in the birth rate has also naturally led to an increase in the number of needy mothers and children." The new BfM was proud to build a home for unwed mothers to house such cases as a pregnant 16-year-old retarded girl who had been raped by a 62-year-old man and was now scheduled for sterilization after the birth.[59]

## The Destruction of Communist Sex Reform

The Reichstag Fire the night of February 27, 1933, led to the outlawing of the KPD, and arrest or swift moves into the underground for many of its activists. Others headed for the borders of France and Czechoslovakia and to the Soviet Union. The underground Communist party made some attempts to keep its sex reform groups alive, at least as service organizations for members who had lost their easy access to birth control. After a period of paralysis, welfare organizations such as International Workers Aid (IAH) and the Red Aid (*Rote Hilfe*), which helped prisoners of the Nazis and their families, and Communist sports groups (*Rote Sport Einheit*) started to function again in 1934, taking directives from leadership in Paris. The workers' sports organizations, closely connected with sex reform, had achieved a membership of over half a million in the Weimar years,[60] and were considered critical to resistance efforts. Youth sport groups were rapidly being integrated into the Hitler Youth, but through 1935 red workers' sports groups still counted about 2,500, mostly young members in Berlin, especially in the working-class districts of Kreuzberg, Friedrichshain, and Prenzlauer Berg.[61]

Sex political groups initially tried to survive by seeking cover in apparently more innocuous associations, and when that failed, in small informal groups that gathered to hear lectures and to distribute contraceptives. Underground reports noted that most new members who paid their 20-pfennig dues were women seeking affordable birth control products, who had no other contact with political antifascist groups. Ironically, the Communist sex reform movement was now indeed reduced to what it had always tried so hard to avoid being, and yet in so many ways had always been: a co-op for buying discount contraceptives and disseminating sex advice. KPD operatives tried to maintain control over distribution and prevent "inexperienced" women from taking over the leadership. At the same time, missives from exile criticized the lack of effort devoted to infiltrating mass Nazi women's organizations and the inability to exploit purportedly widespread outrage—especially among women—over sexual excesses in youth organizations, such as the large number of pregnancies among girls who attended League of German Girls (BDM) camps.

Driven underground, the remnants of Communist sex political groups, which had been so reviled for encouraging sexual bolshevism, and whose literature had been confiscated as obscene, sought to situate themselves as the guardians of sexual morality against Nazi turpitude. They fulminated against heterosexual licentiousness in the girls' organizations and against homosexual perversion "under the whip of sadistic and homosexual youth leaders" in the Hitler Youth. Communist freethinkers who had been attacked as godless propagators of promiscuity now dreamt of organizing women against the Nazi "subversion of the family." Curiously, the party also recommended smuggling in tracts by Wilhelm Reich to compensate for the disappearance of sex education materials.[62] But these efforts could not be sustained as the Communist underground organization was systematically rounded up and incarcerated.

Communists most prominently associated with sex reform fled to the Soviet Union or went underground. Helene Overlach, the former leader of the KPD women's movement against paragraph 218, returned to Germany in 1933 from her Comintern assignment in Moscow to join underground resistance efforts. In her memoirs, she poignantly described her toddler's reaction to the young woman at the train station who was to pose as her mother on the journey across the border to safety with comrades in Switzerland. The little girl began to weep when told, "This is now your Mutti; after all, this was already her third or fourth mother"—a situation typical of the conspiratorial life shared by the young children of resisters. Overlach moved in and out of Nazi jails; mother and child were briefly reunited in 1942 when the by-now-10-year-old returned to Germany only to witness her mother's transport to the women's concentration camp Ravensbrück. The girl was placed in a children's home, and Overlach, who had been so insistent on bearing a child despite all the obstacles presented by party work, barely saw her until after the war had ended.[63]

Friedrich Wolf, still living in Stuttgart after his release from jail in 1931, fled immediately to Moscow via Basel and France. Already in 1929, Martha Ruben-Wolf had predicted to Margaret Sanger "that birth control in Germany will go like politics will go. If one day fascism will conquer Germany, all forms of birth-control will be forbidden."[64] In 1933, she and her husband Dr. Lothar

Wolf sought refuge in the Soviet Union, as did ARSO chief Martha Arendsee. A former member of a Communist youth group in Berlin remembered the long line of taxis waiting outside the Wolfs' suburban home in Niederschön-weide before 1933, and that the cab drivers who had brought women for abortions complained about the loss of business when the Wolfs fled.[65]

## The Crackdown on Abortion

After January 1933, the long-term sex reform goal of legalizing sterilization and guaranteeing physicians' right to perform medically and eugenically necessary abortions was realized by the Nazis, but under conditions that specifically denied any possibility of compatibility between social fitness and individual control, and gave coercive power to doctors and the state. Involuntary sterilizations administered by a system of about 205 hereditary health courts began to be carried out on a mass scale that eventually encompassed up to 400,000 people.[66] At the same time, restrictions on abortion and birth control, which had been on the books since 1871 but had been loosely and irregularly enforced during the Weimar years, were tightened and enforced according to specifically racial and eugenic criteria.[67] While the manufacture and sale of contraception remained legal, prohibitions on display and advertising (paragraph 184.3) were more strictly implemented. On May 26, 1933, seven years after the elimination of paragraphs 219 and 220, which had prohibited any kind of publicity or education regarding abortion or abortifacients, they were reintroduced into the penal code.

The destruction of the sex reform movement, the persecution of Jewish and leftist doctors, and the enforcement of laws criminalizing abortion were all deemed interdependent and necessary to the rebirth of the *Volk*. As the *American Journal of Sociology* observed in 1935 (with remarkable respect for the official version):

> According to the Nazis, a pregnant woman who wished an abortion in those days had no difficulty in finding a midwife or a doctor, particularly a Jew, to perform it for a moderate fee. This condition they have endeavored to correct, driving out of Germany, the Jews who were notorious abortionists, increasing penalties for the performance of abortions except under certain unusual conditions, and keeping a careful lookout through party members to insure respect for the law.[68]

Doctors' anxiety about the changing rules was reflected in a large decline in medical referrals for therapeutic abortions, from about 44,000 in 1932 to 4,131 in 1937.[69] Indeed, some contemporary observers speculated that the post-1933 rise in the birth rate, attributed by the Nazis to such positive incentives as marriage loans and the general sense of psychic renewal, resulted primarily from the crackdown.[70] Sharpened surveillance and the declining availability of therapeutic abortions also seem to have led to an increase in self-induced or quack abortions.[71]

In one telling piece of evidence, Prussian Justice Ministry files for March 1933 contained, on one side of a page, the text of a "New Decree to Combat Lay Abortion," and on the other side, a letter from a lawyer on behalf of a client who wanted a divorce from her Jewish husband and, simultaneously, permission to abort her "mixed blood fetus."[72] The Nazis launched a massive campaign to eliminate voluntary abortions, whether performed by doctors, midwives, or pregnant women themselves; at the same time, abortions deemed medically, and particularly, eugenically or racially necessary, were legalized, tolerated, and in some cases brutally coerced.

Up until recently, our knowledge about abortion policies and practices in the Third Reich has been remarkably limited, and serious research on the subject is only beginning. Based on her path-breaking research on forced sterilization, Gisela Bock has argued that during the Third Reich, "*Gebärzwang* (compulsory childbearing) did not go beyond what was usual before 1933, after 1945 or in other countries," and insisted that the true "novelty" of Nazi policy was its extreme antinatalism.[73] But especially the excellent new (and ongoing) research of the Berlin historian Gabriele Czarnowski is now documenting a far more differentiated and complex situation.

Antinatalist policies were indeed strengthened when the 1933 sterilization law was amended in June 1935 to institutionalize the link between eugenic sterilization and abortion: abortions, even of advanced pregnancies, deemed necessary on medical and mostly eugenic grounds by medical commissions of the *Reichsärztekammer*, were declared legal; if ordered on eugenic grounds, they had to be followed by sterilization, but unlike sterilization, these abortions were technically dependent on women's consent.[74] Provocatively, Bock argues that after the new regulations sanctioning medically and eugenically indicated abortions, "Abortion was now no longer prohibited" in Germany.[75]

However, coercive pronatalism was by no means absent from the Nazi agenda; already in 1930, the NSDAP had introduced a motion in the Reichstag to charge anyone "who artifically block[s] the natural fertility of the German *Volk*" with "racial treason."[76] As Czarnowski aptly puts it, "The prohibition on abortion and directly or indirectly compulsory abortion coexisted."[77] At the same time in 1935 that certain abortions were legalized, midwives and doctors were also required to report all miscarriages, premature births, and terminations for medical reasons. Abortions were strictly regulated by state-appointed medical commissions; state control and the power of certain segments of the medical profession greatly increased. But women's freedom to maneuver, as well as that of physicians who had during Weimar been willing to provide women with affidavits of medical necessity, was drastically reduced.

Furthermore, the "Guidelines for Interruption of Pregnancy and Sterilization on Health Grounds" issued by the *Reichsärztekammer* in 1936 greatly narrowed the medical criteria allowing therapeutic abortions. Whereas in Weimar, medical necessity—sanctioned by the 1927 Supreme Court ruling—had provided sympathetic doctors with a rather large loophole, especially in cases of heart, lung, and psychiatric disorders, the Nazis clearly intended their indications to be primarily eugenic, and medical only in very severe cases. SS Chief Heinrich Himmler established his Bureau to Combat Homosexuality and Abortion in 1936.[78] By 1939, the bureau's card file numbered 8,000 names, including 4,090 women on whom abortions had been performed by 1,020 doctors, 495 midwives, 355 other health workers, and 2,040 other untrained persons.[79]

The notion that abortion was now for the first time legal would have come as quite a surprise to the numerous physicians who were attacked as abortionists, often for referrals and procedures allegedly conducted years earlier, or the many women who found their abortion networks—whether through doctors, midwives, or lay abortionists—under relentless attack. Especially women physicians with their large female clientele, as well as Jewish and politically outspoken doctors who had worked in birth control and sex counseling centers, were subjected to intimidating interrogations and repeated entrapment attempts, both before and after 1935.

Hertha Nathorff, for example, was charged in 1936 with having referred a sickly 17-year-old for an abortion in 1928. Nathorff prided herself on never performing abortions and only making referrals in cases of extreme necessity. Outraged at the accusation that she had provided a so-called *Gefälligkeitsattest* (a dubious certificate of medical necessity given as a favor), she set out for the notorious Alexanderplatz police headquarter's Abortion Division (*Abtrei-bungsdezernat*) with the patient's case history under her arm. Nathorff persuaded the police that, "Never in my entire practice have I touched such a matter." Nevertheless, Nathorff was visited several months later by an elegantly dressed lady offering money for "help."[80] In U.S. exile in 1940, the Hamburg general practitioner Henriette Magnus Necheles described similar experiences:

> That people could be punished for acts committed many years before represented a grave danger. . . . Once a physician was arrested, he could wait for months without a hearing. Then, perhaps, the proceedings would begin. First insurance practice reports going back to 1924 would be scrutinized. If the records revealed too many miscarriages, then the patients would be summoned and questioned about anything and everything. They frequently were told that the physicians had confessed and their testimony was only a formality. Not every woman could withstand such torment, many said yes in order to avoid further interrogation. If, in spite of all this, the accused was released as innocent, his practice had, in the meantime long since vanished.[81]

In January 1941, coercive pronatalism was sharpened by the so-called Himmler police ordinance that banned the importation, production, or sale of any material or instrument likely to prevent or interrupt pregnancy, thus jeopardizing both abortion and contraception. Only condoms were exempted, upon army request, because of their role in combating venereal disease.[82] By 1943, the skyrocketing incidence of illegal abortions under wartime conditions led to the incorporation into paragraph 218 of a regulation that allowed for imposition of the death penalty "if the perpetrator through such deeds continuously impairs the vitality of the German *Volk*." Further restrictions were also placed on contraception and unauthorized sterilization.[83] These penalties were indeed carried out on abortionists during the war, especially—but not only—on Polish women in occupied Poland who performed abortions on "German" women.[84]

The other side of harsh wartime restrictions on abortion and access to contraceptives were secret directives permitting abortions on women defined as prostitutes and "non-Aryans," as well as for the growing number of German women who became pregnant, via consensual sex or rape, by foreign workers or prisoners of war. Already in 1940, the Ministry of Interior issued a secret memo instructing local health offices to consider "voluntary" abortions beyond those legalized by the 1935 amended Law for the Prevention of Hereditarily Diseased Offspring, in "urgent, well-founded" cases where there was suspicion of hereditary defects not already covered, or in cases of rape or undesirable racial mixing (with someone "racially alien," *Artfremd*). Sterilization was recommended as a follow-up.[85] Even so, the ministry worried about abuse and warned that, "The decree is deliberately kept secret so as not to awaken the impression that any expansion of the right to termination of pregnancy is intended."[86]

As the war dragged on and more and more foreign workers from the conquered territories in the East were forced to work in the Reich, coercive abortion policies became more horrific. Until the end of 1942, female forced laborers (about 2 million of 7.7 million POWs and foreign laborers working in the Reich in 1944) who became pregnant were sent home. But in the spring of 1943, the Reich's medical *Führer*, together with the Department of Health and the Reichskommissar for the Consolidation of the German *Volk* (*Festigung deutschen Volkstums*, RKF), began organizing abortions of "unworthy" fetuses on a massive scale. If the father was allegedly of German blood, the decision about whether to perform an abortion on a "foreign worker" (*Ostarbeiterin*) was made by a commission of the Reich's medical chamber together with the SS and RKF. If pregnancies were deemed worth continuing, the newborns were then forcibly taken from their mothers and handed over to *Lebensborn* homes for "Germanicization"; some were placed into special camps where they invariably died of starvation and maltreatment.[87]

By the beginning of 1945 the encroaching Red Army had advanced to such a point that the possibility of mass "violations" of German women by Soviet troops was acknowledged and indeed widely propagandized as part of a campaign to keep both the military and home fronts intact. The Ministry of Interior not only sanctioned extralegal abortions in such cases but even suggested the establishment "in large cities [of] special wards for the care of such women."[88] This suspension of paragraph 218 in cases of alleged rape by "racially alien" Soviet soldiers, coupled with continued insistence on the fundamental criminality of abortion, was, as the last chapter will discuss, to survive the fall of the Third Reich and last into the immediate postwar years.

The most salient feature of Nazi abortion policy therefore was its clear selectivity—both in terms of "race" and decision making. Voluntary abortions, desired by women themselves and not state-sanctioned for reasons of the health of the *Volk*, were severely repressed—up to and including the death penalty for those performing the abortions (including doctors but usually midwives). Abortions on racially, physically, and mentally valuable women were to be stamped out. Abortions on the racially undesirable and "unfit" were coercively performed according to decisions made by the same medical commissions that determined sterilizations, and generally not severely punished if performed illegally.

## The Divided Fate of Medical Sex Reform

Communist, socialist, and Jewish doctors involved with sex reform were of course particular targets of repression on abortion and other charges. Max Hodann, allied with both the KPD and the RV, was arrested at home in the early-morning hours after the Reichstag fire. Prepared for trouble, he had already destroyed the careful referral listings of doctors, midwives, lawyers, and social workers sympathetic to sex reform that he had compiled for the Committee on Birth Control. After several months' imprisonment, he lived illegally in Germany (where his wife had become active in a socialist resistance group) and then fled to Switzerland and England in the fall of 1933.[89]

Dr. Elkan of the Hamburg RV was almost beaten to death in his consultation room in early 1933 by a gang of Nazi thugs. He was dragged from prison to prison, and finally, barely able to walk and with his arm still in a sling, allowed to emigrate to Great Britain.[90] His ironic sense of humor still intact, he wrote to Sanger, "B.C. is a dangerous hobby and more so if it becomes a passion."[91] Dr. Lehfeldt of the Berlin GESEX/RV clinic escaped arrest and fled to the United States, smuggling out his precious clinic records, lest they be used to denounce patients and colleagues.[92]

Dr. Hertha Riese and her husband Walter, a neurologist and sexologist, were both arrested in their Frankfurt home in April 1933. Released a few days later, they quickly packed their suitcases and fled, with their two daughters, across the frontier to Basel and then on to Lyons.[93] Dr. Ernst Gräfenberg, champion of the IUD and director of obstetrics at a municipal hospital in a Berlin suburb, disregarded Lehfeldt's urgent entreaties to join him in exile, hoping to maintain his large private practice on the fashionable Kürfurstendamm. Arrested in 1934, he finally escaped to the United States in 1940 after Margaret Sanger apparently "negotiated his release by paying a large ransom."[94]

By contrast, Hans Harmsen, the only physician prominently associated with sex reform who embraced the Nazi regime, remained in Germany. He continued to work as a population expert for the Protestant charity Inner Mission, and served as consultant for forced sterilization procedures. An ardent admirer of Margaret Sanger, Harmsen had played an important role in the Medical Working Group for Birth Control convened by Kate Stützin, but had remained suspect in the sex reform movement as a whole because, like Stützin, he was staunchly opposed to the legalization of abortion. Indeed, it is worth noting when evaluating questions of continuity and discontinuity from Weimar reform to National Socialist repression that the very few Weimar birth controllers who did explicitly express support for Nazi population policy were all opposed to signficant reform of paragraph 218, the movement's hallmark demand.[95]

Harmsen celebrated the tenth anniversary of his Working Group for the Restoration of the Health of the *Volk* in 1935 with a special issue paying tribute to Germany's "moral renewal."[96] In a 1979 interview, referring to his support for sterilization and his "difficult choice" about whether or not to join the NSDAP, Harmsen recalled:

> Many things which in themselves I considered beneficial and I approved of them, particularly during the early years, and yet . . . all these things, they got to the point where they could no longer be used . . . one always said to oneself: really, in essence all this is exactly what I myself had already demanded years ago.

Despite irritation at the usurpation of his ideas and his successful evasion of party membership, Harmsen supported, together with the Inner Mission, the July 1933 revision—now sanctioning coercion—of the 1932 Prussian sterilization law draft. Working in the "examination of cripples" division attached to the sterilization apparatus in East Frisia, he protested the legalization of eugenic abortions in 1935, tried to save from sterilization those he thought worth saving, worked hard to gain consent from the "unfit," both for their own good and the good of the *Volksgemeinschaft*, but also encouraged forcible sterilization if consent was not forthcoming. Toward the end of the war, when it seemed that his position as a nonparty participant in the racial hygiene project was becoming precarious, Harmsen absented himself as a health officer to the relative safety of Rommel's African campaign. He returned unscathed, and would, as we shall see in the postwar chapter, work enthusiastically to establish family planning on the American model in Western Germany.[97]

Harmsen's antiabortion ally in the Working Group for Birth Control and fellow Sanger confidante Kate Stützin also seems to have made her peace with the regime. Her husband, the sexologist and urologist Johannes Stützin—a Chilean citizen who had fought for the Germans in World War I—was forced out of his position as director of a Protestant hospital because of his Jewish ancestry and given eight days to leave the country. From Spanish exile he expressed to Sanger his shock over expulsion after 45 years of residency: "What is happened to us is too phantastic and too cruel. . . . I never believed that such a fanatism [sic] and brutality would be possible."[98] His wife remained in Berlin with their son. With no apparent second thoughts, she wrote to Sanger in June 1934:

> I think it will be very interesting for you to hear about the new sterilization laws in Germany. It [is] just . . . the point you always considered so very important. I hope this bill will do lots of good in the population questions. . . . Life in Germany is extremely interesting.[99]

Dr. Ilse Szagunn, a League of German Women Doctors (BDÄ) member, director of a Protestant marriage counseling center, and another supporter of paragraph 218, whom Stützin had recommended to Sanger as a reliable source, also reported to her American colleagues:

> We no longer think about the individual but rather about and for the *Volk*. Therefore birth control can no longer ask, what is desirable, helpful or necessary for the individual, but rather: what has to happen for the *Volk* to be protected from the overly strong procreation of the inferior and how we can encourage the procreation of the healthy and fit.[100]

Sanger responded with a polite thank you. Never one to mince words, she then scribbled a note to her secretary about Stützin: "She is a delightful person but a pill and—bows(?) to Hitler." Thereupon the correspondence apparently ended.[101] Sanger's sympathy for anything that was anathema to the Catholic Church initially predisposed her to support the German sterilization law, but when further informed she was quick to grasp its dangerous implications, arguing with those who saw it as one of the "positive" achievements of National Socialism.[102] This made her exceptional among watchful American social hygienists, who greeted the law with near universal approval. Marie Kopp, who had admiringly reported on the rise of marriage and sex counseling clinics in Weimar Germany for the *American Journal of Obstetrics and Gynecology*, returned to Germany in 1935 and pronounced, "that the law is administered in entire fairness" and that there was "little doubt that sterilization of those unfit for procreation is a constructive social measure."[103]

The Nazi takeover abruptly halted German physicians' slow and partial acceptance of birth control as part of medical practice. In 1931, economic crisis, the anti-218 campaign, and the proliferation of clinics had pressured the German gynecology convention to focus on the subject. In 1933, Walter Stoeckel, longtime abortion opponent and cautious supporter of contraception, stepped into the breach left by the exclusion of "non-Aryan" and other reform-minded colleagues. Concerned that the International Gynecology

Congress scheduled for Berlin in 1933 under his chairmanship should go off without a hitch he had "at first only one goal: the unimpeded continuation of the Society for Gynecology and . . . of our irreplaceable scientific and social work." Determined to "[ward] off, on the one hand, every interference into our rights and freedom, and on the other hand [avoid] that the government be provoked into action against us," he was relieved when two "non-Aryan" colleagues, including the noted birth control supporter Dr. Ludwig Fränkel who had played such an important role at the 1931 congress, graciously agreed to withdraw "voluntarily" from the society's board. Stoeckel was enormously pleased with the result of his efforts: Jewish participants from foreign countries could attend and speak; German-Jewish gynecologists "should not speak and remain in their own interest as much as possible in the background."[104]

In his welcoming address, Stoeckel confirmed his opposition to the pre-1933 "degrading of prenatal clinics into concealed sites for birth control," and celebrated "the coming together of all national forces and the unshakeable fanatical faith in Germany's future" at this turbulent time of new "birth"—so much more hopeful than in 1931. Acknowledging the skepticism of some in the audience toward the new regime, he announced:

> We regret that these developments have also hit hard at colleagues whose personalities we highly honor and whose scientific achievements we value highly. We cannot change their fate; they have become the victims of a harshness which has become necessary for the restoration to health of the German *Volk*.[105]

Years later, Stoeckel, a consummate opportunist who had gone on to garner great honors in both postwar Germanies, confided at the end of his remarkably self-congratulatory memoir, that "still I was often filled with shame . . . that we German university professors failed so thoroughly when it came to showing solidarity in hard times."[106]

## The Divided Fate of Women Doctors

Difficult questions about continuity and discontinuity are also raised by the experiences of the pioneering group of women doctors who had staffed municipal or insurance clinics and were organized in the BDÄ. The new state claimed a commitment to improving mothers' status and health, even as it was shutting down health insurance clinics, destroying marriage, sex, and birth control counseling centers, and dismissing precisely those colleagues most concerned with maternal and child welfare initiatives. Younger "Aryan" women doctors, in particular, who did not remember the years of struggle for professional recognition, saw in Hitler's Third Reich, with its stress on sex-segregated social welfare and the selective encouragement of motherhood, the promise of new professional opportunities. Not the least of these were the job openings indicated by the list of Jewish names appearing under the rubric "Resignations" in *Die Ärztin*, the BDÄ journal.

Racially and politically acceptable women physicians found comfortable niches and new spheres of activity working for the League of German Girls, as school and sport physicians or in the new hereditary and racial welfare clinics. By the summer of 1933, over 20 percent of all medical students were female, and medicine had become the most popular course of study for women, surpassing even the humanities.[107] Many women doctors and social workers, exhausted by the struggle against seemingly intractable poverty and hopelessness, welcomed a regime that pledged quick and effective solutions. One doctor reported that whereas under Weimar rule the "Marxist press" would immediately attack as "unsocial" those who refused further treatment for hopeless cases, "today it is a pleasure to work!"[108]

As late as April 1933, *Die Ärztin* published a report from Dr. Hertha Nathorff on her "city-run Women's Counseling Center" and its recommendation of "various kinds of mechanical and chemical methods . . . to avoid unwanted pregnancies."[109] But for Nathorff, April also marked the banishment that contrasted so sharply with what she had felt was the progressive stance of her professional organization. One evening that month at a regular BDÄ meeting, she was confronted by unfamiliar women, some of them already wearing swastikas on their collars, who suddenly informed her and about 25 of her colleagues that the Jewish doctors should "leave the premises, we are now coordinating with the Nazi state." Non-Jewish Communist and Social Democratic colleagues from whom she had expected support no longer dared appear at the meeting.[110]

Two months later, in June, Nathorff's counseling center was closed. The substantial Jewish and socialist membership that had constituted the core of BDÄ connection to the clinic network and the sex reform movement was purged, and *Die Ärztin*, complete with new masthead, announced that, "The general depression which has hung over Germany until the beginning of this year is giving way to new life and new hope."[111] Dr. Lea Thimm, the newly installed National Socialist BDÄ leader, warned her colleagues to relinquish "internationalism . . . democracy and pacifism." In "the new state," she warned, "the issue is not the problem of abortion, but the problem of procreation."[112]

With a militance notably absent when faced with the expulsion of Jewish colleagues, "Aryan" women doctors fought hard and not without success to protect their professional status. Thimm assailed "ruthless" Nazi attacks on "double earners'" eligibility for health insurance reimbursement, which would lead to the "eradication" (*Ausmerzung*) of all women doctors.[113] *Die Ärztin* insisted that two incomes were necessary to maintain an adequate standard of living for their families; furthermore, only married women could truly understand the personal health needs of German women. The BDÄ also argued (correctly) that "competent practical" married women doctors were now more necessary than ever, due to the particularly severe loss of "non-Aryan" physicians in specialties serving female patients.[114]

The essentialist and maternalist ideals that had guided many women sex reform doctors took on a new meaning as the Nazified *Die Ärztin* defended "the mission of the female physician" to "promote the conscious rejection of a mechanistic understanding of life processes" and to introduce into the practice of medicine "womanly kindness, feminine psychological astuteness and feminine tact."[115] As in the Weimar era, women doctors were acceptable because they "generally do not approach medicine as scientists, but more out of a maternal instinct that makes them want to help and take care."[116] The BDÄ justified its "complete willingness to continue . . . work under the changed political conditions and in harmony with the spirit of the new era," as consistent with its longstanding commitment to "promoting the interests of women, children and the family."[117]

But, as the BDÄ vigorously argued, these maternal women physicians were also tough enough for the new Germany: "It is barely possible to organize as many hours out of the day as a woman doctor needs who has a practice, clinic, husband, children and a hospitable home." Role model Dr. Martha Mueller ("a woman doctor as she should be"), for example, had produced three "beautiful, absolutely healthy children" and always showed her pregnant patients that it was possible to "work until the very end, busy from morning till night, without complaint." She also helped her husband with a demanding business and cared for his elderly parents. And when she had guests for dinner and was called to surgery, she rode her bicycle to the clinic so that her husband could use the family car to bring the guests home: the fresh air and exercise helped to keep her fit and calm her nerves! In every town, the reporter noted, there were Martha Muellers who were "triply burdened with career, marriage and worries, and gathered their strength tenfold in order to give of themselves a hundredfold."[118]

The familiar language of maternalism was now fully mobilized to serve goals that went far beyond those that might have previously been deemed necessary to maternal and child welfare by conservative, socialist, or clerical groups. A 1934 report noted that it fell especially to the female doctor to handle the human trauma of the eugenics program. Women were best suited, for example, to explain to other women that they were "unfit" to bear children no matter how deeply they wished to have them:

> For this one needs extraordinary tact and often it is only the psychological sensitivity and warm heart of a motherly woman who can alleviate these apparent hardships and even extract some understanding for the absolute necessity of such measures.[119]

As was the case with so many organizations that capitulated to Nazi *Gleichschaltung* in hopes of preserving their autonomy, the BDÄ's expectations were eventually disappointed, and it was dissolved by the Reich's medical *Führer* in 1936. Acquiescence and professional survival had come at a price. Despite continuing increases in the total number of women physicians, the proportion of nonpracticing female doctors, most of them presumably married and pressured by the double-earner campaign, climbed from 4.8 percent to 17 percent between 1930 and 1937. The coming of the war and the final exclusion of all "non-Aryan" practitioners cemented women's prominent presence in the Nazi (and postwar) medical profession.[120] But the social health experiments in which some of them had played such a leading role were forever destroyed. The doctors who had nurtured those projects were forced out of the profession and out of Germany.

A very few "Aryan" champions of abortion reform and birth control were able to retreat safely into "apolitical" private practice. In February 1933, Anne-Marie Durand-Wever and Hermine Heusler-Edenhuizen, both longtime BDÄ activists, were still calling for reform of paragraph 218. Invoking the rhetoric of Weimar social hygiene, and identifying themselves as members of a "nonpartisan women's league," they maintained that criminalization was counterproductive, asserted their common interest in raising the birth rate, improving prenatal care, and preventing illegal abortions, and insisted that they were anti–paragraph 218, not pro-abortion.[121] On September 6, 1933, however, the Reich Committee for Hygienic Education of the *Volk* wrote to the Ministry of the Interior demanding confiscation of Durand-Wever's book *Rassen-Hygiene, Sterilisation und Nachkommensbeschränkung* (*Racial Hygiene, Sterilization and Limitation of Offspring*) because its "misleading" title obscured the fact that the book discussed contraception and abortion as well as sterilization.[122] Nazis responsible for "hygienic education" were not fooled by semantic similarities and had no trouble distinguishing Durand-Wever's message from their own understandinging of racial hygiene.

Durand-Wever herself retreated from politics into private practice in Berlin's West End. Careful to protect herself from Gestapo spies who tried to entrap her into performing illegal abortions, she stubbornly continued to provide women with contraceptives and perhaps even with abortion advice and referrals. During the war she directed a first aid station for victims of allied bombing attacks.[123]

Another Weimar sex reform activist, the Saxon general practitioner Barbara von Renthe-Fink, briefly fled to Switzerland when threatened with arrest for her activities on behalf of the *Rote Hilfe* as well as the loss of her health insurance eligibility. She shed the doctor husband responsible for her unwanted double-earner status, discontinued all political activities, and moved to Chemnitz with its large population of female textile workers where she fortuitously took over the well-equipped practice of an emigrating Jewish internist. Deemed "unreliable" by the local Agency for the Health of the *Volk*, she nevertheless held onto her health insurance privileges, pursued a busy obstetrics practice, and, according to her memoirs, managed to avoid providing reports on any patient's "hereditary health."[124]

In a bizarre twist of fate, Alice Goldmann-Vollnhals, the dynamic abortion rights advocate and former director of the infant and prenatal clinics of the Berlin Health Insurance League, fled Germany to Shanghai with her husband, the social hygienist Dr. Franz Goldmann, only to return to Nazi Germany in 1936 after her divorce. Unlike her husband, who languished depressed in the Shanghai refugee community, she used her many languages and social skills to quickly build up a busy pediatric and gynecological practice among both the native Chinese and foreign colony in Shanghai.[125] When her marriage collapsed she returned to her son from a previous marriage in Berlin. Thus Alice Goldmann-Vollnhals, well-known birth control campaigner and former employee of the socialist-controlled insurance league, reverted to being Alexa von Klossowski from an aristocratic anti-Semitic white Russian family. Freed of her Jewish mate and once again eligible for health insurance reimbursements, the reinvented Alice/Alexa went straight to the Nazi medical Führer Dr. Leonardo Conti and apparently charmed him into restoring her privileges. She too avoided political activity and established a flourishing general practice in working-class Kreuzberg which she maintained during the war and occupation right up until three days before her death in 1969.[126]

On the other hand, the appearance of acquiescence in Nazi population policy could be at least partially deceiving. Elfriede Paul, a young medical graduate, had been marginally involved in sex reform, especially in the Hamburg BfM, through her social work with delinquent youth. Having passed her licensing exams in April 1933, just when many of the reformers who had inspired her were losing their jobs, she found ample work in the social hygiene field, but under the Nazis and not, as she had expected, under socialists and Communists. Women doctors, she recalled, were especially busy, because so much old staff had been fired and young Nazi doctors spent most of their time going to SA meetings.[127]

Paul seemed fully integrated into the Nazi *Weltanschauung*, moving from concern about proletarian health to efforts on behalf of the health of the *Volk*. In keeping with the Nazi tenet of *Gemeinnutz geht vor Eigennutz* (collective need over individual need), she insisted that physicians' major duty was not to heal the sick and care for the weak but to strengthen preventive care "and solicitude to the healthy and valuable so that their physical characteristics can achieve their full flowering."[128] A BDM physician, Paul wrote a dissertation defending the harsh regimen of the girls' camps, which caused many girls to stop menstruating—certainly a concern for a regime worried about fertility—as a healthy part of a "toughening-up" process. Following a typical career path for a woman doctor in Nazi Germany, she also worked in a hereditary and racial welfare counseling center and as a school physician in Prenzlauer Berg, now renamed after the Nazi martyr Horst Wessel. When her refusal to join the party became a serious obstacle, Paul opened a private practice independent of insurance eligibility or public employment in Berlin's affluent West End, continuing to work part-time for the BDM.

Yet, by 1936, she was also heavily involved in the conspiratorial resistance activities of the Communist Red Orchestra group. Her waiting room hosted meetings; her car, normally used for house calls, was made available for actions and for summer excursions to campsites on the Baltic where cadre relaxed and planned strategy. Arrested in 1942, Paul was one of the few members of the group to survive imprisonment. As we shall see, she became an important figure in the formulation of postwar population policy in the German Democratic Republic (GDR), bringing to her tasks a curious but common melange of Weimar, Soviet, and Nazi notions about social health.[129]

## Nazi Policy and Discourse: The Problem of Continuity

As I suggested in the preface to this book, one cannot evaluate the history of German sex reform and its relationship to National Socialist population and racial policy without looking carefully at the fate of sex reformers after January 1933. Nazi response to sex reform publications or projects that espoused eugenics but by no means met the criteria of Nazi racial hygiene can be particularly revealing in this context. Historians have now (finally) exposed in chilling detail the numerous German racial hygienists and population policy experts, already active during the Weimar Republic, who gained resources and professional prestige after 1933 by collaborating (on different levels and to different degrees) with Nazi programs for sterilization, medicalized killing of the "unfit" ("euthanasia"), and medical experimentation on concentration camp inmates.[130] But with the necessary exception of Hans Harmsen (whose credentials as either a sex reformer or a Nazi are somewhat ambiguous), they were not the same people who were active in the sex reform movement, and this book is not about them.

Certainly sex reformers shared in the motherhood-eugenics consensus, and were committed to hereditarian principles, including support for eugenic sterilization. But to note that most sex reformers, including Communists and Social Democrats, supported some version of eugenics and considered that sterilization might be perpetrated on those too recalcitrant and downtrodden to give their consent, is not to say much. For, in the historical context of the 1920s and 1930s, "eugenical sentiment" was "amazingly widespread," across the political spectrum and over the international map, especially among progressives who believed in the possibility of creating a new and more perfect "race" of human beings.[131] Both Justice and Interior ministry files for the crucial years 1933 to 1935 make clear that the National Socialists themselves were acutely aware that, notwithstanding shared enthusiasm for sterilization of the "unfit" and encouragement of healthy motherhood, support for "racial hygiene" in order to justify legalized abortion or birth control clinics was vastly different from the "racial hygiene" they intended to enforce.

Officials in the Ministry of Interior and Department of Health were bedeviled by would-be Nazis and opportunists who sought to jump on board the new racial project by proclaiming that their work in eugenics demon-strated a long-held belief in Nazi racial ideology.[132] Considerable differences also existed within the Nazi medical and hygiene apparatus, especially be-tween party ideologues who wanted to enforce a vision of a master race and traditionally trained scientists, many of them not even party members, who wanted to carry out what they insisted was a scientifically legitimate project in biological planning. Further differences separated those with a focus on technocratic planning and adherents of organic "natural" medicine.[133] The Committee for Hygienic Education of the *Volk* complained that:

> Repeatedly we determined that writings had been classified as National Socialist by authors who did not in the past and do not now stand on the ground of National Socialist Weltanschauung.[134]

One example was the work of Alfred Grotjahn, the sometime Social Demo-cratic opponent of legalized abortion and holder of the chair in social hygiene at the University of Berlin until his death in 1932. Even the most "radical" of the racial hygienists referred, "before and after 1933, over and over again, to Grotjahn's estimate," that about one-third of the entire population was of "inferior" stock.[135] However, the newly established Reich Committee for Hygienic Education of the *Volk* (*Reichsausschuss für Hygienische Volksbelehrung,* RAHV) refused to sanction continued publication of his work.[136]

Such decisions had far-reaching consequences because the committee ap-proved books for use in schools, feeding a large new market in racial hygiene texts. Indeed, responsibility for social health was increasingly taken away from the Department of Health, which had been so dominated by Social Demo-crats that its newly installed Nazi director complained in 1933 that there were only four NSDAP members in the entire agency.[137] The new director shifted attention to racial research, racial hygiene, and prevention of hereditary dis-eases, rather than general social medicine.[138] But even so, "the health of the *Volk*" became more and more the purview of the Ministry of the Interior. The Special Committee on Population Policy Questions that had been convened by Prussian Interior Minister Severing during the depression was also dissolved on June 1, 1933, and replaced by an ideologically more reliable Committee of Experts for Population and Race Questions.[139]

There are numerous other examples of confusion among and ultimate clash-ing of eugenic discourses. The Jewish founder of social gynecology, Max Hirsch, editor of the *Archiv für Frauenkunde und Eugenik,* was replaced by the Catholic eugenicist Dr. August Mayer, who vowed to "push into the background the previous emphasis on sex research and instead stress heredity, family, and race research." But he worried that "the journal will not be able to survive and that I will only be able to give the adopted Jewish child an Aryan burial."[140]

Dr. Rainer Fetscher, a widely published sterilization proponent who had supported involuntary procedures in certain cases, initially tried to portray himself as a pioneer of National Socialist thinking. But wary Nazi authorities pointed out that, while Fetscher had indeed carried out eugenic sterilizations in his Dresden health insurance marriage counseling center, he had done so for the wrong (social rather than racial) reasons. Moreover, the fact that he had also distributed birth control immediately disqualified him as a participant in the Nazi program.[141] He was dismissed from his post as professor of social hygiene at the Technical University in Dresden and his clinic was closed. Fetscher then opened a private practice in Dresden and, like Elfriede Paul, eventually became deeply involved in resistance activity. He offered his consultation rooms as meeting places for anti-Nazi groups and took great risks on their behalf, certifying soldiers as unfit for duty and smuggling medication and food to forced laborers. In 1943, he became a doctor at police headquarters in Dresden, where he continued his underground work. On May 8, 1945, on his way to making contact with the Red Army on behalf of Communist resistance groups, he was shot to death by the remnants of an SS commando.[142]

Another—and perhaps more problematical—example of deceptive continuities was the fate of a book by the mainstream Weimar feminist Ilse Reicke. *Das Grössere Erbarmen* (*The Greater Compassion*) was originally published in 1929. It was reissued as *Der Weg der Irma Carus: Roman einer Frauenärztin* (*The Path of Irma Carus: Story of a Woman Doctor*) in 1931, at the height of Berlin doctors' involvement in the Wolf/Kienle campaign, and immediately construed as a feminist statement pleading for women's right to contraception and abortion. Irma, the heroine and a prototypical Weimar "new woman," is a young professional, wife, and mother. Busy with a fulfilling medical career, she also shares a companionate marriage with a colleague while mothering two healthy, bright (and very blond) children. Both horrified and touched by the poor "degenerate" women of Berlin's working-class ghettos, and the endless debilitating pregnancies they are forced to endure, Irma and her husband Ludwig open a marriage and birth control counseling service as part of their joint practice. "Can you believe that these coercively-born children are worth anything?" Irma asks. Children brought into the world "only through force of law," she insists will never become "happy human beings." Convinced that "the primary right of every human child must be to be truly wanted and yearned for," she vows to fight the "threatening fist" of "male justice." Very much like her real-life counterpart Else Kienle, Irma cries out, "Ah, men have made the laws, numbers of lecherous men, who wanted power, who wanted human fodder; woman's hand would write different laws."[143]

Radicalized by her work, she also joins in a mass protest meeting sponsored by the BDÄ against paragraph 218. She is, however, repelled by the "politicization" of the issue by a woman doctor representing the KPD, a passionate speaker with frizzy hair—clearly a reference to Dr. Martha Ruben-Wolf. For Irma, the issue is not ideological but a question of social and national health, a "demand of greater compassion and deeper love for Germany."[144] Disillusioned with the "filth" of party politics, Irma withdraws again into her comfortable family and practice. But by the end of the novel, the personally as well as eugenically perfect *völkisch* solution emerges when a wealthy Jewish businessman dies. He had never granted his "Aryan" wife the children she so deeply wanted for fear of burdening them with the stigma of mixed-race blood. He does, however, leave his wife a fortune, which she uses to establish a maternity home in the "light, air and sun" of the German countryside.

Irma and her family escape the degenerate metropolis, and together with Ludwig, Irma takes over the maternity center. She quickly sets up a laboratory for birth control research that will combat the "plagues" of abortion and unhealthy, unwanted children. The pastoral idyll is both intellectually and biologically fertile. The book ends with Irma playing on the lawn with her newborn son, just a few steps away from her laboratory, and dreaming of her German utopia: "no more murderous paragraphs, [but] laws for the protection of mothers."[145] Reicke's version of the motherhood-eugenics consensus managed in one narrative to accommodate racial hygiene and anti-Semitic sentiments, as well as defenses of birth control, abortion under certain circumstances, and women's right to both motherhood and career. From the death of the Jew and the rejection of the decadent city could come a new feminine vision of health and motherhood, one that did not deny women's right to professional fulfillment, but protected her privileges within the context of a system that demanded duty and sacrifice, and both social and biological motherhood.

Nevertheless, the Safari Publishing House prudently stopped public distribution of the renamed book in 1933, citing doubts regarding whether "the book's point of view completely conformed to the goals of National Socialist Germany." Demand for the novel continued, however, and in 1937 the publisher, concerned that "a ban on the book whose sales have up till now been entirely satisfactory, would represent a substantial loss," decided that Reicke's work was open to multiple interpretations. Requesting official permission to redistribute the book, he reminded the Reich Literature Chamber (*Reichsschriftumskammer*) that:

> The book was written at a time when popular opinion, especially in regard to such vital questions, did not conform to the basic biological laws, so that it took a thoroughly upright point of view to bring such a book to the public.[146]

After careful consideration, the Nazi authorities were not impressed by Reicke's version of "biological" thinking. The request was emphatically denied.[147] Even as words remained similar or identical, the underlying meaning of the motherhood-eugenics discourse, so entrenched across the Weimar political spectrum, and the context in which it was now interpreted and enforced, had changed drastically and irrevocably.

The loss of Jewish, socialist, and Communist professionals, as well as the elimination of the pressure once exerted by the working-class movement, and the silencing of all countervailing discussion about the proper nature of the welfare state, fundamentally changed the nature of social welfare and social hygiene projects. The repeated use of the term *wieder* (implying retrieval) in National Socialist decrees was intended to suggest a conservative, restorative quality. Certainly in Berlin and other large cities, and in regard to sex reform, this suggestion of continuity was belied by the radicalism of the changes. The route of social welfare and public health policy from Weimar to National Socialism was convoluted and highly contested. It is not the case that Weimar sex reformers, softened up by years of eugenic discourse and faith in state intervention, paved the way for, or were easily seduced into, support for Nazi population policy. Quite the contrary: their pioneering institutions were systematically liquidated. Weimar sex reformers had to be silenced, fired, arrested (often on abortion charges), killed, driven to suicide, or forced into exile.

# — seven —

# Weimar Sex Reform
# in Exile

Having been a doctor with what I thought was a future yesterday, I
am a sort of gipsy today and heaven knows what I will be tomorrow. I
am not going to give up on B.C. [birth control] even if it has given me
up but at the moment I unfortunately am a very useless member of
the human race.

EDWARD ELKAN, 1934[1]

The Weimar sex reform movement ended in 1933 but the history of Weimar
sex reformers did not. This chapter cannot tell their whole story, for the
recorded history of sex reform splinters and fades as the movement was destroyed. It does follow the life histories of some key figures in the Weimar
movement, both women and men, those who went East as well as West.
Their stories are pieced together from published or unpublished memoirs or
fragments of memoirs, and interviews; for the most part they offer a picture
of continued commitment to social health projects but also of profound disruption and marginalization that contrasts sharply with the sense of efficacy
and possibility that these activists had experienced during the crisis-ridden
Weimar years.

The United States and the Soviet Union had been the most important
models and interlocutors for Weimar sex reformers. With the Nazi seizure
of power, they became the most significant destinations and points of reference as German sex reform went into exile. (Eventually the two countries
would also provide the most powerful models for postwar reconstruction.)
Great Britain and the Scandinavian countries, all with active birth control
movements and a history of participation in the World League for Sex Reform
(WLSR), also received many émigrés.

France and Czechoslovakia served especially as transit stations. By late 1933,
the League of Socialist Physicians (VSA), virtually all of whose members, both

socialist and Communist, had been forced out of Germany, followed the SPD leadership into Czech exile and established itself in truncated form in Prague. Its journal, now called the *Internationales Ärztliches Bulletin (IAB)*, reported critically on the growing repression in Germany, Nazi racial hygiene policies, and conditions in concentration camps, but also on the show trials in the Soviet Union and Stalin's recriminalization of abortion. The journal also documented emigrations, deaths, and medical efforts on behalf of Spanish Civil War fighters. When the Nazis annexed Czechoslovakia in March 1939, the VSA moved to Paris and dissolved within a year as the war scattered its members.[2]

For numerous refugee Weimar sex reformers, contacts from the international birth control and sex reform movement, and especially those established at the Zurich conference organized by Margaret Sanger in 1930, proved decisive in the choice of destination and in the provision of shelter, financial support, and employment. Three women—Margaret Sanger in New York, Elise Ottesen-Jensen, the head of the Swedish sex reform association in Stockholm, and the gynecologist and sexologist Helena Wright in London—all of whom had been in Zurich, were instrumental in organizing refugee aid and in coping with the traumatic sea change that hit world sex reform after 1933.

Committed KPD activists like the physicians Friedrich Wolf and Martha Ruben-Wolf, social welfare (ARSO) chief Martha Arendsee, and women's leader Helene Overlach went to the Soviet Union where they confronted both disillusionment and accommodation, and in some cases, purges and death. Those who survived returned to Germany after the war and in some cases participated in the development of population and social welfare policy in the Soviet occupation zone and subsequently the German Democratic Republic. Refugees in the United States and the British Commonwealth—most of them physicians—became citizens of their host countries. They usually maintained in a reworked, albeit less explicitly ideological fashion their commitments to birth control and social medicine. Together with fellow exiles in Australia, Great Britain, Palestine (Israel), and other countries, they helped to establish International Planned Parenthood after the war. In that context, they also reestablished contact with those few of their former comrades who were trying to reconstruct a birth control movement in both Germanies. Indeed, they served as a crucial conduit for reintegrating Germans into the international movement.

Sex reform refugees who were doctors encountered the particular difficulties of reestablishing professional as well as political identities in unfamiliar worlds. Their fates varied, depending on destination, age, gender, and the date and pattern of their emigration. An unusual feature of this migration, as it had been of the movement, was the relatively large number of women professionals. Women doctors, who had been so prominent in birth control, sex counseling, maternity, and school clinics and in the campaigns for abortion reform, were overrepresented among the stream of "racial" and "political" refugees from Nazi Germany. It has been estimated that 12 percent of the approximately 6,000 physicians who emigrated from Germany were women, a figure that topped both their representation among German doctors as a whole and among German physicians identified as Jews.[3]

For both male and female doctors the story of exile from Nazi Germany is one of loss of status and identity, and of painful and arduous reconstruction. Whereas numerous German refugees eventually established highly successful new careers, sex reformers carried with them the complicated baggage of their identification with birth control and abortion rights, as well as a language of socialism, eugenics, and social medicine, that—particularly in the United States—was becoming increasingly discredited just as they were arriving. Their faith in eugenic hygiene, while certainly widely shared, was necessarily shaken by their experiences in Germany, and became increasingly problematical during the 1930s and 1940s as especially American and British birth controllers distanced themselves from a movement now associated with Nazism.[4]

### Sex Reform in Western Exile: The Role of Gender

Like men, women confronted professional dis- and requalification. But they also faced intense gender discrimination in addition to general prejudices against Jews and foreigners in the medical professions of their host countries. Whether in Shanghai, the Soviet Union, Palestine, England, Australia, or (their most frequent goal) the United States, they found social and family systems and medical establishments much more inhospitable to the combination of personal and professional/political commitments that they had managed in the Weimar Republic. In addition to their struggles for professional recognition, they were also—like all women émigrés—expected to provide material and emotional support for uprooted families and friends. Indeed, for most of these predominantly Jewish and/or socialist and Communist (but very bourgeois) women, the harsh days of emigration were the first time they faced serious resistance as female physicians as well as the daily burdens of domestic drudgery.

Refugee women doctors renegotiated the balance of work, personal life, and politics that they had established in pre-Nazi Germany. They reinvented themselves, sometimes several times, as they moved through several countries and several occupations. Some managed to regain a foothold in the medical profession, but for virtually all of them, reconstruction came at the cost of the rich social and political identities that had been particular to "new women" in Weimar Germany. Precisely the generation of "new women," who had come of age before the depression and had so optimistically established themselves during the innovative stabilization years of the republic, were most disabled. The young adapted more easily, learning the language, acquiring schooling and training in their new homelands or in temporary exile countries like Italy or Switzerland. Although some (perhaps a third—in many ways a surprisingly large number) fiercely determined refugee women doctors were able to revive their medical careers in middle age, usually after years of hardship and struggle, the unique niche that female physicians had carved out for themselves in the Weimar medical profession proved virtually impossible to replace or re-create.

More perhaps than any other group of refugees, socially and politically engaged women doctors expressed (and not only in nostalgic retrospect) a deep sense of satisfaction and pleasure in their professional and personal lives before 1933. Women doctors had been especially prominent not only within sex reform and social medicine but also among the vanguard ranks of Weimar "new women" juggling career, marriage, and motherhood. As middle-class professional women, they enjoyed for a brief and unstable period a peculiar conjuncture of traditional bourgeois privilege (especially household help) and radically expanded, albeit subordinate, employment opportunities. This liminal moment provided an extraordinary opportunity for integrating family and career without overwhelming guilt or exhaustion. Furthermore, for single women, academic study or professional work no longer mandated celibacy, either heterosexual or homosexual. As Charlotte Wolff, an unabashedly open lesbian who combined medical practice by day with a hectic life in Berlin's gay subculture at night, wrote in her memoirs about life as a young clinic physician, "Heaven was not somewhere above us, but on earth, in the German metropolis."[5]

Hertha Nathorff, former director of the Charlottenburg marriage counseling center, who arrived in New York in 1940, well past the October 1936 deadline for New York State recognition of German medical licenses, was bitterly articulate about the loss of her identity as a Weimar "new woman." In her emigration diary she grieved not only for her comfortable home and social position but most especially for her ability to combine meaningful professional work with the life of a wife and mother. Filled with resentment, Nathorff worked as her physician husband's office assistant (even for a while as a singer in a jazz nightclub) and volunteered in the New York refugee community. Seeking to apply her skills, she taught nursing to refugee women seeking domestic employment, started a women's group for the New World Club connected to the German-Jewish newspaper *Der Aufbau*, spoke on radio programs, and wrote columns in the German-language press on such topics as "The Woman as Comrade." Eventually, like many of her peers, she worked as a psychotherapist, all the while mourning her medical career.[6]

In Berlin, with adequate money and servants, in a milieu where doctor couples (albeit with the husband in the superior position) were not uncommon, self-assured successful husbands had not objected to their wives' work, and indeed often expressed pride and pleasure in their companionate marriages. In the uncertainty of exile, men reverted to traditional notions of women's place and gender hierarchy. Nathorff lamented about her displaced husband: "He can't escape from his . . . pride, his stupid pride, that he has to be and will be the family breadwinner, it torments him, but he also torments me."[7]

Nathorff shared her fate with many refugee women doctors. Husbands and colleagues slowly reestablished their practices and their professional circles, their bourgeois identities. The wives, no matter what their original occupation, worked initially as cooks, housekeepers, and nursemaids to support themselves and their family while the men studied for the dreaded foreign-language and medical licensing exams. There was little support for women doctors doing the same, not from the medical profession or the refugee aid societies, which always repeated the discouraging message, "They don't need more doctors here, and certainly not women doctors."[8] There was also no support from husbands, who bereft of status and household help, needed wives to be wives, to help them.

Hertha Riese, the former director of the *Bund für Mutterschutz* Marriage and Birth Control Counseling Center in Frankfurt and an internationally known leader in the sex reform movement, escaped Germany with her husband, the neurologist Walter Riese. Whereas her husband was (barely) able to support himself with grants for displaced scholars from the Rockefeller Foundation, the distinguished Hertha Riese learned that adjustment to the United States meant not only domesticization as a woman but also deradicalization as a sex reformer. Penniless and depressed in New York in 1942, she wrote a poignant letter seeking help from her old comrade Margaret Sanger:

> I do not mean to interfere with the ways Mrs. S. feels she can recommend me and I certainly do not either intend to renegade [sic] my convictions or my past endeavor. The question under the very difficult situation of getting a start within a very complicated set-up . . . is not to put an emphasis on Birth Control.[9]

Walter Riese, having landed a lonely position at the Virginia College of Medicine in Richmond, pleaded to no avail with the Rockefeller Foundation on his wife's behalf:

> Mrs. Riese made innumerable efforts to make use of her capacities. She failed everywhere. For the last months she has been doing a very hard and very primitive physical work, just like any unskilled woman.[10]

Hertha Riese finally found a position as an educational therapist working with "delinquent Negro" children in Richmond. When she asked for aid to support her volunteer mental hygiene work in the juvenile courts, both the Rockefeller Foundation and the National Committee for Resettlement of Foreign Physicians turned her down because her situation did not constitute an "emergency."[11] Exasperated with Hertha Riese's unwillingness to accept her fate as wife of a medical school professor in Richmond, Virginia, the Rockefeller Foundation concluded that, "Mrs. R. is rather difficult."[12]

Following the Nazi takeover in 1933 and into the war years, Sanger was confronted with a stream of desperate and often impoverished colleagues whom she knew from her work in Germany and the international birth control congresses. She did her level best to rescue birth control advocates from Nazi Europe, responding to heartbreaking pleas and persevering in the face of maddening stonewalling from the American authorities. To her faithful and hardworking assistant Florence Rose, she remarked:

> This is a frightful situation and one that if only an affidavit is necessary, I'll sign it. See what can be done—I can't be responsible for any . . . amount, but it is all so horrible not to help is almost as bad.[13]

Dr. Sidonie Fürst, for example, reached New York with the help of an affidavit from Sanger guaranteeing her livelihood. She worked as an assistant at Sanger's Birth Control Bureau for $5 a week to support her dermatologist husband as he studied for his exams and renewed professional contacts. Meanwhile, she also practiced night nursing and tried to keep up with her own studies. The National Committee for Resettlement of Foreign Physicians judged her "very well educated in dermatology," with "excellent experience in sexual science and birth control methods . . . and [a] modest, sincere, and attractive personality." The committee complained, however, that such eminently qualified women doctors were reluctant to accept the usual émigré jobs of governess or domestic servant, and persisted in harboring illusions about rejoining their professions. When Dr. Fürst not surprisingly failed her licensing exams, the committee and her husband were confirmed in their judgment that in America, "Women are extremely difficult to place in the medical profession."[14]

The "setup," as Hertha Riese had put it, was "difficult" and complicated indeed. An organization such as the Rockefeller Foundation, which was explicitly committed to rescuing the flower of European science, was not interested in ordinary medical practitioners, which of course is what women doctors were. But the general committees set up to help refugee physicians, sensitive to depression-era anxieties about an oversupply of doctors, were also unsympathetic to the substantial number of women who hoped to reestablish their medical careers. By 1940, the Rockefeller Foundation Special Research Aid Fund for Deposed Scholars in Medicine had aided 46 refugees. None of them were women. Of the few female scholars aided by the Rockefeller Foundation, none were in medicine.[15]

Women doctors had to confront the double American prejudice against female physicians and foreign professionals, exacerbated by the further double jeopardy of bias against both Jews and Germans. Additionally, the many women who had been active in the campaigns for legalization of abortion and access to birth control services suffered from the American identification (not entirely unjustified) of sex reform with "immorality" and Communism.

Women doctors who had constituted such an important part of the Weimar social welfare network were especially subject (along with many male colleagues in social medicine) to the American Medical Association's explicit fear that refugee doctors, accustomed to a national health insurance system, would subvert the privatized American medical model with notions of (supposedly inferior) "socialized medicine."[16]

For professional women, and indeed for sex reformers in general, exile therefore meant not only a shift from one country to another, from National Socialist persecution to safety, but also expulsion from the avant-garde cultural milieu of large German cities. In the United States, Weimar "new women" were likely to be politically and sexually suspect, adding to the burden of readjustment for women professionals. Exiles brought to America a host of fantasies and preconceptions, both romantic and fearful, derived from the lively Weimar discussions about Americanism and the American model of economic reform and modernity.

Ironically, the America that had often appeared in Weimar as the epitome of all that was "modern," the America that had sent Margaret Sanger to Berlin with funds to help establish birth control clinics, and had provoked extensive debate about the "modern woman" and new forms of companionate heterosexuality, proved in reality—even during the New Deal and the Second World War—to be perhaps efficient but sexually philistine and politically conservative.[17] Former Berlin city councillor and abortion rights campaigner Dr. Käte Frankenthal's "brusque, funny" manner, mannish attire, and conviction that, "I've never been married, I've never had children, I've never had a dog and that's how I like it,"[18] must have fit uneasily into her position as marriage counselor for Jewish Family Services in Manhattan. Even respectably married women like Riese or the Boston pediatrician Alice Nauen rubbed against the current of American ideologies of female maternalism and domesticity dominant during the 1930s and 1940s and certainly in the period after the Second World War when many exiles were just beginning to find themselves as "Americans."

For both married and single professional women the cultural transition reverberated with contradictions. In many ways, both the generational and gender divisions of family life in the United States were less rigid and more egalitarian; middle-class women were active in a broad range of civic and volunteer associations, children spent more time with their parents, and men were known to wash dishes and diaper babies—tasks that had mostly been performed by servants in the bourgeois homes the refugees had left behind. On the other hand, Weimar's women physicians or intellectuals were accustomed to a professional acceptance and openness of sexual discourse and behavior, including a highly unsentimental sense of the differences between sex and love, and a matter-of-fact tolerance of homosexual or bisexual relationships, which was unusual in the United States.[19] As Nauen claimed in a 1971 interview:

Our group has never really needed a Women's lib because professionally in
the past, we had an easier life. I mean we were liberated, the German-Jewish
woman in many ways. . . . But we were much more liberated than our con-
temporaries here. Our sex liberation came earlier. I mean in the academic world,
the sex liberation of my generation was just as limitless if not more so than it is
here.[20]

In England as well, the unmarried Charlotte Wolff's straightforward and
erotic definitions of lesbianism clashed with the genteel world of intense
female friendship in postwar London. In her memoirs, she mused:

Who were we and all those other young women of the twenties who seemed
to know so well what we wanted? We had no need to be helped to freedom
from male domination. We were *free*, nearly forty years before the Women's
Liberation Movement started in America. We never thought of ourselves as
being second-class citizens. We simply were ourselves, which is the only liberation which counts anyway.[21]

An amazing (and ironic) example of deradicalization and adaptation to the
"American way of life" was the fate of Dr. Else Kienle, Dr. Friedrich Wolf's
codefendant and the heroine of the 1931 Communist-led movement to abolish paragraph 218. A fiery defender of women's rights against the male medical establishment, when imprisoned as an abortionist, she had secured her
release through a well-publicized hunger strike. Rescued from Germany by
the charming alcoholic American she expeditiously married, Kienle became
a successful cosmetic surgeon of somewhat dubious respectability in New
York.[22] She quickly transferred her passionate commitment to the betterment
of women from the struggle for birth control and the right to control one's
own body to women's right to bodily self-improvement. In 1940, she published
a book called *The Breast Beautiful* dedicated:

To the medical profession—the specialist as well as the family physician—which
is daily confronted with one of mankind's foremost problems—and—To
women who love beauty and have longed for that heritage which is particularly their own—Beautiful Breasts.[23]

In Kienle's sometimes fanciful and definitely expurgated memoirs, published in the United States in 1957, she reported that John Dillinger once walked
into her office and at gunpoint demanded to have a facial scar removed, only
to flee at the bell of the timekeeper on her autoclave, and told of lecturing
on face-lifts at the Follies Club, an association of ex-showgirls who wanted
to fulfill "woman's dream of a face that never shows its age."[24] She also maintained her faith in the tricks of Weimar sexology, reporting proudly on her
success in alleviating fear of marriage in a young "lesbian" by means of "a
small incision in the hymen," which "guaranteed that her new life would begin

with little or no physical pain." With a touch of contempt for her new homeland, Kienle concluded, "Hazel became a mother twice in three years, and
when I last heard from them she and Teddy were cheerfully conforming to
the American ideal of family life in the suburbs."[25] After numerous other
adventures, including breeding hunting dogs and supervising a 120-animal
farm in New Jersey, Kienle completed her American odyssey by finally establishing "a harmonious union" with her third husband, Wesley Le Roy Robert-
son, a Native American musicologist and fashion designer who sometimes
went by his Choctow name of Isg-ti-Opti.[26]

Many women doctors, probably about two-thirds, never practiced again,
becoming doctors' wives or perhaps their office assistants. Yet, despite the
enormous obstacles, at least one-third—and not only the younger ones—did
return to medicine. They tended to be less well known, less closely identified with sex reform, and less weighed down by the baggage of highly politicized careers in Germany. Some became the feisty tough-minded German-
Jewish pediatricians that might be remembered by those who grew up in
certain postwar American urban neighborhoods. Alice Nauen, who struggled
with tenacity and ultimate success to reestablish herself as a pediatrician in
Boston, reported that the prejudices she faced were "not only towards the
refugee physician . . . but towards the woman." Her colleagues, "didn't like
it. It was the German *and* the woman."[27] Some former activists like Minna
Flake, a veteran of the Berlin VSA, laboriously built a practice on Manhattan's
Upper West Side, drawing her patient pool from old comrades she had counseled while running a refugee aid group in Paris in the 1930s.[28]

Female physicians were of course located, as they had been already in
Germany, in subordinate positions within the profession, practicing general
medicine, less desirable or prestigious specialities such as venereal disease and
tuberculosis treatment, pathology or pediatrics, or in newer and marginal
fields such as public health, psychiatry, and psychoanalysis (especially for
children and family).[29] Thus, women doctors returned to the social service
fields in which they had long been involved, but now they did so in a new
context, in the absence of the large working-class movement and comprehensive national health insurance system that had lent their work financial
security and political significance.

In Germany, women had been prominent in precisely those fields, such
as birth control and social medicine, that were most underdeveloped in the
United States. The American experiment with federally funded maternal and
child welfare clinics, in which many women doctors had found a professional
home, had ended with the repeal of the Sheppard-Towner Act in 1929.
Weimar refugees began arriving in the United States just as economic crisis
was hitting hard and the number of women entering medicine, which had
peaked at about 6 percent of medical school students in 1910, was stagnating
at between 4 and 5 percent.[30] Indeed, whereas Weimar women doctors had
perceived themselves as part of a growing group, the absolute number of

women physicians in the United States was actually declining in the 1930s; in 1930, there were 6,825 women doctors in the United States, 4.4 percent of the total and barely double the total number in much smaller Germany.[31] Refugee physicians, both male and female, faced a situation in which, in Regina Morantz-Sanchez's formulation, the Sheppard-Towner Act's defeat "put the finishing touches on the medical profession's decade-long retreat from social activism."[32]

At the same time, however, as Linda Gordon has so carefully delineated, the birth control movement under the energetic leadership of Margaret Sanger was coming of age in the 1930s and 1940s. Despite the fact that, much to Sanger's irritation, New Deal social welfare policies were very cautious about birth control, the number of birth control clinics in the United States had risen from 55 in 1930 to 800 in 1942, the year the Birth Control Federation of America signaled the turn to medicalized family planning by changing its name to Planned Parenthood Federation of America.[33]

Exiled sex reform physicians' expertise in birth control and sex counseling was perceived as useful by American birth controllers and Sanger did employ several émigrés in her New York Birth Control Research Bureau, but under the professionalized and depoliticized terms that Sanger favored.[34] The link to socialism and the working-class movement had been broken in the United States in the 1920s, but now the combined impact of the depression and the reports of Nazi population policy measures led to a discrediting of eugenic as well as socialist language in favor of "environmentalism," without of course changing, as Gordon points out, the "elitism of the birth controllers."[35] So Weimar sex reformers entered a situation in which birth controllers in the United States were, as Gordon notes, far more concerned with social stability than social justice, suspicious not only of their socialism but also of their hereditarian notions.[36]

Moreover, in an American medical world dominated by private practice, women lost the arenas in which they had been trained to function. They left professional work entirely, resettled into related fields, took low-level clinic and hospital jobs, or adjusted (in many cases reluctantly) to the demands of private practice. Their medical practice, while still primarily in the social caregiver mode, changed meaning and status in the American context where medicine was organized so differently. The ability to find "niches," whether in medicine or in related social service occupations, was absolutely critical.

A significant number of those women doctors who managed to continue their professional careers turned to related nonmedical fields, particularly social work, psycho- or physiotherapy, and psychoanalysis, thus fulfilling in reworked form their Weimar notion of medicine as a holistic social vocation. In the United States, these occupations were subject to less stringent financial and licensing requirements and were considered "womanly" and "caring" in much the same way that general medical practice was viewed in Germany. Psychotherapy in particular was developing into a burgeoning and

relatively open field in the 1940s and 1950s.[37] Forced to suppress both their
socialist and eugenic convictions during and after the Second World War and
later during the Cold War, many women doctors became more Freudian, a
stance they had rejected in Weimar as "antisocial."

Käte Frankenthal initially worked at the Connecticut State Farm for
women, sold socks and Christmas cards door to door, and then established a
psychotherapy practice in New York. She supplemented her earnings by selling Good Humor ice cream in the summer between patients and using her
psychological insights as a nightclub fortune-teller.[38] Exiled sex reformers in
other countries made similar transitions. In France, Lilly Ehrenfried, who had
fled to Paris via Basel when threatened with entrapment on abortion charges,
returned happily to her first love, gymnastics.[39] In London, Charlotte Wolff
became a psychoanalyst specializing in theories of homo- and bisexuality and
graphology; she also became the first person to write a full-length biography
of her old colleague Magnus Hirschfeld.[40] Lotte Fink, the codirector with
Hertha Riese of the Frankfurt *Bund für Mutterschutz* counseling center, became
active in the Australian Racial Hygiene (later Family Planning) Association.
In 1952 she represented Australia at the founding conference of the International Planned Parenthood Federation, organized by Margaret Sanger in
Bombay.

A striking number of women refugees in the United States seem to have
carried their social convictions into a concern for minorities, often working
in black neighborhoods and with African-American families.[41] Hertha Riese
eventually found an outlet for her abundant energy and social concerns as
an advocate for black children in Virginia. On one of her early tours as a door-
to-door saleswoman for perfumes and toiletries, she rang the doorbell of a
wealthy civic-minded woman who was intrigued by the middle-aged woman
with the European accent. In the curious process of immediate personal contact that refugees liked to suggest could happen "only in America," Mrs. Kitty
Dennis became Riese's patron and sponsored her pioneering work in mental
hygiene. By 1942, Riese and Dennis were meeting with black community
leaders and white donors to discuss forming an agency to aid "severely disturbed children." In 1943, the Educational Therapy and Day Care Center
opened in the stack room of the "colored" branch of the Richmond city library.
In 1948, it affiliated with the State Department of Mental Hygiene. By 1960,
Riese's experiment boasted a yearly budget of $63,000; a staff of 18 was treat-
ing about 50 children daily.

In Weimar Frankfurt, Riese had depicted her patients as "wretched victims [who] become a burden to the family and everybody else, and even their
offspring cannot become part of civilized life."[42] Now the former sterilization
enthusiast was committed to the notion that although "disturbed and grossly
neglected children . . . have become indifferent or antagonistic to the avowed
wishes of the community, they are a part of the community and molded
largely by it, and thus they are ours."[43]

Reinvented as a Freudian-oriented child psychotherapist, Riese used 18 years of case histories in the Educational Therapy Center to write a remarkably sensitive and empathic chronicle of children whose emotional crises had everything to do with racism and social and economic deprivation. In her 1962 book *Heal the Hurt Child*, Riese, while still in many ways a radical and certainly an iconoclast in the American context, discarded—like many of her sex reform refugee colleagues—both her socialist and eugenic enthusiasms in favor of a social psychoanalytic approach, insisting:

> In many years of work with the Negro child, I have not found the "Negro" in him. What I found was a greater despondency than in the white child . . . also a deeper hopelessness that talking will not help. . . . But all such more marked negative attitudes are not caused by any "Negro-ness" in these young people— it is generated by particularly damaging pressures and deprivations imposed on them as Negroes.[44]

In her new life, rather than resorting to sterilization as a desperate solution for misery and economic crisis, she aimed to salvage "the hurt child" through social as well as psychiatric intervention. It is clear from reminiscences of those who knew her well that the indominitable Riese paid an enormous price for her successful cultural, political and professional transformation; she gave up her medical career, accepted a reputation as an eccentric, overbearing, and shrill if determined and effective troublemaker, and she alienated her two daughters.[45]

Indeed, revealing again the ways in which gender constrains women more powerfully than men, identities as wives, mothers, sisters, or daughters were clearly more salient than men's as equivalent family members. Women professionals were overburdened with housework and child care. They suffered from the disruption of childbearing and child-raising patterns. They often privileged economic survival and their husbands' psychological and professional reconstruction at the expense of their children—including sending children away to boarding schools or foster homes during the difficult period of adjustment—priorities that later earned them bitter reproach by their offspring.[46]

Single women had in some cases more mobility and less pressure to do menial labor to provide for children and retraining husbands, but often less financial and social support.[47] Helene Stöcker, for example, not a physician but the longtime head of the *Bund für Mutterschutz*, initially fled to Switzerland where she was received by her old friends, the anarchist sex reformers Fritz and Paulette Brupbacher. Stöcker remained in Switzerland, supported by the Brupbachers and refugee funds from the birth control movement and the International Women's League for Peace and Freedom, until 1938 when the German takeover of Austria frightened her across the channel to England.[48] The outbreak of the war then trapped her in Sweden, where she was attending an international congress of PEN (the writers organization). In 1939 the German exile community in Stockholm, including Max Hodann, celebrated her 70th birthday. After the Germans occupied Norway in 1940, Stöcker managed to gain a prized visa for prominent refugees organized with the help of Eleanor Roosevelt. Having finally lost even her remaining luggage at a transit stop in Moscow, she wrote despairingly:

> So one loses one possession after another: home, fatherland, the most important records and books, and then finally even one's clothes. One is like a shipwrecked person who can only save his naked life—which one also has to relinquish at the end.[49]

Gravely ill with breast cancer, Stöcker journeyed across Russia by Trans-Siberian Railroad to Japan, then by ship to the United States, and finally to an apartment on Riverside Drive in New York. In 1942, Hertha Riese described her reunion with Stöcker: "We are still rather lonely and old friends and comrades of thoughts mean a lot to us."[50] In 1943, alone and impoverished, essentially unknown and forgotten, Stöcker died.[51]

The redoubtable Käte Frankenthal, who had resolved her brief temptation to get married in Berlin by "buying some new furniture and hiring a housekeeper,"[52] found herself in conflict with her mentors Harry Stack Sullivan and Clara Thompson at the William Alanson White Institute of Psychiatry over her obdurate insistence that life posed her no problems and certainly none related to being single and childless![53] She died at age 87, in 1976 in New York City, largely isolated from former colleagues and still embittered at being insufficiently appreciated.

A focus on women professionals, especially those most active in sex reform, and the sense of loss they expressed, casts a somewhat different light on the discussion of women's supposedly superior coping skills. Studies of women and emigration from Nazi Europe have stressed that women's familial priorities and the relative weakness of their attachment to public status, as well as their generally greater social flexibility, allowed them to compensate for their losses and adjust to exile better than men.[54] Indeed, professional women as well as housewives carried with them more practical training in modern languages and (and at least minimal) household skills as well as a greater willingness to accept employment beneath their (bourgeois) status.

The fact that, as one refugee woman doctor put it, "It isn't as hard for a woman to cook, as it is for a man to scrub floors,"[55] made women more adaptable to foreign lands, and often turned them into primary and lifesaving breadwinners in the early years of emigration. Women's mediating contacts with social service agencies and educational institutions made them into the primary translators of the new world for their families. But these responsibilities were often fulfilled at great physical and psychological cost and at the price of their own highly developed professional and political—even maternal and sexual—identities.

## Male Sex Reform Doctors in Exile

Men (with some notable exceptions) were generally spared the total disqualification or retooling that many women confronted. But they too had to relinquish professional self-understandings and contexts as well as the eugenic and socialist rhetoric and convictions that had defined their work in Weimar Germany. While most sex reformers did eventually manage the transition, for many it was difficult to distance themselves from practices now associated with Nazism without delegitimating what had been a life's work. They resented the Nazi hijacking of what they still perceived as a progressive social hygiene project inextricably linked to birth control and sex education.[56] In New York in 1951, the sexologist Ludwig Levy-Lenz, who had run the *Liga's* Berlin center, still defended his enthusiasm for sterilization:

> Just as one would remove watches from a lunatic, or take away his knife and fork and only allow him wooden spoons to eat with so one should make sure that he cannot do any harm with his sexual organ.[57]

Dr. Hans Lehfeldt, codirector of the Berlin RV / GESEX clinic, recalled that when he arrived in the United States as a refugee from Nazism, it required Margaret Sanger herself to convince him that the 1933 sterilization law—based, after all, on American models—was not one of the "very few good things that Hitler does," but would be misused for "political purposes."[58] Joined by Austrian refugee physician Christopher Tietze, Lehfeldt became a stalwart of the U.S. birth control movement and one of the founders of the Society for the Scientific Study of Sex as well as an editor with Albert Ellis of the *Journal of Sexual Science*. Maintaining his close friendship with Margaret Sanger, in 1958 he opened the first birth control clinic in a public hospital in New York. The Bellevue clinic was among the first to test the birth control pill on (mostly Hispanic) women in the 1950s and 1960s. Untroubled by charges of recruiting patients as guinea pigs in exchange for free care, Lehfeldt remained proud of his contribution to the development of social medicine in the United States.[59]

Lehfeldt's American success and his integration into the American birth control movement as well as International Planned Parenthood depended on his ability to temper his enthusiasm for some of the central points of the Weimar sex reform program, notably eugenic sterilization, support for homosexual rights, and socialism; what remained consistent was his identity as a crusading non-party-bound physician and his commitment to legal abortion. In 1932, Lehfeldt had published what would become the definitive contemporary account of the lay sex reform movement. In the United States, he also took it upon himself to become the chronicler of sex reform in exile, writing articles about his former colleagues and maintaining contact with young Germans seeking to resuscitate the lost memory of the pre-Nazi movement.[60]

Others found this process of reinvention more difficult. The most notorious example surely was Wilhelm Reich. Drawing on his friendship with the

Danish WLSR activist Hans Leunbach, he had first fled to Denmark; after a
typically peripatetic exile itinerary (Denmark to England to Sweden and finally
to Oslo in 1934), he came to the United States in 1939 with a contract from the
New School for Social Research and settled in Maine. Reich's experiments
with orgone energy eventually led to his incarceration on fraud charges. He
died on November 3, 1957, in an American federal penitentiary in Lewisburg,
Pennsylvania, sympathetically eulogized only by the *Village Voice*.[61]

In England, the activist RV physician Rudolf (Edward) Elkan from Hamburg also had a difficult time adjusting to the "ladies" of the British family
planning movement. In a letter to his old friend Max Hodann, Elkan complained about a ballet benefit for birth control that he felt compelled to attend:
"Of course it is for a good purpose, but I think it's a loathsome affair, and I
am not quite sure for which of my sins I am going to be compelled to go
there."[62] Writing in 1934 to his Danish WLSR comrade Leunbach, Elkan ironically invoked the triumph of the "1,000-Year Reich," wryly noting that he felt
like a "living anachronism" and that "we could have easily waited another
one thousand years for our birth, we wouldn't have missed anything!"[63]

Ernst Gräfenberg, whom Lehfeldt had been unable to persuade to leave
Germany, remained in Berlin because he felt "perfectly safe with wives of high
Nazi officials as his patients." Inevitably—Lehfeldt later noted—"he was
wrong": Gräfenberg was finally ransomed out of a Gestapo jail in 1940 by
Margaret Sanger. He eventually worked under Alan Guttmacher at Mt. Sinai,
and Sanger allowed him to practice—as the only male doctor—at her New
York birth control clinic. But, because she questioned their safety, she would
not let the distinguished Berlin gynecologist prescribe or insert the intrauterine
devices he had developed. Lehfeldt remembered the inventor of the most
widely used IUD, shrugging and saying to his friend, "I'm only working here."[64]

Sanger, Gräfenberg's loyal patron, eventually grew frustrated with his difficulties learning English and adjusting to American informality; she complained that no patient referred to him ever wanted to return.[65] Gräfenberg
died unrecognized in 1957 but his controversial research on the IUD underwent a renaissance in the 1960s. He enjoyed some brief moments of post-
humous fame when his research on female sexual response was used in the
Kinsey Report and by the American sex researchers Masters and Johnson;[66]
indeed the "G" in the title of a 1982 sex advice book on the *G-Spot* honored
Gräfenberg's studies on vaginal orgasm.[67]

Lehfeldt also tried to sustain the international reputation of Felix Theilhaber, his former colleague in the Berlin RV/GESEX clinic who had emigrated
to Palestine in 1935. Along with many other exiles, Theilhaber was instrumental in transferring a specialized and technologically advanced German model
of medical care to a previously medically underserved population in Palestine.
In 1941, he established the Kupat Holim Maccabi health insurance network,
which unlike more strictly socialist plans developed by East European Zion-
ist settlers, provided free choice of doctors. As the reference to the German-

Jewish youth sports organization Maccabi suggested, the insurance plan also aimed to strengthen Zionism through the integration of health, sports, and fitness that Weimar sex reformers had preached; it developed into one of the largest insurance companies in Israel, with Theilhaber serving as its medical director until his death in 1956.[68]

After the war, Lehfeldt was instrumental in reviving connections between American birth controllers and a German movement struggling to reestablish itself in the shadow of the Third Reich. He nurtured contacts with Anne-Marie Durand-Wever and Hans Harmsen, entertaining them on their U.S. tours, and meeting with them at European family planning conferences. As the next chapter will show, the two jointly established the West German family planning organization *Pro Familia*, despite having taken very different paths during National Socialism.[69]

## Exile and the Soviet Union

Those Weimar sex reformers who remained in continental Europe, and especially those who were identified as Communists or outspoken leftists, underwent different kinds of humiliations and transformations. Despite their increasing unease at the ongoing trials and purges in the 1930s, many of them still looked to the Soviet Union as the source of the great social and political experiment that had inspired them to envision a new (human) "race" of sexually and socially healthy women and men, and as the last best hope for defeating a murderous fascism that was ravaging Germany, Italy, and Spain.

For many sex reformers, the recriminalization of abortion in the USSR in 1936 produced the same kind of shock and confusion that the Nazi-Soviet Pact brought their comrades three years later. The most noted KPD campaigner for abortion rights, Martha Ruben-Wolf, who had organized medical study tours to the Soviet Union and represented the views of Soviet physicians at the 1930 Zurich conference, committed suicide in 1939 in the Soviet Union she had so zealously propagandized. She had unsuccessfully protested the 1936 abortion decree, and in 1938 her husband Dr. Lothar Wolf (among many other of her German comrades) had been purged and sentenced as an anti-Soviet spy.[70] Former KPD activist Franziska Rubens, who lived with her two children and surgeon husband in the Comintern Hotel Lux, had just finished a brochure on women in the Soviet Union that referred proudly to the value of the Soviet example of legalized abortion for the 1931 campaign to abolish paragraph 218, when the new law was promulgated: "The brochure, already approved and typeset, was never published."[71]

The June 27, 1936 decree "In Defense of Mother and Child" prohibited abortion except on medical or eugenic grounds, thus abrogating the dramatic reform of November 1920 that made the young Soviet Union the first nation to legalize abortions performed in hospitals by physicians. Recriminalization

came, as it would again in the Soviet-dominated German Democratic Republic, in 1950, after a period of legality justified by a state of (postwar and post-
revolution) emergency. Wrapped into what Wendy Goldman has called a
"larger campaign to promote 'family responsibility,'" the decree also aimed
to "protect" motherhood by expanding maternity benefits, bonuses for mothers of large families, and child-care facilities, as well as tightening divorce restrictions and procedures for collecting alimony—measures that by and large
met with approval among Soviet women.[72]

Given the context of the Soviet revision and the rhetoric of their own campaigns for legal abortion in Weimar Germany, exiled sex reformers should
not perhaps have been as shocked as they professed to be. As was clearly
evident in the extensive German debates, the arguments for legalization,
which frequently referred glowingly to the Soviet model, had always been
ambivalent and conditional. The much-lauded Bolshevik reform had treated
abortion as a necessary evil, and any interruption of pregnancy by laypeople
or midwives remained criminal.

By the beginning of 1924, further restrictions were introduced when the
flood of applications for free abortions led to the establishment of commissions to administer priority lists favoring those judged most needy and worthy: the unmarried and the unemployed. But extensive social data gathered
from the questionnaires required of applicants demonstrated that, just as in
Germany, women terminating unwanted pregnancies were by no means only
the desperate and destitute, but were often employed and married mothers
seeking to limit family size. The women applying to the commissions subverted the tenets of Communist reproductive politics: that in a socialist society the need for abortion would wither away because women with access to
employment and social insurance would be happy to bear children.

Furthermore, in defiance of all the medical and political justifications for
abortion reform, legalization had not stemmed the "epidemic" of illegal abortions or substantially reduced the risks to women's health.[73] Sex reformers'
promise that legalization would reduce injury and morbidity from "quack"
abortions and protect women's health, thereby making them ready to bear
children under improved circumstances, had not been fulfilled. Instead of
providing statistical fuel for progressive German doctors to extoll the medical efficacy of Soviet abortion practice as the KPD had done during the
Weimar years, Soviet physicians were increasingly perturbed about abortions'
negative impact on the birth rate and the hazards the procedure posed even
when performed under the best of circumstances.[74] Their anxieties became
part of the rationale for the 1936 revision.

The 1936 decree was based on contradictory assumptions which were nonetheless consistent with the logic of Communist reproductive politics: on the
one hand, that the social welfare achievements of socialism allowed women
joyfully to undertake both motherhood and waged labor; on the other hand,
that legalization had not attained its stated goals of reducing illegal abortions

and eliminating dangers to health. Furthermore, contrary to the glowing image of Soviet social progress that had been purveyed in Germany not only by the KPD but also by Münzenberg's mass media and by the German Association of Friends of the Soviet Union, cochaired by nonparty members Helene Stöcker and Max Hodann, the decree implicitly conceded the failure of revolutionary reforms such as the family code of 1918 and the 1926 Marriage Reform Law.

Indeed, in many ways the improved provision of child-care and maternity benefits and the tightening of marriage, divorce, and alimony regulations that accompanied the abortion restrictions came as a welcome relief to women who daily contended with menfolk unable to meet the much quoted challenge from a peasant woman at a Bolshevik Congress: "If you love tobogganing, then you have to pull your sled uphill." The 1936 decree promised to alleviate some of the social disorganization produced by war, revolution, civil war, and the New Economic Policy: abandoned wives and children, female unemployment, and men's inability or unwillingness to fulfill their obligation under the 1926 Marriage Law to pay alimony even in de facto unions. Moreover, the new constitution of 1936 proclaimed the complete equality of women and men, and the second Five-Year Plan was resulting in a massive movement of women into the labor force. All these factors mitigated the impact of criminalization; for the vast majority of rural women, legal abortion had been in any case an abstract right not to be deeply mourned. Still, Martha Ruben-Wolf had not been alone in her protest. The decree was preceded by a spirited press debate in which thousands of women vigorously defended the right to abortion they believed the revolution had guaranteed.[75]

Certainly, the edict was experienced as a betrayal by exiled Weimar sex reformers for whom the Soviet example had been so crucial, their shock exacerbated by the simultaneous campaign of terror against German exiles in the Soviet Union and the beginning of the great Moscow show trials. Reporting on the death of Martha Ruben-Wolf, Susanne Leonhard, a Communist activist who spent long years in Stalin's Gulag, bitterly remembered her dismay at what she perceived as the Soviet about-face:

Friedrich Wolf's *Cyankali* was our propaganda piece with which we won over not only working class women but women from all classes and groups for the idea of the liberation of women from the captivity of Paragraph 218. We boasted everywhere about the Soviet Union, the most progressive state in the world in which abortion was permitted.[76]

The exile VSA journal noted that "the language of the Soviet press" defending the decree "can barely be distinguished—it is painfully embarassing to say this—from the Nazi organs in the Third Reich."[77] Although their lives and political identifications would take different turns, both Friedrich Wolf and Max Hodann, arguably the best-known sex reform doctors, responded to the crises of the 1930s by seeking to join the Loyalist forces in Spain. In Hodann's case, and probably in Wolf's, the turn to a cause that seemed to preserve the increasingly shaky humanitarian mission of communism may well have been a way of coping with their confusion and disappointment at the recriminalization of abortion and the show trials and purges. Friedrich Wolf, the focus, together with Else Kienle, of the 1931 anti–paragraph 218 mobilization, had fled Stuttgart in March 1933 as his plays and tracts on natural health and abortion were burned and confiscated. A Communist party member since 1928, he escaped to Switzerland and then to Moscow, where with his wife Else and two sons he occupied a (comparatively palatial) two-room apartment and a dacha in Pereldelkino, near Boris Pasternak. He lived the strange life of a privileged antifascist exile, even as the supposed haven from Nazi persecution became itself an ever more horrific universe of paranoia and denunciation.[78]

Arrests had begun after the assassination in December 1934 of Kirov, the moderate and popular Leningrad party chief, and culminated in the terror of the show trials beginning in August 1936. Despite revived hopes tied to the new Soviet constitution, repression intensified and, "the first large wave of arrests of Germans" came in the summer and fall of 1936;[79] they coincided with promulgation of the new abortion regulations. Franziska Rubens remembered that trusted comrades disappeared because it was "better to arrest one too many than one too few," and those remaining free crossed the street in order to avoid contact with those who might be under suspicion.[80]

As the situation in Moscow became more desperate and greater numbers of German comrades were arrested, Wolf finally managed to leave Moscow for Spain in 1938, when it was already "too late": by February 1939 the war in Spain was over and the international brigades disbanded.[81] Trapped in France, he joined other refugees such as Lion Feuchtwanger, Arnold Zweig, and Franz Werfel in Sanary on the French Mediterranean coast. When the war started, he headed for Paris in order to make contacts with French party officials, but was arrested and interned as a dangerous German and Communist in Le Vernet camp, where he finally met up with the Loyalist fighters he had missed in Spain.[82] Finally, in 1941, the Soviet citizenship secured for him by his wife Else, who had remained in Moscow with their sons, gained his release from internment. He returned to the USSR on the eve of the German invasion, after the worst of the purges was over, and became one of the organizers of the National Committee for a Free Germany, which tried—with little success—to promote Communist and antifascist propaganda among German troops and prisoners of war.[83]

One of his comrades was Martha Arendsee, former Reichstag deputy, head of the KPD social welfare organization ARSO and editor of its journal, with whom he had worked closely during the anti-218 campaign; she broadcast radio programs directed toward German women. Wolf was repatriated in September 1945 to the Soviet Zone where he was honored for his literary work and would add his voice to the revived and by no means resolved debate on paragraph 218 and abortion in post–Nazi Germany. Arendsee also returned to Eastern Germany, where as a party veteran she was appointed to the presidium of the Communist trade union organization.[84]

## Exile in Western Europe

Wolf and Arendsee survived the disappearance and murder of so many party comrades in Stalin's Soviet Union with their faith in communism apparently intact. Max Hodann, on the other hand, who had never publicly joined the KPD and who maintained close contacts to sex reformers in the KPD, SPD, and the nonpartisan Center for Birth Control, had been refused permanent asylum by England, and was debating emigration to the Soviet Union, just as the new abortion decree became public.[85] He resolved his conflict by joining, together with 19 other German physicians, the medical team for the pro-Spanish Loyalist Thälmann Brigade, the German antifascist unit named after the incarcerated former leader of the KPD.[86] In a masterly understatement, he wrote to the British abortion rights activist Janet Chance:

> As you can imagine, the two recent events, the abortion law and the executions, are going to make the new Communist policy of a united front more difficult to achieve at least in the circles of opinion I meet.[87]

In his comprehensive history of sexology and sex reform *History of Modern Morals*, published in England in 1937, Hodann tried to defend the Soviet legislation for a society where "women citizens should have no need to evade motherhood, but can undertake it gladly and safely." Nevertheless, he predicted that, "The renewed sharp penalization of abortion must inevitably lead to a sharp rise in the number of illegal operations, with their train of invalidism and death, in spite of all the contructive work for maternity now promised and planned."[88]

The German novelist and dramatist Peter Weiss, who met Hodann in Swedish exile in the 1940s, has movingly portrayed in his novel *Aesthetik des Widerstands* an ailing but still committed Max Hodann working in field hospitals and convalescent homes in Civil War Spain. Closely following Hodann's own notes, Weiss depicts the physician as plagued by terrible asthma attacks but still filled with "calm" and "happy equanimity" (*vergnüglicher Gleichmut*). Hodann shows off the papers stripping him of his German citizenship and his doctoral degree, tries to cope with the physical, psychological, and not least political problems of wounded and shellshocked casualties in a brigade convalescent home, and negotiates the minefields not only of the war against the Francoist rebels but between Communists and anarchists, and among Communists themselves. In Weiss's version, Hodann tries to turn his clinic

into a site of psychic and intellectual renewal, still believing as he had in his
sex counseling and youth work in Berlin that open and unsentimental discussion—"science and clarity"—could solve all problems.[89]

Max Hodann returned to Norway after his Spanish service and then moved
to Sweden in 1940 just before the German invasion. He was active in the Free
German Cultural Union (*Freier Deutscher Kulturbund*, FDKB), a Communist-
oriented exile organization. Hodann also worked with the Swedish sex reform
organization *Riksförbundet för Sexuell Upplysning* (Swedish Association for
Sexual Enlightenment, RFSU) which had been founded in 1932 in order to press
for birth control and sex education programs from the Social Democrats who
came to power that year. Its head, Elise Ottesen-Jensen, who with Margaret
Sanger would become a cofounder of International Planned Parenthood,
knew Hodann through her work with the WLSR and her participation in the
1930 Zurich conference. She intermittently employed him as an archivist in
her Stockholm headquarters, apparently more as a gesture of solidarity toward
the ailing refugee than because she expected much real work from him.[90]

From 1944 to 1945, Hodann also functioned as a "political adviser" in the
press department of the British Legation in Stockholm. Among his partially
secret activities, Hodann continued the psychological and pedagogical work
with young people that had been his mission in Weimar and then in Spanish
Civil War clinics and field hospitals, and with German Army deserters and
prisoners of war who had escaped to Sweden from Denmark, Norway, and
Finland. His activities, including the publication of a small journal *Der Weg
ins Leben* (*The Path to Life*), were financed by the British, and Hodann came
into increasing conflict with the rest of the FDKB leadership over his contacts to the Western (anti-Communist) allies.

Once the war was over, the German émigré was no longer needed by the
British and he was dismissed in July 1945, a self-described "victim of the de-
mobilization."[91] But his ties to the left were also ruptured: Weiss described
him as profoundly pained by the betrayals of the Soviet Union and Communism, and by the murder of so many old comrades. Willi Münzenberg, under
whose aegis much of Hodann's work had been conducted and publicized and
who had attempted to continue building antifascist popular organizations
during the war, was found dead under an oak tree in a French forest in October 1940. He had apparently been killed either by Stalin's political police
(N.K.V.D.) or local Communist party groups.[92] In a letter to his daughter,
Hodann acknowledged that, "The old slogans have lost their meanings."[93]

Yet, Hodann did move to reestablish his connections with the international
sex reform and birth control movement. He corresponded with Janet Chance
and with his old RV colleague Rudolf (now Edward) Elkan in London—
whereby the two middle-aged and exiled sex reformers warmly shared recollections and ruminations about their many, and not entirely successful,
relationships with women—and with other European birth controllers. He

embarked in 1946 on a grueling lecture tour of Switzerland, after having passed
through Germany by train, and being assaulted by memories "like a bad dream
haunting us."[94] Speaking to groups of Swiss workers, he was criticized for his
insistence that premarital sex was "to be taken for granted";[95] even in Sweden he had been attacked as a "sex-Jew from Weimar" for continuing his
agitation around abortion rights and for his lectures on sexual problems such
as masturbation.[96]

In 1946, still committed to the credo he scribbled in his personal notes for
"openness, responsibility, science; against hypocrisy, mystification and super-
stition,"[97] Hodann was trying to organize a renewed WLSR with a congress
in Switzerland. At least in part due to his death late that year, the conference
was never held; the WLSR could not be revived. At the end, stateless, deeply
depressed, with his health ruined by his year and a half in Spain, he was trying unsuccessfully to start an import/export business. He frantically sent letters to old comrades all over the globe, asking for help in resettling somewhere in a warm climate, which might alleviate his asthma. He died, an
apparent suicide, in Sweden on December 17, 1946, at the age of 52, a broken
and disappointed man. Peter Weiss describes a man in such despair that he
chooses not to inject himself, as he had so often previously, with the vial of
adrenaline that would have calmed his asthma attack. In Weiss's account he
was found, hunched over in the bathroom of his apartment, syringe in hand,
in a "pool of saliva and sweat."[98]

Unlike Friedrich Wolf, Hodann had rejected the possibility of returning
to Germany, having—as he wrote in November 1945—"no desire to now in
comradely fashion rebuild what those barbarians had destroyed in twelve
years."[99] In 1935, Hodann had contributed an obituary for his old mentor
Magnus Hirschfeld to the VSA exile *International Medical Bulletin* published in
Prague. The epitaph he quoted, chosen by Magnus Hirschfeld for himself,
could—11 years later—equally well have applied to Hodann: "Unrecognized,
burnt, banned" (*Verkannt, verbrannt, verbannt*).[100]

The destruction and exile of Weimar sex reform therefore effectively
marked the end of the prewar international sex reform movement in which
German radicals had been so prominent. In August 1946, shortly before his
death, and after the collapse of his plans for a restored WLSR, Max Hodann
still presided over a session at the first postwar conference on birth control.
It had been called by Elise Ottesen-Jensen in Stockholm on behalf of the RFSU,
a lay organization modeled on the defunct RV. With a membership of about
100,000 and a strong lobbying voice in the Swedish government and the public school system, the RFSU was now the only continental European birth
control organization to have survived fascism and world war in a strong position.[101] The Stockholm gathering, which for the first time reunited some activists scattered by war and emigration, became in effect the first meeting of
what would become in 1952 the International Planned Parenthood Federa-

tion. It signaled the sea change in politics and terminology impelled by both the destruction of German sex reform and Stalinist repression: away from sex reform, birth control, and socialism (despite Ottesen-Jensen's protests), to family planning and marriage counseling.

Ottesen-Jensen, a woman very much in the tradition of the mass lay workers' movement, chaired the conference. Margaret Sanger, with her commitment to professionalization and medicalization—whose American financial clout would eventually lend her the upper hand—delivered the keynote address. The contest and collaboration between these two very different but equally committed and charismatic women was expressed in the wrangling over potential titles for the new postwar international movement: sex reform, planned parenthood, or population control. It would also mark the reconstruction and new direction of birth control and sexology in the post–World War II period.

# eight

# No Zero Hour
## *Abortion and Birth Control*
## *in Postwar Germany*

And so once again today, paragraph 218 stands as the flashpoint
(*Brennpunkt*) of all discussions in the states of the Soviet zone and
Berlin.

Delegate to the Saxon Parliament,
June 1947[1]

Work for birth control . . . needs a lot of civil courage, which is rather
rare in this country!

West German lay activist
ILSE LEDERER, June 1954[2]

This book ends with a discussion curiously similar to the one with which it
began: German efforts to cope with defeat and postwar reconstruction and
its perceived effects on women, family, and social health. Once again, the
politics of reproduction and sexuality, and especially questions around abortion, birth control, and marriage and sex counseling, took center stage as a
new welfare state (in this case, two new welfare states) was organized. But
after 12 years of National Socialism, the repression of sex reform in the Soviet
Union, and the exile of many of the most committed exponents of sex
reform, the terms of debate had shifted. Defeat, occupation, and reconstruction could not, indeed deliberately did not intend to, restore what had been
destroyed.

"Zero hour"—the metaphor often used to mark the apparent (but deceptive) collapse of old structures in a devastated postwar Germany—had come
for the German sex reform movement in 1933, not 1945. Yet some veterans of
the Weimar movement played a major role in the formulation of postwar
family planning and social hygiene, as both East and West Germany appropriated, distorted, and renovated different parts of that legacy. Moreover, the

two most important foreign influences—now with physical presences as occupying powers—continued to be the United States and the Soviet Union (in the West, the British also played an important role).

A considerable number of Communist and Social Democratic exiles as well as former inmates of Nazi jails and camps—both Jewish and non-Jewish, and including Friedrich Wolf, Martha Arendsee, and Helene Overlach—initially returned to the East where they claimed the succession to KPD social welfare programs. Supported by the revivified German Communist party (later SED) and the Soviet Military Administration (SMA), they tried to resuscitate such Weimar sex reform initiatives as clinic-based medical care (*Ambulatorien*), legalization of socially necessary abortions, marriage and sex counseling centers, maternal protection, and equality for working women.

In the absence of any significant return of Jewish and leftist professionals to the Western zones, there was, as has now been profusely documented, a great deal of continuity in health and welfare personnel from the Third Reich into the postwar period.[3] In the West, Hans Harmsen and Anne-Marie Durand-Wever both worked to reconstitute a German birth control movement. However, it was Harmsen, the only prominent Weimar sex reformer to collaborate actively with the National Socialists and their sterilization programs, who won the support of Margaret Sanger and the Rockefeller Foundation, and moved relatively seamlessly into the leadership of the postwar family planning organization, *Pro Familia*.

Especially in West Germany, birth control activity was slowly reestablished in the context of a postwar International Planned Parenthood movement that had been stripped of its radical socialist content after the destruction of the Weimar and Soviet experiments. Nonetheless, it remained profoundly influenced—if not without ambivalence—by Weimar sex reform and some of its exiled practitioners. Indeed, in many ways it traced its lineage to the 1930 Zurich conference which had been attended by so many German birth controllers, both those soon exiled and the few, like Harmsen and Durand-Wever, who had remained in Germany.

Thus, this chapter insists—as has the entire book—that the international context was crucial for German domestic developments; it also stresses that the combined—and often not clearly distinguishable—inheritance of Weimar and National Socialist discourses, policies, and personnel profoundly affected postwar developments in both Germanies. The first part discusses the revived abortion debate, especially in the SBZ, where paragraph 218 was abolished and new regulations were instituted. The focus then moves to attempts to reorganize birth control and marriage counseling in both eastern and western sectors of Berlin, the city that continued to be a leader in birth control. Finally, attention shifts to the Federal Republic and the development there of a family planning movement different from both Weimar sex reform and the state-sponsored population policy in the East.

## *Postwar Crisis*

Repeatedly, as a public sphere was reconstituted in the immediate aftermath of May 1945, doctors, health officials, the press, political parties, women's organizations, and church groups rehearsed the debates about abortion, birth control, and marriage and sex counseling that had defined post–World War I and Great Depression discourse about social welfare and population policy. In the wake of war and defeat, calls for reconstruction of "healthy and natural motherliness,"[4] family, and marriage were ubiquitous as was consternation about the birth rate, infant and child malnutrition, invalidism and mortality, the "plagues" of venereal disease, prostitution, tuberculosis, and abortion. This time, familiar anxieties about the health and continued survival of the *Volk* were exacerbated by the physical devastation of warfare on German soil, occupation by four separate victorious powers, the huge influx of German refugees from conquered territories in the East as well as of other displaced persons and concentration camp survivors, and the total collapse—at least publicly—of political and moral legitimacy of the previous regime.

In the much-repeated and diffuse litany of postwar German misery, women variously appeared as the sturdy tidiers of the rubble of war (*Trümmerfrauen*), as villains "who will give themselves for a piece of bread and not think of their husband and children . . . risking the health of the entire *Volk* . . . betraying their children,"[5] and—along with their children—as war's foremost victims who had to cope with the lack of food and fuel, outbreaks of rickets and flu, and the absence or incapacitation of their menfolk. The first call for the establishment of women's councils by the Communist-dominated Berlin *Magistrat* on August 23, 1945, appealed to this community of suffering; while acknowledging women's disproportionate burden of suffering and reconstruction, it relinquished the rhetoric of class oppression for one more adequate to the distress of a defeated and humiliated nation: "Now every household is poor and so is the entire German *Volk*."[6]

The SMA therefore acted quickly to improve health conditions and to counteract the acute shortage of doctors that had been caused by the continuing effects of purges and emigration during the Third Reich as well as by the flight Westward by doctors fearing Soviet retribution. Already on May 28, 1945, the *Magistrat* ordered the reconstitution of the health insurance system. Young sex reform veterans Dr. Elfriede Paul—one of the few survivors of the Red Orchestra resistance group—and Dr. Barbara von Renthe-Fink, who had just become active in the *Bund für Mutterschutz* and RV when the Nazis came to power, joined returning exiles in the Central Health Commission (*Zentralverwaltung für Gesundheitswesen*). Under the direction of Clara Zetkin's physician son Maxim Zetkin, they attempted to rebuild, on the Weimar Berlin Health Insurance League (VKB) model, centralized clinics for prenatal care and to treat tuberculosis, venereal disease, cancer, and mental disorders.[7] Four maternal and infant-care counseling centers, all directed by women doctors, were established.[8]

Women's councils (*Frauenausschüsse*) were quickly formed under SMA auspices to promote democratic political education and organize relief efforts, such as the production of children's winter clothes in sewing circles (*Nähstuben*). They also entered the fray on issues of abortion and birth control, vehemently protesting four-power occupation (*Kontrollrat*) plans to revise paragraph 218 back to its 1926 form. The councils demanded not only the elimination of the draconian Nazi regulations but also the introduction of the social indication, long demanded by Weimar reformers. In another reprise of Weimar programs, they attacked *Kontrollrat* moves to require a doctor's prescription for contraceptives, and proposed instead to combat drastic shortages and the rampant spread of abortion and venereal diseases by contraceptive distribution in clinics and women's advice centers.[9]

Women's council activism in Berlin and the SBZ led in March 1947 to the formation of the Democratic Women's League of Germany (*Demokratischer Frauenbund Deutschlands*, DFD). Anne-Marie Durand-Wever, a bourgeois professional with no clear party affiliation and an "untainted past" as a seasoned women's and birth control rights advocate, agreed to serve as the DFD's first president. She precisely fit the "nonpartisan" image the DFD—which would come increasingly under the control of the Socialist Unity Party (SED) formed by the union of the KPD and SPD in the Eastern zone in April 1946—was trying to project; the reliable SED cadre Käthe Kern took over as vice-chair.[10] Durand-Wever, like many women activists, was attracted to an organization that strove to overcome the political and class divisions that had supposedly weakened the pre-Nazi women's movement, while carrying on the mass organizing tradition of the KPD women's delegate and conference movement. United "against war and militarism," the DFD characterized fascism as patriarchal domination and blamed the war, not the Nazi regime, for victimizing German women and children.[11]

Discussions about health, morality, and abortion in particular, were lent urgency by fears about "alien contamination" of the *Volk* in the form of children resulting from rape (mostly by Soviet soldiers) or from consensual unions (often identified with American, especially African-American, G.I.s). These anxieties melded with concerns over the seductive power of (initially black market) commercial and consumer culture associated with Western occupation forces, the estrangement between long separated spouses, the presence of "surplus" women unable to find partners, and wayward youth. Especially worrisome was venereal disease, which was decried both as a threat to the health of the *Volk* and as a symbol of the general moral degradation, especially among women who had learned to use their bodies as a means of negotiating the postwar chaos.[12] Much to the outrage of the local population which claimed parallels to Nazi policing of sexuality and procreation, the SMA responded by ordering compulsory pelvic examinations of all women aged 16 to 45 working in public establishments, including hair salons, bathing facilities, public toilets, and cinemas, as well as bars, cafes, and restaurants.[13] American authorities in West Berlin also carried out frequent raids to round up potentially infected women.[14]

## Abortion: The Revived Debate and Initiatives in the SBZ

No sooner had the guns been stilled than the politics of reproduction and sexuality—especially abortion—instantly reemerged as a pressing public issue. The chaotic social conditions in defeated Germany and the immediate problem of pregnancies resulting from mass rapes committed by Red Army soldiers as they fought their way west into Berlin forced a harsh confrontation with antiabortion regulations. The Nazi regime had, as we have seen, prepared for the possibility of "extralegal" abortions of "Slav" or "mongol" fetuses. The regime's collapse now led to a virtual suspension of paragraph 218 as doctors worked feverishly in the spring and summer of 1945 to abort pregnancies reported to have been caused by rape.

It has been suggested that perhaps 1 out of every 3 of about 1.5 million women (63 percent of the population) in Berlin at the end of the war were raped—many, but certainly not all, during the notorious days of "mass rapes" from April 24 to May 5 as the Soviets finally secured Berlin. One recent estimate claims that almost 2 million German women were raped by Red Army soldiers.[15] Serious research on this extraordinarily complex and overdetermined topic is just beginning, but for our purposes the significant problem is less the actual scope or experience of the rapes than their immediate public coding as social health and population political problems that required medical intervention.[16]

Already on May 6, 1945, Anne-Marie Durand-Wever emerged from her cellar hideout in bombed-out Berlin and returned to work in a first aid station; she hastened to test women and girls for venereal disease and to ferret out gynecological instruments since, as she noted in her diary, "I guess we'll have to do abortions."[17] Driven by a complicated set of health, eugenic, racist, and humanitarian motives, and with the support of the Protestant bishop, doctors in Berlin quickly decided to suspend paragraph 218 prohibiting most abortions and perform abortions on raped women who wanted them. And as Durand-Wever later reported, "they all wanted them."[18] At a family planning conference in England in 1948 she unflinchingly "confess[ed]" to an applauding audience: "It was a crime, but . . . it was the only thing that we could do at the time."[19] The ad hoc decision was soon institutionalized by a highly organized medical and social hygiene system that had never really broken down, at least not in the cities.

Throughout most of the first year after May 1945, a medical commission composed of three or four physicians attached to district health offices ap-

proved medical abortions—almost up until the last month of pregnancy—
on any woman who certified that she had been raped by a foreigner, usually
but not always a member of the Red Army. With dubious legality but with
virtually full knowledge and tolerance by all relevant—both German and
occupation—authorities, indeed with the consent of the Protestant—although
not the Catholic—church, abortions were performed, it would appear, on a
fast assembly line in the immediate postwar period.

Legal abortions were performed in public hospitals at public cost. The
doctors in charge of the health offices were newly installed antifascists; in
Berlin, several were Jewish. But at least some of the doctors on the commissions approving the abortions, and probably many of those performing them
in hospitals, were former committed Nazi party members who had been (temporarily) suspended from private practice and forced to serve in public positions as part of their denazification proceedings. It seems likely that the techniques used to abort women at extremely late stages of pregnancy had
previously been tested on wartime foreign female forced laborers.[20]

This background has led some historians to characterize these postwar
abortions as a continuation of Nazi race policy.[21] But the picture is more complicated and overdetermined, the discontinuities at least as dramatic as the
continuities. In interpreting the rape experience to officials and also to themselves and their friends or family, and in making their case for abortion in the
affidavits submitted to health offices, women (and the medical authorities
approving the abortions) relied on a mixed legacy of Weimar and National
Socialist population policy discourses, as well as current occupation policy.
They repeatedly referred to both the social and racial/eugenic grounds on
which their abortion should be sanctioned—despite the presumably compelling and popularly known fact that neither of those indications but only rape
by an occupation soldier was recognized as justifying an "interruptio."[22]

Women and their doctors did draw from the Nazi racial hygiene discourse
that banned "alien" offspring (indeed when rapes by other occupation forces
were certified the perpetrator was frequently identified as Negro if American
or North African if French). Rapes by Red Army soldiers had after all not only
been prepared for in Nazi public health policy but also massively prefigured
in Nazi propaganda. Horrific images—notably in newsreels—of subhuman
and animalistic invaders raping German women had been a vital part of the
Nazi war machine's efforts to bolster morale on the Eastern and home fronts.[23]

But women (and their doctors) also hearkened back in narrative terms to
the social hygiene, sex reform, and maternalist discourses of the Weimar welfare state—which predated Nazi racialist formulations and would outlast
them—and framed the abortion issue in terms of medical, social, and eugenic
indications. Women matter-of-factly and pragmatically asserted their right
to terminate pregnancies that were not socially, economically, or physically
viable—in the name of saving the family or preventing the birth of unwanted
or unfit children.

Moreover, in the (successful) affidavits presented to health offices, multiple and overlapping voices all talked at once, often in the same document. In an interesting indication of the dissimultaneity of social welfare understandings in the immediate postwar period, many statements freely mixed the social necessity discourse characteristic of the Weimar 218 debates and the racial stereotypes popularized by the Nazis with threats of suicide or descriptions of serious physical ailments that might have legitimated a medical indication under any regime. A representative letter dated August 20, 1945, and addressed to the Health Office in Berlin Neukölln declared:

> On the way to work on the second Easter holiday I was raped by a Mongol. The abuse can be seen on my body. Despite strong resistance, my strength failed me and I had to let everything evil come over me. Now I am pregnant by this person, can only think about this with disgust and ask that I be helped. Since I would not even consider carrying this child to term, both my children would lose their mother. With kind greetings.[24]

The Berlin special regulation (*Sonderregelung*) on abortions after rape was extended to many Western jurisdictions according to a resolution passed by leading physicians and lawyers in Marburg on May 15, 1945 (*Marburg Beschluss*). But by the end of 1946, with the immediate emergency overcome, and civil and occupation authority more tightly in place, criteria for legal abortion tightened, especially in the Western sector, and the already high illegal abortion rate climbed even further.[25]

Parallel and deeply connected—but without explicit reference—to the postwar rape experience of so many German women, the Weimar debate on abortion that had been abruptly silenced by the Nazi takeover quickly resumed, especially in the SBZ, which took a much more aggressive role than the West in structuring social and population policy. The press was again filled with speak-outs and interviews, women's conferences convened, students debated, and provincial parliaments argued about abrogating paragraph 218 and instituting new regulations.[26]

Friedrich Wolf's drama *Cyankali*, which had inspired such passionate discussion and demonstrations in late Weimar, was restaged almost immediately; this time, as one reviewer noted, the entire *Volk* shared the working-class misery it portrayed.[27] Wolf himself returned from his Soviet exile, interjected himself into the "urgent" debate, and recycled his dramatic call: "A law that makes criminals of 800,000 women a year is no longer a law." But now with socialism supposedly within reach, Communists—as well as Social Democrats—expected that their longtime vision of happy healthy mothers who no longer required abortions would soon be fulfilled.[28] In contrast to Weimar, even for the most committed reformers, the discussion no longer focused on abolition of paragraph 218 but on the limited, contingent, and transient conditions under which abortion would be justified.

On December 8, 1946, the illustrated women's magazine *Für Dich (For You)* published a front-page call for readers' views, modeled on the 1931 abortion speak-out in the Berlin *Volkszeitung*.[29] One of the first responses, published a week later under a large photograph of a *Cyankali* performance, came from Dr. Durand-Wever, probably the most prominent abortion reform advocate to have remained in Germany. Specifically invoking memories of the Nazi years when her commitment to providing contraception almost led her into a Gestapo trap—"the suddenly opened purse clasp and the identity card of a Gestapo agent which fell to the floor saved me from accusation—others were less lucky"[30]—and undoubtedly influenced by necessary but "loathsome" abortions,[31] many performed on rape victims in late stages of pregnancy, Durand-Wever urgently reclaimed her Weimar slogan, "Don't Abort, Prevent!" However, she had revised her corollary pre–1933 call for legalization of abortion. While acknowledging that, "There are cases in which an interruption must be performed,"[32] she was now more skeptical even about necessary legal abortions. "Woman's health," she asserted, "was her most valuable possession . . . also the most valuable capital of the nation";[33] clearly, "No woman's body, no woman's soul can endure such repeated operations."[34]

By the end of the Third Reich and the war, the abortion question was even more difficult to resolve than before. Communists (and socialists) were now more explicit about the limits set on a woman's individual right to control her body. In the 1931 campaign, the KPD had touted the benefits of legalization for female health and fertility, and carried, albeit reluctantly, the banner, "Your body belongs to you." After twelve years of National Socialism and—very importantly, especially for the large numbers of returnees from Soviet exile now in positions of power—the 1936 Soviet retreat on legalized abortion, that old slogan was dismissed as anarchistic and individualistic; the goal now was to construct a law that could reconcile the state's need for the preservation of the "biological and moral foundations for the continuation of the *Volk*" with its need for "realistic" (*lebensnah*) laws.[35] Only a few liberal bourgeois feminists, such as the former Democratic (now Liberal Democratic) party activist Katharina von Kardorff, still insisted as they had during Weimar that paragraph 218 left women with "one leg in the grave and the other in the penitentiary."[36]

Despite some (but remarkably little) direct and much indirect reference to the immediate past of mass rape and Nazi racial policies, postwar public speech for the most part recirculated—in limited and refigured form—Weimar debates about reform and legalization, as well as the easily available model of the Soviet recriminalization. In familiar language, reformers again asserted that women determined to terminate a pregnancy would do so no matter what the cost; noted the irrationality of unenforceable laws, the social health consequences of botched abortions and of unfit or unwanted offspring, the severity of the (temporary) crisis, the necessity of contraception as an alternative to abortion; and assured that under happier circumstances women would certainly revert to their maternal roles.

In the Soviet Zone, where the reform of paragraph 218 was actively pursued, a revamped motherhood-eugenics consensus emerged within the newly formed SED. Rejecting full decriminalization, it favored legalization of the social, in addition to medical, eugenic, and ethical (rape and incest), indication; it also championed extensive pronatalist measures, such as "adequate protection of mothers" and the "establishment of childcare centers."[37] The goal was not "to abolish Par. 218 but to make it superfluous."[38] Adding a nationalist twist to maternalist Weimar KPD and SPD rhetoric about women's natural and only temporarily repressed wish for children, and surely influenced by fears about a population shift to the West, Communists affirmed that, "Germany needs children, if they can be raised under humane conditions, so that they can become carriers of the new democratic life."[39] This "ethic of healthy and natural" motherhood was explicitly conterposed to the militarist (not the racial) intentions of National Socialist ideology.[40] The conflict between individual rights and collective welfare that had so bedeviled Weimar sex reformers was decided in favor of the latter, but in contrast to the Western zones, defined as including—at least under the present unstable conditions—broad access to legal abortions.

Without directly addressing the pressing trauma of rape—throughout the heated public debates about reforming or abolishing paragraph 218 there was no official mention of rape—SED women did urge their comrades to legalize the social and ethical indication. SBZ officials were also prodded by SMA Order Number 234 of October 1947 which called for the rapid reconstruction of German productivity and labor power, both to rebuild Germany and to supply the Soviet Union with desperately needed goods; it provided a major impetus for many reforms including marriage counseling, maternal and childcare programs, and abortion reform.

By the end of 1947, in the Soviet Zone, the longtime sex reform and Communist party goal of abolishing paragraph 218 was achieved—briefly. New laws legalizing socially, ethically, and medically indicated abortions, approved by a commission of doctors and lay representatives from trade unions and women's groups, were promulgated in the separate state parliaments of the SBZ: in Saxony in June, Brandenburg and Mecklenburg in November, and Thuringia in December (only Saxony-Anhalt did not accept the social necessity indication). Paragraph 218, and the subsidiary paragraphs 219 and 220 of the criminal code, were abolished, as well as the 1935 amendment to the sterilization law sanctioning eugenic abortions, the 1943 law that sanctioned a possible death penalty for abortion, and the 1941 police ordinance that restricted access to contraceptives.[41] Additionally, and in dramatic contrast to states in the Western zones that in some cases limited themselves to suspending the Nazi genetic health courts, SMA Order Number 6 of January 8, 1946, formally abrogated the Law for the Prevention of Hereditarily Diseased Offspring.[42]

In March 1947, the Berlin City Council also officially confirmed the de facto rule that no punishment could be imposed or enforced on doctors who performed abortions during the transition period: a decision obviously intended to protect doctors who had certified and performed the many abortions on women who reported having been raped. Although fierce resistance by Christian Democratic (CDU) and some Liberal (LDP) delegates blocked the SED goal of uniform rules, the Soviet Zone nevertheless achieved what Weimar sex reformers had failed to accomplish: the abolition of even the reformed 1926 version of paragraph 218. The SED paper *Neues Deutschland* proudly announced that "the deathknell [hour] of the quack" had sounded.[43]

Yet, the tentative and cautious tone of the debate and the continuing assumption that once conditions had normalized women would willingly bear children for family, state, and *Volk* had set the political and rhetorical paramaters within which the social indication could be eliminated only a few years later by the newly established German Democratic Republic. As in the Soviet Union in 1936, the discourse of social emergency and need that had so often been invoked to justify legalizing abortion and other sex reform measures was now deployed to justify recriminalization. As in the Soviet Union, the necessary conditions for the "healthy upbringing" of children—including the protection and equality of women—were now declared assured, and indeed promoted by a variety of pronatalist benefits, such as baby bonuses for mothers of at least three children, expanded benefits especially for single working mothers, improved child-care and prenatal and maternity facilities, as well as educational and training programs designed to outfit women for the double burden of full-time waged labor and childrearing.[44]

As in the Soviet Union in the 1930s, East German authorities argued that legalization had led to a veritable "abortion addiction; the more applications were granted, the more were submitted."[45] It had failed either to promote the "will to children" or reduce the dangers of illegal abortions.[46] On September 27, 1950, paragraph 11 of the Law for the Protection of Women and Children and for the Rights of Women recriminalized abortion by abolishing the only recently adopted social indication.

Paragraph 11 provoked "very lively" protest from local SED and women's groups at meetings that became so "impassioned and outraged that there was a tumult and a halt had to be called." Women workers attacked the law for expecting them to "bear children only for the state." "Why," they demanded, "do they want so many children—that would be like with Hitler."[47] For their part, DFD and SED officials pointed to the positive measures incorporated in the law and tried to persuade disgruntled women "that we have after all, from the side of the state, done everything possible, to facilitate birth." They contended that, "Our *Volk* has to be renewed, not—like Hitler said it—in order to generate soldiers for war, but in order to . . . assure its continuation in the future."[48]

According to a GDR logic that both appropriated and distanced itself from nationalist and *völkisch* language (and indeed was shared across the border in the Federal Republic), the state's demand for babies was deplorable if made for militarist purposes but acceptable in the name of strengthening the *Volk*.

But the rank and file were apparently not impressed and Communists, especially DFD activists, were hard-pressed to explain the party's turnaround.[49] The conviction that abortions were justified when socially necessary was deeply ingrained among German women, and many in the East remembered the Weimar KPD's singular and resolute position against paragraph 218. As a disappointed Dr. Elfriede Paul noted:

> The thought processes of the law . . . were hard to follow—this must be said in all honesty—especially for those many women and men who had determinedly waged the decades long struggle against Paragraph 218.[50]

Given that the vast social welfare network presumed by the new law was not in fact in place, the DFD was reduced to occasionally intervening—apparently unsuccessfully—on applicants' behalf in the deliberations of commissions determining medical justifications as well as urging members to recruit doctors from the West to staff the counseling centers designed for the "protection" of mothers and children.[51] Functionary Käthe Kern noted, "Especially in regard to Paragraph 11, there is much ideological education to be done."[52] Clearly, SED women were not entirely comfortable with the compromises they forged. As Kern had earlier remarked with some resignation, "These are all very complicated questions. One cannot always do full justice to real life with paragraphs."[53]

## The Debate Over Counseling Centers Revisited

In the immediate postwar years in Berlin, health reformers still worked together across the East/West divide, taking their lead from the Soviet Military Administration's more decisive role in rebuilding social welfare institutions such as polyclinics. Until the summer of 1948, when the introduction of the new currency in the Western sectors and the ensuing Soviet blockade and Allied airlift sealed the division of the city, the four Allied powers jointly ruled Berlin, and it was there that the differing policies of East and West most clearly collided, overlapped, and influenced each other.

Elfriede Paul, von Renthe-Fink, and Durand-Wever had all been initially attracted to the SBZ as the "new and better" Germany where their Weimar-inspired progressive health and social policy visions could best be realized. In fact, seeking direction for the reconstruction of health insurance clinics, Social Democratic public health officials like Barbara von Renthe-Fink and Ernst Schellenberg, a former Communist social worker turned Social Democratic insurance official, studied Weimar municipal guidelines for marriage and birth control counseling and the old VKB yearbooks, with their articles by Alice Goldmann-Vollnhals and Kurt Bendix on maternal and birth counseling.[54] However, with the exception of Paul, for whom the GDR remained the only place where "what had already been discussed in the 1920s could now be ful-filled,"[55] all eventually made difficult decisions to cross over to the West after 1948–1949, when the city officially divided, the Cold War fronts hardened, and the SED and its mass organizations such as the DFD gave up the pretense of popular front work.[56]

Anne-Marie Durand-Wever's leadership position in the DFD fell victim to this increasing polarization. More committed to building birth control ser-vices than either abortion reform or pronatalism, she became increasingly alienated from (and mistrusted by) the East. Especially after her reentry into the international movement at the Cheltenham, England, conference in the summer of 1948, she turned toward Western family planning groups led by her old acquaintance Margaret Sanger. She finally resigned from the DFD in 1950 after the partition of Berlin, just as the organization was in crisis over the GDR's recriminalization of abortion.[57]

In West Berlin, women's counseling centers were established in June 1947 under the auspices of the health insurance network. Once again, doctors, social workers, and party and state officials debated the proper function, scope, and personnel of marriage and sex counseling, agreeing only in the most gen-eral terms on the importance of assuring that "healthy harmonious marriages produced healthy offspring."[58] As in Weimar, they continued to disagree on whether birth control, sex education, and abortion reform benefited or jeop-ardized the reconstruction of stable families. Again, insurance administrators defended clinic services because physicians in private practice were neither qualified nor willing to tend to women's birth control needs. Again, they in-voked paragraph 363 of the national insurance regulations mandating preven-tive care to justify reimbursement for birth control. Invoking well-worn spec-ters, they argued that clinics would combat the "plagues" of hazardous illegal abortions, divorce, and corroded family relations.[59]

Again, clinic-based medicine in general, and birth control and sex coun-seling clinics in particular, faced intense opposition; indeed, conflicts about physicians' proper role and the mandate of paragraph 363 virtually replicated the strikes, counterstrikes, and court settlements of the 1920s. Middle-class women's leaders, who had emerged from a kind of inner emigration to re-claim the conservative feminist heritage of the BDF (Federation of German Women's Associations), quickly distanced themselves from any reminders of the "free" sexuality associated with Weimar sex reform.[60] They condemned clinics as encouraging the current "uninhibited sexual promiscuity" in lan-guage that differed little from that of observers who worried about "degen-eration of mores" (*Verwilderung der Sitten*) after World War I.[61]

The focus of marriage counseling shifted away from birth control and sex advice to dealing with the huge numbers of marriages shattered by wartime separation; this might require sacrificing certain "modern" and egotistical ideas of companionate marriage and sexual satisfaction in the service of children and stability.[62] The renewed sense of "marriage crisis" was fed by journalists' and doctors' oft-repeated stories about husbands who returned to find their wives with an *Onkel* acquired while they were at war or held as prisoners, or wives evacuated to the countryside who returned to find their spouses living with the *Bratkartoffelbraut* (fried potatoes bride) procured to care for men and the household in their absence.[63] In a rather drastic break with Weimar goals, counselors now argued that even newly tough and independent women, faced with "dull, bitter and pessimistic" men, had "to learn that even where their marriages can no longer satisfy their sexual desires . . . they have a chance and duty towards their men and to mankind in general in helping to heal the terrible wounds of war in their own homes."[64]

The Berlin Health Insurance Association (*Versicherungsanstalt Berlin*, VAB), the successor to the Weimar VKB, was not able to revive the pioneering social medicine network of pre-Nazi Berlin. While feminists worried about morality and doctors about their income and freedom to practice, penny-pinching municipal bureaucrats were quick to note that counseling centers now suffered from popular association with National Socialist coercive purposes such as health bans on marriage or sterilization referrals.[65] And in a truly cynical act of "amnesia" about their own responsibility for the fate of the profession and public health during the Third Reich, physicians even conjured up the Nuremberg Trials of Nazi doctors to exemplify the dangers of bureaucratic infringement on the individual competencies of doctors. Deprived of reform-minded socialist, Communist, and Jewish colleagues, the vast majority of those physicians remaining in Berlin, most of them former members of Nazi medical associations, rejected clinics (*Ambulatorien*) as "socialist," authoritarian, un-German, and an import from the Communist East. Increasingly, clinics and counseling centers were treated as a Communist innovation, their history in the Weimar Republic either buried or stigmatized.[66]

By 1950, even in West Berlin—the only place where it had even been seriously attempted—there was general agreement that the development of marriage counseling had been disappointing, and birth control advice was left to a few health insurance centers and later to *Pro Familia* facilities directed by Durand-Wever and her younger colleague Dr. Ilse Brandt.[67] Years later, Renthe-Fink remembered the early postwar period of joint East/West efforts in Berlin as a time when there was "space for ideas, hopes and initiatives."[68] General polyclinics did become the dominant mode of medical service in the East, but in the West, private medicine supported by an extensive social insurance system eventually triumphed, leaving Berlin with only one comprehensive health insurance clinic that survived the 1950s.[69] Moreover, as the second part of this chapter will show, after the Cold War set in during the late 1940s, the initiative for family planning and marriage counseling in the Federal Republic passed to Hans Harmsen and the organization on which he put his stamp: *Pro Familia*.

## From Sex Reform to Pro Familia in the West

The truncated legacy of Weimar sex reform and social medicine was reflected in the rather "pathetic" attempts to resuscitate lay sex reform leagues.[70] Franz Gampe, leader of the old *Reichsverband* (National League for Birth Control and Sexual Hygiene, RV) tried to reincarnate the RV as the League for People's Health and Birth Control (*Bund für Volksgesundheit und Geburtenregelung*) in April 1947. The leader of Weimar's most important sex reform organization now appealed to Margaret Sanger, whom he had met at the 1930 Zurich conference, for literature and "exchange of experiences . . . since the Nazis in 1933 burnt and destroyed everything." Funds and paper were short for a league that again aimed to serve "the poorest of the poor."[71] In Duisburg in northwestern Germany, Willy Karger also gathered Bund members for lectures every other month. Together, Gampe and Karger's groups published a monthly newsletter carefully titled *Die Neue Familie*. They claimed about 2,000 members in 15 local branches, a far cry from the over 100,000 dues-paying members during Weimar.[72]

Birth controllers seeking to revive the Weimar socialist or maternalist lay league tradition confronted multiple obstacles: not only paragraph 218 but in many places the continued existence of the 1941 regulations restricting manufacture, advertisement, sale, or distribution of contraceptives, a medical profession that had overwhelmingly supported National Socialism, the permanent exile of their most progressive colleagues, the resistance of occupation authorities that regularly confiscated shipments of contraceptives from U.S. and British family planning groups,[73] and the generally anti-Communist and Christian-Democratic tenor of postwar West German politics.[74] Last but not least was suspicion, especially of socialist or Communist influence, from the very international, primarily Anglo-American, birth control movement to which German reformers turned for support.

Margaret Sanger, for example, with her long-standing political and financial involvement both during Weimar and with sex reformers in exile, lost little time in dispatching observers to Germany. But they were discomfited by the socialist affiliation and lay character of the fledgling postwar movement. In what surely could have been no surprise to Sanger, her touring representative Margaret Otis lamented, "As you have undoubtedly gathered by this time, if you didn't already know it, that B.C. is a political issue—a dreadful pity, I think."[75] Gampe and his few comrades tried valiantly to resurrect the spirit of the prewar movement, even publishing photographs of the Weimar leaders Magnus Hirschfeld and Max Hodann in their monthly newsletter.[76] But their efforts were quickly discredited as scientifically unreliable, politically suspect, and socially disreputable. The authentic working-class credentials that had legitimated someone like Gampe in a Weimar movement that sought to reconcile medical expertise with a socialist vision now disqualified the former RV leader. The Kassell birth control activist Ilse Lederer described him sympathetically but critically:

He is a workman, a nice man, . . . enthusiastic . . . who spends his free time and money for the idea of birth control . . . his newspaper . . . is written mostly in a simple way to simple people, sometimes with rather a bad taste so that we can't put every copy on our clinic table for our waiting patients.[77]

Looking to the model of the defunct *Bund für Mutterschutz* rather than to the RV, lay women like Lederer in Kassell and Elly Grosser in Coburg almost single-handedly tried to revive the tradition of sex and birth control counseling clinics in West Germany. In the tradition of the lay movement, but more oriented toward women's welfare work than political socialism, they dreamt of re-creating a "European Organization of Motherhood" which would "unit[e] all women of the Western Democracies" in order to "carry on the fight for parental happiness, freedom and peace."[78] Lederer formed a German Society for Conscious Parenting (*Gesellschaft für Bewusste Elternschaft*), and after six weeks of training in England, managed by the end of 1949 to open her Kassel clinic for two hours one night a week. But despite her disavowal of Gampe, she too faced strong opposition, not least because the SED-dominated DFD had propagandized for peace so energetically that in the West it had become virtually a "code-word for Communism."[79]

While British family planners tried to support clinic projects with training, free samples of contraceptives, and intervention with their occupation forces, American—both official and private—support for Lederer was thin due to concern about her socialist connections and pacifist convictions.[80] The U.S. Military Government, later the Office of the High Commissioner on Germany (HICOG), and even "their very useful working branches of Women Affairs," consistently undermined her work,[81] as did the newly established bourgeois moderate women's organizations supported by the Allies, which carefully distanced themselves from the Weimar radicalism associated with Helene Stöcker's BfM.[82] And, totally misapprehending the nature of German party politics and the need for an SPD counterweight to CDU intransigence on birth control, Sanger's deputy Margaret Otis naively reported, "I cannot write to you *too forcefully* what a disaster I think it would be to have B.C. tied to one political party!"[83] In a jaunty description of her adventures seeking out German birth controllers, Otis also described Lederer in terms typical of the casual and genteel anti-Semitism of many American birth control and occupation figures: "I'd thought when I met her, 'Are you Jewish?' but meant in the good sense . . . she says she is a ¼ Jewess. (Just enough to give her drive! The last is my comment.)"[84]

Thus the thorough Nazi repression and stigmatization of the birth control movement as subversively "Bolshevik" and "un-German" continued past the putative zero hour. Unmistakably, if not always explicitly, birth control or any kind of sex reform project was still burdened with the stigma of being "Jewified" (*verjudet*) and degenerate.[85] Frustrated by the thoroughgoing "prejudice and resistance" of his colleagues, one German physician clearly blamed "the fact that the original Birth-Control movement in this country before 1933 was closely united with a rather unpleasant sort of 'sexual s[c]ience' and still has the peculiar flavor of indecency."[86]

After 12 years of National Socialism, it was, in many ways, the Weimar movement, where birth control work "was closely connected with research . . . on sexuality,"[87] not the politics of the Third Reich, that German doctors and politicians—only fitfully denazified or indeed fully trained under the Nazis—as well as Western occupation and family planning officials, treated as the problematic embarrassing past. The few doctors who tried publicly to support birth control quickly learned that, "The older generations of medical men refuse to have anything to do with B.C. unless for strictly medical reasons and the younger representatives do not know enough about it."[88]

Furthermore, in the wake of Nazi population schemes and horror stories about state-controlled reproduction plans to their East in the Soviet Zone, many Germans were uncomfortable with the very notion of planning births and family size. The ubiquitous, hopeful if mechanistic Weimar language of "rationalization" as a desirable feature of modernity had lost its luster. Margaret Otis reported back that Germans "felt Planned Parenthood a bad name for BC in Germany, as they, the Germans, were so sick of planning and certainly didn't want the government to try to plan how many children they should have!"[89] Birth control advocates continually complained that after years of potent pronatalist indoctrination, as well as coercive antinatalist measures, not only doctors but ordinary citizens mistrusted the notion of family limitation.[90] It was no accident that in the early 1950s cautious and beleaguered German birth controllers did not dare embrace even the already deradicalized term "family planning" as a replacement for "sex reform." After experimenting with such terms as "conscious mothering" they adopted the still more benign and obscure (and discreetly Latin as befitted anything to do with sex) name *Pro Familia*.

### Hans Harmsen and West German Family Planning

In a 1979 interview, Hans Harmsen bitterly recalled that in the 1920s he could not get ahead at the Berlin University Hygiene Institute because he was neither a socialist nor a Jew.[91] After 1945, neither of those "liabilities" applied any longer and he embarked on a meteoric career, promoted by Margaret Sanger and especially the Rockefeller Foundation, which had already subsidized his demographic research in the 1920s. He was in rapid order installed as director of the State Hygiene Academy in Hamburg and the Hamburg University Hygiene Institute, president of the German Society for Demography, and in 1952, president of *Pro Familia*.[92] Conveniently, like numerous scientists and technocrats who carried out elements of Nazi policy, he had never formally joined the NSDAP.[93]

To family planning colleagues, Harmsen limited his self-revelations about the recent past to a brief comment in a personal letter to Sanger about the "terrible experiences" his family, like "almost everyone who stayed in the Russian Zone during the first time of occupation, had endured."[94] In any case, his past would not have been a primary consideration in determining American support. As the Rockefeller Foundation noted in a clear-eyed 1947 report, the majority of Germans displayed "no clear conception of the misery inflicted by Nazi Germany on her victims" and were "unwilling to see the present plight of Germany as a consequence of Hitlerism rather than as of Allied mistakes." Nonetheless, it was necessary to extend generous aid lest a stern policy "may in the long run drive many people into the Russian camp."[95] Such thinking served vigorous opportunists like Harmsen well.

With his impeccable anti-Communist credentials, and soon bestowed title as professor of social hygiene at the postwar University of Hamburg, Harmsen made a more congenial partner for the Americans and the international birth control movement than either the old socialist "workman" Gampe or the partially Jewish socialist sympathizer Lederer. Durand-Wever, a physician with a scrupulously non-Nazi past, the daughter of an imperial German diplomat, and a 1910 graduate of the University of Chicago, might have been deemed the perfect candidate for leadership of the reborn German movement; but she had served as first president of the DFD, and was reputed to have a Communist son as well as an unfortunate urge to speak about politics and the evils of the Nazi period.[96]

That such histories or attributes, or indeed too close associations with the "indecent" Weimar lay movement, were considered more "tainted" than Harmsen's open involvement with Nazi population policy may be shocking, but certainly not surprising in the context of postwar German and occupation politics. Indeed, among the many cases of scientists supportive of Nazism who went on to illustrious careers in the Federal Republic, Harmsen's is relatively harmless. It is notable only because unlike more notorious figures such as Auschwitz doctor Josef Mengele's mentor, Otmar von Verschuer, who continued as professor of human genetics at the University of Münster, and with whom Harmsen worked in the Society for Demography, Harmsen had been identified with sex reform and birth control and even became the head of a birth control organization.[97]

In July 1952, the base of the carefully named *Pro Familia*—German Association for Marriage and Family (*Deutsche Gesellschaft für Ehe und Familie e.V.*) was finally established in Ilse Lederer's hometown of Kassel. In attendance were Durand-Wever and Ilse Brandt, who were working with the health insurance clinics in Berlin; Karger and Gampe from lay groups; Dr. Arthur Waldemar Langeheine, who had worked hard in the planning committee; as well as Harmsen and Lederer, bringing with them contrasting political experiences and expectations. Predictably, Harmsen's role produced tension. Lederer did not want to subordinate her working committee for "conscious parenting" to Harmsen and dependence on American support. However, despite her own considerable ambivalence about the medical professionalization of birth control and her appreciation of women's "worthwhile enthusiasm," Sanger recognized the expediency of installing Harmsen as the head of the German organization.[98] Personally sympathetic to women's lay efforts, she tried to mollify Lederer:

> I fully depend upon you to carry the torch, for doctors, no matter how great, are always so conservative and full of fear, because of how much their practice depends upon the gang spirit. . . . So someone else like you, with courage and vision, must receive their private support and advice but not expect them to particularly make a public demonstration, or support of your work.[99]

Civil courage was, however, as Lederer observed, "rather rare in this country."[100] Harmsen was installed as *Pro Familia* president and Dr. Anne-Marie Durand-Wever—whose record under the Nazis was much cleaner—was shunted to the side as vice-president.[101]

## International Connections

Harmsen's ultimate triumph was powerfully influenced not only by the domestic German situation, particularly the increasing necessity that West German birth control activists distance themselves from any "socialist" planning experiments, but by developments—and jockeying for power—within the international movement. Despite intense rivalries among the Americans, British, and Scandinavians about the postwar course of the international movement, the 1946 Stockholm conference organized by Elise Ottesen-Jensen, with which the previous chapter concluded, planned another meeting, on "Population and World Resources in Relation to the Family," to be held in 1948 in Cheltenham, England. This first international conference at which representatives from post–Nazi Germany reappeared as participants signaled the new direction of the postwar family planning movement, as later announced by Sanger: "The big question before the world today is overpopulation," not "sex education, marriage guidance, etc."[102] At that early stage, Durand-Wever—not Harmsen—attended.

Four years after the Cheltenham meeting, and several months after the Kassel gathering, in November 1952, 487 delegates and observers from 14 countries—this time including Harmsen—constituted the International Planned Parenthood Federation at a conference in Bombay, India. "Planned Parenthood" had emerged—after several years of wrangling and a continuing contest for leadership between Ottesen-Jensen and Sanger—as a compromise term that accommodated the sex reform orientation of the Dutch and Scandinavians, the population control interests of the Americans, and the clinic-based family planning approach of the British.[103]

The choice of Bombay, apparently made unilaterally by Sanger, provoked outrage among the planning group, both because it implied a change in focus to third world population control, and because the high travel costs meant that since "mainly American funds were available, . . . the Americans would determine who would attend the conference."[104] Certainly in the German case, Harmsen, with his links to the Rockefeller Foundation, manipulated the limited funding and his personal relationship with Sanger to exclude Durand-Wever and Lederer, the German representatives to the planning group.

Durand-Wever, despite her ill health, had been eager to go to Bombay. At Cheltenham, where she had been personally introduced by the American physician Abraham Stone as an old friend and "one of the leading medical women in Germany," she had made no secret of her pleasure at reassuming her pre-Nazi role in international birth control: "I have been cooped up for such a long time that I do not think anybody can realise what it means to us to get out of Germany."[105] Now she informed Sanger, whom she also considered an old friend: "So once more it is up to you to decide whether my presence [is] worthwhile the cost for the IPPA."[106] Sanger herself was mostly retired and living in Tuscon, Arizona; according to her biographer Ellen Chesler, she was increasingly subject to erratic behavior caused by alcohol and strong painkillers. Her influence in the American family planning movement may have diminished, but—backed by American money—she still loomed large on the international stage.[107] Sanger decided that Harmsen could be more securely relied on to "prefer not to bring up the discussion of ideologies relating to Communism etc," and Durand-Wever stayed in Berlin.[108]

"Thin" and "tense"[109] during his first major foray into the postwar international family planning movement, Harmsen presented a very different message than Durand-Wever had in Cheltenham. Referring to the nightmare of the Nazi years, she had clearly stated:

> Abortion was not ended by the new laws, but was driven into dark channels, and I do not think there was ever such an amount of mortality and morbidity from abortion as during the Hitler years.[110]

Harmsen, by contrast, openly revealed his admiration for much of what had been accomplished by the National Socialist regime he had served. Displaying unabashed contempt for the work of his former sex reform colleagues (one of whom, Lotte Fink, was present as the Australian delegate),[111] he maintained that the Weimar anti-218 movement "unquestionably . . . increased the number of abortions because the recognition of the seriousness and responsibility of interference was systematically blurred." Favorably comparing Nazi "reforms" when "the suppression of abortion" had produced "a considerable increase in the birthrate" to Weimar and post–World War II demographic blight, he assured his international audience that:

The number of abortions fell sharply in the period after 1933 when under well-planned and comprehensive benefit programs every child provided a bonus for the family. These facts were altered only by the difficulties of the post-war years.[112]

Harmsen exploited his presence in Bombay to cement his position as the recognized leader of German family planning. He not only marginalized Lederer's lay activism but successfully edged out Durand-Wever, who as a woman physician in the tradition of the BDÄ's campaigns for women's health was the virtually unanimous favorite of British and Scandinavian IPPF activists. After Bombay, British gynecologist Helena Wright recalled, this "wretched . . . Harmsen creature just came in" and made a "nuisance" of himself by "taking over the leadership of the German organization," and "keep[ing] . . . in the shadow" this "first class woman" who had "worked quietly to the limit." To avid birth controller Wright, Harmsen's credentials were also deeply suspect in another way; he had proudly fathered 10 children by several wives![113]

Indeed, unlike the ailing Durand-Wever, Harmsen was "blessed with a strong constitution and a willingness to work 12–14 hours a day," as one impressed Rockefeller Foundation field worker described him.[114] A grant in 1952 allowed him to tour public health projects in the United States, Canada, and England for three months, and in 1954, the foundation made a major grant of $35,000 for the expansion of the Hamburg Academy of Public Health and to support Harmsen's "able and forward-looking" leadership in "modernizing the public health structure in Germany" and "infusing into it a more democratic spirit and tradition."[115] A glowing 1958 report entitled "Five Years That Were Decisively Influenced by a Grant of the Rockefeller Foundation" described academy research programs on medical and social legislation in the Soviet Zone, the USSR, and the Eastern European countries, which might be useful for the framing of new medical and social legislation "in case of a reunion of Germany."[116]

As *Pro Familia* chief, Harmsen worked to abolish the most restrictive Nazi regulations on contraception, but regularly stonewalled attempts to set up independent birth control clinics. He enthusiastically campaigned for the revival of the sterilization law, albeit with the explicit provisions for coercion removed. He also worked closely with the federal Ministry for Family Affairs on the conditions of refugees from former German territories in Eastern Europe, a position that allowed him to pursue his longstanding "research" interests in Slavs and Gypsies.[117]

By the end of the fifties, Sanger appears to have regretted her choice of Harmsen as German family planning leader and tried to encourage the lay initiatives that he rejected. A bit belatedly, she complained that Harmsen was "so opposed to laymen doing anything . . ." and worried that given how "everyone knows how busy the doctors are in Germany . . . if they are just going to depend upon doctors, they'll get nothing done."[118] But by then *Pro*

*Familia* was firmly set on its elite medical course under Harmsen's leadership. Only in Berlin was his influence somewhat counterbalanced by the presence of Durand-Wever and her increasingly active younger colleague Dr. Ilse Brandt.[119]

A British IPPF official, who "always thought that he [Harmsen] was the most horrible man," summarized her disappointment about the development of *Pro Familia* and the marginalization of Lederer's and Durand-Wever's efforts to make clinics and sex education the focus of postwar birth control: "In almost every country it was started by women and men took over when the money came in."[120] With Harmsen in charge as president, and Durand-Wever still "quietly" doing much of the practical work, the IPPF subsidized the new organization with grants of $1,500 a year throughout the 1950s.[121]

In 1935 Hans Harmsen had demonstrated his power and prestige in Nazi Germany by hosting the World Population Congress in Berlin. In 1957 he celebrated the secure position of *Pro Familia* and its integration into the international family planning movement by cohosting the first conference of the European region of the IPPF in Berlin. Durand-Wever, the vice-president, was thrilled that her "divided city, interesting and nervewracking"—"much changed since your visit in 1928," as she described it to Sanger[122]—was again "one of the few places in Germany where a family planning program can get ahead."[123] Considerable credit went to Durand-Wever's tireless efforts and her cooperation—in the tradition of the BDÄ—with Drs. Renthe-Fink and Ilse Brandt who worked in birth control clinics in the Kreuzberg and Wedding districts.

Harmsen, by now the clear leader of *Pro Familia*, presided over the gathering of some 160 participants, including 62 foreign guests. He also edited the proceedings, which offer a good picture of the postwar family planning movement—both German and international. Harmsen's introduction bypassed most of 12 years of Nazi population policy and deliberately harked back not to the 1930 Zurich meeting, which had been attended by so many of his since-exiled colleagues, but to the 1927 World Population Congress in Geneva where he had first been charmed by Margaret Sanger. Although speakers again invoked the specter of the "abortion scourge" to justify contraception and family planning, the attention and terminology had shifted away from sex reform, birth control, or the rationalization of sexuality and procreation to "The healthy family in ethical, sexological, and psychological perspective."[124]

The Weimar "motherhood-eugenics consensus," which stressed the importance of fertility regulation and heterosexual intimacy leading to healthy offspring and stable marriages, remained. Lost, however, was the sense that heterosexual satisfaction, family stability, and eugenic health were also tied to abortion and homosexual rights or sex counseling for adolescents. The family planners who were meeting in Berlin now acknowledged that available contraceptives or proper sexual techniques alone could not cure the persistent problems of female frigidity and marital disharmony. But retreating from the pragmatic Weimar focus on the "incompetent" man who, like any worker, required training—here in the most productive erotic work flow—they bemoaned the psychic insufficiency of women who resisted relinquishing their "selfish individualistic" clitoral sexuality, thereby threatening healthy reproduction. In the immediate postwar period, counselors confronting the breakdown of male/female relationships had advised women selflessly to bury their own erotic desires in the name of healing men and society.

In the 1950s, the valorization of mutual heterosexual orgasm as the key to a healthy family—which had been such an important part of the Weimar program to rationalize sexuality—had reemerged. But the lines were drawn quite differently. The issue for a decade dominated by a popularized Freudianism was women's willingness to reach for vaginal orgasm, and their ability to "accept" the "phallus" became part of the prescription for healing men made impotent—literally or psychically—by war, defeat, and imprisonment.[125] In an ironic meshing of pre- and postwar prescription, *Pro Familia* condemned condom use as too difficult for weakened men, and recommended the venerable 1920s formula of diaphragm and cream, not, as it had been by Weimar sex reform, to help women know and regulate their bodies, but to help the returning soldier "find his way home"(sic!)[126]

Shortly before her death in 1970, Durand-Wever reflected on her pre-Nazi activism: "Today, forty years later, at the age of eighty and with fifty years experience as a physician, I still stand behind the demands we made then." But, as this chapter has discussed, she and sex reform had changed. In explaining her revised position on abortion, Durand-Wever added a pronatalist spin to her colleague Alice Goldmann-Vollnhals's blunt 1928 statement about women's desperate determination to terminate unwanted pregnancies: "There is nothing a woman will not do to have a wanted child, but she will also stop at nothing if she does not want that child."[127] Durand-Wever's pronouncements on abortion had become more negative; her call for contraceptive alternatives was even more urgent. She now believed only in limited reform of paragraph 218.[128] Despite her misgivings about the legacy of eugenics, she was now willing to join Harmsen in promoting a new federal eugenic sterilization law in which the "voluntary principle will be fundamental."[129]

At the end of the decade, as Sanger's influence declined with her health, her old rival Ottesen-Jensen was elected IPPF president in 1959 at another meeting in India. In 1960 the German Democratic Republic hosted an IPPF regional meeting on abortion at the University of Rostock, which brought together Weimar veterans Hans Lehfeldt from New York, Durand-Wever from West Berlin, and Harmsen from Hamburg.[130] By the beginning of the 1960s, the two old ladies, Sanger and Durand-Wever, had lived to rejoice at the new research on the pill, the first major contraceptive innovation since the diaphragm in the 1880s and the IUD in the 1920s—but not long enough to comprehend that the pill was also not the solution to the social ills they thought adequate birth control would combat.

Durand-Wever's last letter to Sanger, her "dear and beloved pioneer," expressed satisfaction: she had resigned from the board of *Pro Familia* but served as honorary president; Harmsen had been reelected as president, and executive board member Ilse Brandt kept her "well posted." *Pro Familia* was opening more clinics and garnering favorable attention: "So after all these years of hard fighting we have reached a point, where people have begun to talk about us and we are in the public eye."[131] Even Alice Goldmann-Vollnhals —now Alexa von Klossowsi—who practiced in Berlin until three days before her death in 1969, while apparently not active in birth control, sported a doctor's sign that announced, along with consultation hours, "Counseling Center for Women and Girls, Birth Control."[132]

Harmsen remained active in *Pro Familia* as a defender of "voluntary" eugenic sterilizations into a vigorous old age. In 1980, he was, to much honor and applause, elected honorary president at a national meeting in Kassel. Only in 1984 was he forced to resign by a board embarrassed by long-overdue public disclosures about his activities during the Third Reich. Not until the mid-1980s did new leaders change *Pro Familia*'s statement of purpose from the "prevention of abortion" and encouragement of the "will to a child," to simply the provision of sex counseling and family planning, including abortion and sterilization.[133] Not until the mid-1980s did research by a new generation of social and medical historians and pressure from a flourishing alternative media force officials to admit that while Harmsen had never formally been a Nazi, he had in fact "supported forced sterilizations of the mentally handicapped and helped to carry them out in the Protestant Inner Mission institutions for which he was responsible."[134] Moreover, "The organization has to admit self-critically, that it was only forced to this confrontation with itself from the outside and had up till now evaded confronting its own past."[135]

Harmsen steadfastly refused to justify, or apologize for, his positions; efforts at "a clarifying conversation" failed. He insisted "that I advocate—today as then—the sterilization of the hereditarily ill, but reject—today as then— coercive sterilization." Submitting his resignation in the unsteady hand of an 85-year-old, he concluded, "For me, this chapter is hereby painfully terminated."[136] *Pro Familia* called a special internal conference to discuss "this sad end to a much too long delayed confrontation"; it led to critical discussions of the group's relation to the international population control movement and to its own past.[137] A few years later, just short of his ninetieth birthday in 1989, Harmsen died, bitter, disappointed, and unrepentant.

## Conclusion

This final chapter then is meant to suggest that examining postwar debates on population policy, abortion, birth control, and social health can reveal how misleading it is to read—too easily—Weimar discourses on population policy and eugenics as precursors of National Socialism. It is intended to reinforce arguments that have been central to the entire book: that a specific focus on the history of sex reform rather than eugenics and racial hygiene in general gives a different cast to the lines of continuity—of social anxiety and social control—which so preoccupy historians of modern Germany, especially those concerned with welfare and hygiene. Moreover, those same lines of continuity look different when the history of German abortion and birth control politics is followed into exile and the post–World War II period; that is, across the divides of National Socialism and the Holocaust.

When the language of "motherhood-eugenics consensus" and *Volksgesundheit* crossed over from Weimar to National Socialism to the postwar period, it was continually reworked and given different meanings in the context of significantly changed political circumstances; after 1945 the term "racial hygiene" was excised and eugenic notions reconstituted within new power relations determined less by denazification than by the Cold War. The memory of pre-Nazi sex reform disappeared: suppressed in the West by anti-Communism and obsession with reconstructing a healthy "remasculinized" family and society; deformed in the East by the ostensible achievement by 1950 of "absolute equality" of the sexes and economic security that obviated the need for legal abortion and widespread contraception.[138]

The questions of continuity remain difficult and vexed. On the one hand, there is no question that—despite all amply proven continuities in medicine, population policy, and eugenics, and especially among geneticists and racial hygienicists in universities and research institutes, from Weimar through the Third Reich and beyond—the influence of left-wing, mostly Jewish, reformers who advocated abortion reform and birth control and sex counseling, and for whom faith in eugenics and maternalism was part of a commitment to social welfare and sex reform, had been eliminated.

On the other hand, much of the language and even some of the conditions that had, according to some historical accounts, led inexorably to the Nazi seizure of power and the Nazification of medicine and social welfare were indeed present again after the Second World War. The language of "social crisis" and biological disorder, the desire for extensive surveillance and regulation of public health, and the appeal for the recovery of an injured *Volk* were certainly pervasive in both post–World War II Germanies, as they had been during Weimar.[139] But after 1945, these circumstances led not to a National Socialist dictatorship and genocide but to versions of Christian Democratic, Social Democratic, and Communist social welfare states. In different political contexts, the elements of a consensus about motherhood, eugenics, and rationalized sexuality fit together very differently. This must raise for us new questions for the ongoing debates about continuity and discontinuity, peculiarity and comparability, in the development of the modern German welfare state—as well as about differences and similiarities between East and West after 1945.

# Epilogue

As this book goes to press, abortion and paragraph 218 continue to agitate German politics. Current debates and dilemmas in united Germany, in both the "new" and the "old" states of the Federal Republic, about abortion, pronatalism, and social welfare, are shadowed and shaped by the long history of both conflict and consensus—much of it discussed in this book—about the central place in German politics of motherhood and eugenics.

After the upheaval of the immediate postwar years, and the renewed commitment to criminalization in both Germanies after 1950, the issue was relatively dormant until the mid-1960s. By then, the GDR government was urging more lenient interpretation of the law by the abortion commissions, apparently laying the groundwork for relegalization in 1972. It had become clear that broad access to abortion was essential to East Germany's program of economic integration of women into the work force as well as raising the birth rate.[1] In the West also, strict enforcement lapsed in the late 1960s, and the Grand Coalition under Willy Brandt brought renewed attention to abortion politics, both in and out of parliament. But not until the 1970s did a new wave of feminists excavate the history of the Weimar campaigns, reprinting Käthe Kollwitz's and Alice Lex-Nerlinger's posters, and republishing tracts such as *Maria und der Paragraph* to promote their own struggle for abolition of paragraph 218.

In many ways their mobilization bore a remarkable resemblance to the 1931 campaign, recycling many of the same tactics pioneered 40 years earlier, of self-incrimination campaigns and speak-outs in press and rallies, petition drives, and delegate conferences. In June 1971, 375 prominent women announced in the popular magazine *Stern* that they had had abortions. Inspired by simultaneous movements in France and the United States, but clearly influenced by the Weimar heritage just being uncovered, the self-incriminating speak-out set off a wave of summer demonstrations, coordinated by "Action" committees, similar to those that swept Germany in the spring of 1931.[2]

The East Germans relegalized first-trimester abortions in 1972. Like criminalization in 1950, relegalization was accompanied by extensive pro-natalist measures designed to ensure that women carried pregnancies to term. In 1973, West Germans, prodded both by the GDR's action and the women's movement, settled on the so-called indication model that legalized abortions after women submitted to a "counseling session" and two physicians had certified the procedure as medically or socially necessary; *Pro Familia*'s counseling centers played a key role in offering women access to those indications.

In 1974, the Social Democratic/Free Democrat majority in the Bundestag narrowly passed a bill that aimed to legalize—on the GDR model—abortion on demand in the first trimester. In April 1975, the Supreme Court at the behest of Christian Democratic state governments, and the CDU/CSU (Christian Democratic/Christian Socialist) parliamentary faction, overturned the new reform law, and vowed to "uph[o]ld the state's obligation to see pregnancy carried to full term"—and indeed cited the legacy of Nazism as partial justification for that obligation.[3] In East Germany and West Germany, the trimester and indication models continued to confront each other.

When unification came in October 1990, the two parts of Germany could not agree on a single standardized ruling, as the various German states had not been able to agree after 1945. An interim agreement allowed the status quo to continue in both the West and former East for a transitional period of two years. In the summer of 1992, after 14 hours of debate, the Bundestag by a substantial 356 to 283 margin voted in a compromise bill that allowed first-trimester abortions on demand provided that women underwent compulsory counseling.[4]

In May 1993, the German Supreme Court struck down that compromise as unconstitutional on the grounds that it violated the state's obligation to protect human life. According to the court, women had to be informed that "the unborn child has its own right to life," and that abortion was fundamentally illegal even though they and their doctors would not be prosecuted for terminations performed in the first trimester. Outraged women's advocates charged that, in practice, Germany was returning to a situation not dissimilar to that of Weimar Berlin where many abortions were not prosecuted even though they were technically illegal, and where, in the absence of health insurance funding (except in cases of demonstrated rape, medical necessity, or clear expectation that the child would be handicapped), women who paid had access to medical abortions, and all others might be subject to the dubious ministrations of "quacks."[5] This time, however, there is, it seems, no going back and state governments and private foundations quickly responded by establishing funds to assure that no women could be denied an abortion because of lack of money or insurance. The outrage and anxiety seems to have quickly subsided.[6]

Arguably, the lack of clear or aggressive women's response to the May decision and the new regulations it produced has something to do—along with multiple contemporary factors—with the emphasis in current historical scholarship on the anti- rather than pronatalist aspects of Nazi population policy. More attention has recently been focused on forced sterilization and abortion (of the "unfit" and "un-German") rather than on the encouragement of "Aryan" motherhood and the repression of voluntary abortion; there has also been much new publicity about the often brutally late (albeit desired) abortions performed on pregnant German victims of rape by occupation soldiers after World War II. Moreover, interpretations of the new situation are mixed: in a certain sense, the introduction of a trimester model in the West—with compulsory counseling—is an improvement over the previous indication model; the slow introduction of ambulatory vacuum abortion procedures in the East is an improvement over a situation in which women had access to abortion on demand—a benefit they had come to take for granted—but often under uncomfortable and humiliating conditions.

Still the fact remains that abortion for women in Germany today is a favor for the needy, not a right. The Supreme Court of the land has determined that both doctor and woman must be constantly aware that they are committing an illegal—if not prosecutable (*rechtswidrig aber straffrei*, provided the appropriate time and counseling provisions are met)—act of killing which can be sanctioned only if a woman's "level of tolerable burden" (*Opfergrenze*) has been crossed.

The verdict and the guidelines for its enforcement are quite clear in their intent; in the words of the Berlin Senate's Health Administration:

> Counseling is in the service of the unborn child. It must be driven by the effort to encourage women to continue their pregnancy and to open their eyes to the possibilities for a life with the child.[7]

Furthermore, the power of doctors and medical technology over women's lives is only increased by these regulations; doctors performing abortions (who must not have any connection with the institution that did the counseling) now have a greater responsibility to assure that proper counseling has been carried out (at least three days earlier) and that they can take upon themselves the burden of carrying out an illegal, if necessary, act. The stress on term rather than indication requirements places greater pressure on determining the exact stage of pregnancy, which in turn leads to more routine reliance on technology such as ultrasound scans. Finally, physicians are now also called upon to decide whether their patient "can truly personally affirm" the termination of pregnancy (*innerlich bejaht*).[8]

It remains to be seen how long the German electorate, medical profession, courts, and parliament will sustain the current prescription for "illegal but not punishable" abortion. The story is certainly not over. Paragraph 218 remains on the books, and abortion remains an unresolved, highly contested issue in united Germany.

# — notes —

## Preface

1. On the history of eugenics see Sheila Faith Weiss, *Race Hygiene and National Efficiency: The Eugenics of Wilhelm Schallmeyer* (Berkeley: University of California, 1987). For a spirited defense of feminists' use of eugenic ideas see Ann Taylor Allen, *Feminism and Motherhood in Germany, 1800–1914* (New Brunswick, NJ: Rutgers, 1991).

2. I refer to the title by Hans Mommsen, *From Weimar to Auschwitz. Essays in German History* (Princeton: Princeton University Press, 1992). For a critique of the longer-range perspective "from Bismarck to Hitler," see also David Blackbourn and Geoff Eley, *The Peculiarities of German History: Bourgeois Society and Politics in Nineteenth-Century Germany* (New York: Oxford University Press, 1984). See note 4.

3. Atina Grossmann, "The New Woman, the New Family and the Rationalization of Sexuality: The Sex Reform Movement in Germany 1928–1933," Ph.D. dissertation, Rutgers University, 1984.

4. Detlev J. K. Peukert, "The Genesis of the 'Final Solution' from the Spirit of Science," in *Reevaluating the Third Reich*, ed. Thomas Childers and Jane Caplan (New York: Holmes and Meier, 1993), pp. 234–252. See also among many sources, Zygmunt Baumann, *Modernity and the Holocaust* (Ithaca, NY: Cornell University Press, 1989); Gisela Bock, *Zwangssterilisation im Nationalsozialismus. Studien zur Rassenpolitik und Frauenpolitk* (Opladen: Westdeutscher Verlag, 1986); Claudia Koonz, *Mothers in the Fatherland: Women, the Family and Nazi Politics* (New York: St. Martins, 1987); Detlev J. K. Peukert, *The Weimar Republic: The Crisis of Classical Modernity* (New York: Hill and Wang, 1992); the comprehensive study by Paul Weindling, *Health, race and German politics between national unification and Nazism, 1870–1945* (Cambridge: Cambridge University Press, 1989); and Geoff Eley, "Die deutsche Geschichte und die Wider-

sprüche der Moderne. Das Beispiel des Kaiserreiches," *Zivilisation und Barbarei. Die widersprüchlichen Potentiale der Moderne. Detlev Peukert zum Andenken,* ed. Frank Bajohr, Werner Johe, and Uwe Lohalm (Hamburg: Christians, 1991), pp. 17–65. For a rejection of the "modernity" thesis, see Michael Burleigh and Wolfgang Wippermann, *The Racial State: Germany 1933–1945* (Cambridge: Cambridge University Press, 1991).

5. Julius Wolf, *Der Geburtenrückgang. Die Rationalisierung des Sexuallebens in unserer Zeit* (Jena: G. Fischer, 1912). See Peter Weingart, "The Rationalization of Sexual Behavior: The Institutionalization of Eugenic Thought in Germany," *Journal of the History of Biology* 20:2 (Summer 1987):159.

6. See Charles Maier, "Foreword," in *Reevaluating the Third Reich*, pp. XI–XVI. It was at the April 1988 University of Pennsylvania conference documented in this volume that German historians first took collective note of how much the analysis of "biological politics" was influencing interpretations of the Third Reich, and how, in the paraphrased words of the late Tim Mason, for better or worse, attention to the *Volkskörper* was superseding attention to the *Volksgemeinschaft*.

7. See, for example, Atina Grossmann, "Abortion and Economic Crisis: The 1931 Camapign Against Paragraph 218," in *New German Critique* 14 (Spring 1978):119–137, or Wilhelm Reich, *Sex-Pol Essays 1929–1934*, ed. Lee Baxandall (New York: Random House, 1972).

8. See Jane Caplan, "Postmodernism, Poststructuralism and Deconstruction: Notes for Historians," *Central European History* 22:3/4 (1989):260–278; and Isabel V. Hull, "Feminist and Gender History Through the Literary Looking Glass: German Historiography in Postmodern Times," ibid., pp. 279–300.

9. See, for example, the sober and exhaustive study by Weindling, *Health, race and German politics*, p. 430.

10. See among many sources, Weindling, *Health, race and German politics*; Götz Aly and Susanne Heim, *Vordenker der Vernichtung. Auschwitz und die deutschen Pläne für eine neue europäische Ordnung* (Hamburg: Hoffmann und Campe, 1991); Peter Weingart, Jürgen Kroll, and Kurt Bayertz, *Rasse, Blut und Gene. Geschichte der Eugenik und Rassenhygiene in Deutschland* (Frankfurt am Main: Suhrkamp, 1988); Robert N. Proctor, *Racial Hygiene: Medicine Under the Nazis* (Cambridge: Harvard University Press, 1988); Hans-Walter Schmuhl, *Rassenhygiene, Nationalsozialismus, Euthanasie. Von der Verhütung zur Vernichtung "lebensunwerten Lebens" 1890–1945* (Göttingen: Vandenhoeck & Rupprecht, 1987); *Der Griff nach der Bevölkerung. Aktualität und Kontinuität nazistischer Bevölkerungspolitik*, ed. Heidrun Kaupen-Haas (Nördlingen: Greno, 1986).

11. I found Linda Gordon, "Social Insurance and Public Assistance: The Influence of Gender in Welfare Thought in the United States, 1890–1935," *American Historical Review* 97:1 (February 1992):19–54, to be very helpful in thinking through some of these issues. For demonization of the medical profession, see Anna Bergmann, *Die verhütete Sexualität. Die Anfänge der modernen Geburtenkontrolle* (Hamburg: Rasch und Röhring, 1992). For a more balanced but very critical approach to doctors, see Cornelie Usborne, *The Politics of the Body in Weimar Germany: Women's Reproductive Rights and Duties* (Ann Arbor: University of Michigan Press, 1992).

12. Throughout the text, I place eugenic or racial hygiene terms such as "fit," "unfit" or "Aryan" in quotes to mark their dubious meaning and to clearly distance myself from the judgments they imply.

13. For a useful summary of the literature and comprehensive bibliographical notes, see Robert G. Moeller, "The Homosexual Man is a 'Man,' the Homosexual Woman is a 'Woman': Sex, Society, and the Law in Postwar West Germany," *Jour-*

*nal of the History of Sexuality* 4:3 (January 1994):395–429. A new generation of graduate students is also picking up on these issues; I am indebted to a paper by Todd Edelson, History Department, University of Michigan, Ann Arbor.

## Chapter 1

1. Prussian Minister of the Interior Carl Severing (SPD), "1. Sitzung des Reichsausschusses für Bevölkerungsfragen, January 20, 1930," BArch(K) R 86/2369(2), p. 4.

2. Dr. Julius Wolf (1926), *Verhandlungen des Internationalen Kongresses für Sexualforschung*, ed. Max Marcuse (Berlin-Cologne: A. Marcus & E. Webers Verlag, 1927–1928), p. 207.

3. *Statistik des Deutschen Reichs. Volks-, Berufs- und Betriebszählung vom 16 Juni 1925, Die berufliche und soziale Gliederung der Bevölkerung in den Großstädten. Berlin und die ostdeutschen Großstädte* (Berlin: Verlag von Reimar Hobbing, 1931), vol. 406/1, p. 37.

4. Ibid., p. 10.

5. Annemarie Niemeyer, *Zur Struktur der Familie. Statistische Materialien* (Berlin: F. A. Herbig Verlagsbuchhandlung, 1931), identified 1876 as the high point of population growth and noted a steady decline from the 1880s, pp. 164, 70. John Knodel, *The Decline of Fertility in Germany 1871–1939* (Princeton: Princeton University Press, 1975), pp. 38–87, also sees high fertility in the 1870s, and the beginning of a decline in the 1880s, peaking by the beginning of the 1930s. Hans Harmsen, *Praktische Bevölkerungspolitik. Ein Abriss ihrer Grundlagen, Ziele und Aufgaben* (Berlin: Junker & Duennhaupt Verlag, 1931), claimed that unification had actually caused the initial rise in the 1870s, p. 18.

6. According to D. V. Glass, *Population Policies and Movements in Europe* (1940; reprint ed., London: Frank Cass & Co., 1967), the birth rate went down sharply with the inflation starting in 1922, p. 274. See BArch(K) 86/2373(4), on narrowing of birth rate differential; see also Niemeyer, *Struktur der Familie*, p. 88.

7. *Volks-, Berufs- und Betriebszählung*, vol. 406/1, p. 28.

8. See the useful overviews in Cornelie Usborne, *The Politics of the Body in Weimar Germany: Women's Reproductive Rights and Duties* (Ann Arbor: University of Michigan Press, 1992), pp. 1–30; and Paul Weindling, *Health, race and German Politics between national unification and Nazism, 1870–1945* (Cambridge: Cambridge University Press, 1989), pp. 241–304. See also Usborne, "'Pregnancy is the woman's active service': Pronatalism in Germany during the First World War," in *The Upheaval of War*, ed. Richard Wall and Jay Winter (Cambridge: Cambridge University Press, 1988), pp. 389–416.

9. Harmsen, *Praktische Bevölkerungspolitik*, p. 22; 26 years later he still remembered this as a "Novum in the history of the world." See Hans Harmsen, "30 Jahre Weltbevölkerungsfragen," *Beiträge zur Sexualforschung* 13(1958): 2.

10. Tim Mason, "Women in Germany, 1925–1940: Family, Welfare and Work, Part I," *History Workshop Journal* 1 (Summer 1976):96.

11. *Statistisches Jahrbuch des Deutschen Reichs* (Berlin, 1930), p. 32, cited in Usborne, *The Politics of the Body*, footnote 4, p. 230.

12. Margarete Buber-Neumann, *Von Potsdam nach Moskau. Stationen eines Irrweges* (Stuttgart: Deutsche Verlags Anstalt, 1957), p. 55.

13. Harry Kessler, *In the Twenties: The Diaries of Harry Kessler* (New York: Holt, Rinehart and Winston, 1971), p. 108.

14. BArch(K), Reichskanzlei, R43/I/1978, Denkschrift des Preussischen Wohl-fahrtsministers, "Der Geburtenrückgang in Deutschland, seine Folgen und seine Bekämpfung," September 14, 1928, p. 6.

15. Harmsen, *Praktische Bevölkerungspolitik*, p. 22.

16. Mason, "Women in Germany," p. 82.

17. "Der Geburtenrückgang," p. 12.

18. Ernst Kahn, *Der internationale Geburtenstreik. Umfang, Ursachen, Wirkungen, Gegenmassnahmen?* (Frankfurt am Main: Societäts-Verlag, 1930), p. 27.

19. See among many examples "Der Geburtenrückgang," pp. 10–11.

20. Niemeyer, *Struktur der Familie*, p. 82. See also Julius Wolf, *Die neue Sexualmoral und das Geburtenproblem unserer Tage* (Jena: Verlag von Gustav Fischer, 1928); and the government discussions in "Der Geburtenrückgang"; and "Reichsausschuss für Bevölkerungsfragen," BArch(K) R86/2369(2).

21. Ironically Kahn himself insisted that, "Quality, not quantity is decisive." Kahn, *Der internationale Geburtenstreik*, p. 31.

22. *Gesundheitskalendar 1926*, Bearb. Dr. Otto Neustätter, (Munich: Verlag G. Franz'sche Buchdruckerei) 2 Jg. Entry for June. On modernity and technology, see the insightful article by Michael R. Neufeld, "Weimar Culture and Futuristic Technology: The Rocketry and Spaceflight Fad in Germany, 1923–1933," *Technology and Culture* 31:4 (October 1990), especially pp. 744–752. See in general Mary Nolan, *Visions of Modernity: American Business and the Modernization of Germany* (New York: Oxford University Press, 1994); and Tilla Siegel, "Das ist nur rational. Ein Essay zur Logik der sozialen Rationalisierung," in *Rationale Beziehungen? Geschlechterverhältnisse im Rationalisierungsprozess*, ed. Dagmar Reese, Eve Rosenhaft, Carola Sachse, and Tilla Siegel (Frankfurt am Main: Suhrkamp, 1993), pp. 363–396. See also the important early article by Charles S. Maier, "Between Taylorism and Technocracy: European ideologies and the vision of industrial productivity in the 1920s," *The Journal of Contemporary History* 5:2 (1970):27–61.

23. See Young Sun Hong, "Feminity as a Vocation: Gender and Class Conflict in the Professionalization of German Social Work," in *German Professions 1800–1950*, ed. Geoffrey Cocks and Konrad H. Jarausch (New York: Oxford University Press, 1990), pp. 232–251.

24. See Detlev J. K. Peukert, *The Weimar Republic. The Crisis of Classical Modernity* (New York: Hill and Wang, 1989). Some of the most thoughtful recent work on "new women" and "modernity" in Weimar has come from film and literary critics. See especially Andreas Huyssen, "Mass Culture as Woman: Modernism's Other," in *Studies in Entertainment: Critical Approaches to Mass Culture*, ed. Tania Modleski (Bloomington: University of Indiana Press, 1986); Maud Lavin, *Cut with the Kitchen Knife: The Weimar Photomontages of Hannah Höch* (New Haven, CT: Yale University Press, 1993); Linda Mizejewski, *Divine Decadence: Fascism, Female Spectacle, and the Makings of Sally Bowles* (Princeton, NJ: Princeton University Press, 1992); Patrice Petro, *Joyless Streets: Women and Melodramatic Representation in Weimar Germany* (Princeton, NJ: Princeton University Press, 1989). For a good general summary, see Ute Frevert, *Women in German History: From Bourgeois Emancipation to Sexual Liberation* (Providence, RI: Berg Press, 1989), pp. 149–204.

25. See Renate Bridenthal, "Beyond 'Kinder, Küche, Kirche': Weimar Women at Work," *Central European History* 6:2 (1973):148–166; Renate Bridenthal and Claudia Koonz, "Beyond *Kinder, Küche, Kirche*: Weimar Women in Politics and Work," in *When*

*Biology Became Destiny: Women in Weimar and Nazi Germany*, ed. Renate Bridenthal, Atina Grossmann, and Marion Kaplan (New York: Monthly Review, 1984), pp. 33–65; Dörte Winkler, *Frauenarbeit im "Dritten Reich"* (Hamburg: Hoffman und Campe, 1977), pp. 20–23; Annemarie Tröger, "The Creation of a Female Assembly-Line Proletariat," in *When Biology Became Destiny*, pp. 237–270; and especially the remarkable contemporary articles, Marguerite Thibert, "The Economic Depression and the Employment of Women," *International Labor Review* 27:4 (April 1933):443–470 and 5 (May 1933):620–630; and Judith Grunfeld, "Rationalization and the Employment and Wages of Women in Germany," *International Labor Review* 29:5 (May 1934):605–632.

26. See among many sources, Mason, "Women in Germany I," p. 77. Niemeyer, *Struktur der Familie*, notes on p. 23 that there are 2,804,474 widows vs. only 876,289 widowers in Weimar Germany. On social policy implications see Karin Hausen, "The German Nation's Obligations to the Heroes' Widows of World War I," in *Behind the Lines. Gender and the Two World Wars*, ed. Margaret Randolph Higonnet, Jane Jenson, Sonya Michel, and Margaret Collins Weitz (New Haven: Yale University Press, 1987), pp. 126–140. On the social history of women during the war, see Ute Daniel, "Women's work in industry and family: Germany, 1914–18," in *The Upheaval of War*, pp. 267–295.

27. *Jahrbuch der Krankenversicherung* (Berlin: Verlagsgesellschaft deutscher Krankenkassen, 1928), p. 5. See also Clifford Kirkpatrick, *Nazi Germany. Its Women and Family Life* (Indianapolis: Bobbs-Merill, 1938), pp. 126–130; Friedrich Burgdörfer, *Zeitschrift für Sexualwissenschaft und Sexualpolitik* 14 (April 1, 1927):13; Niemeyer, *Struktur der Familie*, p. 28.

28. Niemeyer, *Struktur der Familie*, p. 76, cautioned that many illegitimate children were born to stable unmarried couples. Numerous memoirs and personal reminiscences testify that this was not only an elite phenomenon.

29. See Atina Grossmann, "Girlkultur or Thoroughly Rationalized Female: A New Woman in Weimar Germany?" *Women in Culture and Politics: A Century of Change*, ed. Judith Friedlander, Blanche Cook, Alice Kessler-Harris, and Carroll Smith-Rosenberg (Bloomington: Indiana University Press), 1986, pp. 62–80.

30. In 1907, 34.7 percent of the female population was married; in 1910, 36.1 percent; in 1925, 39.4 percent; and in 1933, 42.7 percent. Helen Boak, "Women in Weimar Germany: The 'Frauenfrage' and the Female Vote," in *Social Change and Political Development in Weimar Germany*, ed. Richard Bessel and E. J. Feuchtwanger (Totowa, NJ: Barnes and Noble, 1981), p. 171, footnote 45.

31. Niemeyer, *Struktur der Familie*, p. 27.

32. Harmsen, *Praktische Bevölkerungspolitik*, p. 17. See also "Der Geburtenrückgang," p. 7.

33. See the excellent discussion in Peukert, *The Weimar Republic*, pp. 7–9.

34. On right-wing pronatalist politics in Weimar, see Usborne, *The Politics of the Body*, pp. 69–101; also her "The Christian churches and the regulation of sexuality in Weimar Germany," in *Disciplines of Faith*, ed. Jim Obelkevich, Lyndal Roper, and Raphael Samuel (New York: Routledge and Kegan Paul, 1987), pp. 99–112.

35. Friedrich Syrup, *Hundert Jahre Staatliche Sozialpolitik 1839–1939*, (Stuttgart: Kohlhammer, 1957), p. 371. See also *Statistik des Deutschen Reichs. Die Krankenversicherung im Jahre 1931*, Band 431 (Berlin: Verlag von Reimar Hobbing, 1933), pp. 14–16.

36. Ludwig Preller, *Sozialpolitik in der Weimarer Republik* (Stuttgart: Franz Mittelbach Verlag, 1949), pp. 139–145.

37. Eve Rosenhaft, "Working-Class Life and Working-Class Politics: Communists,

Nazis and the State in the Battle for the Streets, Berlin 1928–1932," in *Social Change and Political Development in Weimar Germany*, p. 210.

38. "Denkschrift über die gesundheitlichen Verhältnisse des Deutschen Volkes," in *Stenographische Berichte der Verhandlungen des Reichtags* 451:1224 (November 4, 1931), pp. 26–27.

39. Prewar housing was much cheaper, in part due to rent control laws. See Dan Silverman, "A Pledge Unredeemed: The Housing Crisis in Weimar Germany," *Central European History* 3:1/2 (March/June 1970):118; Adelheid von Saldern, "The Workers Movement and Cultural Patterns on Urban Housing Estates and in Rural Settlements in Germany and Austria During the 1920s," *Social History* 15:3 (October 1990):333–354.

40. For discussion of impact of modernity and rationalization in lives of working-class women, see Mary Nolan, "'Housework Made Easy': The Taylorized Housewife in Weimar Germany's Rationalized Economy," *Feminist Studies* 16:3 (Fall 1990): 549–577. See also Michael Honhart, "Company Housing as Urban Planning in Germany, 1870–1940," *Central European History* 23:1 (March 1990):3–21; James Wickham, "Working-class movement and working-class life: Frankfurt am Main during the Weimar Republic," *Social History* 8:3 (1983):315–343; Barbara Orland, "Emanzipation durch Rationaliserung? Der 'rationelle Haushalt' als Konzept institutionalisierter Frauenpolitik in der Weimarer Republik," in *Rationale Beziehungen?*, pp. 222–250.

41. See Syrup, *Hundert Jahre Staatliche Sozialpolitik*, pp. 374–375; Glass, *Population Policies*, pp. 272–273. See also the excellent discussion of "state and society" in *The State and Social Change in Germany, 1880–1980*, ed. W. R. Lee and E. Rosenhaft (New York: Berg, 1990), pp. 1–33.

42. Paul Weindling, *Health, race, and German politics*, p. 409. An undergraduate paper by Jenna Schwartz, Barnard College, highlighted this quote for me.

43. Paul Weindling, "Eugenics and the Welfare State During the Weimar Republic," in *The State and Social Change*, p. 131.

44. See correspondence in BArch(P) RMI 11178. See *Verhandlungen des Internationalen Kongresses für Sexualforschung*, ed. Max Marcuse (Berlin-Cologne: A. Marcus & E. Webers Verlag, 1927–1928); *Proceedings of the Second International Congress for Sex Research. London 1930*, ed. A. W. Greenwood (London-Edinburgh: Oliver & Boyd, 1931).

45. BArch(P) RMI 9185, GESOLEI 1926 file. See also RMI 11176 GESOLEI 1926-1927, Bd.3. GESOLEI stood for "Gesundheit, Soziale Wohlfahrt, Leistung."

46. See BArch(P) RMI 11175. See in general Sandra J. Coyner, "Class Consciousness and Consumption: The New Middle Class During the Weimar Republic," *Journal of Social History* 10:3 (Spring 1977):311–331. On health propaganda, see also Weindling, *Health, race and German politics*, pp. 409–418.

47. Runderlass des Ministeriums für Volkswohlfahrt, February 27, 1926, betr. Einrichtung ärztlich geleiteter Eheberatungsstellen in Gemeinden und Kreisen, in *Volkswohlfahrt. Amtsblatt des Preussischen Ministeriums für Volkswohlfahrt*, vol. 7 (1927), pp. 299–307. See also RMI to RGA February 27, 1926, in BArch(K) R 86/2372/3 (Gesundheitszeugnisse für Ehebewerber); Max Hodann, *Geschlecht und Liebe in biologischer und gesellschaftlicher Beziehung* (Berlin: Büchergilde Gutenberg, 1932), p. 249; Weindling, *Health, race and German politics*, pp. 424–425.

48. RGA to RMI, March 31, 1927, in BArch(K) R 86/2373(3). Of the 77 centers, 20 were in cities and 47 in small towns and rural areas. For the 111 figure, see Marie E.

Kopp, "The Development of Marriage Consultation Centers as a New Field of Social Medicine," *American Journal of Obstetrics and Gynecology* 26 (July 1933):130.

49. The example of the official Frankfurt marriage counseling center and its relationship to a local Bund für Mutterschutz center, which did offer birth control advice, documents this very clearly. See Stadtarchiv Frankfurt am Main, Magistrats-Akte R 1536.

50. The decree officially sanctioned the activity of a center that had been operating privately in Dresden since 1923 under the direction of Dr. Rainer Fetscher. See BArch(K) R 86/2372(3), especially "Denkschrift des Sächsischen Arbeits- und Wohlfahrtsministeriums über Ehe- und Sexualberatung," Dresden, December 20, 1927, and "Aus dem Bericht über die Sitzung des Fachausschusses für Mutterschutz, Säuglings- und Kleinkinderfürsorge, November 15, 1927."

51. Unlike most other Prussian state-run centers, the Berlin site was willing to make referrals for birth control if there were compelling medical or genetic (eugenic) grounds. Scheumann in *The Practice of Contraception: An International Symposium and Survey*, ed. Margaret Sanger and Hannah Stone (Baltimore: Williams and Wilkins, 1931), pp. 249–254.

52. *Berliner Tageblatt* (1927), n.d., in BArch(K) R86/2373(4). See also *Vossische Zeitung*, June 14, 1927, in R86/2373(4). On counseling centers, see also the clippings in R86/2373(4) (Eheberatung 1923–1931); R86/2373(2) (Heiratspolitik); R86/2373(3) (Ehezeugnisse). On government centers, see also R86/2373(7) (Ehegesetze 1913–1927); and R86/2371(1) (Rassenhygiene-Eugenik).

53. See Hugh Wiley Puckett, *Germany's Women Go Forward* (New York: Columbia University Press, 1930; reprint ed., New York: AMS Press, 1967), pp. 288–293. For text of law, see BArch(K) R86/1063.

54. For KPD critique of the law as stigmatizing and repressive, see GStA, Rep. 84a/868 and 84a/869. For general sex reform objections see *Neue Generation* (NG) 24(1) (January 1928):1–5. See also Elizabeth Meyer Renschhausen, "The Bremen Morality Scandal," in *When Biology Became Destiny*, pp. 87–108.

55. For debate on condom automats in Berlin *Magistrat* see GStA, Rep. 84a/869, especially report of November 6, 1930. See also *Mitteilungen AfVG* No. 3 (February 1931) and *Innere Mission* 25(9) (April 1930):57–58. By 1932, 1,600 condom vending machines had been installed in Germany. See James Woycke, *Birth Control in Germany 1871–1933* (London, New York: Routledge, 1988), p. 113.

56. See Detlev Peukert, "Der Schund-und Schmutzkampf als Sozialpolitik der Seele" in *"Das War ein Vorspiel nur..." Bücherverbrennung in Deutschland 1933, Voraussetzungen und Folgen* (Berlin-Vienna: Medusa Verlagsgesellschaft, 1983), pp. 51–64; Margaret F. Stieg, "The 1926 German Law to Protect Youth Against Trash and Dirt: Moral Protectionism in a Democracy," *Central European History* 23:1 (March 1990):22–56; Klaus Petersen, "The Harmful Publications (Young Persons) Act of 1926: Literary Censorship and the Politics of Morality in the Weimar Republic," *German Studies Review* 15:3 (October 1992):505–523.

57. See Max Hirsch, *Mutterschaftsfürsorge. Kritische Darstellung der wissenschaftlichen Grundlagen, praktischer Einrichtungen und gesetzgeberischer Massnahmen. Grundlegung der Sozialgynäkologie* (Leipzig: Kabitzsch, 1931), pp. 79–93; BArch(K) R86/2373(3) for text. See also Puckett, *Germany's Women*, pp. 300–307; Syrup, *Hundert Jahre*, p. 362; Irene Stoehr, "Housework and motherhood: debates and policies in the women's move-

ment in Imperial Germany and the Weimar Republic," in *Maternity and Gender Policies: Women and the Rise of the European Welfare States, 1880s–1950s* (New York: Routledge, 1991), pp. 228–229.

58. Dr. Alice Goldmann-Vollnhals of the Berlin health insurance system's prenatal and infant-care service estimated that only one-quarter of eligible women took advantage of the law's provisions. Hirsch, *Mutterschaftsfürsorge*, p. 93.

59. Antonio Gramsci, "Americanism and Fordism," in *Selections from the Prison Notebooks* (New York: International, 1971), pp. 305, 297.

60. *Die Neue Linie* 1:6 (March 1930).

61. Fritz Giese, "Die Wiedergeburt des Körpers und das technische Zeitalter," in *Das Reich des Kindes*, ed. Adele Schreiber-Krieger (Berlin: Deutsche Buch-Gemeinschaft, 1930), p. 387.

## Chapter 2

1. Reprinted in H[ans] Lehfeldt, "Die Laienorganisationen für Geburtenregelung," *Archiv für Bevölkerungspolitik, Sexualethik und Familienkunde* 2 (1932):67–68.

2. Dr. Hans Lehfeldt, *Sexual-Hygiene. Offiz. Organ des Reichsverbandes für Geburtenregelung und Sexualhygiene (SH)* 4:11 (November 1932):1.

3. Lehfeldt, "Die Laienorganisationen," p. 64.

4. 150,000 was an often-cited figure for official membership. See *Proletarische Sozialpolitik. Organ der Arbeitsgemeinschaft sozialpolitischer Organisationen (PS)*5:8 (1932):353. See also police estimates in BArch(K) R58 (Reichssicherheitshauptamt)757/1, p. 47. The total number of adherents may well have been considerably higher; official figures underestimated the impact of the lay leagues among those who were not formal members. Cornelie Usborne, in *The Politics of the Body in Weimar Germany. Women's Reproductive Rights and Duties* (Ann Arbor: The University of Michigan Press, 1992), p. 117, cites (without attribution) a figure of 400,000 members in lay groups "by the end of the 1920s."

5. BArch(P) RMI 1501/9351, p. 143.

6. See D. V. Glass, *Population Policies and Movements in Europe* (reprint, London: Frank Cass, 1967 [1940]), p. 277; Dr. Erich Goldberg, "Über Empfängnisverhütung," *Zeitschrift für Sexualwissenschaft* 18:5 (October 25, 1931):282; Paul Heiser, "Das Fiasko der Schutzfrage," *SH* 1:6 (March 1929):44–45; James Woycke, *Birth Control in Germany 1871–1933* (London, New York: Routledge, 1988), pp.113, 246; Usborne, *The Politics of the Body*, p. 112; and reports in BArch(K) R86/1685(3).

7. See BArch(P), RMI 1501/9351.

8. Magnus Hirschfeld, *Sittengeschichte des 20 Jahrhunderts* (reprint, Hanau am Main: Verlag Karl Schustek, 1966), p.198.

9. See James P. Steakley, *The Homosexual Emancipation Movement in Germany* (New York: Arno Press, 1975); W. U. Eisler, *Arbeiterparteien und Homosexuellenfrage. Zur Sexualpolitik von KPD und SPD in der Weimarer Republik* (Berlin: Verlag Rosa Winkel, 1980).

10. BArch(P) 70 In1, vol. 3, "Institut für Sexualwissenschaft. Fragezettel bei Verhütungsfragen."

11. Magnus Hirschfeld, *Sex in Human Relationships* (London: John Lane the Bodley Head, 1935), pp. XVI–XVII. For a critical view of Hirschfeld, see John Fout, "Sexual

Politics in Wilhelmine Germany: The Male Gender Crisis, Moral Purity and Homophobia," *Journal of the History of Sexuality* 2:3 (1992):388–421; for an admiring biography by a colleague, see Charlotte Wolff, *Magnus Hirschfeld: A Portrait of a Pioneer in Sexology* (London: Quartet, 1986).

12. See *Sexualreform und Sexualwissenschaft. Vorträge gehalten auf der I. Internationalen Tagung für Sexualreform auf sexualwissenschaftlicher Grundlage in Berlin*, ed. A. Weil (Stuttgart: Julius Püttmann Verlagsbuchhandlung, 1922). See also Jeffrey Weeks, *Sex, Politics and Society: The Regulation of Sexuality Since 1800* (New York: Longman, 1981), p. 184.

13. See Christl Wickert, *Helene Stöcker 1869–1943. Frauenrechtlerin, Sexualreformerin und Pazifistin. Eine Biographie* (Bonn: Dietz, 1991); Amy Hackett, "Helene Stöcker: Left-Wing Intellectual and Sex Reformer" in *When Biology Became Destiny. Women in Weimar and Nazi Germany*, ed. Renate Bridenthal, Atina Grossmann, and Marion Kaplan (New York: Monthly Review, 1984), pp. 109–130; Ann Taylor Allen, *Feminism and Motherhood in Germany 1800–1914* (New Brunswick, NJ: Rutgers University Press, 1991).

14 See Istvan Deak, *Weimar Germany's Left-Wing Intellectuals: A Political History of the Weltbühne and Its Circle* (Berkeley: University of California Press, 1968), on the "homeless left." See also Helene Stöcker, "Fünfundzwanzig Jahre Kampf für Mutterschutz und Sexualreform," *Neue Generation (NG)* 26:3/4 (March/April 1930):47–55.

15. See Marielouise Janssen-Jurreitt, "Nationalbiologie, Sexualreform und Geburtenrückgang—über die Zusammenhänge von Bevölkerungspolitik und Frauenbewegung um die Jahrhundertwende," and Ulrike Prokop, "Die Sehnsucht nach Volkseinheit: Zum Konservatismus der bürgerlichen Frauenbewegung vor 1933" in *Die Überwindung der Sprachlosigkeit. Texte aus der neuen Frauenbewegung*, ed. Gabriele Dietze (Darmstadt: Luchterhand, 1979), pp. 139–175, 176–202; Richard Evans, *The Feminist Movement in Germany 1894–1933* (London, Beverly Hills: Sage, 1976), esp. ch. 4.

16. See Lehfeldt, "Laienorganisationen," p. 63.

17. Lehfeldt, "Laienorganisationen," pp. 63–65.

18. There has been remarkably little research on consumer culture in Weimar. See Lynn Abrams, "From Control to Commercialization: The Triumph of Mass Entertainment in Germany 1900–25?" *German History* 8:3 (1990):278–293.

19. See the correspondence on business scandals involving the contraceptive cream Patentex and personal intrigues in the Institute for Sexual Science, and Max Hodann's subsequent resignation as director of its counseling center in BArch(P), 70 Int. vol. 1.

20. The Federation for Sex Reform (*Bund für Sexualreform*), centered in Chemnitz, also had branches in Bavaria, Thuringia, and western Saxony, and published the journal *Sexualhygiene*. The Sexual Hygiene Association (*Verein Sexualhygiene*), based in Dresden, covered central and eastern Saxony, and published its own journal *Sexualhygiene und Lebensreform*. Silesian groups in the *Verein Sexualhygiene* split off in 1925 to form their own People's Federation for the Protection of Mothers and Sexual Hygiene (*Volksbund für Mutterschutz und Sexualhygiene*); its journal *Weckruf (Reveille)* quickly boasted 19,000 subscribers.

21. See *SA* 3:4 (April 1928):1; *Die Kommune* 10:3 (February 1930):27–28; Bernd Bublitz, "Die Stellung des Vereins Sozialistischer Ärzte zur Frage der Geburtenregelung von 1923–1933," M.D. diss., Kiel, 1973.

22. In a mid-1920s realignment, more conservative Social Democrats broke away

to establish an *Arbeitsgemeinschaft Sozialdemokratischer Ärzte*. See Usborne, *The Politics of the Body*, p. 128; for a slightly different version, see also Robert Proctor, *Racial Hygiene: Medicine Under the Nazis* (Cambridge: Harvard, 1988), pp. 255–261..

23. This account of the pre-1928 years of the sex reform movement primarily relies on Lehfeldt, "Laienorganisationen," pp. 63–87, which remains the most comprehensive available source. Contemporary discussions (e.g., *Mitteilungen der Arbeitsgemeinschaft für Volksgesundung*, August 20, 1932) as well as later studies such as Glass, *Population Policies*, pp. 276–277, used Lehfeldt, himself a member of GESEX and active in the RV, as the authority on the German sex reform movement. Franz Neumann in turn quotes Glass in *Behemoth: The Structure and Practice of National Socialism 1933–1944* (reprint New York: Harper Torchbook, 1966 [1944]), pp. 147–148. The details as reported by Lehfeldt, although confusing and perhaps not entirely accurate, are essentially confirmed by RGA and police records as well as contemporary articles and books, and the interviews I conducted.

24. See *Zuchthaus oder Mutterschaft. Beiträge zum Sexualproblem* (Berlin: Verlag der Syndicalist, 1929), pamphlet documenting a 1925 GESEX rally against paragraph 218, which featured Schöffer as a speaker.

25. See Kurt Nemitz, "Julius Moses und die Gebärstreik-Debatte, 1913," *Jahrbuch des Instituts für deutsche Geschichte* 2 (1973):321–325; Anneliese Bergmann, "Frauen, Männer, Sexualität und Geburtenkontrolle: Die Gebärstreikdebatte der SPD im Jahre 1913," in *Frauen suchen ihre Geschichte*, ed. Karin Hausen (Munich: C. H. Beck, 1983), pp. 81–108; Karl-Heinz Roth, "Kontroversen um Geburtenkontrolle am Vorabend des ersten Weltkrieges: eine Dokumentation zur Berliner 'Gebärstreik Debatte' von 1913," *Autonomie* 12 (1978):78–103; Daniel S. Nadav, *Julius Moses und die Politik der Sozialhygiene in Deutschland* (Gerlingen: Bleicher, 1985), pp. 135–136.

26. *SH* 4:8 (August 1932):63.

27. Dr. R. Elkan, Hamburg, "'Birth Control' ein Weg aus der Wirtschaftskrise," *Volksgesundheit* 42:7 (1932):89; also in *SA* 8 (1932):82.

28. *SH* 2:14 (November 1930):106.

29. Recommended literature included cheap 50-pfennig editions of Maria Winter, *Abtreibung oder Verhütung der Schwangerschaft*; Fritz Brupbacher, *Kindersegen, Fruchtverhütung, Fruchtabtreibung*; Luise Otto, *Vorbeugen, nicht abtreiben*, and the somewhat more expensive and sophisticated Emil Höllein, *Gegen den Gebärzwang, der Kampf um die bewusste Kleinhaltung der Familie*; Magnus Hirschfeld and Richard Linsert, *Empfängnisverhütung, Mittel, und Methoden*; even August Forel, *Die Sexuelle Frage*, the prewar sexology classic now available in a relatively inexpensive people's edition; and finally Van de Velde's standard trilogy, *Die Vollkommene Ehe, Die Abneigung in der Ehe*, and *Die Fruchtbarkeit in der Ehe*, which unlike Max Hodann's popular version, *Geschlecht und Liebe*, was thought to be written in language inaccessible to the working class.

30. Hans Lehfeldt, *Das Buch der Ehe. Wegweiser für Männer und Frauen* (Berlin: Aufklärungs Bücherei. Beiträge zum Problem der Geburtenregelung, n.d), p. 3.

31. "Nicht nur fort sollst Du Dich pflanzen, sondern hinauf." Nietzsche was often quoted as a motto in sex reform publications, for example, *SH* 2:12 (September 1930), or in *Neue Generation*, edited by his great admirer Helene Stöcker. See Hackett, "Helene Stöcker," pp. 109–130.

32. *SH* 4:9 (September 1932):2.

33. Wolff, *Magnus Hirschfeld*, pp. 92, 94.

34. *SH* 4:4 (April 1932):28.

35. *Volksgesundheit. Monatsschrift für Gesundheitspflege, Heilkunde, Lebensreform, Freikörperkultur* 43:1 (January 1933):8.

36. *SH* 2:8 (May 1930):69; *SH* 1:11 (August 1929):87.

37. Lehfeldt, "Laienorganisationen," p. 85.

38. "Aus der Bewegung," *Sexualnot. Zeitschrift für Kleinhaltung der Familie, für Hygiene, Eugenik und Kultur der Ehe und des Liebeslebens. Offizielles Organ des Bundes der Geburtenregelung Deutschlands* 2:7 (July 1928), report from Bochum, in BArch(K) R86/2379(5).

39. Eight courses with 15 students each had been held by 1932, and interest was growing. Lehfeldt, "Laienorganisationen," p. 67.

40. *Liebe und Leben*, no. 4, (1929), in BArch(K) R58/336 Beiheft 11.

41. See, e.g., Wilhelm Reich, "Sexual Misery of the Working Class," in *Sexualnot und Sexualreform. Verhandlungen der Weltliga für Sexualreform. IV Kongress, abgehalten in Wien vom 16 bis 23 September 1930*, ed. H. Steiner, (Vienna: Elbemühl, 1931), p. 86.

42. Marie E. Kopp, "The Development of Marriage Consultation Centers as a New Field of Social Medicine," *American Journal of Obstetrics and Gynecology* 26 (July 1933):125.

43. Dr. Edward Elkan, personal interview, London, January 27, 1981.

44. *SH* 2:13 (October 1930):103.

45. Lehfeldt, "Laienorganisationen," p. 66.

46. *SH* 3:12 (December 1931):91. The term "Vernichtung lebensunwerten Lebens" in reference particularly to "euthanasia" was first popularized by law professor Karl Binding and professor of medicine Alfred Hoche in their *Die Freigabe der Vernichtung lebensunwerten Lebens* (Leipzig: F Meiner, 1920 [1922]). Interestingly, when Dr. Elkan was questioned about lectures with that title, he said, "That meant sterilization and of course abortion. But the 'Vernichtung lebensunwerten Lebens' was also carried on by the Nazis. I can't very well imagine that we would have a meeting under that flag . . . Well . . . Under the Weimar Republic, these things were in the air." Elkan interview, January 27, 1981.

47. Dr. Hans Lehfeldt, personal interviews, New York City, September 14, 1977; October 1, 1980. See also Lehfeldt, "Laienorganisationen," p. 68.

48. Dr. Hans Lehfeldt, *SH* 4:11 (November 1932):1.

49. Lehfeldt, *Das Buch der Ehe.*

50. *SH* 3:2 (February 1931):12

51. Lehfeldt, "Laienorganisationen," p. 85.

52. *SH* 1:5 (February 1929):37; 6 (March):46; 7 (April):51; 12 (October):1, 6.

53. *SH* 2:12 (September 1930):90.

54. *SH* 2:6 (March 1930):46–47.

55. Friedrich Wolf Archiv (FWA), folder 392, radio lecture text, 1926.

56. Report on public health congress of the Verband Volksgesundheit at the International Hygiene Exhibition, June 21–24, 1930, Dresden, in BArch(P) RMI 26235, pp. 225–234.

57. Friedrich Wolf, *Der Schwache Punkt der Frau. Gesunde Mädchen, Glückliche Frauen* (Stuttgart: Süddeutsches Verlagshaus, 1930), pp. 17–19.

58. *Ideal Ehe*, no. 2 (December 1927):43. See also Hertha Riese, *Geschlechtsleben und Gesundheit, Gesittung und Gesetz* (Berlin: Der Sturm, 1932).

59. Friedrich Wolf, *Herunter mit dem Blutdruck. Schlaganfall, Verlust der Arbeitskraft, Vorzeitiges Altern sind vermeidbar. Lies dieses Buch* (Stuttgart: Süddeutsches Verlagshaus, 1929), p. 20.

60. See the photographs in journals such as *Ideal Ehe (Lebensbund)*, *Der Eheberater*, *Liebe und Ehe*, or the film *Wege zu Kraft und Schönheit*, in BArch(K) film archive.

61. For discussion of the politics of nudism during Weimar, see Wilfried van der Will, "The Body and the Body Politics as Symptom and Metaphor in the Transition of German Culture to National Socialism," in *The Nazification of Art*, ed. Brandon Taylor and Wilfried van der Will (Winchester: The Winchester Press, 1990), pp. 14–52.

62. *Die Freikörperkultur. Amtliches Organ des Reichsverbandes für Freikörperkultur*, no. 5 (May 1927).

63. See Max Hodann, *Bub und Mädel. Gespräche unter Kameraden über die Geschlechterfrage* (Rudolstadt: Greifenverlag, 1929, first ed. 1923–1924).

64. *SH* 4:5 (May 1932):39.

65. *SH* 4:10 (October 1932):86.

66. *SH* 4:6 (June 1932):45.

67. See, e.g., *SH* 3:10 (October 1931):78; 5 (May 1931):39.

68. *SH* 3:9 (September 1931):71.

69. Th. van de Velde, *Die vollkommene Ehe. Eine Studie über ihre Physiologie und Technik* (Leipzig: Benno Konegen Medizinscher Verlag, 1928, [Dutch 1926]).

70. *Ideal Lebensbund* 3:4 (April 1929):105.

71. See *Ideal Lebensbund* 2:1–10 (1928); no. 4 was a special issue on *Erotik des Lebens*; no. 6 on *Ehe-Schulung* (marriage education). Nos. 2 and 6 were confiscated on grounds of obscenity.

72. See Wilhelm Reich, *People in Trouble* (New York: Farrar, Strauss and Giroux, 1976).

73. *Ideal Lebensbund* 3:4 (April 1929):104–105.

74. *Die Aufklärung. Monatschrift für Sexual-und Lebensreform*, no.5 (June 1929), p. 59.

75. *Volksgesundheit* 40:6 (June 1930):151.

76. Quotes and stories that follow from *Sexualnot* 2:7 (July 1928):191–196, in BArch(K) R86/2379(5).

77. *Sexualnot* 2:7 (July 1928):191–196, in BArch(K) R86/2379(5).

78. From *SH* clippings, August 20, 1928; February 13, 1929; December 9, 1928, in FWA folder 153/2.

79. See Wilhelm Reich, "Sexual Misery"; Max Hodann, *Geschlecht und Liebe* (Rudolstadt: Greifenverlag, 1927); Hertha Riese, *Die Sexuelle Not Unserer Zeit* (Leipzig: Hesse und Becker Verlag, 1927).

80. *Sexualnot* 2:7 (July 1928):191–196.

81. The Böse Bund had tried to negotiate an affiliation with the RV in 1928 but had been unwilling to relinquish its commercial connections. In 1929, however, the Hanover-based Bund für Geburtenregelung joined with the Böse groups to form the *Liga*, with Hans Hexel as chair and Hugo Oehlschlaeger of the former *Bund für Geburtenregelung* as business manager. See BArch(K) R86/2379(5), and Lehfeldt, "Laienorganisationen," p. 68.

82. Oberregierungsrat Hesse (the RGA's regular observer of the sex reform movement) to RMI, June 1929, in BArch(K) R86/2379(5). According to a police report of April 5, 1931, in BArch(K) R58/548(6), the *Liga* had some 22,000 members throughout the Reich and considered itself nonpartisan. The police suspected that business manager Oelschlaeger was a member of the anarchist-oriented Communist Workers Party (KAPD), but agreed that unification had led to the purging of many radical elements.

KPD members might well have preferred moving into the more apolitical (and therefore more susceptible to infiltration) *Liga* than the sophisticated RV.

83. BKR to RGA, October 24, 1928, BArch(K) R86/2379(5).

84. RGA to RMI, June, 1929, R86/2379(5), BArch(K); see also RMI to RGA, October 16, 1929, R86/2369(1), and police report, R58/548(8), p. 162.

85. Abbreviated transcript of the verdict, *Grosse Strafkammer des Landgerichts Bochum*, December 2, 1930, in BArch(K) R58/548, pp. 49–51.

86. *Juristische Wochenschrift*, no. 43 (January 10, 1930), in BArch(K) R86/2379(5).

87. *Liebe und Leben*, no. 3 (1929), and *Der Abend*, no. 473, August 10, 1929, both in BArch(K) R86/2379(5).

88. Dr. Hans Lehfeldt, personal interviews, September 14, 1977, October 1, 1980, New York City.

89. See Levy-Lenz, *Die Schwangerschaftsunterbrechung. Ihre Voraussetzungen und ihre Technik* (Berlin-Hessenwinkel: Albert Baumeister, 1932), reviewed in *Archiv für Bevölkerungspolitik* 7 (1932):308.

90. Ludwig Levy-Lenz, *The Memoirs of a Sexologist: Discretion and Indiscretion* (New York: Cadillac Publishing Co. Inc., 1951), p. 200.

91. See Atina Grossmann, "The New Woman and the Rationalization of Sexuality in Weimar Germany," in *Powers of Desire: The Politics of Sexuality* (New York: Monthly Review, 1983), pp. 153–171.

92. Max Hodann, *History of Modern Morals* (London: William Heinemann, 1937), p. 134.

93. Max Hodann, *Geschlecht und Liebe in biologischer und gesellschaftlicher Beziehung* (Berlin: Büchergilde Gutenberg, 1932), front piece, and p. 28.

94. Dr. R. Fetscher, *Soziale Medizin* 2:5 (1929):250.

95. Levy-Lenz, *Memoirs*, p. 253.

96. BArch(Sapmo) I 2/701/28 ZK der KPD, Abt. Frauen, Kampagne gegen die Par. 218/219. This "Schriftwechsel Abt. Frauen mit der Parteiführung 1921–23" also shows that plans were already forged in the early 1920s to infiltrate the BfM.

97. On KPD women's politics, see also Sylvia Kontos, *Die Partei kämpft wie ein Mann* (Basel/Frankfurt am Main: Stroemfeld Roter Stern, 1979).

98. See Helmut Gruber, "Willi Münzenberg's German Communist Propaganda Empire 1921–1933," *The Journal of Modern History* 38:3 (September 1966):278–297. ARSO was founded at a meeting in October 1927 but first went public in 1928. On ARSO generally, see Elfriede Foelster, "Die Arbeitsgemeinschaft sozialpolitischer Organisationen (ARSO) von 1927–1929. Zur Geschichte der Sozialpolitik der KPD, "*Beiträge zur Geschichte der Arbeiterbewegung* 20:2 (1978):222–236. For detailed information collected by the police and government, see Geheimes Staatsarchiv Preussischer Kulturbesitz Dahlem (GStA) Landeskriminalamt Berlin (Rep. 219)/56–59. See also BArch(K) R58/336 (10, 11, 13), 548(5–13), 757, 775 (14–17), 776; R58/700 on other mass cultural organizations; BA R 134/67, 70, 73, 40; R86/2306, 2369(1); and for KPD material, BArch (Sapmo) I 4/11/2.

99. In a continually changing and overlapping system, the *Interessengemeinschaft für Arbeiterkultur* (IFA) was responsible for general welfare and youth; *Internationaler Bund für die Opfer der Arbeit und des Krieges* (IB) aided war victims and other disabled pensioners; *Rote Hilfe* (RH) provided legal and other aid to prisoners and ex-prisoners; *Rote Frauen und Mädchen Bund* (RFMB) was in charge of outreach to bourgeois women's

organizations; the KPD itself handled workers' rights and unemployment; the *Kommunistischer Jugend Verband Deutschlands* (KJVD) shared responsibility for youth and children together with the *Internationale Arbeiter Hilfe* (IAH).

100. *PS* 1:3 (August 1928):94–95. This meeting was followed by a Population Political Congress in Berlin in February 1929. See *PS* 2:1 (January 1929).

101. See first issue of *PS* 1:1 (May 1928).

102. For KPD critique, see GStA, Rep. 84a/868, 869.

103. *PS* 2:12 (December 1929):380.

104. German participants included Helene Stöcker, Auguste Kirchhoff, and Dr. Hertha Riese from the BfM, KPD jurist Felix Halle, and Dr. Max Hodann. See *2nd Sexualreform Kongress—WLSR. Copenhagen July 1–5, 1928*, ed. H. Riese and J. H. Leunbach (Leipzig: Georg Thieme Verlag, 1929); see also *NG* 24:8/9 (August/September 1928):274–278; *PS* 1:4 (September 1928):124–125.

105. *SH* 15 (1930):116; the RV journal meticulously chronicled WLSR activities.

106. Lehfeldt, "Laienorganisationen," p. 73; see also Jeffrey Weeks, *Sex, Politics and Society*, p. 185.

107. See *3rd Sexual Reform Congress—WLSR. London, September 8–14, 1929*, ed. N. Haire (London: Kegan, Paul, Trench, Trubner & Co., 1930). See Dora Russell, *The Tamarisk Tree. My Quest for Liberty and Love* (London: Virago, 1977), pp. 219–220, for a description of her excitement at viewing a Russian film on the dangers of illegal abortions and the benefits of legalization.

108. Margaret Sanger papers, Library of Congress (LC), Volumes 9–15. I am grateful to Ellen Chesler, author of *Woman of Valor: Margaret Sanger and the Birth Control Movement in America* (New York: Simon and Schuster, 1992), for having steered me to this material. Smedley had come to Berlin with her common-law husband, an Indian nationalist leader. See Janice R. MacKinnon and Stephen R. MacKinnon, *Agnes Smedley: The Life and Times of an American Radical* (Berkeley: University of California Press, 1988), pp. 69–133.

109. See Mary Nolan, *Visions of Modernity*.

110. Grotjahn's seminar began in 1915; his students included the radical birth control advocates Max Hodann and Alice Goldmann-Vollnhals. See Grotjahn Papers, Humboldt University Archives, Berlin, and his memoir, *Erlebtes und Erstrebtes. Erinnerungen eines sozialistischen Arztes* (Berlin: Kommissions-Verlag F. A. Herbig, 1932). See also Hodann's affectionate sketch of Grotjahn and the seminar in Hodann papers, vol. 1(2), Arbetarrörelesens Arkiv, Stockholm (HARA).

111. Hans Harmsen, "30 Jahre Bevölkerungsfragen," *Beiträge zur Sexualforschung* 13 (1958):1–5. See *Proceedings of the World Population Conference: Geneva, August 29–September 3, 1927* (London: Edward Arnold and Co., 1927), ed. M. Sanger and E. How-Martyn; M. Sanger, *An Autobiography* (New York: Norton, 1938), pp. 384–387. Further world population conferences were held in Rome in 1931, in Berlin in 1935 under the direction of Hans Harmsen, in Paris in 1937, and then again in Geneva in 1949.

112. Dr. Hans Harmsen, personal interview, April 17–18, 1979, Benesdorf near Hamburg.

113. See correspondence in Sanger LC, as noted in note 108.

114. Report by Harmsen on meeting in Grotjahn's office on August 1, 1929, to discuss Sanger's problematic activities in Germany. See also his mixed report on Sanger's lecture in Berlin on December 6, 1927, and letter to Eugen Fischer, December 9, 1929. Hans Harmsen papers, NL 336/146, BArch(K). I am grateful to Sabine Schleiermacher

who is writing a dissertation on Harmsen for facilitating my access to these as yet uncatalogued materials.

115. Sanger to Kate Stützin, October 21, 1929. In Harmsen NL 336/146. Sanger was also discouraged by the "great opposition of the women's movement in Germany," sadly referred to by Lida Gustava Heymann (who felt that in contrast to official feminism, "many enlightened men and women will be overjoyed") in a letter to Sanger, March 3, 1929. Sanger LC.

116. Harmsen to Eugen Fischer, December 9, 1929. See reports on meetings on May 28, 1928, August 8 and 24, 1929, and February 9, 1930. Those attending included Dr. Karl von Behr-Pinnow, head of the moderate eugenic organization *Deutscher Bund für Volksaufartung und Erbkunde*, founded in Berlin in 1926 (who sent the original invitation), Harmsen, Grotjahn, Friedrich Burgdörfer, Anne-Marie Durand-Wever, and Kate Stützin. In Harmsen NL 336/146.

117. Sanger to Stützin, October 21, 1929. In Harmsen NL 336/146.

118. Dora Russell, *Tamarisk Tree*, p. 217. Also present in London were Marie Stopes from Great Britain, Hannah Stone from the United States, Madeleine Pelletier from France, and Elise Ottesen-Jensen from Sweden.

119. *Volksgesundheit* 39:12 (December 1929):245.

120. *The Practice of Contraception. An International Symposium and Survey*, ed. Margaret Sanger and Hannah Stone (Baltimore: Williams and Wilkins, 1931), pp. 175, 196, apologetically justified inclusion of papers on abortion due to their research value. See also Sanger, *Autobiography*, pp. 409–410.

121. Sanger to Smedley, September 30, 1930. Sanger LC.

122. Sanger and Stone, *Practice of Contraception*, p. XIII.

123. This description is taken from Harmsen's personal notes on the conference, in NL 336/146.

124. Elkan interview.

125. Dr. Arthur Baum, in *Sexualnot*, p. 195. See also *SH* 2:15 (1930):115–116; *Volksgesundheit* 40:12 (1930):272–273. The eight women present delivered 9 of the total 78 papers.

126. Linda Gordon, *Woman's Body, Woman's Right: A Social History of Birth Control in America* (New York: Viking, 1976, revised 1990), pp. 253–254. See also James Reed, *From Private Vice to Public Virtue* (New York: Basic Books, 1978).

## Chapter 3

1. Clipping from newspaper *Montag Morgen*, sent to Margaret Sanger by Agnes Smedley from Berlin, in vol. 15, Sanger Papers, Library of Congress (LC).

2. Sample announcement in Dr. R. Fetscher, "Ehe- und Sexualberatung," *Soziale Medizin*, no. 5 (1929):250.

3. The term is borrowed from Carole Joffe's insightful contemporary study, *The Regulation of Sexuality: Experiences of Family Planning Workers* (Philadelphia: Temple University Press, 1986).

4. Paul Weindling, "Eugenics and the Welfare State During the Weimar Republic," in *The State and Social Change in Germany, 1880–1980*, ed. W. R. Lee and Eve Rosenhaft (New York: Berg, 1990), p. 133.

5. Marie E. Kopp, "The Development of Marriage Consultation Centers as a New Field of Social Medicine," *American Journal of Obstetrics and Gynecology* 26 (July

1933):124. See also Edna Noble White, "Experiments in Family Consultation Centers," *Social Forces* 12 (May 1934):557–562.

6. In contrast to the Association of Socialist Physicians (VSA), the KPD Proletarian Health Service (*Proletarischer Gesundheitsdienst*) and many Social Democratic insurance physicians initially supported the strike and criticism of the clinics as factories with long waits and insufficient personnel. See BArch(Sapmo) VSUF 408 (PGD), and *Seit über einem Jahrhundert . . . : Verschüttete Alternativen in der Sozialpolitik*, ed, Eckhard Hansen, Michael Heisig, Stephan Leibfried, and Florian Tennstedt (Düsseldorf: Bund Verlag, 1981), pp. 413–459.

7. *Statistik des deutschen Reichs*, vol. 431, pp. 10–11. By 1928 the annual cost was about 5,800 million RM. In 1911 there were 22,000 funds with an average of only 455 members each; by 1932, 6,600 funds with an average of 2,833 members each. See Deborah A. Stone, *The Limits of Professional Power: National Health Care in the Federal Republic of Germany* (Chicago: University of Chicago Press, 1980), p. 79. Of the 20,175,000 people (one-third of the population as opposed to only one-tenth in 1885) insured in 1925, 7 million were female and 13 million were male, a ratio of about 62 women to 100 men. See Charlotte Wolff, "Die Fürsorge für die Familie im Rahmen der Schwangerenberatung der Ambulatorien des Verbandes der Berliner Krankenkassen" (M.D. dissertation, Friedrich Wilhelm University, Berlin, 1928), p. 25. See also Friedrich Syrup, *Hundert Jahre Staatliche Sozialpolitik 1839–1939* (Stuttgart: Kohlhammer, 1957), p. 371; and Ludwig Preller, *Sozialpolitik in der Weimarer Republik* (Düsseldorf: Athenenäum/Droste, 1949, reprinted 1978), pp. 330, 384–385.

8. *Jahrbuch der Ambulatorien des Verbandes der Krankenkassen Berlins 1926/27*, p. 15.

9. See *Jahrbuch der Ambulatorien 1928/29*, p. 15. In 1929 the clinics provided 70,431 orthopedic gymnastic, 18,495 prenatal, and 5,574 sex and marriage counseling consultations.

10. See Dr. Alice Goldmann-Vollnhals, "Mutterschutz," in *Jahrbuch der Krankenversicherung 1929* (Berlin: Verlagsgesellschaft deutscher Krankenkassen, 1930), pp. 173–182; Dr. Alice Vollnhals, "Die Schwangerenfürsorge in den Ambulatorien in den Jahren 1926 und 1927," *Jahrbuch der Ambulatorien 1926/1927*, p. 67.

11. *Die Frau* 11:9 (September 1935):148. See also *Reichsmedizinalkalendar*, 1932. On female physicians and health insurance, see Beate Ziegeler, *Weibliche Ärzte und Krankenkassen. Anfänge ärztlicher Berufstätigkeit von Frauen in Berlin 1893–1935* (Weinheim: Deutscher Studien Verlag, 1993), especially pp. 95–110.

12. This figure is based on names collected by the Berlin *Jüdischer Frauenbund* (Jewish Women's League) in January 1934. I am indebted to Sharon Gillerman for material from File B 1, *Verband Berlin des Jüdischen Frauenbundes*, E. V., Gesamtarchiv der deutschen Juden, BArch(P), Aussenstelle Coswig.

13. In 1931 they did 25,000 consultations. *Jahrbuch der Ambulatorien 1930/31*, p. 13. On five women VKB doctors, see also Charlotte Wolff, *Hindsight. An Autobiography* (London: Quartet Books, 1980), p. 101. The five municipal centers were in Friedrichshain, Neukölln, Reinickendorf, Wedding, and Charlottenburg.

14. Vollnhals, "Die Schwangerenfürsorge," *Jahrbuch der Ambulatorien 1926/27*, p. 66.

15. Vollnhals was also motivated by the desire for a higher independent income to support her son from a previous marriage when she married Franz Goldmann, with whom she had studied in Grotjahn's social hygiene seminar. Unpublished papers, courtesy of her daughter-in-law, Itta Vollnhals, Berlin.

16. See Karen Hagemann, *Frauenalltag und Männerpolitik. Alltagsleben und gesell-*

*schaftliches Handeln von Arbeiterfrauen in der Weimarer Republik* (Bonn: Verlag J. H. W. Dietz, 1990) for a critique of SPD social conservatism. See Cornelie Usborne, *The Politics of the Body in Weimar Germany: Women's Reproductive Rights and Duties* (Ann Arbor: The University of Michigan Press, 1992) for a substantially more sympathetic analysis of the SPD position on birth control and abortion reform.

17. Unless otherwise documented, the following account of the activities of the Committee for Birth Control is strongly indebted to the correspondence between Margaret Sanger and Agnes Smedley, preserved in the Sanger papers, Library of Congress, volumes 9–20.

18. See Margaret Sanger, *An Autobiography* (New York: Norton, 1938), pp. 388–389. See also Hans Harmsen's somewhat nervous notes on her militant lecture, BArch(K) NL 336/146.

19. Smedley to Sanger, April 6, 1926. Sanger LC.

20. See Smedley to Sanger, April 6, 1926. Sanger LC. Smedley wrote that Heusler-Edenhuizen "has a clinic also—but of that I do not wish to speak; such things are illegal." See also Wolff, *Hindsight*, pp. 95–111.

21. Smedley to Sanger, May 18, 1928. Sanger LC.

22. Smedley to Sanger, March 18, 1928. See also May 18, 1928. Sanger LC.

23. Smedley to Sanger, April 3, 1928. Sanger LC. Dührssen later withdrew due to illness and was replaced by a KPD physician.

24. Sanger, *Autobiography*, pp. 388–389. See also Sanger to Smedley, March 30, 1928. Sanger LC.

25. May 18, 1928, Smedley to Sanger. Sanger LC.

26. March 18, 1928, Smedley to Sanger. Sanger LC.

27. Part of the problem may have derived from Schmincke's conflicts with Social Democratic city and district officials. Dr. Käte Frankenthal reported that she was specifically appointed municipal physician (*Stadtarzt*) in Neukölln to frustrate his Communist schemes. See Käte Frankenthal, *Der dreifache Fluch: Jüdin, Intellektuelle, Sozialistin. Lebenserinnerungen einer Ärztin in Deutschland und im Exil* (Frankfurt/Main: Campus Verlag, 1981), pp. 122–126.

28. Nov. 2, 1928, Smedley to Sanger. Sanger LC.

29. Smedley to Sanger, June 16, 1928. Sanger LC.

30. *Neue Generation* 24:8/9 (August/September 1928):303–304.

31. Smedley to Sanger, July 7, 1928. Sanger LC.

32. Dr. Käthe Becher, "Jahresbericht der Fürsorge- und Beratungsstelle Spandau," *Jahrbuch der Ambulatorien 1928/29*, p. 36.

33. See above, chapter 2, for Hodann's criticism of Hirschfeld's business dealings, in BArch(P) 70In1.

34. Ruben-Wolf to Sanger, August 9, 1930. Sanger LC. Sanger also supported Henriette Fürth, a Frankfurt sex reform activist and mother of eight, while she struggled to write a book on birth control. See Henriette Fürth, *Die Regelung der Nachkommenschaft als eugenisches Problem* (Stuttgart: J. Puttmann, 1929).

35. Smedley to Sanger, November 2, 1928. Sanger LC.

36. Ibid.

37. Dr. Kurt Bendix, "Bericht über die Ehe- und Sexualberatungsstellen des Verbandes der Krankenhassen Berlin," *Jahrbuch der Ambulatorien 1928/29*, p. 17. Of the first visits (out of a total 6,425 patient contacts), 2,028 were for birth control, 102 for sex counseling, 59 for marriage counseling, 290 for pregnancy tests, 68 for abortion

certifications, and 68 were miscellaneous; 83 percent of the clients were identified as working-class. This compares to the 5,000 new patients annually that Margaret Sanger's Birth Control Clinical Research Bureau (established in 1923) was seeing at the end of the 1920s. Sanger's clinic was open five days a week including evening sessions and recorded about 20,000 client contacts annually. See Ellen Chesler, *Woman of Valor: Margaret Sanger and the Birth Control Movement in America* (New York: Doubleday/Simon and Schuster, 1992), p. 282.

38. In 1929, there were 18,495 prenatal consultations. *Jahrbuch der Ambulatorien 1928/1929*, p. 15.

39. Of 5,574 clients, 66.7 percent asked for birth control, 25 percent requested abortion referrals, and only 11 percent marriage counseling and eugenic advice. Dr. Kurt Bendix, "Der Stand der Geburtenregelung in Berlin, Referat. WLSR, London, Sept. 1929," *NG* 25 (October 10, 1929):282–286. See also Bendix, "Bericht," *Jahrbuch der Ambulatorien 1928/29*, pp. 17–25.

40. Dr. Alice (Goldmann-) Vollnhals reported that out of 2,482 pregnant women counseled in 1926, 300 asked for abortions: 25 had their pregnancies terminated for medical reasons and 7 of them were also sterilized. In most cases the reason cited was tuberculosis. "Die Schwangerenfürsorge," *Jahrbuch der Ambulatorien 1926/27*, pp. 81–83. See also Dr. Martin Hirschberg, "Unterbrechung der Schwangerschaft aus medizinischer Indikation," *Jahrbuch der Ambulatorien 1928/29*, pp. 74–84.

41. See *PS* 2:2 (February 1929):59–60; *NG* 24:12 (December 1928):435; Ruben-Wolf in *The Practice of Contraception: An International Symposium and Survey*, ed. Margaret Sanger and Hannah Stone (Baltimore: Williams and Wilkins, 1931), pp. 234–239. For government responses see RGA reports to RMI, May 26, 1929, in BArch(K) R86/2369(1). See critical reports such as Hans Harmsen's in *Die Medizinische Welt*, no. 31 (1930). Sanger's funds paid for printing the proceedings.

42. Dr. Lydia Ehrenfried, unpublished memoirs, Leo Baeck Institute, New York, p. 141.

43. *NG* 25:2 (February 1929):77–78.

44. *SH* 1:4 (February 1929):99.

45. Kristine von Soden, *Die Sexualberatungsstellen der Weimarer Republik 1919–1933* (Berlin: Edition Hentrich, 1988), p. 105. A study commissioned by the BfM estimated that already by the end of the expansive year 1928, Berlin boasted 15 active birth control and sex counseling clinics, open at least a few hours every week, one for every 200,000–300,000 people. Lotte Neisser-Schroeter, *Enquete über die Ehe und Sexualberatungsstellen in Deutschland mit Berücksichtigung der Geburtenregelung* (Berlin-Nikolassee: Verlag der Neuen Generation, 1928), pp. 7–8.

46. *Berliner Morgenpost*, July 11, 1930, in BArch(K) R86/2372(4).

47. Durand-Wever in *Contraception*, p. 86. See also Dr. Annie H. Friedländer, "Die Frau in der Eheberatung," *Schaffende Frau* 1:8 (May 1930):261–262. By 1933, most all-women centers were religiously run; 50 by the Catholic Church, 13 by Protestants, and 2 by the *Jüdischer Frauenbund* (one in Berlin and one in Frankfurt). They offered housework courses, aid for child raising, some legal advice for married women, but certainly no birth control. See Kopp, "Marriage Consultation," p. 125.

48. See responses to 1931 *Gemeinde Tag* survey on *Eheberatungsstellen* in BArch(K) R36/1364 and 1365.

49. Such professional anxieties and the tight job market for young physicians fueled antifeminist and anti-Semitic sentiments, helping to account for the enthusi-

asm with which most "Aryan" doctors later greeted National Socialism, as well as the large number who joined the SA and SS. See Michael H. Kater, "Physicians in Crisis at the End of the Weimar Republic," in *Unemployment and the Great Depression in Weimar Germany*, ed. Peter D. Stachura (Basingstoke and London: Macmillan, 1986), pp. 49–77; "Hitler's Early Doctors: Nazi Physicians in Predepression Germany," *The Journal of Modern History* 59:1 (March 1987):25–52; "Professionalization and Socialization of Physicians in Wilhelmine and Weimar Germany," *Journal of Contemporary History* 20 (1985):677–701; *Doctors Under Hitler* (Chapel Hill: University of North Carolina Press, 1989).

50. See reports in *Archiv für Wohlfahrtsplege*, February and March 1932 in BArch(K) R36/955.

51. See, for example, *Jahrbuch der Ambulatorien 1928–1929*, p. 5.

52. Jacques Donzelot, *The Policing of Families* (New York: Pantheon, 1979) p. 173. Paul Weindling correctly points out that public health officials often preferred "conveniently cheap" programs of education and inspection to more substantial investments in, for example, school meals. See "Eugenics and the Welfare State" in *The State and Social Change*, p. 147. See David F. Crew, "German socialism, the state and family policy, 1918–33," *Continuity and Change* 1:2 (1986):235–263, for a considerably more positive assessment of Social Democratic efforts in social welfare.

53. See the series of articles on "Sexualberatung, Eheberatung, Geburtenregelung. Sollen die Krankenkassen sich daran beteiligen?" in the journal of health insurance–affiliated doctors, dentists, and pharmacists, *Soziale Medizin*, no. 1–8, 1929.

54. "Verhandlungen der Deutschen Gesellschaft für Gynäkologie, Frankfurt, 27–30 May, 1931," *Archiv für Gynäkologie* 144 (1931):366.

55. "Verhandlungen," *Archiv für Gynäkologie* 144 (1931):127, 379–383.

56. Ibid., p. 376.

57. Hugo Sellheim, *Zeitschrift für Sexualwissenschaft* 18:6 (December 31, 1931):344.

58. *Die Welt am Abend*, November 8, 1926, in BArch(K) R86/2372(4).

59. "Verhandlungen," *Archiv für Gynäkologie* 144 (1931):369–370.

60. Dr. Ludwig Fränkel, quoted in J. Marcuse, "Die deutschen Gynäkologen und die Geburtenregelung," *Sozialistischer Arzt* 6 (1930):184.

61. *Statistik des Deutschen Reichs*, vol. 431, pp. 18–19. See also *Denkschrift über die gesundheitlichen Verhältnisse des deutschen Volkes*, reports for 1925 to (especially) 1931, in *Stenographische Berichte der Verhandlungen des Reichstags*, vol. 451; and collected in BArch(K) R86/931 and R43/I/1978.

62. *Soziale Medizin* No.7 (1929):347.

63. *Zeitschrift für Sexualwissenschaft* 18:4 (1931):232.

64. See, for example, Julius Wolf, *Die neue Sexualmoral und das Geburtenproblem unserer Tage* (Jena: Verlag von Gustav Fischer, 1928), p. V.

65. *Denkschrift des Sächsischen Arbeits-und Wohlfahrtsministeriums über Ehe-und Sexualberatung. Aus dem Bericht der Sitzung des Fachausschusses für Mutterschutz, Säuglings-Kleinkinderfürsorge, am 5 November 1927*, in BArch(K) R86/2372(3), pp. 28, 32.

66. Dr. F. K. Scheumann, *Die Aufgaben der Eheberatung* (Leipzig: Voss, 1932), p. 89.

67. For example, Lehfeldt in *SH* 4:11 (November 1932):1.

68. *SA* 4:1/2 (August 1928):34. See also Neisser-Schroeter, *Enquete*, p. 21.

69. See Dr. Alfred Korach, "Probleme der Eheberatung," *Soziale Medizin*, no. 1 (1929), pp. 35–40.

70. See Scheumann, *Eheberatung als Aufgabe*, p. 20.

71. See Kopp, "Marriage Consultation," p. 128. See also Dr. Grumach, "Wer soll Eheberater sein?" *Soziale Medizin*, no. 3 (1929), pp. 127–128.

72. Elise Ottesen-Jensen in *Contraception*, p. 28. See also Dr. Hans Lehfeldt in *3rd Sexual Reform Congress—WLSR. London, September 8–14, 1929*, ed. N. Haire (London: Kegan Paul, Trench, Trubner & Co., 1930), p. 126; arguments in *SH* 2:11 (August 1930):87.

73. Dr. Hertha Nathorff, personal interview, New York City, June 16, 1980.

74. *SA* 5:1 (March 1929):19.

75. See Ludwig Fränkel *Die Empfängnisverhütung. Biologische Grundlagen, Technik und Indikationen. Für Ärzte bearbeitet* (Stuttgart: Ferdinand Enke, 1932), pp. 112–133.

76. L. v. Nida, *Geburtenregelung—eine ethische und wirtschaftliche Forderung* (Oberursel: Reich, 1928), p. 15. As mentioned in Chapter 2, Magnus Hirschfeld was accused of colluding with von Nida to promote Antibion. See BArch(P) 70In1.

77. Dr. Lotte Fink, for example, claimed on the basis of six years of clinic experience with 600 cases that a Ramses diaphragm combined with Contrapan cream was the optimal method. *Archiv für Gynäkologie* 144 (1931):335–336.

78. "Verhandlungen," *Archiv für Gynäkologie* 144 (1931):345–347. See also Hans Lehfeldt on Gräfenberg in the *Mt. Sinai Journal of Medicine* 42:4 (July / August 1975):347.

79. Else Kienle, *Frauen. Aus dem Tagebuch einer Ärztin* (Berlin: Gustav Kiepenhauer Verlag, 1932), p. 431.

80. See Ziegeler, *Weibliche Ärzte*, pp. 111–130; Susanne Zeller, *Volksmütter. Frauen im Wohlfahrtswesen der zwanziger Jahre* (Düsseldorf: Schwann, 1987), pp. 68–71.

81. Erna Glaesmer, *Eheberatungsstellen und Geburtenverhütung* (Stuttgart: Enke, 1932), pp. 7–8. In fact, women directed only 5 of the 16 municipal counseling centers in Berlin; the rest were run by male physicians close to the Social Democratic or Communist parties. Outside of Berlin, women doctors worked in 15 of 47 clinics. See Scheumann, *Eheberatung als Aufgabe*, pp. 39, 78ff.

82. Ehrenfried memoirs, p. 49.

83. *NG* 26:9/10 (1930):240. See also presentations by Dr. Hertha Riese, Dr. Reni Begun, and lay activists Ottesen-Jensen and Kirchhoff in *Contraception*, pp. 28–32.

84. Goldmann-Vollnhals, "Mutterschutz," *Jahrbuch der Krankenversicherung* (1929), p. 182.

85. Auguste Kirchhoff in *NG*, no. 9/10 (1930):240.

86. Nathorff interview, New York City, June 16, 1980.

87. Smedley to Sanger, January 3, Friday the 13th (no exact date, probably 1928). Sanger LC.

88. Nathorff interview, June 16, 1980.

89. Becher, "Spandau," *Jahrbuch der Ambulatorien 1928–1929*, p. 38.

90. Wolff, *Hindsight*, p. 97.

91. Linda Gordon, *Heroes of Their Own Lives* (New York: Viking, 1988). See also Joffe, *Regulation* on American family planning workers. David F. Crew describes a similar process (although without focusing on gender) in his study of family welfare in Düsseldorf during the Weimar Republic, "German socialism," especially pp. 246–255.

92. Dr. Elisabeth Prinz, "Zur Frage der Ethik und Diätetik des Privatlebens," *NG* 27:7/8/9 (1931):159.

93. See among innumerable examples, the film *Mutter Krausen's Fahrt ins Glück*, 1929, directed by Piel Jutzi, with collaboration by Käthe Kollwitz, Hans Baluschek, and Otto Nagel, [see Rudolf Freund and Michael Hanisch, *Filmprotokoll und Materialien*

(Berlin: Henschelverlag, 1976)]; Hertha Riese, *Die Sexuelle Not Unserer Zeit*, (Leipzig: Hesse und Becker Verlag, 1927); idem, *Geschlechtsleben und Gesundheit, Gesittung und Gesetz* (Berlin: Der Sturm, 1932); Otto Rühle, *Illustrierte Kultur- und Sittengeschichte des Proletariats* (Berlin: Neuer Deutscher Verlag, 1930); Alexander Graf Stenbock-Fermor, *Deutschland von unten. Reisen durch die proletarische Provinz, 1930* (1931, reprint edition, Luzern and Frankfurt: Verlag C. J. Bucher, 1980 [1931]).

94. Wolff, "Die Fürsorge für die Familie," p. 42.

95. Lotte Fink, "Wirkung der Verhütungsmittel: Erfahrungen aus der Ehe- und Sexualberatung Frankfurt," *Archiv für Gynäkologie* 144 (1931):336.

96. Paul Levy in *SA*, no. 1/2 (1928):11, quoted in Bernd Bublitz, "Die Stellung des Vereins sozialistischer Ärzte zur Frage der Geburtenregelung von 1927 bis 1933," M.D. dissertation, Kiel, 1973, p. 1. See also, for example, the statistics in Hans Harmsen, *Praktische Bevölkerungspolitik. Ein Abriss ihrer Grundlagen, Ziele und Aufgaben* (Berlin: Junker & Dünnhaupt Verlag, 1931), p. 78.

97. Riese, *Die Sexuelle Not Unserer Zeit*, p. 46.

98. Cited by Hans Lehfeldt, "VII Internationaler Kongress für Geburtenregelung, Zürich 1–5 September, 1930," *Zentralblatt für Gynäkologie* 2 (1931):117.

99. See, for example, Fränkel, *Empfängnisverhütung*, pp. 27–108, on sterilization methods.

100. The Protestant social welfare agency *Innere Mission* clearly supported (voluntary) sterilization. See, for example, Hans Harmsen, *Bevölkerungspolitik*. On his career in the church, see Heidrun Kaupen-Haas, "Eine deutsche Biographie-der Bevölkerungspolitiker Hans Harmsen," in *Heilen und Vernichten im Mustergau Hamburg. Bevölkerungs-und Gesundheitspolitik im Dritten Reich*, ed. Angelika Ebbinghaus, Heidrun Kaupen-Haas, and Karl Heinz Roth (Hamburg: Konkret, 1984), pp. 41–44. The Catholic eugenicist Hermann Muckermann was also staunchly pro-sterilization. See the discussions in the Preussischer Staatsrat, July 2, 1932, recorded in "Die Eugenik im Dienste der Volkswohlfahrt," in GStA, Rep. 84a/871. The history of sterilization in the Weimar Republic has been widely addressed in recent literature, albeit usually in the context of background to the 1933 National Socialist sterilization law. See especially Gisela Bock, *Zwangssterilisation im Nationalsozialismus. Studien zur Rassenpolitik und Frauenpolitik* (Opladen: Westdeutscher Verlag, 1986), and for a fine summary, Paul Weindling, *Health, race and German politics between national unification and Nazism, 1870–1945* (Cambridge: Cambridge University Press, 1989), pp. 388–393, 441–457.

101. Harmsen, *Bevölkerungspolitik*, p. 86.

102. Margaret Sanger, *An Autobiography*, p. 389.

103. Harmsen, *Bevölkerungspolitik*, p. 86.

104. Riese, *Die Sexuelle Not Unserer Zeit*, p. 46.

105. Riese in *Contraception*, pp. 116–117. For a thoughtful discussion of the conflict "between the idea of individual human beings as historically determined, concrete and particular in their needs, and the ideology of 'individualism,'" see Rosalind Pollack Petchesky, "Reproductive Freedom: Beyond 'A Woman's Right to Choose,'" *Signs* 5:4 (Summer 1980):663.

106. Fränkel, in "Verhandlungen," p. 91. Frankenthal warned that the political right-wing supported sterilization and opposed birth control because, "They need a big surplus of people because they consider it their physician's duty to murder the inferior." Käte Frankenthal, "Ärzteschaft und Faschismus," in *SA* 7 (1931):104, quoted in Bublitz, "Stellung," p. 44.

107. *Volksgesundheit* 41:10 (1931):195–196.

108. The complex and ambiguous relationship between the twentieth century left and eugenics has produced a lively discussion among historians, especially of Britain and Germany. See, for example, Sheila Rowbotham, *A New World for Women: Stella Browne—Socialist Feminist* (London: Pluto Press, 1977), especially pp. 18–19; Loren R. Graham, "Science and Values: The Eugenics Movement in Germany and Russia in the 1920s," *American Historical Review* 82:5 (December 1977):1133–1164; Michael Freeden, "Eugenics and Progressive Thought: A Study in Ideological Affinity," *The Historical Journal* 22:3 (1979):645–671, with rejoinder by Greta Jones, "Eugenics and Social Policy Between the Wars," *The Historical Journal* 25:3 (1982):717–728; Diane Paul, "Eugenics and the Left," *Journal of the History of Ideas* (October 1984):567–590. For Germany, see the excellent summary by Sheila Faith Weiss, "The Race Hygiene Movement in Germany 1904–1945," in *The Wellborn Science: Eugenics in Germany, France, Brazil and Russia*, ed. Mark B. Adams (New York: Oxford University Press, 1990), pp. 8–68.

109. *Jahrbuch der Ambulatorien 1930/31*, pp. 12–13.

110. Ibid., p. 10.

111. Sanger to Helene Stöcker, August 5, 1931. Sanger LC. On Slee's financial troubles, see Chesler, *Woman of Valor*, pp. 336–337.

112. Ruben-Wolf to Sanger, July 5, 1929. Sanger LC.

113. Dr. P. Gornick, "Die Schwangerenfürsorge in den Ambulatorien in den Jahren 1928 und 1929," *Jahrbuch der Ambulatorien 1928/29*, p. 43.

114. Vollnhals, "Die Schwangerenfürsorge," p. 82.

115. *SA* 7:5/6 (May/June 1931):192.

## Chapter 4

1. Kurt Tucholsky, "Die Leibesfrucht spricht," in *Gesammelte Werke*, vol. 3 (Hamburg, 1983), p. 983, translated as "The Embryo Speaks" by Harold Poor.

2. "Arbeiterfrauen antworten dem Papst," *Arbeiter Illustrierte Zeitung (AIZ)* 10:5 (1931):84–85.

3. "On Christian Marriage," in *Sixteen Encyclicals of Pius IX* [XI] (Washington, DC: National Catholic Welfare Council, n.d.), pp. 23–24, quoted in William Schneider, "Toward the Improvement of the Human Race: The History of Eugenics in France," *Journal of Modern History* 54 (June 1982):286. Cornelie Usborne suggests that the encyclical may have been partly a response to dissent within German Catholic ranks about prohibitions on birth control. See "The Christian Churches and the regulation of sexuality in Weimar Germany," in *Disciplines of Faith*, ed. Jim Obelkevich, Lyndal Roper, and Raphael Samuels (New York: Routledge and Kegan Paul, 1987), p. 108.

4. Carroll Smith-Rosenberg, "The Abortion Movement and the AMA, 1850–1880," in *Disorderly Conduct: Visions of Gender in Victorian America* (New York: Alfred A. Knopf, 1985), p. 214.

5. Volker Berghahn, *Modern Germany: Society, economy and politics in the twentieth century* (Cambridge: Cambridge University Press, 1982), pp. 119–120.

6. See the KPD anticlerical pamphlet, Johannes Karl König, *Seid fruchtbar und mehret euch! Zur Enzyklika des Papstes Pius XI. Für Paragraph 218 und gegen die werktätigen Frauen* (Berlin: 1931), in BArch(K) ZSg 1 (Zeitgeschichtliche Sammlung) 61/33(1). On KPD anticlericalism, see also police reports in BArch(K) R58/509 and 677 on the KPD

and the Freethinkers (*Freidenker*), and the series "Der Papst gegen die notleidenden Frauen," *Die Kämpferin*, especially no. 2 (1931):6–7 and no. 7 (1931):11.

7. Communists were especially impressed with the growing participation of women in strikes and strike support in the predominantly Catholic Ruhr and Upper Silesian regions where the men had tended to vote Communist and their wives Center. See Brian Peterson, "The Politics of Working-Class Women in the Weimar Republic," *Central European History* 10:2 (June 1977):87–111.

8. At the Berlin Congress in November 1930, over half the delegates were identified as housewives. See BArch(K) R134/70, p. 140. See also *Die Kämpferin*, no. 14 (1931):4.

9. Resolution passed at Second Reich Women's Conference of the IAH (International Workers Aid) in Halle, March 14–15, 1931, reported in BArch(K) R58/684.

10. See correspondence in BArch(Sapmo) ZK der SED. I 2/701/28 Abt. Frauen.

11. *SH* 3:8 (August 1931):57.

12. The meeting also proposed an arbitration court to regulate conflicts. See Hans Lehfeldt, "Die Laienorganisationen für Geburtenregelung," *Archiv für Bevölkerungspolitik, Sexualethik, und Familienkunde* 2 (1932):65, 73–75.

13. Dr. Hans Lehfeldt, personal interview, New York City, October 1, 1980.

14. *Die Frau* 38:9 (July 1931):569. The Center for Birth Control's membership in turn overlapped with that of a purely medical Experts' Conference Group for Birth Control (*Fachkonferenz für Geburtenregelung*) that first met on June 25, 1930, at the invitation of Harmsen's Working Group for Restoration of the Health of the *Volk* (*Arbeitsgemeinschaft für Volksgesundung*, AfVG) and the Population Policy Committee (*Bevölkerungspolitischer Ausschuss*) of the RGA. The Experts' Group, directed by University of Berlin Professor of Obstetrics and Gynecology Walter Stoeckel, drew an elite membership that included leading gynecologists, university professors, social hygienists, and prominent women physicians (who were separately listed). It voiced cautious support for contraception, provided that it was controlled and administered by doctors. See Hans Harmsen, "Ärztliche Aufgaben auf dem Gebiet der Geburtenregelung," *Medizinische Welt*, no. 21 (1931):1–11.

15. The festivities included an open meeting for reform of the sex crimes code, with an address by homosexual rights campaigner Kurt Hiller and a banquet whose honored guests included Magnus Hirschfeld and the Social Democratic Reichstag president Paul Löbe. See *NG* 26:5/6 (May/June 1930):109–124, and police reports in GStA Rep. 84a/8232.

16. Helene Stöcker, in *NG* 26:3/4 (March/April 1930):53. See also her foreword to Lotte Neisser-Schroeter, *Enquete über die Ehe und Sexualberatungsstellen in Deutschland mit Berücksichtigung der Geburtenregelung* (Berlin: Verlag der Neuen Generation, 1928), p. 1.

17. See, for example, the Münzenberg mass circulation publication *Arbeiter Illustrierte Zeitung* (*AIZ*)7:30 (1928), with full-page spread on sex reformers, with photos of Hodann, Hirschfeld, Stöcker, Heinrich Meng, and Havelock Ellis.

18. See material on KPD organizing around the Scottsboro boys and American racism in the small Magnus Hirschfeld collection, Kinsey Institute for Research in Sex, Gender and Reproduction, Indiana University, Bloomington, Indiana.

19. See Elfriede Foelster, "Die Arbeitsgemeinschaft sozialpolitischer Organisationen (ARSO) von 1927–1929. Zur Geschichte der Sozialpolitik der KPD," *Beiträge zur Geschichte der Arbeiterbewegung* 20:2 (1978), 252. Clara Zetkin herself urged young

activists disillusioned by party rigidity to join mass organizations like the IAH that were more hospitable to women. See correspondence with Maria Reese, Kleine Erwerbungen 379/1 (Maria Reese) in BArch(K). On IAH, see also extensive police reports in BArch(K) R134/50, 67 and R58 (Reichssicherheitshauptamt)/497, 539, 539, 649 (41, 43, 44, 45), and 674.

20. On changes in Soviet views, see Wendy Goldman, "Women, Abortion and the State 1917–1936," in *Russia's Women: Accommodation, Resistance, Transformation*, ed., Barbara Evans Clements, Barbara Alpern Engel, and Christine D. Worobec (Berkeley: University of California Press, 1991), pp. 243–265.

21. See Cornelie Usborne, *The Politics of the Body in Weimar Germany: Women's Reproductive Rights and Duties* (Ann Arbor: University of Michigan Press, 1992), pp. 156–181.

22. Ibid., p. 174.

23. See, for example, Emil Höllein, *Gegen den Gebärzwang! Der Kampf um die bewusste Kleinhaltung der Familie* (Berlin-Charlottenburg: Selbst Verlag, 1928).

24. See Usborne, *The Politics of the Body*, pp. 173–174. See also D. V. Glass, *Population Policies and Movements in Europe* (reprint ed.; London: Frank Cass & Co. Ltd., 1967 [1940]), pp. 280–281.

25. Friedrich Wolf, *Cyankali*, vol. 2, *Gesammelte Werke* (Berlin: Aufbau Verlag, 1960), p. 342. I first discussed this campaign in "Abortion and Economic Crisis: The 1931 Campaign Against Par. 218 in Germany," *New German Critique* 14 (Spring 1978):119–137. See also Hans Jürgen Arendt, "Eine demokratische Massenbewegung unter der Führung der KPD im Frühjahr 1931. Die Volksaktion gegen den Paragraphen 218 und gegen die päpstliche Enzyklika 'Casti Connubi,'" *Zeitschrift für Geschichtswissenschaft* 19:1 (1971):213–223. This extraordinarily well-documented mobilization can be followed in the reports and clippings collected in BArch(K) R86/2379(5); police reports in BArch(K) R58/548(7, 8); GStA Rep. 219/57; *SH* 3 (1931), especially nos. 3, 4, 6; *NG* 27:1, 2, 3 (Jan., Feb., Mar. 1931); and *SA* 7(1931); *PS* 4 (1931), as well as in the daily newspapers and the collected papers of Friedrich Wolf, Friedrich Wolf Archiv (FWA), Akademie der Künste, Berlin. See also the special (and not very funny) issue of the KPD satirical magazine *Der Eulenspiegel. Zeitschrift für Scherz, Satire, Ironie und tiefere Bedeutung*, no. 4 (April 1931).

26. See Friedrich Wolf, *Sturm gegen Paragraph 218. Unser Stuttgarter Prozess* (Berlin: Kampfausschuss gegen Paragraph 218, 1931), in BArch(K) ZSg 2/178(1).

27. See Istvan Deak's lively account of Weimar intellectuals' "revolt against conventional morality," in *Weimar Germany's Left-Wing Intellectuals: A Political History of the Weltbühne and Its Circle* (Berkeley: University of California Press, 1968), p. 129. See also Willem Wesling, "A New Morality: Left-Wing Intellectuals on Sexuality in Weimar Germany," *Journal of Contemporary History* 25 (1990):69–85.

28. The "Committee for Self-Denunciation" (*Komitee für Selbstbezichtigung gegen den PP 218*) was led by Dr. Heinrich Dehmel (son of the expressionist poet Richard Dehmel); other notable members were Ernst Toller, Thea von Harbou, and Margarete Kaiser, editor of *Die Schaffende Frau*. The call for openly stating, "I have had an abortion" or "I have performed an abortion," was first raised by anarcho-syndicalists who rejected KPD and sex reform organization tactics of parliamentary and electoral action.

29. It was expressly noted that among over 2,500 people at the rally, many were women. See *SA* 7:3 (March 1931):67–69; reports (March 16, 1931) on rally in Prussian Herrenhaus on March 7, 1931, in BArch(K) R86/2379(5) and BArch(K) R58/548(8), p. 134.

30. *NG* 27:7/8/9 (July/August/September 1931):164–167. The forum began March 1, 1931. See also BArch(K) R58/548(8), p. 140.

31. *Die Welt am Abend*, March 5, 1931, letter to "Öffentliche Anklage," in FWA folder 393/1. The paper's "Open Protest Against Paragraph 218" started on February 28, 1931; it also sponsored numerous protest meetings. See BArch(K) R58/548(8), p. 129.

32. *Vossische Zeitung*, March 8, 1931, p. 2.

33. Kate Stützin to Margaret Sanger, February 24, 1931, Sanger LC.

34. *Berliner Tageblatt* 59:118 (March 11, 1930) in BArch(P) Reichsjustizministerium (RJM, Ministry of Justice) 6233/vol. 2 (March 1, 1931 to October 21, 1934), p. 265. See Renny Harrigan, "Die Sexualität der Frau in der deutschen Unterhaltungsliteratur 1918–1933," *Geschichte und Gesellschaft* 7:3/4 (1981):412–437, for a brief description of abortion as a theme for popular literature.

35. FWA, folder 285 on *Cyankali* and folders 393 and 378 on the 1931 anti-218 campaign.

36. *Paragraph 218. Gequälte Menschen*, in BArch(K) ZSg 2/178(2), was based on Carl Credé-Hörder, *Volk in Not! Das Unheil des Abtreibungsparagraphen* (Dresden: Carol Reissner Verlag, 1927). A third anti–paragraph 218 play was Hans Jose Rehfisch's *Der Frauenarzt (The Gynecologist)* (Berlin: 1928–1929). The three authors reflected the different political tendencies that coalesced around the abortion issue: Wolf, a Communist; Credé, a eugenically oriented Social Democrat; and Rehfisch, a liberal bourgeois lawyer.

37. Weinert's poem "Die Arbeiterfrau" was published in 1930, Brecht's "Herr Doktor" and Tucholsky's "Die Leibesfrucht spricht" in 1931. An earlier version of Tucholsky's under the pseudonym Theobald Tiger was published in *Die Kämpferin*, no. 2 (1929):6.

38. Bertolt Brecht, "Herr Doktor," in *Gesammelte Werke*, vol. 8 (Frankfurt/Main: 1967), p. 382.

39. Franz Krey, *Maria und der Paragraph* (Vienna, Berlin, Zurich: Internationaler Arbeiter Verlag, 1931; [reprint ed. Berlin: Verlag Neuer Kurs, 1972]), was first published as volume 5 of the *Rote Eine Mark Reihe*, with a foreword by Friedrich Wolf, and immediately serialized in *AIZ* 10 (1931).

40. Petra Schneider, *Weg mit dem PP 218. Die Massenbewegung gegen das Abtreibungsverbot in der Weimarer Republik* (Berlin: Oberbaumverlag, 1975), p. 86. "Workers literature" from the League of Proletarian Revolutionary Writers consistently used abortion themes as a metaphor for general class and sex oppression, usually involving a white-collar heroine whose work in the office of a large factory conveniently puts her in contact with class-conscious (male) industrial workers. See, for example, Rudolf Braune, *Das Mädchen an der Orga Privat. Ein Kleiner Roman aus Berlin* (reprint ed. Berlin: Verlag Neues Leben, 1975 [1932]), serialized in the *AIZ* spin-off for women *Der Weg der Frau* 1 (June 1931); also Willi Bredel, *Rosenhofstrasse. Roman einer Hamburger Arbeiterstrasse* (1930; reprint ed. Berlin: Oberbaum Verlag, 1974). Contemporary nonfiction accounts told similar stories, for example, Otto Rühle's description of towns in "Württemberg, where the female population of entire villages was implicated in investigations and brought up on charges" in his *Illustrierte Sittengeschichte des Proletariats*, vol. 2 (reprint ed., Lahn-Giessen: Focus Verlag, 1977 [1930]), pp. 61–62.

41. *Kuhle Wampe* (1931), directed by Slatan Dudow, written by Bertolt Brecht and Ernst Ottwald. See *Kuhle Wampe. Protokoll des Filmes und Materialien*, ed. Wolfgang Gersch and Werner Hecht (Frankfurt am Main: Suhrkamp Verlag, 1969).

42. *Frauen in Not. Internationale Ausstellung, 9. Oktober bis 1. November 1931, im Haus der Juryfreien, Berlin* (catalogue). I am grateful to Maud Lavin for this document. See also Emmy Wolff, "Frauen in Not. Betrachtungen zu einer Kunstausstellung," *Die Frau* 39:2 (November 1931):99–104.

43. Alice Lex-Nerlinger (1893–1975) joined the KPD and the ASSO (*Association revolutionärer bildender Künstler Deutschlands*) in 1928. Her "Par. 218" is owned by the Märkisches Museum, Berlin. In 1977 a group of feminist artists in Berlin re-created the 1931 show and added new works protesting the continued presence of paragraph 218 in the German legal code. See *Par. 218—Bilder gegen ein K(l)assengesetz. Materialien zu einer Ausstellung,* ed. "Arbeitsgruppe Par. 218" (Berlin: 1977).

44. See Grossmann, "Abortion and Economic Crisis," pp. 71–75.

45. *SH* 3:3 (March 1931):22.

46. *Die Frau* 38:7 (April 1931):439–440. See also *Die Schaffende Frau* 2:3 (March 31, 1931):79.

47. See her prison diary, *Frauen. Aus dem Tagebuch einer Ärztin* (Berlin: Gustav Kiepenhauer Verlag, 1932), and her unreliable memoirs, written in U.S. exile (which do not even mention her arrest and involvement in the 1931 campaign): Else K. LaRoe, *Woman Surgeon* (New York: Dial Press, 1957).

48. See Kienle's own account, "Der Fall Kienle," in *Die Weltbühne* 14 (April 14, 1931):535–539. *Die Weltbühne* also published related articles by Carl von Ossietzky (March 3, 1931):301–303, and Friedrich Wolf (March 24, 1931):413–418.

49. Kienle, "Fall Kienle," p. 535. Reprinted in Ingrid Zwerenz, *Frauen. Die Geschichte des Par. 218* (Frankfurt am Main: Fischer Taschenbuch, 1980), p. 194.

50. Kienle, *Frauen,* p. 296. See also "Der Fall Kienle"; letters in FWA, folder 153; *Die Kämpferin,* no. 7 (1931): 4.

51. Kienle, *Frauen,* p. 309.

52. Ibid., pp. 307, 310.

53. Kienle and her lawyer Alfred Apfel also spoke at the "nonparty political" rally in the Admiralpalast; see BArch(K) R58/548(8), p. 140. Unlike most of her allies, von Harbou went on to join the Nazi party after Fritz Lang had fled to the United States. See her *Reichskulturkammer* file, Berlin Document Center. Thea von Harbou's strong involvement in the campaign may have been influenced by her close friendship with her cousin Dr. Anne-Marie Durand-Wever (personal conversation with Madeleine Durand-Noll, Durand-Wever's granddaughter, Cochem an der Mosel, January 12, 1993).

54. See, for example, Gertrud Bäumer, "Frauenprogramm: Neuer Aufbruch oder?" *Die Frau* 39:12 (September 1932):730–732. For background on abortion and the BDF, see also Ann Taylor Allen, *Feminism and Motherhood in Germany 1800–1914* (New Brunswick, NJ: Rutgers University Press, 1991), especially ch. 10; Richard Evans, *The Feminist Movement in Germany 1894–1933* (London, Beverly Hills: Sage, 1976). See also Renate Bridenthal, "Professional Housewives" in *When Biology Became Destiny* (1984); and Nancy Reagin, "Bourgeois Women, Local Politics and Social Change: The Women's Movement in Hanover, 1880–1933," Ph.D dissertation, Johns Hopkins, 1990 (forthcoming 1995, University of North Carolina Press).

55. *Die Schaffende Frau. Zeitschrift für modernes Frauentum* 2:2 (March 1931):57; see also 2:3 (April 1931). Margarete Kaiser, the editor, was also author of a sex manual *Die Liebe als Kunst* (Berlin: Ibis Verlag, 1932) and a regular speaker at anti-218 rallies.

56. K. Stützin to M. Sanger, 1931, n.d., Sanger LC. Sanger avoided a direct reply. The divisons in the Center for Birth Control were foreshadowed in 1926 when Kate Stützin's husband Dr. Johann Stützin and his sexologist colleague Albert Moll did not invite "sex radicals" Hirschfeld and Stöcker to the Sex Research Congress in Berlin, and continued in the center's relationship to Stoeckel's Experts' Conference Group for Birth Control. See note 13 above. Moll defended "Der 'reaktionäre' Kongress für Sexualforschung" and criticized Hirschfeld for confusing agitation with science in his "Institut für Unwissenschaft" in *Zeitschrift für Sexualwissenschaft* 13:10 (1927):321–331.

57. Women doctors' response to desperate women patients was also a major theme in Weimar popular fiction. See, for example, Vicki Baum, *Stud. Chem. Helene Willfuer* (Berlin: Ullstein, 1928), and Braune, *Mädchen an der Orga Privat.*

58. Käte Frankenthal, *Der dreifache Fluch: Jüdin, Ärztin und Sozialistin. Lebenserinnerungen einer Ärztin in Deutschland und im Exil* (Frankfurt am Main: Campus Verlag, 1981), pp. 115, 119.

59. Henriettte D. Magnus Necheless, "Reminiscences of a German Jewish Woman Physician," unpublished manuscript (Chicago: 1940), translated by Ruth F. Necheless (New York: 1980), pp. 27–28. I am grateful to Eleanor Riemer for giving me a copy of this memoir. Original in Houghton Library, Harvard University.

60. Alice Goldmann-Vollnhals, "Die Schwangerenfürsorge in den Ambulatorien in den Jahren 1926 und 1927," *Jahrbuch der Ambulatorien des Verbandes der Krankenkassen Berlins 1926/1927*, p. 83.

61. Dr. Elisabeth Prinz, "Zur Frage der Ethik und Diätetik des Sexuallebens," *Die Neue Generation* 27:7/8/9 (1931):162.

62. "Paragraph 218. Furchtbare Tatsachen," *Welt am Abend*, March 31, 1931, in FWA, folder 393/1.

63. *Die Frau* 37:10 (July 1930):600. The petition attracted police attention and evoked a storm of response. See BArch(K) R58/548(6), and GStA Rep. 84a/8232. For response from the medical profession, see statement by *Deutscher Ärzte-Vereinsverband Potsdam* to Reichstag Criminal Justice Committee, February 14, 1931, in R86/2379(5).

64. The KPD resolution calling for social as well as medical and eugenic indications lost by only seven votes. By contrast, in March 1928, the Prussian Medical Society had reaffirmed that pregnancies could only be terminated if the mother's life was endangered. On the Berlin Medical Society debates, see BArch(K) R58/548(6), p. 118; R86/2369(1); R86/2379(4); *Die Frauenwelt. Eine Halbmonatsschrift* (SPD), no. 8 (1929):178; *Ideal Lebensbund* 3 (January 1929):28; and the summary in *Zuchthaus oder Mutterschaft. Beiträge zum Sexualproblem* (Berlin: Verlag der Syndikalist, 1929).

65. Charlotte Wolff, "Die Fürsorge für die Familie im Rahmen der Schwangerenberatung der Ambulatorien des Verbandes der Berliner Krankenkassen," M.D. dissertation, Friedrich Wilhelms University, Berlin, 1928, p. 11.

66. *Die Frau* 37:10 (July 1930):600.

67. Hertha Riese in *3rd Sexual Reform Congress—WLSR. London, September 8–14, 1929*, ed. Norman Haire (London: Kegan, Paul, Trubner and Co., 1929), pp. 220–221.

68. *Die Frau* 37:11 (August 1930):662. On conflicts among doctors, see Cornelie Usborne, "Abortion in Weimar Germany—the debate amongst the medical profession," *Continuity and Change* 5:2 (1990):199–224.

69. *SH* 4 (May 1932):37–39. A national survey conducted by the BDÄ directly after the Wolf/Kienle arrests confirmed that compared to male colleagues, female physi-

cians were more likely to oppose paragraph 218. The overwhelming majority of the 1,406 (of 2,761, slightly less than half) women who responded to the questionnaire favored liberalization. Only 86 (6.4 percent) supported existing regulations, 283 (20.9 percent) supported complete decriminalization, and the largest number favored combined consideration of medical and social indications. Most of the reform-minded were from large cities, between the ages of 30 and 40, and had completed their training during or after the war, giving them at least 10 years of experience. Presumably they were also the ones most likely to respond; the survey certainly demonstrated urban women doctors' commitment to reform. See *Weg der Frau* 2:3 (March 1, 1932):28; also *Die Frau* 39:5 (February 1932):312.

70. *Weg der Frau*, the Münzenberg women's journal spawned by the *AIZ* began publication in June 1931 with a front-page interview with Dr. Else Kienle under the headline "Dein Körper Gehört Dir": *Weg der Frau* 1 (June 1931):1.

71. BArch(K) R58/548/8, pp. 167–176.

72. Wolf, *Sturm gegen Paragraph 218*, pp. 23–24.

73. See, e.g., Hans Harmsen, "Die Russischen Erfahrungen mit der Freigabe der Abtreibung. Die Bewegung zur Beseitigung des Abtreibungsparagraphen in Deutschland," in Arbeitsgemeinschaft für Volksgesundung (AfVG), *Sinn und Problematik des Abtreibungsparagraph*, pp. 5–22; A. B. Genss, *Was lehrt die Freigabe der Abtreibung in Sowjetrussland* (Vienna: Agis, n.d.), reviewed in *Mitteilungen der Arbeitsgemeinschaft für Volksgesundung* 29 (December 9, 1929):2.

74. The attack on fascist population policy, in contrast to Soviet achievements, is especially well documented in *Referenten Material für die Volksaktion gegen den Par. 218 und Verteidigung Friedrich Wolfs* (Berlin: Kampfausschuss, 1931). See Victoria de Grazia, *How Fascism Ruled Women* (Berkeley: University of California Press, 1992), especially pp. 41–76.

75. Report on Wolf's speech, March 7, 1931, at rally in Prussian Herrenhaus. March 16, 1931, in BArch(K) R86/2379(5). See also Georg Kubik, "Dr. med. Friedrich Wolf als Arzt und Kommunist im Kampf der deutschen Arbeiterklasse für die Geburtenregelung gegen den PP 218 des bürgerlichen Strafgesetzbuches und dessen Anwendung in der Weimarer Republik," Ph.D. diss., Rostock University, 1968.

76. Friedrich Wolf, *Sturm*, pp. 23–24.

77. Höllein, *Gebärzwang*, p. 187.

78. See BArch(K) NS 26/810 for KPD membership statistics. See also Gabrielle Bremme, *Die politische Rolle der Frau in Deutschland. Eine Untersuchung über den Einfluss der Frauen bei Wahlen und ihre Teilnahme an Partei und Parlament* (Göttingen: Vandenhoek & Ruprecht, 1956), p. 73; Maurice Duverger, *The Political Role of Women* (Paris: UNESCO, 1955), pp. 54–65; Peterson, "The Politics of Working-Class Women."

79. Manes Sperber, personal interview, Paris, February 1, 1978.

80. Käte Frankenthal, *PP 218 streichen—nicht ändern* (Berlin: E. Laubsche Verlagsbuchhandlung, 1931). In October 1931, Frankenthal quit the SPD in protest against its weak position, and became one of the founding members of the Sozialistische Arbeiter Partei (SAP), a left-splinter group; see Frankenthal, *Dreifache Fluch*. On the SPD, see also Renate Pore, *A Conflict of Interest: Women in German Social Democracy 1919–1933* (Westport, CT: Greenwood Press, 1981), pp. 78–80; Alfred Grotjahn, *Erlebtes und Erstrebtes. Erinnerungen eines sozialistischen Arztes* (Berlin: Kommissions-Verlag F. A. Herbig, 1932); Werner Thoennessen, *The Emancipation of Women: The Rise and Decline*

*of the Women's Movement in German Social Democracy 1863–1933* (London: Pluto Press, 1973), and most comprehensively, Karen Hagemann, *Frauenalltag und Männerpolitik. Alltagsleben und gesellschaftliches Handeln von Arbeiterfrauen in der Weimarer Republik* (Bonn: Verlag J. H. W. Dietz, 1990). For a more favorable view of the SPD, see Usborne, *The Politics of the Body.*

81. Sperber interview, February 1, 1978.

82. Helene Overlach, speech at the Sportpalast, Berlin, June 1929, BArch(Sapmo) 1/1/25 Parteifragen.

83. Helene Overlach, personal interview, Berlin, GDR, January 11, 1979.

84. Even the Catholic Church, which had a powerful public political voice in the Center party, never mounted a "Right to Life" campaign, but rather denounced abortion as one of many social evils to be combated, including sexual immorality and women's emancipation, listed in the papal encyclical.

85. *Ideal Lebensbund* 3 (March 1929):68–69.

86. Hodann, *Geschlecht und Liebe in biologischer und gesellschaftlicher Beziehung* (Berlin: Büchergilde Gutenberg, 1932), pp. 149–157. The desperate suicide was a regular theme for the "Frau in Not" story. *PS* 5:10 (1932):302 reported 1,000 suicides in Berlin in the first half of 1932. According to the "Denkschrift über die gesundheitlichen Verhältnisse des deutschen Volkes" in *Stenographische Berichte der Verhandlungen des Reichstags* 451: 1224 (November 4, 1931), p. 17, as with every catastrophic statistic, Berlin had the highest suicide rate: 4.22 per 10,000 people. The average national rate was 3.8 for men and 1.5 for women; women's rate was increasing faster than men's. Arendt, "Eine demokratische Massenbewegung," p. 31, quotes the *Statistisches Jahrbuch für das Deutsche Reich* (1933), p. 43, as recording 18,625 female suicides in 1931, the highest figure for all of Europe. Women of chidbearing age from 30 to 40 were especially vulnerable, a fact often connected with unwanted pregnancy, the illegality of abortion, and the "surplus woman" problem.

87. *Die Kämpferin* 2 (1931):10. See also Kommission für die Überwachung der öffentlichen Ordnung, BArch(K) R134/70, p. 206.

88. By 1931, the RGA noted a decrease in child-bed fever mortality in large cities, generally attributed to improved techniques by abortionists. See *Denkschrift über die gesundheitlichen Verhältnisse 1931*, p. 10; BArch(K) R86/920/15 (Ursachen der Sterbefälle), p. 7; *Statistik des Deutschen Reichs* 393, pp. 123–124.

89. RV physician Hans Lehfeldt remembered that in Berlin indications for dilation and curettage were "very liberally interpreted. We got a certificate from one of the doctors saying that the woman requires the operation and you put it into your charts and you were entitled to do an operation." Interview, New York City, October 1, 1980.

90. Dr. Hertha Nathorff, personal interview, New York City, September 25, 1980.

91. Mischket Liebermann, *Aus dem Ghetto in die Welt* (Berlin [East]: Verlag der Nation, 1977), p. 65.

92. Wolf, *Cyankali*, p. 134.

93. Renee Strowoba to Friedrich Wolf, February 9, 1930, in FWA, folder 285.

94. See, for example, James Mohr, *Abortion in America: The Origins and Evolution of National Policy* (New York: Oxford University Press, 1978); Smith-Rosenberg, "Abortion Movement, pp. 217–244; Barbara Brookes, *Abortion in England 1900–1967* (London: Croom Helm, 1988).

95. See the careful study by Sigmund Peller, *Fehlgeburt und Bevölkerungsfrage. Eine medizinisch-statistisch und sozial-biologische Studie* (Stuttgart / Leipzig: Hippokrates Verlag, 1930), pp. 77–125.

96. Smith-Rosenberg, "Abortion Movement," p. 218.

97. Claire Waldorff: "Die Grossstadt Pflanze," on "Es gibt nur ein Berlin und das ist mein Berlin," Electrola (records) historical cuts.

98. Irmgard Keun, *Gilgi—eine von uns* (reprint ed.; Düsseldorf: Claassen Verlag, 1979 [1931]), pp. 175–176.

99. The image of a "new woman" resolving the abortion dilemma by leaving a weak lover and having the baby on her own was also powerfully evoked in the 1927 Soviet film *Bed and Sofa* directed by Avram Roon.

100. Vicki Baum, *Stud. chem. Helene Willfuer* (Berlin: Ullstein, 1928), pp. 96, 99–100, 104.

101. Ibid., p. 126.

102. Ibid., pp. 136–137.

103. See also Braune, *Mädchen*, and Ernst Ottwaldt, *Denn Sie Wissen Was Sie Tun. Ein Deutscher Justiz-Roman* (reprint ed.; Berlin: Verlag Klaus Guhl, 1978 [1931]), p. 47.

104. See complaints about influence of lay leagues and anti-218 propaganda in BArch(P) RMI 1501 / 9351, pp. 186–187.

105. The first RGA file, BArch(K) R86 / 2379(1), May 6, 1917–November 17, 1921, recorded early discussions on new laws proposed after the war and the revolution. R86 / 2379(2), November 15, 1919–August 7, 1923, covered discussions about the fine differences between abortifacients or contraceptives and noted the lucrativeness of the illegal abortion business in postwar Germany. R86 / 2379(3), August 7, 1923–March 16, 1927 as well as files in R86 / 931 (8, 9, 10, 11), and annual health reports, covering the stabilization period, focused on supposedly large increases in illegal abortions, perhaps due to improved record keeping and the resolution of the immediate postwar health crises of TB, VD, and malnutrition. R86 2379(5), September 6, 1929–December 31, 1932, the last and thickest file, portrayed a crisis period when government attention was directed toward the political struggles around abortion, and the RGA demanded more information from provincial authorities on birth control and abortion practices. See also R86 2373(2), Heiratspolitik 1913–1929; R 86 / 931 (11–15), local health reports; R86 / 920(15) Ursachen der Sterbefälle 1929–1932; *Reichsgesundheitsblatt* 1926–1932. See, furthermore, Prussian Ministry of Justice, GStA, Rep. 84a / 8232, 8233, and BArch(P), RMI 1501 / 9351, 9352.

106. *Frauenwelt*, no. 9 (May 3, 1930):20. See also Annemarie Niemeyer, *Zur Struktur der Familie. Statistische Materialien* (Berlin: F. A. Herbig, 1931), p. 97; Anne-Marie Durand-Wever, "Umfang und Ursachen der Geburtenbeschränkung," *Medizinische Welt* 5, no. 7 (February 14, 1931):244. David Glass, trying to make sense of the statistical data in 1940, concluded that abortions increased at a fairly steady rate from 1908 to 1932. Despite considerable variations, even the lowest rates for the years prior to 1933 were very high. See Glass, *Population Policies*, p. 277, and table 25, p. 280.

107. For example, the Berlin Charité reported that 91.2 percent of its cases resulted from criminal abortions, while a hospital in Catholic Münster insisted that 100 percent of its interrupted pregnancy cases were spontaneous miscarriages! *Reichsgesundheitsblatt*, no. 50 (1930):925.

108. Some physicians advised women to start self-aborting and then go, bleeding and feverish, to a hospital where physicians would then be compelled to finish the

job, in order to save the woman's life or health. During Weimar (unlike under the Nazis), doctors were not required to notify the authorities in such cases. See Glass, *Population Policies,* p. 285.

109. See also Heiser's defense in Apotheker Paul Heiser, "Das Fiasko der Schutzfrage," *SH* 1:6 (March 1929):44–45.

110. See clippings and other information on trial from BArch(K) R86/2373(2) Bevölkerungspolitik 1913–1929. As frequently happened, Heiser, the founder of the lay Workers Association for Birth Control (*Arbeitervereine für Geburtenregelung*), succeeded in turning his trial into a prosecution of the abortion paragraph rather than the abortionist. An all-male Berlin jury managed to uphold the letter of the law and still declare a virtual acquittal; they found him technically guilty, and sentenced him to two years in jail, but since he had already spent 14 months in pretrial detention, he was immediately released on probation. There are numerous examples of physicians testifying on behalf of accused colleagues. In 1929, for example, a Thuringian court acquitted a physician when three expert medical witnesses, Professors Wilhelm Liepmann and Hugo Sellheim, and sex reform physician Felix Theilhaber, testified that he had merely "helped" in a "humane and social" if not "wise manner" in 25 cases of extreme need. *Welt am Abend,* March 12, 1931; also *Berliner Tageblatt,* November 14, 1929.

111. See Alfred Grotjahn, "Eine PP 218 Kartothek und ihre Lehren," *Medizinische Welt* 5:4 (1931); also *Archiv für Bevölkerungspolitik* 7 (1932):308.

112. Friedrich Wolf, FWA, folder 153/2, cited Julius Wolf to claim one death for every 50 "miscarriages" adding up to at least 6,000 female deaths annually, so that in greater Berlin, "At the sexually most active age between 20 and 40 years, abortion kills almost as many as one third of the victims of tuberculosis, this angel of death." See Julius Wolf, *Mutter oder Embryo? Zum Kampf um den Abtreibungsparagraphen* (Berlin: Carl Heymanns Verlag, 1930), p. 7; *Zeitschrift für Sexualwissenschaft* 16:5 (October 10, 1929); Niemeyer, *Zur Struktur der Familie,* p. 97. Also important to the debate was interpretation of Soviet data; depending on their point of view, observers pointed to the low mortality rate of legal abortions or to the very high number of legal abortions as well as the continuing high number of illegal abortions. See Susan Gross Solomon, "The Soviet Legalization of Abortion in German Medical Discourse: A Study of the Use of Selective Perceptions in Cross-Cultural Scientific Relations," *Social Studies of Science* 22: 3 (August 1992):455–485. Generally on these "statistical acrobatics," see Usborne, *The Politics of the Body,* p. 187.

113. From 1882 to 1890, for example, there were only 225 convictions a year for illegal abortions. See Peller, *Fehlgeburt,* p. 136. In 1909, 1,030 people of 1,322 prosecuted were convicted; in 1913, 1,518 of 1,879; in 1919 in the new republic, 988 of 1,274; in 1925— the high point—7,193 of 8,402; in 1927 after the reform, 5,313 of 6,142. See Niemeyer, *Struktur der Familie,* p. 97. As chapter 6 details, arguments about the relative extent of abortion prosecutions during Weimar continue today. See Gisela Bock, "Antinatalism, maternity and paternity in National Socialist racism," in *Maternity and the Rise of the European Welfare States, 1880s–1950s,* ed. Gisela Bock and Pat Thane (London and New York: Routledge, 1991), p. 242; Usborne, *Politics of the Body,* p. 174.

114. Brookes, *Abortion in England,* p. 51. See also Diana Gittins, "Women's Work and Family Size Between the Wars," *Oral History* 5:2 (Autumn 1977):84–100.

115. Margaret Sanger, *An Autobiography* (New York: Norton, 1938), p. 284.

116. Oberamtsarzt, Rothweil (Württemberg) to RGA, April 10, 1926, BArch(K) R86/931/12.

117. See Dr. Martin Hirschberg, "Unterbrechung der Schwangerschaft aus medizinischer Indikation" in *Jahrbuch der Ambulatorien 1928/29*. pp. 78–84.

118. Only 15 percent of the respondents were gynecologists. See *SA* 7:1 (January 1931):23; Helene Boerner, "Zum Hamburger Fragebogen über den Paragraphen 218," *Deutsches Aerzteblatt* 60:4:57; "Welche Wünsche hat die Hamburger Ärzteschaft für die Änderung des PP 218?" in *Medizinische Welt* 5:2 (1931):59; Kubik, "Dr. med. Friedrich Wolf," p. 117. On the whole, general practitioners were friendlier to reform than specialists. Carl Credé estimated, in his own defense, that three-quarters of all German general practitioners sometimes performed abortions. See Credé, *Volk in Not*, p. 3.

119. Paul Weindling by contrast stresses that the campaign "distracted away from the risks of placing eugenics and racial hygiene in the hands of an authoritarian state" and weakened "the grip of pro-natalism." Paul Weindling, *Health, race and German politics between national unification and Nazism 1870–1945* (Cambridge: Cambridge University Press, 1989), p. 461.

120. See, for example, Mathilde Kelchner, *Kummer und Trost jugendlicher Arbeiterinnen. Eine sozialpsychologische Untersuchung an Aufsätzen von Schülerinnen der Berufschule* (Leipzig: Verlag von C. L. Hirschfeld, 1929), or Günter Krolzig, *Der Jugendliche in der Großstadtfamilie. Auf Grund von Niederschriften Berliner Berufsschüler–und schülerinnen* (Berlin: F. A. Herbig Verlagsbuchhandlung, 1930).

121. The 1932 catalogue for the *Gesunde Frau, Gesundes Volk* exhibition exhorted women to refuse "this unnatural step, so contrary to the essence of women's body and soul." The strong woman and brave mother was defined by the courage to resist the pressures of selfish men and "old wives" networks. See catalogue, March/April 1932, p. 25, BArch(K) R86/888.

122. Reichsausschuss für Bevölkerungsfragen, January 20, 1930, in BArch(K) R86/2369(2), especially pp. 9–17, 33–76.

123. A. Gottstein, A. Grotjahn to RGA, Berlin, June 18, 1931. Only four days earlier, Grotjahn had submitted a similarly grounded resignation protesting the emergency decree cutbacks in child benefits (*Kinderzulagen*), Grotjahn to Gottstein, June 4, 1931. In BArch(K) R86/2369(2).

124. Dr. Max Hirsch, "Die Volkshygienische Bedeutung der Fruchtabtreibung und die Mittel zu ihrer Bekämpfung" (n.d.), Referat wissenschaftlicher Beirat, Prussian Ministry for Social Welfare, in BArch (K) R86/2371(1).

125. Maria Monheim, *Rationalisierung der Menschenvermehrung. Eine Studie zur praktischen Bevölkerungspolitik* (Jena: Verlag von Gustav Fischer, 1928), pp. 64, 50.

126. Alexander Graf Stenbock-Fermor, *Deutschland von unten. Reisen durch die proletarische Provinz 1930* (reprint ed., Luzern and Frankfurt am Main: Verlag C. J. Bucher, 1980 [1931]), p. 24.

127. Personal communication, Henry Pachter (comment on my undergraduate paper, City College, 1973).

128. *Denkschrift über gesundheitliche Verhältnisse* (1931), p. 3.

129. "Der Papst gegen die notleidenden Frauen," *Die Kämpferin*, nos. 2 (1931):5–7 and 7 (1931):11. The journal reappeared on June 15 (no. 10) in larger and yet more rhetorical format, strengthened in accusations of "social fascism" by the fact that the ban had been ordered by the SPD Prussian Interior Minister Grzesinski.

130. Police report, June 3, 1931, BArch(K) R58/548(8), p. 173. Wolf and Kienle's trial was repeatedly postponed, and by the time the police started looking for them again

after January 1933, Kienle had already fled the country and the case against Wolf could not be prosecuted in her absence. Berlin police report, February 4, 1933, p. 228.

## Chapter 5

1. "Notverordnungen im ureigensten Sinne des Worte, denn sie verordnen Not und steigern die schon vorhandene Not," quoted in Stefan Bajohr, *Die Hälfte der Fabrik. Geschichte der Frauenarbeit in Deutschland 1914 bis 1945* (Marburg: Verlag der Arbeiterbewegung und Gesellschaftswissschaften, 1979), p. 195.

2. See Eve Rosenhaft, *Beating the Fascists? The German Communists and Political Violence 1929–1933* (Cambridge: Cambridge University Press, 1983); Anthony McElligott, "Street Politics in Hamburg, 1932–3," *History Workshop* 16 (Autumn 1983):83–90.

3. Rosenhaft, *Beating the Fascists*, pp. 13–14.

4. See Hermann Weber, *Die Wandlung des deutschen Kommunismus. Die Stalinisierung der KPD in der Weimarer Republik* (Frankfurt am Main: Europäische Verlagsanstalt, 1969); Ossip Flechtheim, *Die KPD in der Weimarer Republik* (Frankfurt am Main: Europäische Verlagsanstalt, 1969); Helmut Gruber, "Willi Münzenberg's Communist Propaganda Empire 1921–1933," *The Journal of Modern History* 38:3 (September 1966):278–297.

5. See Detlev Peukert,"The Lost Generation: Youth Unemployment at the End of the Weimar Republic," in *The German Unemployed: Experiences and Consequences of Mass Unemployment from the Weimar Republic to the Third Reich*, ed. Richard Evans and Dick Geary (London: Croom Helm, 1987), pp. 172–193; Elizabeth Harvey, "Youth Unemployment and the State: Public Policies towards Unemployed Youth in Hamburg during the World Economic Crisis," Ibid., pp. 142–171; Eve Rosenhaft, "Organizing the 'Lumpenproletariat': Cliques and Communists in Berlin During the Weimar Republic," in *Social Change and Political Development in Weimar Germany*, ed. Richard Bessel and E. J. Feuchtwanger (Totowa, NJ: Barnes and Noble, 1981), pp. 207–240.

6. The film *Kuhle Wampe* (1931), for example, strongly (if obliquely) suggests that the young heroine Anni is "helped" out of her desperate search for an illegal abortion by comrades in the local party youth group.

7. BArch(Sapmo) I 2/701/28 Abt. Frauen.

8. On the history of the KPD and the politics of Bolshevization, see Weber, *Die Wandlung der KPD in der Weimarer Republik*; Ossip Flechtheim, *Die KPD in der Weimarer Republik* (Frankfurt am Main: Europäische Verlagsanstalt, 1969). Sylvia Kontos, *Die Partei kämpft wie ein Mann* (Basel-Frankfurt am Main: Stroemfeld, Roter Stern, 1979), discusses policy on women, especially pp. 25–91.

9. The newly formed RFMB gained 4,000 members in six weeks. See BArch(K) R134/30 (Reichskommission für die Überwachung öffentlicher Ordnung, Nachrichtensammelstelle im Reichsministerium des Innern), p. 21. See also R134/30/33/37 and R58/757 (Reichssicherheitshauptamt). Police records provide excellent source material for the RFMB (and all KPD organizations dealt with here), since they consist to a large extent of material produced by the organizations themselves (internal reports, memoranda, annual programs, leaflets, etc.).

10. Helene Overlach memoirs, BArch(Sapmo) EA 1053.

11. Ibid.

12. See *Die Kämpferin. Organ der Gesamtinteressen der arbeitenden Frauen, 1927–1932*. In 1928, 17 percent of 130,000 KPD members (and 21 percent of 867,671 SPD members) were women; in large cities, the figure was closer to 25 percent. See Karen Hagemann, "Men's Demonstrations and Women's Protest: Gender in Collective Action in the Urban Working-Class Milieu during the Weimar Republic," *Gender and History* 5:1 (Spring 1993):105–106.

13. Overlach's memories are from a personal interview, Berlin-GDR, January 11, 1976, and her unpublished memoirs, BArch(Sapmo) EA 1053.

14. Rosa Meyer-Leviné, *Inside German Communism: Memoirs of Party Life in the Weimar Republic* (London: Pluto Press, 1977), pp. 142–143. See also her collected papers, BArch(K).

15. Overlach interview, January 11, 1976.

16. Overlach interview and memoirs.

17. In her extremely expurgated memoir, Kienle portrayed the trip as mainly an escape from marital problems and a miscarriage that had left her infertile. She also claimed to have been briefly arrested in Moscow. Else K. La Roe, *My Life as a Surgeon* (New York: Dial Press, 1957), pp. 194, 178.

18. See *Stenographische Berichte der Verhandlungen des Reichstags*, vol. 451, KPD-Antrag no. 1201, October 16, 1931; *Die Kämpferin*, no. 15 (1931):4. See also Richtlinien: Frauen and Mädchen Staffeln Gegen den Faschismus, police report October 26, 1932, in BArch(K) R134/75, pp. 159–174.

19. The comprehensive *Gesetz über Arbeitsvermittlung und Arbeitslosenversicherung* guaranteed unemployment benefits as a right without eligibility or need provisions to be jointly financed by employer and employee. It also established the state as an employment agency through the establishment of a *Hauptstelle der Reichsanstalt für Arbeitsvermittlung und Arbeitslosenversicherung* (Central Agency for Employment Referrals and Unemployment Insurance). When established in 1927, it supported 586,000 workers; in the hard winter of 1928–1929 the number had risen to over two million, and by 1930–1932 threatened to burst the coffers of state benefits. See B. Weisbrod, "The Crisis of German Unemployment Insurance in 1928/29 and Its Political Repercussions," in *The Emergence of the Welfare State in Britain and Germany 1850–1950*, ed. W. J. Mommsen (London: Croom Helm, 1981), pp. 188–204; Friedrich Syrup, *Hundert Jahre Staatliche Sozialpolitik 1839–1939* (Stuttgart: Kohlhammer, 1957), pp. 330–345.

20. Women were especially hurt by an emergency decree that redefined many jobs occupied by women as "minor occupations" ineligible for insurance coverage. See in general Marguerite Thibert's remarkably cogent contemporary analysis, "The Economic Depression and the Employment of Women," *International Labor Review* 27:4 (April 1933): 620–630; Annemarie Tröger, "Die Dolchstosslegende der Linken: 'Frauen haben Hitler an die Macht gebracht,'" in *Frauen und Wissenschaft. Beiträge zur Berliner Sommeruniversität für Frauen, Juli 1976* (Berlin: Courage Verlag, 1977), pp. 324–355; Karin Hausen, "Unemployment also Hits Women: The New and Old Woman on the Dark Side of the Golden Twenties in Germany," in *Unemployment and the Great Depression in Weimar Germany*, ed. Peter D. Stachura (London: Macmillan, 1986), pp. 78–120; Helgard Kramer, "Frankfurt's Working Women: Scapegoats or Winners of the Great Depression?" in *The German Unemployed: Experiences and Consequences of Mass Unemployment from the Weimar Republic to the Third Reich*, ed. Richard J. Evans and Dick Geary, (New York: St. Martin's Press, 1987), pp. 108–141.

21. A December 8, 1931, decree cut wages back to the 1927 level, with particularly stringent cuts for civil servants, particularly devastating for single, self-supporting women teachers and postal workers. A fifth decree on June 14, 1932, mandated cutbacks of at least 300 million RM in pension and other insurance payments. Finally, in fall 1932, the Papen government included marriagelike relationships in the restrictions on eligibility applied to married workers.

22. Marie Jahoda, Paul Lazarsfeld, and Hans Zeisel, *Marienthal: A Sociology of an Unemployed Community* (reprint ed., Chicago: Aldine Atherton, 1971 [1933]).

23. See Tröger, "Legende," and Hausen, "New and Old Women."

24. See issues of *AIZ*, 1929–1933, and *Weg der Frau* 1931–1933. For the Soviet-German comparison, see "24 Stunden aus dem Leben einer Moskauer Arbeiterfamilie," *AIZ* 10:38 (1931). The Russian Filipows were compared to the "Bauarbeiterfamilie Fournes in der Kösliner Strasse"; and "Mutter Fournes Arbeitstag," no. 48, p. 968. See also police reports on IAH filmstrip, Berlin, September 27, 1932, and June 3, 1932, BArch(K) R58/614. For views of housework, see the comic stories about Frau Gründlich and Frau Grämlich in *Weg der Frau*.

25. ARSO to Marianne Gundermann, 5 April 1931 in BArch(Sapmo) I 4/11/1, "Revolutionäre Massenorganisationen, ARSO."

26. Text of IAH filmstrip, Neue Deutsche Lichtbildstelle, in BArch(K) R58/614. The RGO (trade union opposition) set up housewives' groups in 1932. See R134/81, pp. 219–220.

27. *Arbeiter Kalender*, January 1932, in BArch(K) ZSg 1, 61/5(5).

28. Similar, or more benighted, stories have been told for the SPD. See Karen Hagemann's exhaustive study of the Hamburg SPD, *Frauenalltag und Männerpolitik: Alltagsleben und gesellschaftliches Handeln von Arbeiterfrauen in der Weimarer Republik* (Bonn: J. H. W. Dietz, 1990); also her "Men's Demonstrations and Women's Protest," pp. 101–119; Helmut Gruber, *Red Vienna: Experiment in Working Class Culture 1919–1934* (New York: Oxford University Press, 1991).

29. Käthe Duncker, "Die Familie im Wandel der Zeiten," *PS* 4:6 (June 1931):176.

30. Hilde Wirisch on her play *Nora 1932*, performed by *Junge Volksbühne*, December 26, 1932, in BArch(K) R58/613. See Mary Nolan, *Visions of Modernity: American Business and the Modernization of Germany* (New York: Oxford University Press, 1994) for discussion of the left's infatuation with technology.

31. BArch(K) NS26/10. See also R58/684, 674, 504, 401, and R134/10 as well as the journals *Die Frauenwacht*, *Frauen in Front*, and *Der Vormarsch*.

32. Maria Reese papers, Kleine Erwerbungen 379/1, BArch(K).

33. *Der Vormarsch* 2:2 (January 1933):10–14, in BArch(K) R58/649(44).

34. Medical examinations of tenants in the Maierhof, Ackerstrasse, Berlin, took place January 22, 1933. See *Der Vormarsch* 2:3 (February 1933):20, and leaflet "Frauen an die Front," calling on women to rally on March 8, 1933, in BArch(K) R58/684. See also R58/336/10; R134/70,71.

35. *Volksgesundheit* 42:12 (1932):82. See ARSO Rundschreiben, Essen, January 30, 1931, in BArch(K) R58/757(4), p. 97. ARSO attempted to infiltrate a long list of organizations dealing with health and social welfare: homeopathic medicine, temperance, antiimmunization, war invalids, the handicapped, pensioners, tenants, welfare recipients, as well as the unemployed councils. See police report, October 1, 1930, R58/757(1), p. 47. See also ARSO Rundschreiben, no. 11, in police report from February 13, 1931, in BA R134/70, pp. 179–185.

36. *PS* 4:1 (1931):27–29. See BArch(K) R58/548(5), on sex-political demands, and discussion in Chapter 2.

37. See BArch(K) R36/991, correspondence of *Archiv für Wohlfahrtspflege* for discussion on how to handle the upstart but growing ARSO. See also BArch(Sapmo)I 4/11/1–3. On ARSO, see also Chapter 2.

38. The group was also sometimes called *Einheits Verband* (or *Komite*) *für proletarischen Mutterschutz und Sexualreform*. See *Liebe Verboten. Einheitsverband für proletarische Sexualreform und Mutterschutz* (Berlin: Verlag für Arbeiterkultur, n.d. [1931]), p. 17, in BArch(K) ZSg 1, 65/77(4); Hans Lehfeldt, "Die Laienorganisationen für Geburtenregelung," *Archiv für Bevölkerungspolitik, Sexualethink und Familienkunde* 2 (1932), pp. 80–81; BA R58/757(1), p. 46.

39. Dr. Hans Lehfeldt, personal interview, New York City, September 14, 1977. Wilhelm Reich used the same term in his description, *People in Trouble*. Volume 2 of *The Emotional Plague of Mankind* (New York: Farrar, Strauss and Giroux, 1976), p. 155.

40. Lehfeldt, "Laienorganisationen," p. 81, and interviews, New York City, September 14, 1977, and October, 1, 1980.

41. Dr. Martha Ruben-Wolf, in *PS* 2:12 (December 1929):380. For KPD critique of rival groups, see also *PS* 4:5(May 1931):151–154; 4:6 (June):169–170; 4:7 (July):223; 4:8 (August):253–255.

42. BArch(K) R 58/497; see also *PS* 5:8 (August 1932):253–256; *SH* 3:3 (March 1931).

43. *SH* 4:9 (September 1932):2.

44. The police explicitly noted the parallel response to failure in "consolidating existing groups." See, for example, report from Berlin, May 28, 1932, GStA, Rep. 219/57, p. 81.

45. *PS* 4:8 (August 1931):254, and *Liebe Verboten*, p. 18.

46. Letter from Elkan to Mrs. How-Martyn, Hamburg, December 15, 1931, in International Planned Parenthood Federation Archive, David Owen Centre for Population Studies, University of Wales, Cardiff (IPPFA).

47. *Liebe Verboten*, p. 10.

48. Ibid., p. 14.

49. Ibid., p. 4.

50. Ibid., p. 17.

51. The phrase is Paul Weindling's, *Health, race and German politics between unification and Nazism 1870–1945* (Cambridge: Cambridge University Press, 1989), p. 441.

52. Rundschreiben der EpS an alle proletarischen Organisationen, Cologne, July 8, 1931, in BArch(K) R58/548(6), p. 48. See also *Zwei Jahre Brüningdiktatur. Von Brüning zu Papen. Handbuch der kommunistischen Reichstag fraktion* (Berlin: KPD, April/Mai 1932).

53. Abschrift. Winter Arbeitsplan 1931/32 (EpS), in GStA Rep. 219/57, pp. 61–64.

54. GStA, Rep. 219/57, p. 77. See also BArch(K) R58/548(6), p. 60.

55. The EpS also sponsored meetings (*Stubenversammlungen*) only for women to facilitate their discussions. BArch(K) R58/757(4), p. 126. R58 and R134 files contain police reports but also much original material confiscated by both Weimar and National Socialist police forces.

56. GStA, Rep. 219/57, p. 60. See also police report, Cologne, November 3, 1931, BA R58/548(6). On Luise Dornemann who ran the EpS center in Düsseldorf, see her memoir in BArch(Sapmo) EA 1653.

57. David Crew, "German socialism, the state and family policy, 1918–1933," *Continuity and Change* 1:2 (1986):248, 257, 258.

58. Ibid., p. 257.

59. By July 1932, it would be 632,224. See Harvey, "Youth Unemployment," p. 291.

60. BArch(K) R58/757(4), p. 126.

61. GStA, Rep. 219/57, pp. 85–89.

62. *Die Warte* (January 1932):3–4.

63. Ibid., p. 10.

64. Ibid., p. 14.

65. Ibid., p. 11.

66. Reich, *People in Trouble*, pp. 149–157.

67. See, for example, Hans-Peter Gente, ed. *Marxismus, Psychoanalyse, Sexpol*, vol. 1 (Frankfurt am Main: Fischer Taschenbuch Verlag, 1970); Wilhelm Reich, *Sex-Pol Essays 1929–1934*, ed. Lee Baxandall (New York: Random House, 1972); David Boadella, *Wilhelm Reich: The Evolution of his Work* (Plymouth, England: Vision Press, 1973); Bertell Ollman, *Social and Sexual Revolution: Essays on Marx and Reich* (Boston: South End Press, 1979), especially pp. 159–161, 172–173. For a somewhat more critical view, see Paul A. Robinson, *The Freudian Left: Wilhelm Reich, Geza Roheim, Herbert Marcuse* (New York: Harper and Row, 1969).

68. Lehfeldt interview, October 1, 1980.

69. When told that Reich had supposedly gone insane toward the end of his life, Dr. Elkan, formerly of the Hamburg RV retorted, "Well, he always was." Interview with Dr. Edward Elkan, London, January 27, 1981.

70. See especially Max Hodann, *Bub und Mädel. Gespräche unter Kameraden über die Geschlechterfrage*, 1929, [first ed. 1924]), and *Bringt uns wirklich der Klapperstorch?* (both Rudolstadt: Der Greifenverlag zu Rudolstadt, Thür.)

71. Annie Reich, *Das Kreide-Dreieck. Der Verein erforscht die Geheimnisse der Erwachsenen* (Berlin: Verlag für Sexualpolitik, 1932).

72. Wilhelm Reich, *Der Sexuelle Kampf der Jugend* (reprint ed. Graz: Verlag O, n.d., [1932]). See, for example, *NG* 27: no. 4/5/6 (April/May/June 1931):103–108, for description of a youth meeting to discuss Nikolai Bogdanov's novel about adolescent love and sex, *Das erste Mädel* (reprint ed., Munich: Damnitz Verlag, 1974). On the KJVD, see BArch(K) R58/563, 587, 600, 601, 629, 654, 657–662/2, 680/1, 683, 727, 1172 (7), and 1173 (8).

73. *Sexualnot und Sexualreform. Verhandlungen der Weltliga für Sexualreform. IV Kongress, abgehalten in Wien vom 16. bis 23. September 1930*, ed. H. Steiner (Vienna: Elbemühle Verlag, 1931), pp. 72–87.

74. *Rote Fahne*, April 11, 13, 1931, announced lectures by Reich on "Marxist Sexual Economy and Sexual Politics" on Mondays at 8 P.M. at MASCH, Gartenstrasse 25. See also BArch(K) R134/70, for police report. A young domestic servant in the KJVD, who attended the MASCH lectures, remembered them as "weird but stimulating." Interview with Lore Diener, Berlin West, November 11, 1977.

75. Reich, *People in Trouble*, p. 152.

76. See above Chapter 3. On Reich in Vienna, see Anson Rabinbach, *The Crisis of Austrian Socialism: From Red Vienna to Civil War 1927–1934* (Chicago: University of Chicago Press, 1983), pp. 66–72. See also Wilhelm Reich, "Erfahrungen und Probleme der Sexualberatungsstellen für Arbeiter und Angestellte in Wien," *SA* 5:3 (September 1929):98–102. Helmut Gruber's useful discussion in *Red Vienna* situates Reich as a rebel in the context of Austro-Marxist sexual politics and claims that he opened six sex advice clinics in Vienna in 1929, pp. 155–179, especially pp. 161–62.

77. Reich, *People in Trouble*, p. 145.

78. Ernest Bornemann, *Die Ur-Szene. Eine Selbstanalyse* (Frankfurt am Main: S. Fischer, 1977), p. 23.

79. Max Hodann, *Bub und Mädel*, p. 43.

80. Bornemann, *Ur-Szene*, p. 24. He claimed that his work with Reich contributed to the fact "that I never in my life had a single sexual problem with the exception of simple horniness," p. 24.

81. On Adler and his importance to sex reform, see Manes Sperber, *Die Vergebliche Warnung. All das Vergangene . . .* (Vienna: Europaverlag, 1975); Alice Rühle-Gerstel, *Die Frau und der Kapitalismus* (Leipzig: Verlag von S. Hirzel, reprint ed.; Frankfurt am Main: Verlag Neue Kritik, n.d. [1932]); Sofie Lazarsfeld, *Erziehung zur Ehe* (Vienna and Leipzig: Verlag von Moritz Perles, 1928); Russell Jacoby, *Social Amnesia: A Critique of Conformist Psychology from Adler to Laing* (Boston: Beacon Press, 1975); and Adler himself; see *The Individual Psychology of Alfred Adler: A Systematic Presentation in Selections from his Writings*, ed. Heinz L. and Rowena R. Ansbacher (New York: Harper & Row, 1964).

82. Reich, *People in Trouble*, pp. 108–110. At the Vienna WLSR in 1930, he reported that based on his sample among proletarian youth groups, 50 percent of men and 90 percent(!) of women had some kind of dysfunction of the ability to fully enjoy sex, *Sexualnot*, p. 81.

83. Reich, *People in Trouble*, pp. 110–111.

84. On right-wing and clerical response to the "crisis of the family," see Usborne, *The Politics of the Body*, pp. 69–101, and idem, "The Christian Churches and the regulation of sexuality in Weimar Germany," in *Disciplines of Faith*, ed. Jim Obelkevich, Lyndal Roper, and Raphael Samuels (New York: Routledge and Kegan Paul, 1987), pp. 99–112.

85. "Erhebung über Sexualmoral," *Mitteilungen der Arbeitsgemeinschaft für Volksgesundung* (edited by Hans Harmsen), 1 (January 15, 1931), p. 285.

86. See Rosenhaft, "Organizing the 'Lumpenproletariat.'"

87. See *Lenin ruft die werktätigen Frauen* (1926), in BArch(K) ZgS, 1 61/28(5). See also Clara Zetkin, "My Recollections of Lenin: An Interview on the Woman Question," in *Feminism. The Essential Historical Writings*, ed. Miriam Schneir (New York: Vintage, 1972), pp. 335–343. Zetkin herself went to some pains to reassure an obviously distressed associate of Hirschfeld's Institute for Sexual Science that Lenin had not intended in the conversation she recounted to imply that Communist youth organizations should tabooize sexuality. She insisted that comrades Zinoviev and Krupskaya (Lenin's wife) both checked her recollections before publication and would have rejected an antisex position as "un-Leninist." Zetkin, for her part, insisted that Lenin saw "sexual enlightenment and education on the basis of reliable scientific findings, as well as coeducation, as social necessities that should not have to wait until after the revolution." Clara Zetkin correspondence, NL 5/83, letter to Richard Linsert, September 27, 1930, BArch(Sapmo).

88. *Lenin ruft die werktätigen Frauen*, p. 23.

89. See, e.g., *Arbeiterjugendbewegung in Frankfurt 1904–1945. Materialien zu einer verschütteten Kulturgeschichte*, ed. Holtmann, Pokorny, and Werner (Lahn-Giessen: Anabas Verlag, 1978); Gerhard Roger, *Die Pädagogische Bedeutung der Proletarischen Jugendbewegung Deutschlands* (Frankfurt am Main: Verlag Roter Stern, 1971), pp. 97–99.

90. See Wilhelm Reich, *Sexuelle Kampf der Jugend*; and *Sexualerregung und*

*Selbstbefriedigung. Beantwortung sexueller Fragen* (reprint ed., Graz: Verlag O, 1976); Bornemann, *Ur-Szene*, pp. 22–25.

91. At approximately the same time, Peter Martin Lampel's play, *Revolte im Erziehungshaus*, about the appalling conditions in a reform school and the rebellion of its inmates, focused public attention on the sad fate that might have awaited the young Krantz had not the leftist intelligentsia rallied to his defense. See *NG* 25, no. 2 (February 1929):83–84. Krantz emigrated to the United States and became a professor of comparative literature at the University of Oklahoma. See Max Fürst, *Talisman Scheherezade. Die schwierigen Zwanziger Jahre* (Munich: Karl Hanser Verlag, 1976), pp. 242–255, especially pp. 245–246.

92. Henry Jacoby, *Von des Kaisers Schule zu Hitlers Zuchthaus. Eine Jugend links-aussen in der Weimarer Republik* (Frankfurt am Main: dipa Verlag, 1980), pp. 55–56.

93. See E. Rose Ewald, "Jugend Berät Jugend," *Mutter- und Kinderland* (August 1929):23–24.

94. Fürst, *Talisman*, pp. 252, 250–251.

95. Fürst, ibid., p. 251.

96. See *SA* 5:2 (June 1929):69–73; *NG* 27:1/2/3 (January/February/March 1931):49; *NG* 24:3 (March 1928):84–85. See also the memoirs of Max Fürst, *Talisman;* Jacoby, *Jugend links-aussen;* Sperber, *Die vergebliche Warnung;* Gisela Konopka, *Group Work in the Institution—A Modern Challenge* (New York: Association Press, 1954); idem, *Courage and Love* (Edina, MN: Burgess Printing, 1988).

97. *NG* 27:1/2/3 (January/February/March 1931):49. The Frankfurt BfM also offered youth counseling one hour a week; requests for birth control were referred to the regular clinic, run by Drs. Riese and Fink. See *NG* 25:3 (March 1929):131; also Karl Reimann's reminiscence in *Arbeiterjugendbewegung in Frankfurt*, p. 143.

98. See *Die Welt am Abend*, December 29, 1931; *PS* 5:6 (June 1932):182; see also reports by Erna Gysi on Jugendberatungsstelle in nos. 8( August 1932):244–248 and 10 (October 1932):317–319. The potential appeal of IAH centers is indicated by the fact that in 1931, *Die Welt am Abend*, a Münzenberg "mass" organ, had a circulation of 229,000; see Helmut Gruber, "Willi Münzenberg's German Communist Propaganda Empire 1921–1933," *The Journal of Modern History* 38:3 (September 1966): 288, footnote 31. See also "Richtlinien für Jugendberatungsstellen," in BArch(K) R58/685.

99. *PS* 5:9 (September 1932):266.

100. Max Hodann, *Geschlecht und Liebe in biologischer und gesellschaftlicher Beziehung* (Berlin: Büchergilde Gutenberg, 1932). See, for example, *Leipziger Volkszeitung*, March 2, 1932, in BArch(K) R86/2373(4); also Wolf's lecture notes, FWA folder 153.

101. Reich, *People in Trouble*, p. 151.

102. Ibid., p. 150. The IAH and other groups typically complained that proletarians came to the organization for short-term selfish and not political reasons. See *Der Vormarsch* 2:2 (January 1933):14, in BArch(K) R58/649(44).

103. Reich, *People in Trouble*, p. 145.

104. Ibid., p. 155.

105. See *Die Kämpferin* No. 7 (1932), and BArch(K) R134/71, pp. 196–233; R134/67, pp. 231–236. KPD membership reached unprecedented heights in 1931; in December 1931, 2,768 women had been recruited: 13,4 percent of total new members. But by 1932, with the anti-218 euphoria gone, the membership picture was gloomy again. See BArch(K) NS26/810, p. 4.

106. GStA, Rep. 219/57, p. 77; see also BArch(K) R58/548(6).

107. See BArch(K) R58/548(6), p. 103; also R58/757 and R58/336(11). It may well be that this picture of frenetic activity is somewhat distorted as a result of stepped-up police surveillance and documentation.

108. BArch(K) R86/2269(2), p. 226. See also *Korrespondenz des Informationsbüros für Geburtenregelung*, no. 1 (January 1932) and no. 2 (March 1932).

109. Lehfeldt, "Laienorganisationen," p. 81. The AfG (*Arbeitervereine für Geburtenregelung*) had grown from Heiser's group. It had published the *Freies Geschlecht* and was centered in Berlin.

110. *PS* 5:8 (August 1932):253.

111. EpS report on Landeskonferenz, April 16–17, 1932 (police report dated April 26, 1932), GStA, Rep. 219/57, pp. 85–89. By July 27, 1932, however, Essen police claimed that membership was declining and they saw no danger; GStA, Rep. 219/57, p. 99.

112. Police report May 23, 1932, GStA, Rep. 219/57, p. 77; see also *Rote Fahne*, May 24, 1932.

113. Report, Berlin, May 23, 1932, GStA, Rep. 219/57, p. 81.

114. The police counted 300 and 400 in the audience at the two January meetings. See BArch(K) R58/336/10 (AMSO), pp. 39–75.

115. Sperber, *Die vergebliche Warnung*, p. 210. Besides working as a psychological consultant at the central Berlin Welfare Agency (*Zentrale für Wohlfahrtspflege*), the 27-year-old Sperber lectured in youth reformatories, spent hours daily as a private therapist, went to meetings at night, and sheltered homeless runaways in his apartment.

116. Even the watchful police could detect no political content to the meeting and did not attempt to interfere. Report October 15, 1932, BArch(K) R58/757.

117. BArch(K) R58/336/11.

118. *Liga* to Polizei Praesidium Berlin, October 22, 1932, in BArch(K) R58/757(1).

119. See the *Liga*'s letter (October 24, 1932) protesting the closing by the Prussian Culture Ministry (revamped after the July coup). The decision was said to have affected 4,316 members, including 2,300 unemployed workers, who had exercised there for free. See also text of ban, October 31, 1932, all in BArch(K) R58/757(1).

120. Kate Stützin to Sanger, March 10, 1932. Sanger LC.

121. Sanger to Stützin, March 23, 1932. Sanger LC.

122. Stützin to Sanger, September 7, 1931. Sanger LC. Stützin was also dreaming about leaving her husband and flying away to a suffrage conference in Athens. See her husband Dr. Johann Stützin's letter to Sanger about his restless wife, March 3, 1932.

123. Lehfeldt, "Laienorganisationen," p. 85.

124. Marie E. Kopp, "The Development of Marriage Consultation Centers as a New Field of Social Medicine," *American Journal of Obstetrics and Gynecology* 26 (July 1933):124–125.

125. *Korrespondenz des Informationsbüros für Geburtenregelung*, no.2 (March 1932), p. 10.

126. Elkan to Mrs. How-Martyn, Hamburg, July 30, 1932, IPPFA.

127. *NG* 20:11/12 (1932):175–179.

128. *SH* 4:11 (November 1932):82.

129. Police report, February 13, 1932, on February 12 EpS meeting, Berlin, BArch(K) R58/548(6), pp. 69–70.

## Chapter 6

1. Rudolf Elkan to Mrs. How-Martyn, Hamburg, July 30, 1932. International Planned Parenthood Federation Archives, David Owen Centre for Population Studies, University of Wales, Cardiff (IPPFA).

2. *Verwaltungsbericht der Bezirksverwaltung Mitte für die Zeit vom 1 April 1932 bis 31 März 1936 (unter Berücksichtigung der Geschehnisse in der Zeit vom 1 April 1928 bis 31 März 1932)*, Heft 9 (Berlin 1937), p. 21.

3. *Verwaltungsbericht Treptow 1 April 1932 bis 31 Marz 1936*, Heft 23 (Berlin 1936), p. 17.

4. For a clear and concise summary of these laws, see Michael Burleigh and Wolfgang Wippermann, *The Racial State: Germany 1933–1945* (Cambridge: Cambridge University Press, 1991), pp. 44–51.

5. Kate Stützin to Margaret Sanger, April 21, 1933; Sanger's note on the letter. Sanger papers LC.

6. For example, in March 1933, Berlin's Lichtenberg district elected 10 KPD and 10 SPD (as well as 15 NSDAP) delegates to the local council. A year later, the entire district council had been eliminated. *Landesarchiv* Berlin (LAB East, formerly *Stadtarchiv*) Rep. 47-09, Sign. 111.

7. See Siegfried Ostrowski, "Vom Schicksal jüdischer Ärzte im Dritten Reich. Ein Augenzeugenbericht aus den Jahren 1933–1939," *Bulletin des Leo Baeck Institutes* 24 (1963):313–351.

8. See among many other sources, Michael N. Kater, *Doctors Under Hitler* (Chapel Hill: University of North Carolina Press, 1989); Michael N. Kater, "Hitler's Early Doctors: Nazi Physicians in Predepression Germany," *Journal of Modern History* 59:1 (March 1987):25–52. For specific figures on percentages of Jewish doctors, see Berliner Geschichtswerkstatt, *Der Wedding. Hart an der Grenze. Weiterleben in Berlin Nach dem Krieg* (Berlin: Nishen Verlag, 1987), p. 75. Over 65 percent of all doctors in Berlin were classified as "non-Aryan." See *Medizin und Nationalsozialismus. Tabuisierte Vergangenheit-Ungebrochene Tradition?* ed. Gerhard Baader and Ulrich Schultz (Berlin West: Verlagsgesellschaft Gesundheit, 1980), p. 65.

9. *Verwaltungsbericht der Bezirskverwaltung Wedding für die Zeit vom 1 April 1932 bis 31 Marz 1936* (including 1928–1931), Heft 11 (Berlin 1936), p. 29.

10. *Verwaltungsbericht Mitte*, p. 20. In Kreuzberg, the second largest district in Berlin (after Charlottenburg), all 43 doctors (two full-time and the rest part-time) on the district payroll were Jews ("Ein Beweis, wie Israel für einander bürgt"). *Verwaltungsbericht des Bezirksbürgermeisters des Verwaltungsbezirks Kreuzberg der Stadt Berlin 1932–1935*, Heft 14 (Berlin 1936), p. 16.

11. LAB East, Rep. 47-09. Sign. 109. See also Eve Rosenhaft, "Working-Class Life and Working-Class Politics: Communists, Nazis and the Battle for the Streets, Berlin, 1928–1932," in *Social Change and Political Development in Weimar Germany*, ed. Richard Bessel and E. J. Feuchtwanger (New York: Barnes and Noble, 1981), pp. 207–240.

12. Kater, "Hitler's Early Doctors," pp. 25–52. See also Robert Proctor, *Racial Hygiene. Medicine Under the Nazis* (Cambridge: Harvard University Press, 1988), especially pp. 223–250.

13. For detailed discussion, see Alfons Labisch and Florian Tennstedt, *Der Weg zum "Gesetz über die Vereinheitlichung des Gesundheitswesens" vom 3 Juli 1934. Entwicklungslinien und-momente des staatlichen und kommunalen Gesundheitswesens in Deutschland*

(Düsseldorf: Schriftenreihe der Akademie für öffentliches Gesundheitswesen in Düsseldorf, vol. 13, 1985).

14. It is worth quoting the original Nazi language: "Unbrauchbare und politisch unzuverlässige Bedienstete wurden ausgemerzt und durch einwandfreies Personal ersetzt." In Lichtenberg in 1933, 129 employees were fired and replaced by 89 new ones. LAB East, Rep. 47-09, Sign. 109, Lichtenberg. See, in general, Thomas E. J. de Witt, "The nazification of welfare: organization and policy, 1930–39," *Societas* 7:4 (Autumn 1977):303–327.

15. *Verwaltungsbericht 1 April 1928 bis 31 März 1936. Der Bezirksbürgermeister des Verwaltungsbezirks Horst Wessell der Reichshauptstadt Berlin* (formerly Friedrichshain), p. 18.

16. *Verwaltungsbericht Mitte*, p. 22.

17. In the prestigious Auguste Viktoria Hospital in Schöneberg, the number of patients declined from 9,875 patients, for a total of 236,973 days in 1931, to 8,773, in 210,924 days, in 1935. *Verwaltungsbericht der Bezirksverwaltung Schöneberg für die Jahre 1932–1935* Heft 19 (Berlin 1936), p. 16.

18. See Christian Pross and Rolf Winau, *Nicht Mishandeln. Das Krankenhaus Moabit* (Berlin: Edition Hentrich, 1984), especially pp. 180–226.

19. *Verwaltungsbericht der Bezirksverwaltung Charlottenburg, April 1932 bis 31 März 1936*, Heft 15 (Berlin 1937), p. 27.

20. See Gisela Bock, "Keine Arbeitskräfte in diesem Sinne: Prostituierte im Nazi-Staat" in Pieke Biermann, *"Wir sind Frauen wie andere auch!" Prostituierte und ihre Kämpfe* (Reinbek bei Hamburg: Rowohlt, 1980), pp. 70–106.

21. Paul Weindling, *Health, race and German politics between unification and Nazism, 1870–1945* (Cambridge: Cambridge University Press, 1989), p. 430. In other publications I have translated *Erb-und Rassenpflege* as Gene and Race Care. Here I use Weindling's translation, "hereditary and racial welfare."

22. *Verwaltungsbericht Kreuzberg*, p. 16. The *Zeitschrift für Gesundheitsverwaltung und Gesundheitsfürsorge*, no. 10 (May 20, 1933), p. 240, announced that the chief mayor had closed all municipal marriage counseling centers until further notice, that is, until new guidelines were issued and appropriate doctors hired.

23. In 1900, one in three German women bore a child; in 1933 only one in 10, in Berlin one in 20. See Marie E. Kopp, "Legal and Medical Aspects of Eugenic Sterilization in Germany," *American Sociological Review* 1:5 (October 1936):762.

24. BArch(K) (*Deutsche Gemeindetag*) R36/884. Grundsätze für die Verleihung der Ehrenpatenschaften der Stadt Berlin, April 20, 1934.

25. On Marital Health Law of October 1935, see Gabriele Czarnowski, *Das Kontrollierte Paar. Ehe-und Sexualpolitik im Nationalsozialismus* (Weinheim: Deutscher Studien Verlag, 1991).

26. For example, in the Berlin Lichtenberg *Beratungsstelle*, 100 applications for sterilizations were processed in 1934, 400 in 1935, and 545 in 1936. By contrast, 240 eugenic marriage certificates were provided and only 16 baby bonuses for third and fourth children approved. It does seem that the positive measures were handled more grudgingly than the negative. LAB East, Rep.47-09, Sign.108. On Nazi antinatalism, see Gisela Bock, "Equality and difference in National Socialist racism," in *Beyond Equality and Difference: Citizenship, feminist politics and female subjectivity*, ed. Gisela Bock and Susan James, (New York: Routledge, 1992), pp. 89–109; "Antinatalism, maternity and paternity in National Socialist racism," in *Maternity and the Rise of the European Wel-*

*fare States, 1880s–1950s,* ed. Gisela Bock and Pat Thane (London and New York: Routledge, 1991), pp. 233–255; Bock, *Zwangssterilisation im Nationalsozialismus. Studien zur Rassenpolitik und Frauenpolitik* (Opladen: Westdeutscher Verlag, 1986).

27. *Medizin und Nationalsozialismus,* ed. Baader and Schultz, p. 79.

28. Elfriede Nemitz (Moses' companion), personal interview, Berlin West, March 23, 1979. See also Daniel S. Nadav, *Julius Moses und die Politik der Sozialhygiene in Deutschland* (Gerlingen: Bleicher, 1985), p. 309.

29. Eckhard Hansen, et al., *Seit über einem Jahrhundert . . . Verschüttete Alternativen in der Sozialpolitik* (Cologne: Bund Verlag, 1981), pp. 464, 486. The firings did not go completely smoothly. The career bureaucrat in charge of the purges did not proceed with enough dispatch and proved entirely too willing to reinstate contractual obligations. On the Führer's birthday, April 20, money had to be spent to buy swastika flags for the clinics because only the black, red, and gold flags of the republic were to be found. Eight doctors, seven of whom had lifetime tenure, actually sued in labor court against their dismissals. See BArch(P), RAM (Reich Arbeitsministerium) 5382, pp. 59–61, reproduced in ibid., pp. 474, 485–487.

30. Ibid., p. 468.

31. See Paul Weindling, "Eugenics and the Welfare State During the Weimar Republic," in *The State and Social Change in Germany, 1880–1980,* ed. W. R. Lee and Eve Rosenhaft (New York: Berg, 1990), pp. 131–160. Peter Weingart, "The Rationalization of Sexual Behavior: The Institutionalization of Eugenic Thought in Germany," *Journal of the History of Biology* 20:2 (Summer 1987):159–193, lumps together (p. 179) such diverse groups as the RV and the *Bund der Kinderreichen* as "transmitters of race-hygiene." See also Götz Aly, *Die Restlose Erfassung. Volkszählen, Identifizieren, Aussondern im Nationalsozialismus* (Berlin: Rotbuch, 1984).

32. Konrad Kühne, "Zum Gesetz zur Verhütung erbkranken Nachwuchses von 14.7.1933." *Vertrauensarzt und Krankenkasse,* no. 3 (September 1933):60, quoted in Hansen, *Seit über einem Jahrhundert,* p. 468.

33. Kristine von Soden, *Die Sexualberatungsstellen der Weimarer Republik 1919–1933* (Berlin: Edition Hentrich, 1988), p. 157, uses the term "seamless" (*nahtlos*). Gisela Bock, *Zwangssterilisation,* p. 186, uses "without a break" (*bruchlos*), referring to the work of the counseling centers. She cites the example of Dr. F. K. Scheumann in Prenzlauer Berg, but his counseling center was one of those embraced by the Prussian 1926 decree and not run by muncipality or health insurance.

34. See especially Cornelie Usborne, *The Politics of the Body in Weimar Germany: Women's Reproductive Rights and Duties* (Ann Arbor: The University of Michigan Press, 1992), pp. 148–155, 204–205; Paul Weindling, *Health, race and German politics,* pp. 383–393, 450–457; Gisela Bock, *Zwangssterilisation.* See also my discussion in preface and Chapter 3.

35. The RGA cited the need for family statistics in the industrialized and urbanized post–World War I era. RGA president to RMI, November 8, 1922, in BArch(K) R86/2371(1), "1907–1927 Rassenhygiene—Eugenik." (RGA files had always combined "Racial Hygiene" and "Eugenics.") See also R86/2371(2), 1927–1932. In 1923 expert consultants to the Interior Ministry (RMI) reluctantly conceded that establishing a section for the study of race (*Abteilung für Rassenlehre*) was prohibitively expensive. RMI meeting report, January 22, 1923. See also the RGA's careful response (August 4, 1927) to a Bavarian query about possibilities for sterilization of mixed race "Rhineland bastards," R86/2371(1).

36. *Bund für Volksaufartung und Erbkunde* acknowledgment to RGA, June 2, 1926, BArch(K) R86/2371(1).

37. Exhibition catalogue, (Ausstellung für Erbkunde und Eugenik, April 26–May 15, 1927), BArch(K) R86/2371(1).

38. Protokoll (marked *Vertraulich*), Berlin, February 28, 1929, BArch(K) R86 2371(2), p. 4.

39. See minutes of February 28 and November 14, 1928, sessions in R86 BArch(K) R86/2371(1) and R86/2374(2) on "Unfruchtbarmachung geistig Minderwertiger."

40. Preussischer Staatsrat, "Eugenische Materialien für die Beratung in Gemeindeausschüssen," in BArch(K) R86/2371(2), 1931, pp. 1–4.

41. Prof. Dr. Lange, *Die Eugenik im Dienste der Volkswohlfahrt* (1932), *Preussischer Staatsrat*, July 2, 1932, in GStA, Rep. 84a/871, pp. 30–35.

42. See discussion in *Preussischer Staatsrat*, January 20, 1932, and in *Preussischer Landesgesundheitsrat*, July 2, 1932, in *Geheimes Staatsarchiv*, Rep. 84a/871. See pamphlet "Die Eugenik im Dienste der Volkswohlfahrt," published by *Preussischer Staatsrat*, July 2, 1932.

43. *Volksgesundheit* 43 (January 1933):7.

44. Scheumann, "Entwurf und Diskussion zum Gesetz," p. 73; see also Hans Harmsen's relatively cautious comments, pp. 81–82, Preussischer Landesgesundheitsrat, July 2, 1932, in GStA, Rep. 84a/871.

45. Gesetz zur Verhütung erbkranken Nachwuchses, in *Reichsgesetzblatt*, no. 86, Berlin, July 25, 1933, in GStA, Rep. 84a/871. See Weindling, *Health, race and German politics*, pp. 523–525.

46. Cornelie Usborne, *The Politics of the Body*, p. 205. Indeed, the July 14, 1933, Law for the Prevention of Hereditarily Diseased Offspring was based not only on the 1932 discussions in the Prussian Health Council but followed guidelines set in the United States by the Model Eugenical Sterilization Law promulgated by Dr. Harry Laughlin, superintendent of the Eugenic Record Office in Cold Spring Harbor, Maine, in 1922. See Allan Chase, *The Legacy of Malthus. The Social Costs of the New Scientific Racism* (New York: Knopf, 1976), p. 13; also Stefan Kuhl, *The Nazi Connection: Eugenics, American Racism, and German National Socialism* (New York: Oxford University Press, 1994). On German reaction to American and Scandinavian sterilization programs, see BArch(K) R86/2371 (1,2) R 86 /2374(1). On the distinctions between 1932 and 1933 provisions, see Jeremy Noakes's excellent (and neglected) article, "Nazism and Eugenics: The Background to the Nazi Sterilization Law of 14 July 1933," in *Ideas into Politics*, ed. R. J. Bullen, H. Pogge von Strandmann, and A. B. Polansky (London: Croon Helm, 1984), pp. 75–94.

47. See discussions in Staatsrat, January 20, 1932, and in Landesgesundheitsrat, July 2, 1932, in GStA, Rep. 84a/871; followed by text of "Gesetz zur Verhütung Erbkranken Nachwuchses," *Reichsgesetzblatt*, no. 86, Berlin, July 25, 1933, and material on "Sterilisierung im Interesse der Volkswohlfahrt," 1932–1934, all in GStA, Rep. 84a/871. See also "Erbgesundheitsgerichte," 1933–1934, Rep. 84a/872, and "Reinerhaltung der Rasse," 1933–1934, Rep. 84a/873.

48. Magnus Hirschfeld to George Sylvester Viereck, October 30, 1933. Hirschfeld Collection, Kinsey Institute, Bloomington, Indiana. Dr. Henriette Necheles, who had campaigned for abortion reform, expressed similar sentiments in her exile memoir, noting that the law "would have been often welcomed as an idea if it had been car-

ried out by wise lawmakers." Essay in Houghton Library, Harvard University, E.C.A. Mi. 90-3281, p. 26.

49. See police records in BArch(K) R58/328, including extensive lists of confiscated literature, and Gestapo reports in R58/776. See also the lengthy list of *Zersetzungserscheinungen* (subversive activities) in Geheimes Staatspolizeiamt Berlin, August 9, 1933. Poignant testimony to this process can be found in the old catalogues of the Staatsbibliothek Berlin (East), where many sex reform or sexological titles were adorned with a little note: "missing as of May 1933."

50. The Geheimes Staatspolizeiamt report, May 30, 1933, in BArch(K) R58/776, on this action notes that Theilhaber was nowhere to be found. However, Hans Lehfeldt M.D., "Felix A. Theilhaber—Pioneer Sexologist," *Archives of Sexual Behavior* 15:1 (1986):9 reports that he was arrested (perhaps at another point). Lehfeldt confirmed this story in an interview in New York, November 2, 1992, as did Theilhaber's son Adin Talbar (who remembered watching out the window as his father was hustled into a car by two men in trenchcoats), personal interview, Jerusalem, Israel, August 25–26, 1993.

51. Hexel's confession is in a statement to police on June 8, 1933, BArch(K)R58/776. The *Liga* in Bavaria was smashed in March 1933; the Berlin branch changed its name to *Gemeinschaft für Gesundheitspflege* but was closed by police on June 7, 1933. See also Berlin police report, August 3, 1936, R58/328.

52. See especially Detlev J. K. Peukert, "The Genesis of the 'Final Solution' from the Spirit of Science," in *Reevaluating the Third Reich*, ed. Thomas Childers and Jane Caplan (New York: Holmes and Meier, 1992), pp. 234–252; and idem, *Inside Nazi Germany* (New Haven: Yale University Press, 1989).

53. *Geheimes Staatspolizeiamt Berlin*, August 9, 1933, BArch(K) R58/328.

54. Introduction by Norman Haire, p. VII to Magnus Hirschfeld, *Sex in Human Relationships* (London: John Lane the Bodley Head, 1935), quoting *Der Angriff* (May 6, 1933). See also Gerhard Sauder, ed., *Die Bücherverbrennung. Zum 10 Mai 1933* (Berlin: Carl Hanser Verlag, 1983), pp. 162-166. Many rumors have suggested that the institute's destruction was also intended to protect Nazis who had been its clients; one account speculates that some of the institute's records were not really burned but confiscated by the Gestapo and "used one year later in the murder of Röhm and other SA leaders." Erwin J. Haeberle, "Swastika, Pink Triangle, and Yellow Star: The Destruction of Sexology and the Persecution of Homosexuals in Nazi Germany," in *Hidden from History: Reclaiming the Gay and Lesbian Past*, ed. Martin Bauml Duberman, Martha Vicinus, and George Chauncey, Jr. (New York: New American Library, 1989), p. 369; *The Journal of Sex Research* 17:3 (August 1981):270–287.

55. See Magnus Hirschfeld, *Men and Women: The World Journey of a Sexologist* (New York: G. P. Putnam's Sons, 1935). Haeberle says Hirschfeld watched the burning of the institute on a newsreel screen in Paris, "The Destruction of Sexology," p. 368.

56. Charlotte Wolff, *Magnus Hirschfeld: A Portrait of a Pioneer in Sexology* (London: Quartet Books, 1986), p. 414. Remarkably, this homage by his old Berlin colleague remains the only full-length biography.

57. Dora Russell, *The Tamarisk Tree: My Quest for Liberty and Love* (London: Virago, 1977), p. 219.

58. Leunbach to Sanger, May 2, 1934. Sanger papers, LC.

59. See BArch(K)R 36/1148, report of Deutscher Bund für Mutterschutz to Deutsche Städtetag, August 1934; Christl Wickert, *Helene Stöcker 1869–1943, Frauen-*

*rechtlerin, Sexualreformerin und Pazifistin. Eine Biographie* (Bonn: Verlag J. H. W. Dietz Nachf, 1991), p. 135.

60. Volker Berghan, *Modern Germany: Society, economy and politics in the twentieth century* (Cambridge, England: Cambridge University Press, 1982), p. 86.

61. BArch(Sapmo) KPD ZK Politburo 1/2/3/252.

62. "Bericht über die Arbeit der Bezirksleitung der Berliner Roten Kulturfront," August 26, 1935. BArch(Sapmo) KPD ZK Politburo. 1/2/3/252.

63. BArch(Sapmo) EA 1053. Interview, Berlin GDR, January 12, 1976.

64. Martha Ruben-Wolf to Margaret Sanger, July 5, 1929, Sanger LC. This comment came in the context of a plea for money for the Committee for Birth Control. Ruben-Wolf continued hopefully, "When socialism will become stronger, birth control will grow stronger too."

65. Lore Diener, personal interview, West Berlin, November 11, 1977.

66. See especially Bock, "Equality and difference," p. 96.

67. Henry P. David, Jochen Fleischhacker, and Charlotte Höhn, "Abortion and Eugenics in Nazi Germany," *Population and Development Review* 14:1 (March 1988):85–86, note that by 1933 over 30,000 women were registered in criminal police files as having served some (mostly brief) time in detention for illegal abortions; the Nazis used some of these records to charge doctors.

68. P. K. Whelpton, "Why the Large Rise in the German Birth-Rate?" *American Journal of Sociology* 41:3 (November 1935):300; see also Frank H. Hankins, "German Policies for Increasing Births," *American Journal of Sociology* 42:5 (March 1937):630–652.

69. James Woycke, *Birth Control in Germany 1871–1933* (London, New York: Routledge, 1988) p. 74. David et al., "Abortion and Eugenics," also say that requests declined "sharply" from 34,690 in 1932 to 4,391 in 1936 and 3,400 in 1937, p. 93.

70. See Whelpton, "Why the Large Rise," pp. 299–313. See also Clifford Kirkpatrick, *Nazi Germany: Its Women and Family Life* (Indianapolis, New York: The Bobbs-Merril Press, 1938).

71. See Czarnowski, *Das Kontrollierte Paar*, pp. 155–156.

72. *Erlass zur Bekämpfung der Laienabtreibung*, March 1933; letter, March 21, 1934, in GStA Rep. 84a/8232.

73. Bock, "Antinatalism, maternity and paternity," p. 242. The confusion and lack of accurate knowledge is exemplified by the remarkable inconsistency of statements on the subject made by Gisela Bock, perhaps the most prominent researcher on Nazi population policy. In "Racism and Sexism in Nazi Germany: Motherhood, Compulsory Sterilization, and the State," *Signs* 8:3 (Spring 1983):400–421, the article that presented her original nuanced analysis of Nazi population policy as selectively pro- or antinatalist for the "fit" or the "unfit," she maintained that there was "a 65% increase in yearly convictions between 1932 and 1938, when their number reached almost 7,000." (See also David et al., "Abortion," p. 93.) By 1986, Bock had retreated from that position and now claimed (using different sources) that, "During the ten years 1933–42 there were one sixth *fewer* (my ital.) convictions for abortions than during the ten years 1923–1932 (39,902 to 47,487)," *Zwangssterilisation*, p. 161. "Antinatalism" is an English-language summary of *Zwangssterilisation*.

74. See Kopp, "Legal and Medical Aspects," p. 764.

75. Bock, *Zwangssterilisation*, p. 99.

76. David et al., "Abortion," pp. 85–86.

77. Gabriele Czarnowski, "Frauen als Mütter der 'Rasse'. Abtreibungsverfolgung und Zwangssterilisation im Nationalsozialismus," in *Unter anderen Umständen. Zur Geschichte der Abtreibung*, ed. Gisela Staupe and Lisa Vieth (Dresden/Berlin: Deutsches Hygiene Museum/Argon Verlag, 1993), p. 59. See also Michaela Garn, "Zwangsabtreibung und Abtreibungsverbot. Zur Gutachterstelle der Hamburger Ärztekammer," in *Heilen und Vernichten im Mustergau Hamburg. Bevölkerungs- und Gesundheitspolitik im Dritten Reich*, ed. Angelika Ebbinghaus, Heidrun Kaupen-Haas, and Karl Heinz Roth (Hamburg: Konkret Literatur Verlag, 1984), pp. 37–40.

78. For evidence that abortion was sometimes prosecuted in conjunction with homosexual offenses, see, for example, Universitätssrat files, Humboldt University Archives, Berlin, which record prosecutions of physicians who had received degrees from Humboldt. On Nazi persecution of homosexuality, see especially Geoffrey J. Giles, "'The Most Unkindest Cut of All': Castration, Homosexuality and Nazi Justice," *Journal of Contemporary History* 27 (1992):41–61; Claudia Schöppmann, *Nationalsozialistische Sexualpolitik und weibliche Homosexualität* (Pfaffenweiler: Centaurus-Verlagsgesellschaft, 1991). For excellent bibliography, see Robert G. Moeller, "The Homosexual Man Is a 'Man,' the Homosexual Woman Is a 'Woman': Sex, Society, and the Law in Postwar West Germany," *Journal of the History of Sexuality* 4:3 (January 1994):395–405.

79. David et al., "Abortion," p. 95.

80. *Das Tagebuch der Hertha Nathorff: Berlin–New York, Aufzeichnungen 1933–1945*, ed. Wolfgang Benz (Frankfurt: Fischer, 1988), pp. 82–83. Also pp. 28 and 31 of the original essay, Houghton Library, Harvard.

81. Henriette D. Magnus Necheles, "Reminiscences of a German-Jewish Woman Physician," Chicago, 1940, original deposited in Houghton Library, Harvard University; reworked and translated by Ruth F. Necheles, New York, 1980, p. 49. Additional women physicians reporting such experiences included Edith Kramer and Lydia Ehrenfried (unpublished memoirs, Leo Baeck Institute, New York), and Minna Flake (interview with daughter Renee Barth, Chester, CT, July 18, 1990). See also note, June 25, 1937, in BArch(K) R22/967, p. 175, on Dr. Georg Manes, formerly active in Hamburg RV and BfM, held in preventive detention since June 6, 1937, for investigation of abortions allegedly performed in 1930–1931.

82. Hans Harmsen, "Notes on Abortion and Birth Control in Germany," *Population Studies* 3 (1950):402–405, p. 402; David et al., "Abortion," p. 96.

83. David et al., "Abortion," p. 97.

84. Capital punishment was also imposed on "commercial abortionists" in the *Altreich*; see Czarnowski, "Frauen als Mütter," pp. 67–68. See also David, "Abortion," p. 98.

85. RMI, September 19, 1940, secret memo to health offices and local governments. BArch(K), Schumacher collection, 399. I am grateful to Gabriele Czarnowski for copies of these materials.

86. RMI, February 11, 1941, BArch(K) R22/5008, p. 21.

87. See Burleigh and Wippermann, *Racial State*, p. 73 See also Czarnowski, "Frauen als Mütter," pp. 68–71; Garn, "Zwangsabtreibung," p. 39.

88. RMI to RMJ, express letter, Berlin, February 26, 1945, in BArch(K) R22/5008, pp. 107–108.

89. Interview, Renate Saran, daughter of Max Hodann, London, July 10, 1984.

See also Mary Saran, *Never Give Up* (London: Oswald Wolff, 1976) (his wife's memoir), and Max Hodann, *History of Modern Morals*, translated by Stella Browne (London: William Heinemann, 1937). The Communist district health commissioner in Neukölln, Dr. Richard Schmincke, was also arrested the night of the Reichstag fire; released from prison the end of the year, he spent several years in the Communist underground, lost his license to practice in 1939, and committed suicide in August 1939. See von Soden, *Sexualberatungsstellen*, p. 156.

90. Dr. Edward Elkan, personal interview, London, January 27, 1981.

91. Rudolf Elkan to Margaret Sanger, October 12, 1933, Sanger LC.

92. Dr. Hans Lehfeldt, personal interviews, New York City, September 14, 1977, October 1, 1980, November 2, 1992.

93. Beatrice Riese (daughter of Hertha), personal interview, New York City, July 7, 1992.

94. Hans Lehfeldt, "Ernst Gräfenberg and His Ring," *Mount Sinai Journal of Medicine* 42:4 (July/August 1975):346.

95. To my knowledge, the only (and marginal) exception would be Thea von Harbou, the screenwriter active in the 1931 anti-218 campaign, who later joined the NSDAP.

96. "Der Kampf um innere und äussere Volksgesundung. Zehn Jahre Veröffentlichung der Arbeitsgemeinschaft für Volksgesundung. Ein Quellenbericht zu bevölkerungspolitischen, sozialhygienischen und sozialethischen Tagesfragen," ed. Dr. Hans Harmsen, *Schriften zur Volksgesundung*, no. 21 (June 1935). In BArch(K) R86/2373(12).

97. Quotes from interview with Dr. Hans Harmsen, Benesdorf near Hamburg, April 17–18, 1979. Further information from his personal papers and Reichsärztekammer file, Berlin Document Center. See also Sabine Schleiermacher, "Die Innere Mission und ihr bevölkerungspolitisches Programm" and Heidrun Kaupen-Haas, "Die Bevölkerungsplanner im Sachverständigenbeirat für Bevölkerungs- und Rassenpolitik" in *Der Griff nach der Bevölkerung. Aktualität und Kontinuität nazistischer Bevölkerungspolitik*, ed. Kaupen-Haas (Nördlingen: Franz Greno, 1986), pp. 73–102, 103–120. See also Kaupen-Haas, "Eine deutsche Biographie—der Bevölkerungswissenschaftler Hans Harmsen," in *Heilen und Vernichten im Mustergau Hamburg. Gesundheits- und Bevölkerungspolitik im Dritten Reich*, ed. Kaupen-Haas, Angelika Ebbinghaus, and Karl Heinz Roth (Hamburg: Konkret, 1984), pp. 41–44.

98. Johannes Stützin to Margaret Sanger, April 26, 1933, Sanger LC.

99. Stützin to Sanger, June 5, 1934, Berlin. Sanger LC.

100. Frau Dr. med. Ilse Szagunn to Miss Helen F. Harper, Berlin, September 14, 1936. Sanger LC. Szagunn became editor of *Die Ärztin* until it was ordered to cease publication in 1942.

101. Letter to Szagunn, October 23, 1936. Also handwritten note from Margaret Sanger to Miss Rose, Sanger LC.

102. Lehfeldt interviews, New York City, September 14, 1977, October 1, 1980, November 2, 1992.

103. Kopp, "Legal and Medical Aspects," pp. 766, 788. Citing the 1927 U.S. Supreme Court decision in *Buck v. Bell*, she noted (p. 770): "It is better for all the world if instead of waiting to execute degenerate offspring for crime or to let them starve for their imbecility, society can prevent those who are manifestly unfit from continuing their kind. Three generations of imbeciles are enough."

104. Walter Stoeckel, *Erinnerungen eines Frauenarztes* (Munich: Kindler Verlag, 1966), p. 391.

105. Speech by Geh. Rat Prof. Stoeckel, "XXIII. Tagung der Deutschen Gesellschaft für Gynäkologie in Berlin vom 11–14 Oktober 1933," *Zentralblatt für Gynäkologie,* no. 2, (1934):88, 91.

106. Stoeckel, *Erinnerungen,* p. 436.

107. Kater, *Doctors Under Hitler,* p. 98. In 1933–1934, 4,619 women were studying medicine, compared to 2,701 in philology. See also Barbara Cohors-Fresenborg, *"Frau Onkel Doktor." Untersuchung über die Anfänge des Frauenstudiums in der Medizin anhand von Fragebögen und Interviews mit Ärztinnen* (Münster: Medizin und Gesellschaft Bd.5, 1989), p. 6.

108. Quoted in Gabriele Czarnowski, "Ehe- und Sexualpolitik im Nationalsozialismus. Medizin und Politik in Ihrer Bedeutung fuer das Geschlechterverhältnis," Diss. Freie Universität Berlin, 1989, pp. 182–183. On social workers' welcoming of National Socialism, compare the two books published by Lisbeth Franzen-Hellersberg before and after 1933: *Die jugendliche Arbeiterin, ihre Arbeitsweise und Lebensform. Ein Versuch sozialpsychologischer Forschung zum Zwecke der Umwertung proletarischer Tatbestände* (Tübingen: Mohr, 1932), and *Jugendpflege und Jugendrecht im neuen Staat* (Tübingen: Mohr, 1934).

109. *Die Ärztin* 9:4 (April 1933):80.

110. This is a composite of three very slightly different versions of the same event related by Hertha Nathorff, once in an interview in New York on June 16, 1980, and earlier in her essay "My life before and after 1933" submitted to Harvard University researchers in 1940 (in Houghton Library, Harvard University, no. 162), and finally in her published diary, *Das Tagebuch der Hertha Nathorff. Berlin-New York Aufzeichnungen 1933 bis 1945,* ed. Wolfgang Benz (Frankfurt am Main: Fischer Taschenbuch Verlag, 1988), p. 40.

111. *Die Ärztin* 9:6 (June 1933):120. About 270 of Berlin's 720 women doctors were Jewish, a very high percentage even for a profession in which Jews were heavily represented relative to their less than 1-percent proportion within the population as a whole.

112. *Die Ärztin* 9:6 (June 1933):120–121. See BArch(P) RMI 26229 for material advocating adoption instead of abortion, especially on the *Bund Kinderland,* which organized adoptions of illegitimate children from racially fit mothers, pp. 143–144.

113. *Die Ärztin* 10:8 (August 1934):140. Only about 115 women were affected by a January 1934 edict barring married women from insurance practice. See Kater, *Doctors Under Hitler,* pp. 92–93, 103.

114. *Die Ärztin* 9:12 (December 1933):262. Eighty percent of married women doctors responding to a query from the journal insisted that combining career and motherhood did not pose a problem.

115. Mathilde Kelchner, "Die Sendung des weiblichen Arztes," *Die Ärztin* 11:1 (January 1935):3, 5.

116. Rotraut von d. Sperl, "Die Frau als Ärztin" in *Deutsche Frauen an der Arbeit* in BArch(P) DAF 62-03/7089.

117. *Die Ärztin* 9:6 (June 1933):2, 118. The umbrella Federation of German Women's Associations (BDF), of which the BDÄ was a member, had avoided *Gleichschaltung* and Aryanization by dissolving. See memo from BDF to RMI, May 5, 1933, signed by Agnes Zahn-Harnack, in which she states that the BDF would prefer to conduct its own dissolution. In BArch(P) RMI 26332, Frauenfragen Allg. 5.5.33 to 1934, Bd. 1, pp. 5–8.

118. Else Luz, "Eine Ärztin Wie Sie Sein Soll," October 4, 1934, in BArch(P), DAF (Deutsche Arbeitsfront) 62-03.

119. Ibid. Claudia Koonz, *Mothers in the Fatherland: Women, the Family and Nazi Politics* (New York: St. Martins, 1987), argues that, "Far from being helpless or even innocent, women made possible a murderous state in the name of concerns they defined as motherly," p. 5. See also Gisela Bock's harsh critique of Koonz and the opposing argument that it was precisely "unmotherly" women who worked with the regime in "Die Frauen und der Nationalsozialismus: Bemerkungen zu einem Buch von Claudia Koonz, " *Geschichte und Gesellschaft* 15 (1989):563–579; also idem, "Antinatalism, maternity and paternity," p. 250. On the bitter debates about women's agency and complicity in Nazi racial hygiene, see also Atina Grossmann, "Feminist Debates about Women and National Socialism," *Gender and History* 3:3 (Autumn 1991):350–358; Claudia Koonz, "Erwiderung auf Gisela Bocks Rezension von *Mothers in the Fatherland*"; Bock, *"Ein Historikerinnenstreit?" Geschichte und Gesellschaft* 18 (1992):394–404; and idem. "Frauen und Geschlechterbeziehungen in der nationalsozialistischen Rassenpolitik, in *Nach Osten. Verdeckte Spuren nationalsozialistischen Verbrechen* (Frankfurt am Main: Neue Kritik, 1992), pp. 99–133. On women's conflicts about sterilization, see Koonz, "Eugenics, Gender, and Ethics in Nazi Germany: The Debate about Involuntary Sterilization, 1933–1936," in *Reevaluating the Third Reich*, pp. 66–85, and idem. "Ethical Dilemmas and Nazi Eugenics: Single-Issue Dissent in Religious Contexts," *Journal of Modern History* 64 Supplement (December 1992):S8-S31.

120. Kater, *Doctors Under Hitler*, pp. 92–93, 108.

121. Letter to Deutschen Städtetag, February 14, 1933, BArch(K) R36/1145.

122. BArch(P) RMI 26244/4, "Vererbungslehre und Rassenhygiene 1933," p. 406.

123. Interview with Dr. Durand-Wever's daughter, Annemarie Florath, Berlin Johannistal, December 12, 1991. See Reingard Jäkl, "1945—Eine politische Chance für Frauen?" in *"Ich bin meine eigene Frauenbewegung." Frauen-Ansichten aus der Geschichte der Grossstadt* (Berlin: Edition Hentrich, 1991), pp. 268–297. Interview with Dr. Helena Wright, London, January 26, 1981, and letter from Joan Rettie of International Planned Parenthood to Dr. Wright, February 1981, also testified to Durand-Wever's quiet courage.

124. Barbara von Renthe-Fink, *So alt wie das Jahrhundert. Lebensbericht einer Berliner Ärztin* (Frankfurt am Main: R. G. Fischer, 1982), pp. 32–37.

125. See BArch(P) RMI 26402, "Nichtarische Ärzte" for reports on German doctors and dentists in China.

126. I am indebted to Itta Vollnhals, Berlin, for generously sharing memories and memorabilia of her mother-in-law, as well as to Christine Antoni, Institute for the History of Medicine, Free University Berlin, for information on Franz Goldmann (who became a lecturer at the Harvard School of Public Health).

127. See Elfriede Paul Papers, NL 229/10, Barch(Sapmo).

128. Lecture May 23, 1935, on "Robert Koch und unsere Zeit" in Paul Papers, BArch(Sapmo).

129. See also her memoir, Elfriede Paul, *Ein Sprechzimmer der Roten Kapelle*, ed. Vera Küchenmeister (Berlin: Militärverlag der DDR, 1981).

130. See discussion of historiography in preface.

131. Diane Paul, "Eugenics and the Left," *Journal of the History of Ideas* (October 1984):569, footnote 5. As Stephen Jay Gould has noted in regard to the "diverse and powerful movement of eugenics, . . . . Politics always makes strange bedfellows but

the range of eugenical support must have generated some legendary pillow fights before 'lights out.'" "Does the Stoneless Plum Instruct the Thinking Reed?" *Natural History* 4:92: 16–17.

132. See especially BArch(P) RMI 26 243, Bd. 3 (January 1,1931–July 1933).

133. See Proctor, *Racial Hygiene*, pp. 223–250, and especially Weindling's careful discussion in *Health, race and German politics*, pp. 489–496.

134. Reichsausschuss für Volksgesundheitsdienst, October 25, 1933, Barch(P), RMI 26228, p. 194.

135. Bock, *Zwangssterilisation*, p. 45.

136. Barch(P) RMI 26 243, Bd. 3, p. 397.

137. See letter from newly appointed director Dr. Reiter to Interior Minister Frick, October 9, 1933, BArch(P) RMI 26-288, Bd. 2, 1933–1934 (*Reichsgesundheitsamt Allgemeines*), pp. 40–41. The longtime director Dr. Hamel had been forcibly retired on October 1, 1933, see p. 28.

138. Barch(P) RMI 26 288, Bd. 2, June 1933–1934, (Reichsgesundheitsamt Allgemeines), pp. 26–41.

139. This committee, which included prominent Weimar eugenicists such as Burgdorfer and Lenz, also soon lost power to the Ministry of Interior, and eventually to the Nazi party and SS. See Burleigh and Wippermann, *Racial State*, p. 57; Weindling, *Health, race and German politics*, pp. 489–522.

140. BArch(P), RMI 26 244 Bd. 4, p. 302. Ironically, Dr. Hirsch's eugenic guidelines for the bride and groom and his marriage fitness questionnaires continued to be used by the Nazis long after their author had emigrated to England in 1933. Czarnowski notes that many couples simply threw the leaflets on the steps of the Rathaus. See Czarnowski, *Das Kontrollierte Paar*, pp. 77, 121.

141. See statement from Saxon Ministry of Interior, February 18, 1934, unfavorably comparing Fetscher to the Zwickau sterilizer Dr. Boeters who had been treated as a "crackpot" by the Weimar Department of Health but was now taken more seriously, in BArch(P) RMI 26 250, Bd. 3 (1934, Sterilisationsgesetze), pp. 163–171. Compare Bock, *Zwangssterilisation*, p. 50.

142. Conversation with Mrs. Henny Brenner, Berlin, July 1993. See also Kater, *Nazi Doctors*, p. 78, and *Medizin, Faschismus und Widerstand*, ed. Barbara Bromberger, Hans Mausbach, and Klaus-Dieter Thomann (Cologne: Pahl-Rugenstein, 1985), pp. 313–312.

143. Ilse Reicke, *Das Grössere Erbarmen. Roman* (Berlin-Zürich: Eigenbroedler Verlag, 1929), pp. 182, 77, 165.

144. Ibid., p. 183.

145. Ibid., p. 256.

146. Safari Verlag GMBH Berlin to the *Reichsschrifttumskammer*, July 7, 1937, Ilse Reicke File, *Reichsschrifttumskammer*, Berlin Document Center.

147. SS Obersturmführer Herbert Menz to the Reichsführer SS, Chef des Sicherheitshauptamtes, Abt. Presse, July 22, 1937, Reicke File.

## Chapter 7

1. Edward Elkan to Elise Ottesen-Jensen, 1934. I am grateful to Doris Linder, College of San Mateo, for giving me copies of this correspondence.

2. Robert Proctor, *Racial Hygiene: Medicine under the Nazis*, (Cambridge: Harvard University Press, 1988), pp. 263, 278–279. See *Internationales Ärztliches Bulletin*.

*Zentralorgan der Internationalen Vereinigung Sozialistischer Ärzte. Jahrgang I-VI (1934–1939)*, reprint, ed. Florian Tennstedt, Christian Pross, and Stephan Leibfried (Berlin: Rotbuch Verlag, 1989).

3.  Hans Peter Kröner, "Die Emigration deutschsprachiger Mediziner 1933–1945. Versuch einer Befunderhebung," *Exilforschung. Ein internationales Jahrbuch* 6 (1988):83–97, claims on p. 86 that women constituted 10.5 percent of all Jewish physicians in Germany and 8.5 percent of all physicians in 1933 (my own figures are closer to 6.5 percent), and on p. 90 that 84 percent of all exiled German physicians eventually landed in the United States, Great Britain, and Palestine / Israel. See also Atina Grossmann, "The Americanization of Weimar Sex Reformers: New Women in Exile," in *Dancing on the Volcano: Essays on the Culture of the Weimar Republic*, ed. Thomas W. Kniesche and Stephen Brockmann (Columbia S.C.: Camden House, 1994), pp. 195–211; idem, "New Women in Exile: German Women Doctors and the Emigration," in *Between Sorrow and Strength. Women Refugees of the Nazi Period*, ed. Sibylle Quack (New York: Cambridge University Press, 1995, pp. 215–238). In general, see Kathleen Pearle, "Ärzteemigration nach 1933 in die USA. Der Fall New York," *Medizinhistorisches Journal* 19:1/2 (1984):112–137; Paul Weindling, "The Contribution of Central European Jews to Medical Science and Practice in Britain, the 1930s–1950s," in *Second Chance: Two Centuries of German-speaking Jews in the United Kingdom*, ed. Werner E. Mosse and Julius Carlebach (Tübingen: Mohr, 1991), pp. 243–254; Doron Niederland, "Deutsche Ärzte-Emigration und gesundheitspolitische Entwicklungen in 'Eretz Israel' (1933–1948)," *Medizinhistorisches Journal* 20:1/2 (1985):149–184; Sabine Fahrenbach, "Ausgegrenzt und vertrieben—Jüdische Ärzte 1933 bis 1941," in *Faschismus und Rassismus. Kontroversen um Ideologie und Opfer/ Arbeitsgruppe Faschismusforschung*, ed. Werner Röhr (Berlin: Akademie Verlag, 1992), pp. 168–178.

4.  On this development within U.S. Planned Parenthood see especially Linda Gordon, *Woman's Body, Woman's Right: Birth Control in America* (New York: Penguin, 1974, revised 1990), pp. 337–385. On British family planning see Beryl Suitters, *Be brave and angry. Chronicles of the International Planned Parenthood Federation* (London: International Planned Parenthood Federation, 1973).

5.  Charlotte Wolff, *Hindsight: An Autobiography* (London: Quartet, 1980), p. 66.

6.  Interviews with Hertha Nathorff, New York City, June 16, 1980, September 25, 1980. See also Miriam Koerner, "Das Exil der Hertha Nathorff," *Dachauer Hefte* 3:3 (November 1987):232–249.

7.  Wolfgang Benz, ed., *Das Tagebuch der Hertha Nathorff. Berlin–New York Aufzeichnungen 1933–1945* (Frankfurt am Main: Fischer Taschenbuch Verlag: 1988), pp. 189–190.

8.  Quoted in Koerner, "Das Exil," p. 239.

9.  Hertha Riese to Miss [Florence] Rose (Sanger's assistant), February 10, 1942, MSPS.

10.  Walter Riese to Robert A. Lambert, M.D., December 3, 1942. Rockefeller Foundation Center Archives (RF), R.G. 1.1. Series 200, Box 97, Folder 1180.

11.  Robert A. Lambert, memorandum, April 29, 1943. R.F. R.G. 1.1. Series 200, Box 97, Folder 1180.

12.  Robert A. Lambert, memorandum, December 1, 1944. R.F. R.G. 1.1. Series 200, Box 97, Folder 1180.

13.  Note to Rose attached to letter to Sanger from Dr. Ludwig Chiavacci, Octo-

ber 25, 1938, MSPS. Sanger and Rose's efforts are well (and sometimes tragically) documented in her papers; they led co-workers to refer to a "Refugee Department" headed by Rose. See *Margaret Sanger Papers Project Newsletter* 5 (Spring 1993):2. Once the war and the immediate danger was over, Sanger indicated that she could no longer afford to find jobs for refugee doctors who did not speak good English and adjust to American ways. See Sanger to Rose, January 6, 1947, MSPS.

14. Vocational Summary from Physicians Committee, November 1940, included with letter to Sanger from Community Service Society of New York, April 14, 1941, MSPS. On the general fate of refugee physicians specializing in sexually transmitted diseases, see Alfred Hollander, "The Tribulations of Jewish Dermatologists under the Nazi Regime," *The American Journal of Dermatology* 5:1 (1983):19–26.

15. A list of displaced (not yet funded) medical scholars compiled in London in 1936 included eight women, mostly at the assistant or researcher level. See material on the Emergency Committee in Aid of Displaced Foreign Physicians in R.F. R.G 2, Series 717, as well as on the Rockefeller Foundation Special Research Aid Fund for Deposed Scholars in R.F. R.G. 1.1, Series 200. These papers, as well as the Margaret Sanger papers, also provide ample evidence for the intense (although often genteel) anti-Semitic prejudice directed against refugee scholars and professionals.

16. See Pearle, "Ärzteemigration," pp. 127–128.

17. On Weimar views of America, see Mary Nolan, *Visions of Modernity: American Business and the Modernization of Germany* (New York: Oxford University Press, 1994). Many refugees had read accounts promising that American women were spoiled by men who did housework and pushed baby carriages. See Fritz Giese, *Girlkultur. Vergleiche zwischen amerikanischen und europäischen Rhythmus und Lebensgefühl* (Munich: Delphin 1925), p. 106. At the same time, Nolan, pp. 116–117, 127, points to the central role many German observers assigned to "puritanism" in forming the American character.

18. Personal communication from Dr. Erika Fromm to Kathleen Pearle, May 16, 1950. I am grateful to Professor Stephan Leibfried for providing this material on Frankenthal.

19. Sibylle Quack also makes some of these points in her "Bericht über die Konferenz 'Women in the Emigration after 1933' 25–27. 11.1991 in Washington," *Feministische Studien* 1 (1992), p. 150. On the United States, see Elaine Tyler May, *Homeward Bound: American Families in the Cold War Era* (New York: Basic Books, 1988).

20. Alice Nauen, interview conducted by Herbert A. Strauss, Boston, June 12, 1971, transcript, p. 42. By kind permission of Research Foundation for Jewish Immigration, Inc.

21. Wolff, *Hindsight*, p. 106.

22. Verena Steinecke in *Sie musste erst Rebellin werden. Das abenteuerliche Leben von Else Kienle* (Stuttgart: Schmetterling Verlag, 1992), p. 65, footnote 58 cites Christine Wittrock, *Egelsbach in politisch bewegter Zeit, 1914–1950* (Frankfurt/Main: 1991), as noting that Kienle's haste to leave was forced not only by her pending case with Wolf but also by another accusation of illegal abortion with fatal outcome in Frankfurt in 1932.

23. Else K. La Roe, M.D. *The Breast Beautiful* (New York: House of Field, 1940), dedication page.

24. Else K. La Roe, *Woman Surgeon* (New York: Dial Press, 1957), pp. 244–245, 276.

25. Ibid., p. 353.

26. Ibid., p. 367.

27. Nauen interview, p. 23. For discussion of the barriers against women, especially married women and mothers, in the American medical profession in the 1930s and 1940s, see Regina Markell Morantz-Sanchez, *Sympathy and Science: Women Physicians in American Medicine* (New York: Oxford University Press, 1985), pp. 232–350.

28. Interview with Renee Barth, daughter of Minna Flake, Chester, CT, July 18, 1990.

29. Among émigré male doctors, psychiatry/neurology and pediatrics followed right after internal medicine as the dominant specialties. The distribution among émigré doctors was disproportionate to the percentages among German doctors as a whole (10 percent were psychiatrists and neurologists compared to 2 percent of all German doctors; 5.8 percent were pediatricians compared to 2 percent), reflecting the tendency of Jews as well as women to cluster in new and/or marginal specialties. Refugee psychiatrists had a significant impact on the development of mental health programs in state hospitals and institutions for the criminally insane where many of them found employment. See Kröner, *Exilforschung*, p. 90.

30. Morantz-Sanchez, *Sympathy and Science*, p. 234. The percentages would only rise significantly again in the 1970s.

31. Susan Ware, *American Women in the 1930s: Holding Their Own* (Boston: Twayne Publishers, 1982), p. 73. According to the *Ärztliche Mitteilungen*, May 27, 1933, there were 3,400 women licensed as doctors in Germany. See Helene Börner, "Zur Frage der Berufstätigkeit der Frau," *Die Ärztin* 9, no. 11 (1935):234. See also Atina Grossmann, "German Women Doctors from Berlin to New York: Maternity and Modernity in Weimar and in Exile," *Feminist Studies* 19, no. 1 (Spring 1993):65–88.

32. Morantz-Sanchez, *Sympathy and Science*, p. 309; see also pp. 266–311.

33. See Gordon, *Woman's Body, Woman's Right*, pp. 297–383. See also May, *Homeward Bound*, pp. 149–50; James Reed, *From Private Vice to Public Virtue: The Birth Control Movement and American Society Since 1830* (New York: Basic Books, 1978).

34. Dr. Hans Lehfeldt, personal interviews, New York City, September 14, 1977; October 1, 1980; November 2, 1992. See also Ellen Chesler, *Woman of Valor: Margaret Sanger and the Birth Control Movement in America* (New York: Doubleday/Simon and Schuster, 1992), p. 289.

35. Gordon, *Woman's Body*, p. 298. See also May, *Homeward Bound*, pp. 298–299.

36. Gordon, *Woman's Body*, p. 338.

37. On the growing importance of psychotherapy and psychoanalysis, see May, *Homeward Bound*, and Nancy Chodorow's interviews with women psychoanalysts in *Feminism and Psychoanalystic Theory* (New Haven: Yale University Press, 1989), pp. 199–218.

38. Käte Frankenthal, *Der dreifache Fluch: Jüdin, Ärztin und Sozialistin. Lebenserinnerungen einer Ärztin in Deutschland und im Exil* (Frankfurt am Main: Campus, 1981); Afterword by Kathleen Pearle and Stephan Leibfried, pp. 252–253.

39. Dr. Lydia Ehrenfried, memoirs, Kfar Saba and Paris, 1968, in Leo Baeck Institute, New York. I am grateful to Christian Pross, M.D., for donating a copy of this unpublished manuscript.

40. See Charlotte Wolff, *Love Between Women* (New York: St. Martin's, 1971); *Bisexuality. A Study* (London: Quartet, 1979); *The Hand in Psychological Diagnosis* (New York: Philosophical Library, 1952); *Magnus Hirschfeld* (London: Quartet, 1986).

41. Alice Nauen prided herself on having a practice that was 15 percent "Negro";

and Harlem Hospital in New York City employed several refugee physicians. Hilde Lachmann-Mosse, daughter of the publisher of the *Berliner Tageblatt* and a pediatrician, cofounded the Lafargue Clinic in Harlem, the first free mental health clinic in the eastern United States. See her papers in the Leo Baeck Institute, New York.

42. Dr. Hertha Riese, *Die Sexuelle Not Unserer Zeit* (Leipzig: Hesse and Becker Verlag, 1927), p. 46.

43. Hertha Riese, *Heal the Hurt Child: An Approach Through Educational Therapy with Special Reference to the Extremely Deprived Negro Child*, foreword by Nathan W. Ackerman (Chicago: University of Chicago Press, 1962), p. XVIII.

44. Ibid., p. XIII.

45. Interview with Riese's daughter, Beatrice Riese, New York City, July 7, 1992. See also Riese's memorial to her husband, *Historical Explorations in Medicine and Psychiatry*, ed. Hertha Riese (New York: Springer, 1978).

46. See, for example, Benz, *Das Tagebuch der Hertha Nathorff*. Memoirs and interviews suggest that refugee women also often made difficult decisions to forego having children, or to have only one child when they might have wished to have more.

47. Examples of single professional women who had been well established in Germany and then died impoverished, underrecognized, and lonely in the early years of exile include Alice Salomon and Helene Stöcker. See Christine Backhaus-Lautenschläger, . . . *Und standen ihre Frau* (Pfaffenweiler: Centaurus-Verlagsgesellschaft, 1991), pp. 275–284. For a more upbeat perspective, see Erna Barschak, *My American Adventure* (New York: I. Washburn, 1945).

48. See Christl Wickert, *Helene Stöcker 1869–1943. Frauenrechtlerin, Sexualreformerin und Pazifistin. Eine Biographie* (Bonn: J. H. W. Dietz Nachf., 1991), pp. 135–140. In Zurich, Stöcker lived near Anita Augspurg and Lida Gustava Heymann of the Women's International League for Peace and Freedom with whom she had cooperated in the fight against paragraph 218, but apparently there was little contact among the elderly women. In 1943, the two longtime companions Heymann and Augspurg committed dual suicide in their Swiss exile, where they had remained when the Nazi takeover had caught them on a trip abroad. See their memoirs, Lida Gustava Heymann and Anita Augspurg, *Erlebtes-Erschautes. Deutsche Frauen kämpfen für Freiheit, Recht und Frieden 1850-1940* (Meisenheim am Glan: Verlag Anton Hain, 1977).

49. Cited in Wickert, *Helene Stöcker*, p. 152.

50. Riese to Miss Rose, April 15, 1942. MSPS.

51. The remnants of her papers and the memoir that she still tried valiantly to complete are in the Peace Collection, Swarthmore College Archives.

52. Frankenthal, *Der dreifache Fluch*, p. 110.

53. Ibid., pp. 251–255.

54. See Backhaus-Lautenschläger, *Und standen*, and Quack, *Between Sorrow and Strength*.

55. Nauen interview transcript, p. 33.

56. See among numerous examples, Dr. Silva, "Von der neudeutschen Gesundheitspolitik," *Internationales Ärztliches Bulletin* 2:1 (January 1935):1–3.

57. Ludwig Levy-Lenz, *Memoirs of a Sexologist: Discretion and Indiscretion* (New York: Cadillac Publishing Co. Inc., 1951), pp. 281–282.

58. Lehfeldt interview, New York City, September 14, 1977.

59. Lehfeldt interview, New York City, November 2, 1992. Lehfeldt died in New

York in June 1993; until then he had participated in New York University Medical School activities.

60. See Hans Lehfeldt, "Felix A. Theilhaber—Pioneer Sexologist," *Archives of Sexual Behavior* 15:1 (1986):1–12; "Ernst Gräfenberg and His Ring," *Mt. Sinai Journal of Medicine* 42:4 (July/August 1975):345–352. In the 1980s Lehfeldt traveled to Berlin to lend support to the newly established Magnus Hirschfeld Gesellschaft.

61. See Ilse Ollendorff Reich, *Wilhelm Reich: A Personal Biography* (New York: St. Martin's Press, 1969), p. 149; also Paul A. Robinson, *The Freudian Left: Wilhelm Reich, Geza Roheim, Herbert Marcuse* (New York: Harper and Row, 1969).

62. Letter to Hodann, May 1, 1936. Max Hodann Papers, Arbetarrörelsens Arkiv, Stockholm. Acc. Nr. 70/008 (hereafter HARA), vol. 2. Also personal interview with Dr. Edward Elkan, London, January 27, 1981.

63. Elkan to Hans Leunbach, postcard, August 30, 1934, HARA, vol. 10.

64. Lehfeldt interview, October 1, 1980, New York City.

65. Sanger to Florence Rose, January 6, 1947. MSPS.

66. Lehfeldt, "Gräfenberg," p. 347, claims that Gräfenberg's own sexual history was published in the *Kinsey Report*.

67. Alice Kahn Ladas, Beverly Whipple, John D. Perry, *The G-Spot and Other Recent Discoveries About Human Sexuality* (New York: Holt, Rinehart and Winston, 1982) relied on Ernst Gräfenberg, "The Role of the Urethra in Female Orgasm," *International Journal of Sexology* 3 (1950):145–148.

68. Hans Lehfeldt, "Theilhaber," pp. 9–10. See Niederland, *"Ärzte-Emigration"* on the influence of German-Jewish refugees on medical practice and organization in Israel. I am grateful to Adin Talbar, Theilhaber's son, for information and material, interview, Jerusalem, August 26 and 27, 1993. See also Renate Heuer, "Der Untergang der deutschen Juden. Felix A. Theilhaber's Darstellung der jüdisch-deutschen Identitätsproblematik," *Archiv Bibliographia Judaica, Jahrbuch* 1 (1985):73–84.

69. In her travel diary, Durand-Wever reported her pleasure at seeing Lehfeldt and the warm reception she received at the fiftieth anniversary of her graduation from the University of Chicago: "I had been a little afraid. One never knows how one will be received as a German," "Amerika nach 50 Jahren," unpublished manuscript (c. 1960), p. 13, with kind permission of Dr. Madeline Durand-Noll.

70. Dr. Lothar Wolf was "driven to his death" on September 9, 1940. *Internationales Ärztliches Bulletin*, and p. XI. On Martha Ruben-Wolf, see also Susanne Leonhard, *Gestohlenes Leben. Schicksal einer Politischen Emigrantin in der Sowjetunion* (Frankfurt am Main: Europäische Verlagsanstalt, 1956), pp. 48–49.

71. Franziska Rubens memoir, EA 0787, BArch(Sapmo). The SED officially solicited these memoirs from party veterans in the 1950s and 1960s. As Rubens herself wrote, "It is not easy to write about the memories from that time, to write about them honestly." However distorted, these memoirs collected in the SED Archives are a valuable source. On the horrors of life in the Hotel Lux during the purges, see Ruth von Mayenburg, *Hotel Lux. Das Absteigequartier der Weltrevolution* (Munich: Piper, 1991).

72. Wendy Goldman, "Women, Abortion and the State, 1917-1936" in *Russia's Women: Accommodation, Resistance, Transformation*, ed. Barbara Evans Clements, Barbara Alpern Engel, and Christine D. Worobec (Berkeley: University of California Press, 1991), p. 244. See also Janet Evans, "The Communist Party of the Soviet Union and the Women's Question: The Case of the 1936 Decree 'In Defense of Mother and Child,'" *Journal of Contemporary History* 16:4 (October 1981):757–775.

73. Many women, especially rural women, continued to resort to illegal abortions, avoiding the inconvenience and delay of applying to commissions and the pain of hospital abortions (which were performed without anesthesia). See Goldman, "Women, Abortion and the State," pp. 249–250. Goldman notes on p. 250 that, "almost 85 percent of Russian women lived in the countryside, but 85 percent of the abortions occurred in the towns."

74. Evans, "Communist Party," pp. 762–763. Susan Gross Solomon has also pointed out that the 1920 legalization of abortion "added new impetus to the medical criticism of legalization." See her "The Demographic Argument in Soviet Debates Over the Legalization of Abortion in the 1920s," *Cahiers du Monde Russe et Sovietique*, no. 1 (1992), p. 2. For a contemporary American medical perspective, see Frederick J. Taussig, M.D., *Abortion Spontaneous and Induced: Medical and Social Aspects* (St. Louis: The C. V. Mosby Company, 1936), p. 396.

75. Evans, "Communist Party," p. 770. See also Wendy Zeva Goldman, "Women, the Family, and the New Revolutionary Order in the Soviet Union," in *Promissory Notes: Women in the Transition to Socialism*, ed. Sonia Kruks, Rayna Rapp, and Marilyn Young (New York: Monthly Review, 1989), pp. 125–143.

76. Susanne Leonhard, *Gestohlenes Leben*, p. 48. See also the extraordinary memoirs of her son, Wolfgang Leonhard, *Child of the Revolution* (Chicago: H. Regnery, 1958).

77. *Internationales Ärztliches Bulletin* 4:4/5 (May/June 1937):59. See also Proctor, *Racial Hygiene*, p. 278.

78. Along with the children of many other refugees, Wolf's two sons attended the German Karl Liebknecht School and the Ernst Thälmann summer camp. They would attain considerable fame of their own: Konrad Wolf as a noted GDR filmmaker, and Markus, who beautifully preserved this story in the memoir *Die Troika. Geschichte eines nichtgedrehten Films. Nach einer Idee von Konrad Wolf* (Berlin: Aufbau, 1989), as the now notorious East German Staasi "spymaster." As a counterstory, see Leonhard, *Child of the Revolution*.

79. David Pike, *German Writers in Soviet Exile 1933–1945* (Chapel Hill: University of North Carolina Press, 1982), pp. 355–356.

80. Rubens, EA 0787, BArch(Sapmo).

81. Else Wolf and Walter Pollatschek, *Wolf. Ein Lesebuch für unsere Zeit* (Berlin: Aufbau-Verlag, 1974), p. XLVI. Markus Wolf in *Troika*, p. 226, suggests (apparently erroneously) that his father was already in Spain when the abortion law took effect and specifically refers to the family's consternation about its impact on the author of *Cyankali*. Friedrich Wolf was however outside the Soviet Union for some of the period, even before his departure for France in 1938 (among other trips, he attended a writers' congress in the United States in 1935). See Pike, *German Writers*, p. 357. Pike estimates on pp. 355–356 that at least 70 percent of the about 170 German cultural exiles in the Soviet Union were arrested.

82. See Wolf and Pollatschek, *Wolf. Ein Lesebuch*, especially p. XLVI.

83. According to Pike, *German Writers*, p. 152, footnote 81, "Wolf was something of an outcast" among the exiled Germans in the Soviet Union and many of his plays were not published or produced. He quotes on pp. 327–328 a letter from June 9, 1941, in which Wolf complains to the Soviet Central Committee that, "After twenty-two years of not exactly unsuccessful activity as a dramatist it is impossible for me to find work in the Soviet Union as a playwright." Letters written by Wolf recorded his, and especially his wife Else's, attempts to help the companions and children left behind

when people disappeared. It cannot be an accident that Wolf tried so hard to leave Moscow during this period.

84. Martha Arendsee, EA 0017, BArch(Sapmo).

85. See correspondence in HARA, vol. 10.

86. From 1936 to 1939, 5,000 Germans fought in the international brigades in Spain; 3,000 lost their lives. See Barbara Bromberger and Hans Mausbach, "Ärzte im Widerstand: Zur Geschichte des antifaschistischen Widerstandes 1933–1945," in *Medizin, Faschismus, Widerstand*, ed. Bromberger, Mausbach, and Thomann (Cologne: Pahl-Rugenstein, 1985), p. 264.

87. Hodann to Janet Chance, August 24, 1936. She responded: "What dreadful news from Russia on abortion . . . " November 25, 1936. Elkan also suggested to Hodann that his "asthma [was] a hint that you shouldn't go to Russia." Elkan to Hodann, August 8, 1936. The correspondance in vol. 10 HARA reveals Hodann's anguish about the Soviet situation; it was exacerbated by the fact that his former wife Traute was in the Soviet Union and demanding child support for one of his daughters. In one letter, May 5, 1936, she threatens to take him to court: "What should I do with the child? Should I put her on the train to you? Should I hang her? Should I stop feeding her? I have to ask you so blandly because you write to me so blandly."

88. Max Hodann, *History of Modern Morals*, translated by Stella Browne (London: William Heinemann, 1937), p. 295.

89. Peter Weiss, *Die Aesthetik des Widerstands* (Frankfurt am Main: Suhrkamp, 1983), pp. 169, 223–243. Max Hodann is also a central character in Weiss's *Notizbücher 1971–1980* (Frankfurt am Main: Suhrkamp, 1981) and (as Hoderer) in his autobiographical novel *Fluchtpunkt* (Frankfurt am Main: Suhrkamp, 1973). See also Hodann's notes, "Bemerkungen zum Sexual Problem in der Armee," vol. 3, HARA. Weiss seems to have carefully studied and followed fairly faithfully the documents he found in Hodann's papers. I am grateful to Robert Cohen for his help on Weiss's references to Hodann; see his *Bio-Bibliographisches Handbuch zu Peter Weiss' "Ästhetik des Widerstands"* (Hamburg: Argument Verlag, 1989).

90. Doris H. Linder, "Elise Ottesen-Jensen and the Emergence of the International Planned Parenthood Federation 1945–1953." Paper presented to the Seventh Berkshire Conference on the History of Women, June 19–21, 1987, Wellesley College, p. 24, footnote 10. Ottesen-Jensen also served in the 1940s as head of the Stockholm office of the New York–based International Relief and Rescue Committee. I am grateful to Professor Linder for sharing with me her rich knowledge of the Scandinavian and international birth control movement.

91. Hodann to Dr. S. Lehmann (Ben Schemen, Palestine), October 23, 1945, HARA. See Helmut Müssener, *Exil in Schweden. Politische und kulturelle Emigration nach 1933* (Munich: Carl Hanser Verlag, 1974). especially pp. 201–209, 256–262.

92. Pike, *German Writers*, p. 341, and Weiss, *Notizbücher*, vol. 2, p. 153.

93. Letter to his daughter Renate Saran in London, December 12, 1945, HARA, vol. 1. See also his former wife Mary Saran's memoir, *Never Give Up* (London: Oswald Wolff, 1976), pp. 30–35.

94. "Wiedersehen mit der Schweiz nach 12 Jahren," November 17, 1946, typescript manuscript in HARA, vol. 1.

95. Letter to Neumann (Zurich), October 21, 1946, HARA.

96. Müssener, *Exil in Schweden*, p. 205.

97. HARA, vol. 8.

98. Weiss, *Notizbücher*, p. 61. See also *Aesthetik*, p. 267. See also notes in HARA, vol 8. Robert Cohen, in his *Bio-Bibliographisches Handbuch*, p. 83, says that Hodann committed suicide.

99. November 17, 1945, in HARA, vol. 2.

100. Dr. Max Hodann, "Magnus Hirschfeld zum Gedächtnis," *Internationales Ärztliches Bulletin* 2, no. 5/6 (May–June 1935):73–76 (reprint, 1989).

101. Linder, "Elise Ottesen-Jensen," p. 24, footnote 10, and pp. 4–5.

## Chapter 8

1. Frau Wenk, Liberal Democratic Party delegate to the Saxon Landtag, during debate, June 18, 1947, in BArch(Sapmo) Zentralkomite (ZK) der SED, IV/17/28, p. 109.

2. Lederer to Mr. (William) Vogt (president of Planned Parenthood Federation of America), June 2, 1954, File 8.4 (Germany), International Planned Parenthood Federation Archive, David Owen Centre for Population Studies, University of Wales, Cardiff (IPPFA).

3. This is being increasingly detailed for virtually every professional group in Germany. On population and health policy in the Federal Republic, see Robert Proctor, *Racial Hygiene: Medicine under the Nazis* (Cambridge: Harvard University Press, 1988), pp. 298–312; Paul Weindling, *Health, race and German politics between unification and Nazism 1870–1945* (Cambridge: Cambridge University Press, 1989), pp. 558ff, and in general Robert G. Moeller, *Protecting Motherhood: Women and the Family in the Politics of Postwar Germany* (Berkeley: University of California, 1993). See also Geoffrey Cocks, "Repressing, Remembering, Working Through: German Psychiatry, Psychotherapy, Psychoanalysis, and the 'Missed Resistance' in the Third Reich," *Journal of Modern History* 64, suppl. (December 1992):S204–216.

4. Richtlinien für Ehe-und-Sexualberatungsstellen, September 17, 1946, in Landesregierung Sachsen, Ministerium für Arbeit und Sozialfürsorge 35/1, no. 1810 (Ministerium für Gesundheitswesen), Staatsarchiv Dresden (SAD).

5. First session of antifascist Women's Council, March 21, 1946, in BArch(Sapmo), ZK SED IV 2/17/54 (Saxony); for discussion of social crisis and "depraved" women (*Verwilderung der Sitten, Verfall der Frau*), see also IV 2/17/55 (Berlin) and SAD 35/1.

6. BArch(Sapmo) ZK SED, IV 2/17/55.

7. Paul was briefly minister for work and welfare in Hanover before moving east in 1946. Colleagues in the Health Commission included returned exiles Erwin Marcusson (from Kazachstan), Carl Coutelle (China), Rudolf Neumann (Mexico), Eva Schmidt-Kolmer (England), and Erwin Friedeberger (USA). See Elfriede Paul, *Ein Sprechzimmer der Roten Kapelle*, ed. Vera Küchemeister (Berlin: Militärverlag der DDR, 1981); and Paul's papers in BArch(Sapmo) NL 229. See also Peter Mitzscherling, "Auf dem Wege zu einer 'sozialistischen' Sozialpolitik? Die Anfänge der Sozialpolitik in der SBZ/DDR," in *Sozialpolitik nach 1945. Geschichte und Analysen*, ed. Reinhart Bartholomäi, Wolfgang Bodenbender, Hardon Henk, and Renate Hüttel (Bonn-Bad Godesberg, Verlag Neue Gesellschaft, 1977), p. 94.

8. Barbara von Renthe-Fink, "Aus der Nachkriegsgeschichte der Gesundheitspolitik in Berlin," in *Sozialpolitik nach 1945*, pp. 69–70. For Saxon initiatives, see also SAD 35/1, no. 1810.

9. Abt. Frauenausschüsse to Deutsche Zentralverwaltung für das Gesundheitswesen in der Sowjetischen Besatzungszone, August 22, 1946, in BArch(Sapmo), ZK
der SED, IV 2/17/28.

10. Interview with Dr. Durand-Wever's daughter, Annemarie Florath, Berlin
Johannistal, December 12, 1991, and her granddaughter Dr. Madeline Durand-Noll,
Cochem an der Mosel, January 12, 1993. See Reingard Jäkl, "1945—Eine politische
Chance für Frauen?" in *"Ich bin meine eigene Frauenbewegung." Frauen-Ansichten aus der
Geschichte der Grossstadt* (Bezirksamt Schöneberg Berlin: Edition Hentrich, 1991), pp.
268–297.

11. Drs. Elfriede Paul and Barbara von Renthe, and the moderate Weimar feminist Else Lüders also attended the founding congress. See *Protokoll Gründungskongress
des Demokratischen Frauenbundes Deutschlands Berlin 7–9 March 1947*, p. 32, in Demokratischer Frauenbund Deutschlands, Archive (DFDA, BArch (Sapmo). See also former
ARSO leader Martha Arendsee, *Schriften zur Ideologischen und kulturellen Arbeit der
Frauenausschusse 1:1.* (Berlin: Volk und Wissen Verlag, n.d).

12. Observers estimated that at the end of the war there were over seven million "surplus" women, six million of marriageable age, and that almost half of the German population was on the move. See Barbara Willenbacher, "Zerrüttung und
Bewährung der Nachkriegsfamilie," and Nori Möding, "Die Stunde der Frauen? Frauen
und Frauenorganisationen des bürgerlichen Lagers," in *Von Stalingrad zur Währungs-
reform. Zur Sozialgeschichte des Umbruchs in Deutschland*, ed. Martin Broszat, Klaus-
Dietmar Henke, and Hans Woller (Munich: R. Oldenbourg, 1988), pp. 620–621,
595–618. Robert G. Moeller points out that, "More than three million German soldiers were killed in the war, and in 1945 nearly two million more remained in pris-
oner-of-war camps," *Protecting Motherhood*, p. 27; see his excellent survey of postwar
conditions, pp. 8–37. See also Eva Kolinsky, *Women in Contemporary Germany: Life,
Work and Politics* (Providence: Berg, rev. ed. 1993), pp. 24–40.

13. Order no. 030 by Marshall Shukow, Supreme Commander SMA, February
12, 1946, and order no. 273 on combating venereal disease among the German population in the SBZ, December 11, 1947. Men aged 16 to 55 in similar situations were also
affected; Soviets, of course, were exempted, much to German displeasure. See, for
example, complaints collected in SAD 35/1.

14. See Landesarchiv Berlin (LAB) Rep 214/2814/217.

15. *Befreier und Befreite. Krieg, Vergewaltigungen, Kinder*, eds. Helke Sander and Barbara Johr (München: Verlag Antje Kunstmann, 1992), pp. 48, 54–55. Sander estimates
that at least 110,000 women were raped, many more than once, in Berlin, of whom
up to 10,000 died or suffered serious health consequences. The numbers cited for Berlin vary wildly: from 20,000 to 100,000 to almost one million, with the actual number
of rapes respectively higher because many women were attacked repeatedly. See also
Erich Kuby, *Die Russen in Berlin 1945* (Bern/Munich: Scherz, 1965), pp. 312–313.

16. My own current research focuses on rape and abortion in the early postwar
period. See Atina Grossmann, "A Question of Silence: The Rape of German Women
by Occupation Soldiers," *October* (April 1995). See also the pioneering studies by Ingrid
Schmidt Harzbach, "Eine Woche im April. Berlin 1945. Vergewaltigung als Mas-
senschicksal," *Feministische Studien* 2 (1984):51–65; Erika M. Hoerning, "Frauen als
Kriegsbeute. Der Zwei-Fronten Krieg. Beispiele aus Berlin," in *"Wir kriegen jetzt andere
Zeiten." Auf der Suche nach der Erfahrung des Volkes in nachfaschistischen Ländern.
Lebensgeschichte und Sozialkultur im Ruhrgebiet 1930 bis 1960*, ed. Lutz Niethammer and

Alexander von Plato (Bonn: Verlag J. H. W.Dietz Nachf., 1985), pp. 327–346; Annemarie Tröger, "Between Rape and Prostitution: Survival Strategies and Chances of Emancipation for Berlin Women after World War II," in *Women in Culture and Politics: A Century of Change* (Bloomington: Indiana University Press, 1986), pp. 97–117; also more recently, Albrecht Lehmann, *Im Fremden ungewollt zuhaus. Flüchtlinge und Vertriebene in Westdeutschland 1945-1990* (Munich: C. H. Beck, 1991), pp. 151–169.

17. Anne-Marie Durand-Wever, "Als die Russen kamen. Tagebuch einer Ärztin," unpublished diary, entry May 6, p. 32. With kind permission of Dr. Madeline Durand-Noll.

18. Dr. Anne-Marie Durand-Wever, "Mit den Augen einer Ärztin. Zur Kontroverse zwischen Prof. Nachtsheim und Dr. Volbracht," *Berliner Ärzteblatt* 83:14 (1970): Sonderdruck (n.p.n).

19. *Proceedings of the International Congress on Population and World Resources in Relation to the Family. August 1948. Cheltenham, England* (London: H. K. Lewis, n.d.), p. 102.

20. See Michael Burleigh and Wolfgang Wippermann, *The Racial State: Germany 1933-1945* (Cambridge: Cambridge University Press, 1991), p. 263.

21. See especially Schmidt-Harzbach, "Eine Woche im April," and Hoerning, "Frauen als Kriegsbeute."

22. See the remarkable files on "Interruption of Pregnancy" in LAB Rep. 214/2814 (Bezirksamt Neukölln), discussed in Grossmann, "A Question of Silence."

23. See, for example, Deutsche Wochenschau no. 739/46/1944, 754/9/1945, 755/10/1945, in BArch(K).

24. LAB Rep. 214/2814/220.

25. See the useful summary of the legal situation in East and West in Michael Gante, *Par. 218 in der Diskussion. Meinungs-und Willensbildung 1945–1976* (Düsseldorf: Droste Verlag, 1991), pp. 24–55.

26. For example, "Diskussionen um den Paragraphen 218," *Neue Zeit*, December 25, 1946. See the extensive collections of press clippings in BArch(Sapmo) ZK SED IV/2/17/29.

27. Walter Lennig, *Berliner Zeitung*, March 3, 1947, in BArch(Sapmo) ZK SED IV 2/17/29, p. 63.

28. Dr. Friedrich Wolf, "Der Par. 218 und die soziale Indikation," *Neues Deutschland*, December 17, 1946 in BArch(Sapmo) ZK SED IV 21/17/29. See also Paul Ronge and Friedrich Wolf, *Problem Par. 218* (Rudolstadt: Greifenverlag, n.d.[1946–1947]).

29. *Für Dich* 1:17 (December 8, 1946). See also the simultaneous discussion "For and Against the Social Indication" in the SED paper *Neues Deutschland*, November 30, 1946, in BArch(Sapmo) ZK SED IV/2/17/29.

30. *Für Dich* 1, no. 18. p. 3.

31. Durand-Wever used this terminology in "Als die Russen kamen."

32. Durand-Wever in DFD Bundesauschuss, September 24, 1948. DFDA.

33. Ibid.

34. Anne-Marie Durand-Wever, *Bewusste Mutterschaft durch Geburtenregelung* (Rudolstadt: Greifenverlag, n.d, 1946 or 1947), p. 30. See also her other brochure *Normale und Krankhafte Vorgänge im Frauenkörper. Schriften zur Ideologischen und Kulturellen Arbeiten der Frauenausschüssen* (Berlin/Leipzig: Volk und Wissen Verlag, 1946).

35. *Für Dich*, 1:18 (December 12, 1946):3.

36. *Kurier*, December 13, 1946, in BArch(Sapmo) ZK SED, IV 2/17/29. A few other dissenting voices pleading for women's right to decide, at least within the first tri-

mester, appear in the letters' column or in SED files. See long letter from Anni König, a former nurse for BDÄ abortion rights advocate Dr. Hermine Heusler-Edenhuizen, in IV 2/17/29.

37. Käthe Kern, December 19, 1946, BArch(Sapmo) ZK SED, IV 2/17/28. See also *Für Dich* 1:19 (December 22, 1946):8 and 1:20 (December 29, 1946):4.

38. Notes in Käthe Kern's collected papers, BArch(Sapmo), NL 145/50, p. 213.

39. Dr. Eva Kolmer, "Frauenschutzgesetz—nicht Par. 218," January 29, 1947, in *Pressedienst*, BArch(Sapmo) ZK SED IV 2/17/28. For similiar statements, see Käthe Kern, collected papers, NL145, and her statement, December 19, 1946, in ZK der SED IV 2/17/28.

40. For example, in Saxon marriage counseling guidelines, September 17, 1946, SAD 35/1, no. 1810.

41. Paragraph 219 banned advertising of abortifacients and paragraph 220 banned advertising of abortion services. See also Kirsten Poutrus, "'Ein Staat, der seine Kinder nicht ernähren kann, hat nicht das Recht, ihre Geburt zu fordern.' Abtreibung in der Nachkriegszeit 1945 bis 1950," in *Unter anderen Umständen. Zur Geschichte der Abtreibung* (Berlin/Dresden: Argon Verlag/Deutsches Hygiene Museum, 1993), pp. 73–85.

42. Numerous doctors resisted elimination of the sterilization law, insisting on the respectable pre-Nazi history of eugenic sterilization. Moreover, doctors continued to want to report, as they had been ordered to in 1935, all suspicious miscarriages. It may be relevant here that, in contrast to the Western zones, the scarcity of doctors in the SBZ led to their exemption from denazification. See discussion in the Saxon Ministerium für Arbeit und Sozialfürsorge 2144, Ministerium für Gesundheitswesen no. 290, SAD. There seems to have been a good deal of confusion, deliberate and otherwise, about which regulations were still in effect.

43. *Neues Deutschland*, September 27, 1947, in BArch(Sapmo), IV2/17/29, p. 83. Crimes justifying ethical indication had to be reported within two weeks and abortions after the first trimester had to be strictly medically indicated. Saxony Anhalt adopted a law in February 1948 that stressed aid, such as the provision of linens, for women and newborns. The CDU, and on occasion the LDP, were not above invoking Nazi crimes against "unfit life" as a reason for keeping abortion illegal, or likening legal abortion to the Nazi "euthanasia" programs. See, for example, transcripts of debates in the Saxony-Anhalt Landtag in 1947, in Käthe Kern NL 145/50, p. 43.

44. See the necessary conditions for recriminalization laid out by Chief Prosecutor Hilde Benjamin, "Juristische Grundlagen für die Diskussion über den par. 218. Abt. Frauenausschusse bei der Deutschen Verwaltung für Volksbildung in der SBZ," *Mitteilungen der juristischen Arbeitskommission im Zentralen Frauenausschuss*, 3 Folge, Berlin, February 27, 1947, in DFDA. For a good summary, see *Ende der Selbstverständlichkeit? Die Abschaffung des par. 218 in der DDR. Dokumente*, ed. Kirsten Thietz (Berlin: Basis, 1992). On the contrasting development of a domestic model in the West, see Moeller, *Protecting Motherhood*.

45. See Dr. K. H. Mehlan, "Die Abortsituation in der DDR," in *Internationale Abortsituation. Kongress 5–7 Mai 1960* (Leipzig: Georg Thime, 1961), pp. 52–63. In 1950, for example, the SBZ recorded 311,000 births, 26,360 legal abortions, and c. 84,000 illegal abortions. In 1951, after passage of the law, the birth rate rose only modestly to 318,000, but the number of legal abortions dropped drastically to 5,037, the estimated number of criminal abortions to 68,000 (p. 59).

46. Ibid., p. 57.

47. SED Landesverband Brandenburg reports on factory meetings to ZK SED, Frauenabt., Potsdam, October 26, 1950 and October 18, 1950, in BArch(Sapmo) IV 2/17/30, pp. 129, 128.

48. Jenny Matern, Bundesvorstandssitzung, June 11–12, 1951. DFDA BArch(Sapmo).

49. See DFD Bundesvorstandssitzung, June 11–12, 1951, Berlin, DFDA. See letters and discussion in BArch(Sapmo) ZK SED IV 2/17/30.

50. Notes in Elfriede Paul Papers, BArch(Sapmo), NL 229/13.

51. DFD Meeting, Berlin, June 11–12, 1951, DFDA. See reports of DFD efforts in Ministerium für Arbeit und Sozialfürsorge 2145. Ministerium fur Gesundheitswesen no. 29, SAD.

52. Käthe Kern, DFD Bundesvortstandssitzung, October 19–20, 1950, DFDA.

53. Notes for Women's Conference speech, May 28, 1947, in Kern NL 145/50, p. 125. As an example of the intense interest in the abortion issue among SED activists, see the 35-page bibiliography listing over 800 books, articles, and dissertations, *Par. 218 StGB als rechtspolitisches Problem. Eine Literaturübersicht*, ed. Dr. Guenther Berg (Jena: 1947), included among Kern's papers.

54. Renthe-Fink, *So alt*, p. 72. See also Renthe-Fink, "Aus der Nachkriegsgeschichte der Gesundheitspolitik in Berlin," in *Sozialpolitik nach 1945*, p. 69. See also Landesgesundheitsamt Berlin, February 24, 1948, in LAB Rep. 12/1641/271.

55. Paul specifically traced her lineage through such reform-minded physicians as Georg Manes, a Hamburg BFM physician arrested on abortion charges in 1937; Rainer Fetscher, the Dresden eugenicist who had joined the Communist resistance; and Hans Lehfeldt of the Berlin RV, who had, as we have seen, become a gynecologist and Planned Parenthood advocate in New York. In 1949, Paul became director of the central health insurance office in (east) Berlin where she worked closely with Martha Arendsee, another veteran of the anti-218 campaign and former leader of the KPD social welfare organization, ARSO. In an experiment unusual for the GDR, Paul then established birth control and marriage counseling clinics in Magdeburg directly modeled on her experiences with the *Bund für Mutterschutz*. See Paul, *Sprechzimmer*, and her BArch(Sapmo) NL 229.

56. On the difficult transition from East to West in 1949, see Barbara von Renthe-Fink, *So alt wie das Jahrhundert. Lebensbericht einer Berliner Ärztin* (Frankfurt am Main: R. G. Fischer Verlag, 1982), pp. 47–92. In 1960 she became an SPD health senator in West Berlin, and after her retirement, vice-president of the (West) German Red Cross.

57. Durand-Wever had resigned the chair of the DFD in April 1948 ostensibly for health reasons, an unlikely claim given her increasing isolation as "bourgeois" and her simultaneous growing involvement in the "western-oriented" international family planning movement. See letter Maria Weiterer to Emmy Koenen (Demerius) referring to Durand-Wever, June 20, 1947; also Durand-Wever's statements in minutes of Vorstand meeting, April 6, 1948, and Arbeitsbesprechung, April 14, 1948, DFDA.

58. Ilse Brandt, "Auswertung von 4000 Fällen der Berliner Beratungsstellen," in *Die gesunde Familie in ethischer, sexualwissenschaftlicher und psychologischer Sicht. Beiträge zur Sexualforschung 13*, ed. Hans Harmsen (Stuttgart: Ferdinand Enke Verlag, 1958), pp. 135–136.

59. Brandt, "Auswertung," noted that again, "It has become customary for women to get rid of an unwanted pregnancy," pp. 135–136. See also memo on "Beratungsstellen für Frauen und Mädchen bei der VAB [successor to the Weimar League] Berlin, Landesgesundheitsamt, Berlin, February 12, 1947, LAB Rep. 12/1641/271.

60. See Gabriele Strecker, *Überleben ist nicht genug. Frauen 1945–1950* (Freiburg: Herder, 1981), p. 76. See also Möding, "Stunde der Frauen."

61. Agnes von Zahn-Harnack (former BDF leader), "Vertrauensstellen für Verlobte und Eheleute," in LAB Rep. 12/1641/271.

62. Memo by Frau Dr. Kuhr, Gesundheitsamt Neukölln, June 17, 1948, LAB Rep. 12/1641/271.

63. For an "Onkel" story, see *Für Dich* 1, no. 8. (October 1946), p. 4. For occupation view, see, for example, LAB Rep. 210/840/88 "Militaerregierung, Gesetze, Verordnungen 1945–50. Zehlendorf."

64. Stefanie Hirt, "Marriage Guidance in Berlin," *The International Journal of Sexology* (May 1949):1–3.

65. Memo, Landesgesundheitsamt, Berlin, February 24, 1948, in LAB Rep. 12/1641/271. See also decision of Finanzabteilung, Magistrat von Gross-Berlin, July 23, 1948, LAB Rep. 12/1641/271, that counseling centers should not be established as part of local district health offices, although those already in existence continued to function. A very diverse group of women worked in these centers, including Durand-Wever's friend and birth control advocate Stefanie Hirt (in Schöneberg), as well as Dr. Ilse Szagunn (in Steglitz), who had been an outspoken National Socialist.

66. See "Spuren der Erinnerung—Ein Nachtrag: Die Konflikte um die Ambulatorien in Berlin 1947 bis 1953," in Eckhard Hansen et al., *Seit über einem Jahrhundert— Verschüttete Alternativen in der Sozialpolitk* (Cologne: Bund Verlag, 1981), pp. 504, 509–510.

67. Minutes, Landesgesundheitsamt meeting, Berlin, January 22, 1949, LAB Rep. 12/1641/271.

68. Renthe-Fink, "Aus der Nachkriegsgeschichte," in *Sozialpolitik nach 1945*, p. 70.

69. See Georg Weyhmann, "Die Geschichte des Ambulatoriums der AOK Berlin," in *Sozialpolitik nach 1945*, pp. 57–64. See also "Spuren der Erinnerung," pp. 500–546.

70. The American birth controller Margaret Otis used the term "pathetic" to describe Willy Karger of the lay *Bund für Volksgesundheit und Geburtenregelung* in a letter to Dorothy Brush, June 20, 1952, MSPS.

71. Gampe to Sanger, February 13, 1949. See also Gampe's letter to the (British) Family Planning Association, July 30, 1949, File 8.4 (Germany, folder Bavaria) IPPFA.

72. Vera Houghton, "Birth Control in Germany," *Eugenics Review* 43:4, p. 187. In a letter to Houghton, of the International Committee for Planned Parenthood, London, October 8, 1950, Gampe claimed 1,800 members. In File 8.4, IPPFA.

73. See Dr. Arthur Waldemar Langeheine (Göttingen) to (Miss Helen) Donnington (international secretary, Family Planning Association, London), January 15, 1948, on his inability to retrieve shipments of Volpar paste from customs in File 8.4, IPPFA. See also Dr. Anne-Marie Durand-Wever's report in *Proceedings . . . Cheltenham*, p. 104, on her use of private APO addresses for clandestine shipments of contraceptives to Berlin.

74. Sensational abortion trials with large numbers of women rounded up and interrogated by police were again being reported, especially in southern Germany. See Vera Houghton, "Birth Control in Germany," *The Eugenics Review* 43(4):185–187. At the same time, purely commercial groups with similar-sounding names, such as *Reichsverband für Familienplanung*, sprung up in Bavaria, further reducing lay credibility. On sexual repressiveness, see also Heide Fehrenbach, "The Fight for the 'Christian West': German Film Control, the Churches, and the Reconstruction of Civil

Society in the Early Bonn Republic," *German Studies Review* 14 (1991):39–63; Robert G. Moeller, "The Homosexual Man is a 'Man,' the Homosexual Woman Is a 'Woman': Sex, Society and the Law in Postwar West Germany," *Journal of the History of Sexuality* 4:3 (January 1994):395–429.

75. Margaret Otis to Dorothy Brush (Sanger's friend and supporter), June 20, 1952, MSPS.

76. Gampe to Houghton, January 14, 1951. File 8.4 IPPFA.

77. Ilse Lederer to Vera Houghton, November 3, 1950, File 8.4, IPPFA.

78. Quote from Elly Grosser, in report by Vera Houghton for the International Committee on Planned Parenthood, October 23, 1950, in File 8.4, IPPFA.

79. Leonore Mayer-Katz, *Sie haben zwei Minuten Zeit. Nachkriegsimpulse aus Baden* (Freiburg, 1981), p. 136, quoted in Möding, "Die Stunde der Frauen?" p. 634.

80. Lederer to Houghton, May 4, 1950, and November 3, 1950. See also the extensive correspondence between Dr. Arthur Waldemar Langeheine (Göttingen) with Helen Donington (international secretary, Family Planning Association, London, and International Committee on Planned Parenthood) about the tremendous difficulties of getting support for birth control from physicians, authorities, and the general population, in 8.4 IPPFA. See also Ilse Lederer's painfully frustrating correspondence, especially with Protestant Church officials, about birth control clinics, in the fascinating folder containing Lederer's papers in Hans Harmsen collection, BArch(K) NL 336/344/1. I am immensely grateful to Sabine Schleiermacher, who is writing a biography of Harmsen, for having facilitated access to this as yet uncatalogued material.

81. Lederer to Houghton, November 3, 1950, File 8.4, IPPFA.

82. On U.S. policy toward women, see Gabrielle Strecker, *Überleben ist nicht genug. Frauen 1945–1950* (Freiburg im Breisgau: Herder, 1981), and Hermann-Josef Rupieper, "Bringing Democracy to the Fräuleins: Frauen als Zielgruppe der amerikanische Demokratisierungspolitik in Deutschland 1945–1952," *Geschichte und Gesellschaft* 17 (1991):61–91, especially pp. 76–77.

83. Otis to Brush, June 20, 1952, MSPS.

84. Otis to Brush, June 20, 1952, MSPS. In fairness, it should be noted that Sanger's representatives also automatically suspected anyone Catholic as anti–birth control.

85. On the connection between postwar anti-Communism, anti-Semitism, and anti-Americanism, see Wolfgang Benz, "Nachkriegsgesellschaft und Nationalsozialismus. Erinnerung, Amnesie, Abwehr," *Dachauer Hefte* 6:6 (November 1990):12–24. See also Frank Stern, *The Whitewashing of the Yellow Badge: Anti-Semitism and Philosemitism in Postwar Germany* (Oxford: Pergamon Press, 1992).

86. Dr. A. W. Langeheine (Deutsche Gesellschaft für Familienfragen, Vorbereitendes Komite, Göttingen) to (Miss) Donington, January 23, 1949, File 8.4, IPPFA.

87. Langeheine to Donington, December 14, 1948, File 8.4, IPPFA.

88. Langeheine to Donington, January 23, 1949, File 8.4, IPPFA. See his similiar remarks at the 1948 Cheltenham conference, *Proceedings . . . Cheltenham*, p. 97. A report by Vera Houghton, October 7, 1950, noted that Dr. Langeheine had been barred from insurance practice apparently on account of his birth control work. File 8.4, IPPFA.

89. Otis to Brush, June 20, 1952. MSPS.

90. See, for example, Ilse Lederer's poignant letters to the British Family Planning Association and Durand-Wever's "Report to ICPP," n.d. (probably 1955) in File 8.4, IPPFA. See also Durand-Wever's complaint that, "At present the word 'heredity' bears a stigma" and while "We are slowly bringing people back to see that there are

hereditary diseases," Hitler "had made such havoc with the idea that it lost all credit." *Cheltenham . . . Proceedings*, p. 103.

91. Harmsen claimed to have been so informed by his mentor and professor, Alfred Grotjahn. Personal interview, Benesdorf bei Hamburg, April 17–18, 1979.

92. See Sabine Schleiermacher, "Racial Hygiene and Deliberate Parenthood: Two Sides of Demographer Hans Harmsen's Population Policy," *Issues in Reproductive and Genetic Engineering* 3:3 (1990):201–210; also Heidrun Kaupen-Haas, "Eine deutsche Biographie—der Bevölkerungswissenschaftler Hans Harmsen," in *Heilen und Vernichten im Mustergau Hamburg. Gesundheits- und Bevölkerungspolitk im Dritten Reich*, ed. Kaupen-Haas, Angelika Ebbinghaus, and Karl Heinz Roth (Hamburg: Konkret, 1984), pp. 41–44.

93. See Harmsen's Reich Medical Chamber (*Reichsärztekammer*) file, Berlin Document Center.

94. Harmsen to Sanger, February 11, 1948, File 8.4, IPPFA.

95. "A Summary Report on Conditions of Science in Germany," by N. Artin and R. Courant, August 1947. RF RG 2, File 717 Germany, Folder 2627. Rockefeller Foundation Center Archives, Pocantico Hills, New York (RF).

96. Otis to Brush, June 20, 1952, MSPS. Curiously for all the concern about Durand-Wever's Communist family ties, her own very public early leadership of the women's organization in the Soviet Zone, the DFD, was never directly mentioned.

97. See, for example, Proctor, *Racial Hygiene*, pp. 306–308.

98. Sanger to Harmsen, November 8, 1957, MSPS.

99. Sanger to Lederer, January 25, 1952, MSPS.

100. Lederer to (William) Vogt (president of Planned Parenthood Federation of America), June 2, 1954, File 8.4 IPPFA. "Civil courage" was seemingly also in short supply in the United States; Lederer's planned official tour to the United States was apparently canceled when she expressed interest in seeing Sanger's Birth Control Research Bureau. See also the excellent (and witty) official history by Beryl Suitters. *Be brave and angry: Chronicles of the International Planned Parenthood Federation* (London: International Planned Parenthood Federation, 1973), p. 100.

101. Lederer to Planned Parenthood Federation of America, August 5, 1952, MSPS. For a slightly different version of the rather confusing series of events that led to the establishment of *Pro Familia*, see Suiters, *Be brave*, p. 12ff.

102. Sanger to Durand-Wever, October 24, 1951, MSPS. On Sanger and Cheltenham, see also Ellen Chesler, *Woman of Valor: Margaret Sanger and the Birth Control Movement in America* (New York: Doubleday / Simon and Schuster, 1992), pp. 407–411.

103. Suitters, *Be brave*, pp. 9–14.

104. Suitters, *Be brave*, p. 48.

105. Durand-Wever, *Proceedings . . . Cheltenham*, p. 100.

106. Durand-Wever to Sanger, June 25, 1952. Durand-Wever was grateful to Sanger for care packages sent to her after the war. See Durand-Wever to Sanger, April 14, 1951, MSPS.

107. Chesler, *Woman of Valor*, pp. 417–419. See also Linda Gordon, *Woman's Body, Woman's Right: A Social History of Birth Control in America* (New York: Viking, 1976, revised 1990), pp. 337–354.

108. It should be noted that for Sanger the "etc." included "all these ideologies: Communism, Catholicism, Nazism and Fascism [which] should all be grouped to-

gether as enemies of Freedom and Democracy." Sanger to Harmsen, July 26, 1952, MSPS. See also Durand-Wever to Sanger, June 25, 1952, noting that about politics, "we had a great deal of experience during the Hitler regime and now in the Soviet zone." MSPS.

109. Suitters, *Be brave*, p. 54.

110. Durand-Wever in *Proceedings . . . Cheltenham*, p. 101. See also Suitters, *Be brave*, p. 31.

111. Harmsen later claimed that when another German-Jewish refugee, the Israeli delegate Dr. Beate Davidson, refused to shake his hand, Lotte Fink intervened, saying that Harmsen had helped her emigrate to Australia and was "all-right." Interview, April 17–18, 1979.

112. Hans Harmsen, "The Medical Evil of Abortion," in *Third International Conference on Planned Parenthood. Report of the Proceedings 24–29 November 1952, Bombay* (Bombay: Family Planning Association of India), p. 151. For similarly positive invocations of Nazi measures, see Moeller, *Protecting Motherhood*, on West German discussions in the 1950s about "money for children" (*Kindergeld*) and maternity protection (*Mutterschutzgesetz*), pp. 109–179.

113. Dr. Helena Wright, personal interview, London, January 26, 1981.

114. Diary notes by RPB on June 23, 1953, visit with Harmsen in Hamburg. In RF RG 1.2, 717 (Hamburg Academy of Public Health. Teaching Program 1951-1955).

115. R.F. R.G. 1.2 717. The Rockefeller Foundation was especially pleased that in Hamburg, Harmsen could cooperate with the conservative family sociologist Helmut Schelsky. On Schelsky, see Moeller, *Protecting Motherhood*, pp. 117–120.

116. *Jahresbericht Hamburg Akademie für Staatsmedizin 1957*, pp. 4, 30. See also *Akademie für Staatsmedizin in Hamburg 1958*, edited by Dr. Hans Harmsen, Hamburg 1959.

117. See Kaupen-Hass, "Eine deutsche Biographie," On the conservative politics of the Ministry and its chief Franz-Josef Wuermeling, see Moeller, *Protecting Motherhood*, pp. 101–103, 197–199.

118. Sanger to Rufus Day, January 9, 1959. See also her chastising letter to Harmsen, November 8, 1957. MSPS.

119. In spring 1952, in a whirlwind style reminiscent of Sanger's highly publicized visit in 1927–1928, her rival Ottesen-Jensen gave five lectures to overflow audiences in Berlin. See Durand-Wever to Sanger and Houghton, May 1, 1952, MSPS. Dr. Clarence Gamble also apparently sent funds to Berlin in the 1950s to assure that birth control work could continue on a private basis even under a Christian Democratic administration. Suitters, *Be Brave*, p. 100.

120. Personal conversation, Joan Rettie, former secretary of the European region, IPPF, Kew Gardens, Surrey, July 9, 1984. It is clear that the British family planning activists intensely disliked and mistrusted Harmsen, although their ire was more directed at his imperious shunting aside of Durand-Wever and his privileged connection to American finances than his Nazi past. However, IPPF staffers did wonder, when he disappeared during a conference in South America, whether he had gone to meet old Nazi comrades. Personal interview, Dr. Helena Wright, London, January 26, 1981.

121. Durand-Wever to Finance Committee of the IPPF, January 6, 1959, MSPS. See also Durand-Wever "Report on Activities, *Pro Familia* Deutsche Gesellschaft für Ehe und Familie e.V. to IPPF" (n.d.).

122. Houghton to Sanger, May 7, 1956, MSPS.

123. Durand-Wever to Sanger, May 8, 1957 (on *Pro Familia* letterhead), MSPS.

124. Hans Harmsen, "30 Jahre Weltbevölkerungsfragen" in *Die gesunde Familie in ethischer, sexualwissenschaftlicher und psychologischen Sicht*, ed. Harmsen (Berlin: IPPF, 1957), pp. 1–5. See also typescript of his remarks in MSPS.

125. Edward F. Griffith, "Die Bejahung der Sexualität in der Ehe," in Harmsen, *Die gesunde Familie*, p. 16.

126. Ibid., p. 34.

127. Durand-Wever, "Mit den Augen."

128. Ibid. Specifically, she opposed the trimester solution being adopted in the GDR, preferring a medical, social, age (too young or too old), ethical, and eugenic indication model.

129. Anne-Marie Durand-Wever, "Ärztliche Indikationen zur Empfängnisverhütung," in Harmsen, *Die gesunde Familie*, p. 128.

130. See *Internationale Abortsituation. Kongress 5–7 Mai 1960*, ed. Dr. F. K. Mehlan.

131. Durand-Wever to Sanger, November 25, 1961, MSPS.

132. Shortly before her death she was honored by local Berlin television as an honored elderly citizen. Still spry and brusque she warned viewers to toughen themselves, and not to take too many medications or complain too much. Videotape courtesy of Itta Vollnhals, Berlin.

133. *Sexualpädagogik und Familienplannung (pro familia* magazine) 4/84, p. 25.

134. Report by Monika Simmel-Joachim and Elke Kiltz to the National Board of Pro Familia, May 16, 1984. *Die tageszeitung (TAZ)* reported, February 2, 1984, that the honorary president of *Pro Familia* was part of "the old guard of fighters for liquidation (*Ausmerze*)und racial improvement (*Aufartung*)." Also instrumental was Heidrun Kaupen Haas's exposé, "Hans Harmsen—eine deutsche Biographie," published in 1984. See also Sabine Schleiermacher, "Die Innere Mission und ihr bevölkerungspolitische Programm," in *Der Griff nach der Bevölkerung. Aktualität und Kontinuität nazistischer Bevölkerungspolitik*, ed. Heidrun Kaupen-Haas (Nördlingen: Greno, 1986), pp. 73–102. I am grateful to Schleiermacher for supplying me with copies of the internal correspondence quoted here and below.

135. *Pro Familia Informationen* (internal section of *Sexualpädogik und Familienplannung),* 6/84 (June 1984), p. 21.

136. Harmsen to Jürgen Heinrichs (president of Pro Familia), August 4, 1984. See also his letter, July 1, 1984.

137. "Bericht des Bundesvorstandes zur Mitgliederversammlung der PF am 8 und 9 Juni 1985 in Bad Bevensen." After much hesitation, *Sexualpädagogik und Familienplannung* published Schleiermacher's critical evaluation, "Hans Harmsens hierarisches Gesellschaftsmodell: Auszüge einer sozialdarwinistischen Familienpolitik," 1/[19]90, pp. 28–29.

138. I borrowed the term "remasculinization" from Robert Moeller; he refers to Susan Jeffords, *The Remasculinization of America: Gender and the Vietnam War* (Bloomington: University of Indiana Press, 1989). The influence of church-oriented social hygienists such as Harmsen and Hermann Muckermann—pronatalist but by no means antieugenic—profited mightily from the whitewashing of the church's role in the Third Reich. See Weindling, *Health, race and German politics*, pp. 565–582. See also Proctor, *Racial Hygiene*, pp. 298–312, and Moeller, *Protecting Motherhood*, p. 5.

139. See, for example, the pride with which health insurance doctors in postwar Berlin reported on their extensive records of several hundred thousand index cards. Weyhmann, "Die Geschichte des Ambulatoriums," in *Sozialpolitik nach 1945,* p. 61.

## Epilogue

1. See confidential memo Re. Par. 11, Gesetz über den Mutter und Kinderschutz und die Rechte der Frau vom September 27, 1950, March 1965, Ministerium für Gesundheitswesen, in DFDA.

2. See Joyce M. Mushaben, "Feminism in Four Acts: The Changing Political Identity of Women in the Federal Republic of Germany," in *The Federal Republic at Forty,* ed. Peter H. Merkl (New York: New York University Press, 1989), pp. 76–109.

3. Mushaben, "Feminism," p. 92. For an excellent analysis of the 1974 decision, helpful also in understanding the 1993 verdict, see Douglas G. Morris, "Abortion and Liberalism: A Comparison Between the Abortion Decisions of the Supreme Court of the United States and the Constitutional Court of West Germany," *Hastings International and Comparative Law Review* 11 (1988):159–245.

4. Ferdinand Protzman, "Germany Widens Abortion Rights After Fierce Debate in Parliament," *New York Times,* June 26, 1992. For a brief summary of the abortion debate since the 1970s, see Myra Marx Ferree, "The Rise and Fall of 'Mommy Politics': Feminism and Unification in (East) Germany," *Feminist Studies* 19:1 (Spring 1993): 89–115.

5. Stephen Kinzer, "German Court Restricts Abortion, Angering Feminists and the East," *New York Times,* May 29, 1993, p. 1.

6. Mechthild Küpper, "Nach Weimar führt kein Weg zurück," *Wochenpost,* no. 34 (August 19, 1993):8.

7. Senatsverwaltung für Gesundheit Berlin, "Die Neuregelung der Beratung bei Schwangerschaftskonflikten nach dem Urteil und der Anordnung des Bundesverfassungsgerichts vom 28 Mai 1993," p. 5. This language is remarkably similar to the cozy tone of the letters of rejection sent to GDR women requesting medically or eugenically indicated abortions after 1950: "We are sure that after you have recovered from the initial shock, you will look forward to your little child (*Kindchen*)." See BArch(P), DQ 1, DDR Ministerium für Gesundheitswesen.

8. Ibid., p. 14. See also the full text of the verdict, "Das Urteil des Bundesverfassungsgerichts zum Schwangerschaftsabbruch vom 28. Mai 1993," *Juristen Zeitung* (Sonderausgabe, June 7, 1993).

# — index —